THE SOCIAL MACHINE

THE SOCIAL MACHINE

Designs for Living Online

Judith Donath

The MIT Press
Cambridge, Massachusetts
London, England

MIT Press books may be purchased at special quantity discounts for business or sales promotional use. For information, please email special_sales@mitpress.mit.edu.

This book was set in Minion and Scala Sans by the MIT Press. Printed and bound in the United States of America.

Library of Congress Cataloging-in-Publication Data

Donath, Judith, 1962–.
The social machine : designs for living online / Judith Donath.
pages cm
Includes bibliographical references and index.
ISBN 978-0-262-02701-4 (hardcover : alk. paper)
1. Online social networks. 2. Social media. I. Title.
HM742.D56 2014
006.7'54—dc23
2013035294

10 9 8 7 6 5 4 3 2 1

CONTENTS

PREFACE

WHY THE TITLE "THE SOCIAL MACHINE: DESIGNS FOR LIVING ONLINE"?

Why did I choose "The Social Machine: Designs for Living Online" as the title of this book? The "machine" in the title is the computer. In its incarnation as a "social machine," its abstract binary digits are programmed to transform it into a communication medium and a setting for interactions, an electronic place to see and be seen.

There is a long history of naming computers as machines for various functions, a tradition that reveals the changing scope of the computer's domain.[1] Herman Hollerith's nineteenth-century "Tabulating Machine," built to help with the US Census, became IBM's twentieth-century general-purpose "Business Machine." Alan Turing, in his 1950 essay "Computing Machinery and Intelligence," predicted that future computers would be "thinking machines," their responses indistinguishable from those of a human. Today they are "social machines"; people use computers to meet friends, play games, collaborate on projects, commiserate, and argue.

This book's title also refers to "The Architecture Machine Group" (ArcMac), the MIT research laboratory founded in 1967 by Nicholas Negroponte that was the precursor of the Media Lab.[2] I began my graduate studies in ArcMac, and was there (and subsequently at the Media Lab) immersed in a culture devoted to inventing technologies to transform how people think, learn, and communicate. It was also a culture—very different from most computer science departments at the time—that emphasized the sensory experience of the computer interface, that it should not be a cramped readout, but a fully inhabitable environment. Many of the ideas in this book stem from my time there.

Other "Machines" also resonate with this book's title. *Dream Machines* is Ted Nelson's visionary tract about the computer as source of an infinite variety of new media. He wrote, "What matters is the design and workability of the media we create and choose. This is an enormous responsibility and an excitement." The title also echoes architect Le Corbusier's famous saying, "The house is a machine for living in." A machine, he said, is something we build to solve a problem; for example, the airplane is a machine that solves the problem of flying. As for the house, he said, "The problem of the house has not yet been stated." Le Corbusier's *Toward a New Architecture* (Le Corbusier 1986 [1931]) is about distilling what problems the house should solve and how it should do so.

What is the problem of the social machine? To decide what we should build, we need to understand what makes society function, what people want to know about each other, and the way this knowledge changes our behavior. This book looks at these fundamental questions about how we want to live online and reviews experimental designs that explore new ways of being and communicating with each other.

The word "machine" also has harsher overtones. "Thinking machine," "dream machine," "social machine"—these phrases are provocative because they sound self-contradictory. A machine is inherently sterile, inanimate, automated, unthinking. The "social machine" under its sinister interpretation processes people for their data; it automates relationships, atrophying the human dimension. As designers and users of these technologies, we need to recognize this darker side to ensure we are instead creating tools for the benefit of those who use them.

STRUCTURE OF THE BOOK

The Social Machine consists of an introduction and twelve linked design and theory chapters. Each chapter in a pair addresses a common topic, approached from a different perspective.

Chapter 1, "Introduction: Design Shapes Society," lays out the premise of the book and outlines three design goals for online spaces:

- Be innovative: Go "beyond being there" to create new ways of interacting, seeing others, and presenting oneself.
- Be legible: Interfaces should provide meaning and structure to the abstract online world.

TABLE 0.1

	Design	Theory
	1. Introduction: Design Shapes Society	
Visualizing social data	2. Visualizing Social Landscapes	3. Interfaces Make Meaning
Social networks	4. Mapping Social Networks	5. Our Evolving Super-Networks
Interactions among people	6. Visible Conversations	7. Contested Boundaries
Individuals and their data	8. Data Portraits	9. Constructing Identity
Virtual bodies	10. Embodied Interactions	11 Privacy and Public Space
The transformation of everyday life	12. Social Catalysts	

• Be beneficial: The interface design has a profound effect on the user's experience and on the evolution of online culture.

Chapter 2, "Visualizing Social Landscapes," introduces the goal of creating informative and intuitive interfaces by visualizing social patterns; the fundamental design problems are identifying the socially meaningful data and depicting it legibly and intriguingly. These social visualizations can map the overall structure of a community or communities ("long shots," discussed in this chapter and in "Mapping Social Networks"), show the interactions among a group of people ("medium shots," discussed in "Visualizing Conversations"), or depict an individual ("close-ups," discussed in "Data Portraits").

Chapter 3, "Interfaces Make Meaning," delves deeper into the problem of creating a legible, interesting depiction. It explains how people use metaphors to understand abstract concepts—and because the online world is inherently abstract, we rely on interface metaphors to understand it. Other topics include the expressive elements of interactivity and the problem of making the affordances of a new medium intuitively understandable.

Chapter 4, "Mapping Social Networks," returns to visualizing the structure of a community (the "long shot") while focusing on mapping the network of relationships among a large number of people. It discusses what we can learn from these maps, how we can depict what flows through the connections, and how network maps can help us track changes in social connectivity—a particularly relevant issue as social media accelerate these changes.

Chapter 5, "Our Evolving Super-Networks," addresses the question of what social network structure makes sense in our mobile, information-centric world. Our networks grow as we meet more people and have the means to stay in touch with them more easily; yet at the same time, our need for these networks diminishes as markets increasingly provide the support and services for which we once relied on family and friends.

Chapter 6, "Visible Conversations," looks at the design of the "medium shot"—depicting interactions among people. Such visualizations help establish social mores, provide context for the conversation, and illuminate the complex history of online group interaction. To design them, one needs to understand the many social functions of conversation, beyond the mere exchange of information.

Chapter 7: Any conversation or interaction is a bounded situation with some barriers, whether physical or purely social and conventional, limiting who joins in and how the situation is defined. "Contested Boundaries" examines the challenge of creating these boundaries online, where there are no walls and identity is fluid.

Chapter 8, "Data Portraits," is about the close-up: the depiction of an individual through data by and about him or her. Framing this visualization design problem as "portraiture" highlights how such works answer to the often competing desires of artist, audience, and subject—including when, as is often the case online, the "artist" is the machine.

Chapter 9, "Constructing Identity," looks closely at how we form impressions of each other. Online identity is malleable, and it is easy to fake many of the familiar external signals of identity, such as race, gender, and age. Can we—and do we want to—design interfaces that replace these physically based cornerstones of identity with other signals such as knowledge markers, history of reactions, and so on?

Chapter 10, "Embodied Interaction," discusses the design of new interaction interfaces. It traces the tension between recreating the experience of face-to-face interaction versus creating new types of experiences, that is, "going beyond being there." Its focus is on the representation of the participants and the translation of physical actions into online behaviors.

Chapter 11, "Privacy and Public Space," focuses on the control of personal data, that is, the tension between subject and viewer. It is often difficult to gauge whether an online space is private or public—whether one's remarks will be recorded, searchable, and liable to appear in unintended contexts.

Making this legible is essential for helping people decide how they wish to act and maintain control of their self-presentation.

Chapter 12, "Social Catalysts," looks at projects that move social interaction from the individual screen and into public space. Its focus is on how these works act as "social catalysts"—transforming the dynamics of a space and bringing some of the online world's open sociability to public space by bringing physically distant people into contact or by providing people with new knowledge about or new means to interact with each other.

ACKNOWLEDGMENTS

For a decade starting in 1997, I directed the Sociable Media Group at the MIT Media Lab, working with an extraordinary group of students. Many of the ideas and examples in this book come from projects we designed and built there. Throughout the book, examples marked with an asterisk are from work this group created. My warmest thanks to Karrie Karahalios, Fernanda Viégas, Roy Rodenstein, Rebecca Xiong, David Chiou, danah boyd, Dana Spiegel, Kelly Dobson, Hyun-Yeul Lee, Scott Golder, Ethan Perry, Christine Liu, Andrew Fiore, Aaron Zinman, Drew Harry, Orkan Telhan, Francis Lam, Dietmar Offenhuber, Alex Dragulescu, Yannick Assogba, Matt Lee, Joey Rozier, Rodrigo Leroux, Derek Tang, Raffi Krikorian, and Jawad Laraqui. Special thanks to my mentors at the Media Lab, Andy Lippman and Nicholas Negroponte.

Ken Goldberg has been a wonderful collaborator and colleague. I have learned a great deal from many conversations with Martin Wattenberg, Sherry Turkle, Jeremy Bailenson, Natalie Jeremijenko, Ben Shneiderman, Pattie Maes, Michael Naimark, Paul Dourish, Jeffrey Huang, Gilad Lotan, Eric Paulos, Keith Hampton, Ken Perlin, Christina Yang, Marc Smith, George Fifield, Robin Dunbar, and many others. I owe a debt of inspiration to Barry Wellman and Jim Hollan.

I have had the excellent fortune to be a fellow at Harvard's Berkman Center for Internet and Society for the last several years. It is the yin to the Media Lab's yang, embracing technology but also questioning it. I am especially grateful to the group of fellow book-writing Fellows who have provided criticism, encouragement, and much-needed interim deadlines: Ethan Zuckerman, David Weinberger, Doc Searls, Colin Maclay, Eszter Hargittai,

Christian Sandvig, Wendy Seltzer, Jason Kaufman, Lokman Tsui, Zeynep Tufecki, and Reynol Junco. Members of the Social Media Collective at Microsoft New England also graciously read a draft and provided helpful advice—thank you to Nancy Baym, Kate Crawford, Mary Gray, Kate Miltner, Hector Postigo, Megan Finn, and Jean Burgess. Thank you also to Lisa Randall for insightful comments and camaraderie.

Doug Sery, my editor at the MIT Press, has been wonderfully patient and encouraging as this book grew from a short text on designing social media to a deeper, more analytical and also longer (both in words and, especially, in writing time) book. Doug has an unsurpassed network of scholars and writers in the areas of new media and design, and he found excellent reviewers for this manuscript. I would like to thank these anonymous critics for their thorough readings; they improved this book tremendously with their insightful comments. Margy Avery was an excellent guide through the thicket of the publishing process and Judy Feldmann provided precise copyediting. One of this book's key arguments is that appealing designs encourage people to linger longer and delve more deeply—I am very grateful to Yasuyo Iguchi for the beautiful design of these pages.

I am very grateful for the support and humor of many friends. Thank you to Debbie, Joanne, Laura, Susan, Claire, and many others for both encouragement and much welcome distraction.

My warmest thanks to my family—my partner John and my children Van and Anya—for their love and patience (and some motivating impatience). The joy of their presence made writing this book a pleasure.

1

INTRODUCTION: DESIGN SHAPES SOCIETY

THE MAKING OF A COMMUNITY MAP

In 1991, the Web had not yet been invented and the Internet was much less social than it would become years later. Still, it was far from uninhabited, and the centralized, multiuser computers that were then common functioned as social centers, places where people came to check their email, read news, and see who else was around.

At the MIT Media Lab, where I was a graduate student at the time, the central computer was called "media-lab," and its users were a superset of the people who inhabited the Media Lab building; all the current students and faculty were on it, as were some alumni and other associates, who might be anywhere in the world. You could run a command called "who" to see who was logged in and for how long had they been idle. If you were working at the lab late at night, it was a good way to see who else was around, or if you were there during the day, to see if a colleague was easily reachable.

I spent the summer of 1991 working in Japan. It was fascinating, but also lonely. The company was in a far suburb of Tokyo and few of my coworkers spoke English. When I logged in to media-lab to check my email, I would also look at who else was active on the machine. When it was mid-afternoon for me, it was the middle of the night in Cambridge, and only one or two night owls would be present. But on nights that I worked late, I could watch the tide of distant log-ins rise, as people arrived to work in the Lab's morning.

Running the "who" command printed a list of names and their idle times, but it did not give an intuitive feel for the flow of activity. What I really wanted was a window that would show me who was online and who was active. I wanted it to be very much like a real window onto a central plaza, which one might look out of occasionally to see who was passing by.

When I returned to Cambridge, I began designing this window—and immediately faced the problem of how to arrange all the names. The most obvious and easy solution would be to arrange them in alphabetical order. But this was unsatisfactory: such a layout would provide no context about the people—their role in the lab, whether they were residents or distant affiliates. Furthermore, such an arrangement was too reminiscent of the list of names on a committee program or memorial. Another solution would be to arrange the names by hand. I could use a floor plan of the lab and place all the residents in their offices, with the other affiliates floating in space outside. But this would be a tremendous amount of work, and would require constant updating as new people joined. Plus, the nonresident community was large—in the thousands—and growing, with many members I did not know. Where to place all of them? Instead, I decided to write a program that would automatically place each person in a meaningful location on the screen. To do this, I needed a database containing relevant information about everyone who had a media-lab account.

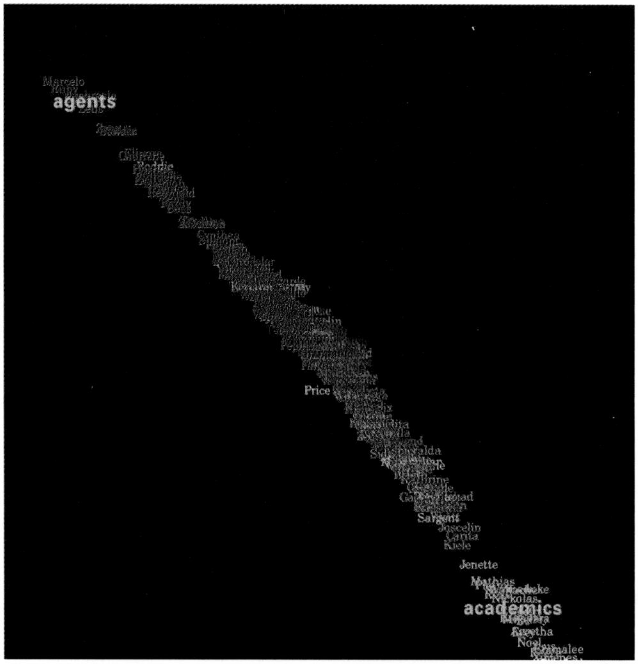

FIGURE 1.1
Judith Donath, *Visual Who* (1995). Roles and relationships mode, two anchors. This mode, shows all members of the community (names changed for privacy). Brightness shows strength of ties to the anchors.

The mail-alias file, which contained all of the Media Lab's group email lists, was just this sort of database. Email was integral to the lab's culture. When someone joined the community, he or she received a media-lab email address and was added to the appropriate official lists: there were lists for staff, faculty, and students. Each research group had its own mailing lists, as did the softball team and those interested in cryptography. People planning a ski trip made a mailing list for it, as did those who worked on a research project together and those who shared a love of cooking or tennis or esoteric computer music. Over time, each person created a self-portrait in mailing lists, telling of his or her interests, responsibilities, and roles at the Media Lab.

With the mailing list data, I created *Visual Who*,[*1] an interactive visualization that depicted this community. Starting with a few user-chosen mailing lists as anchors, it grouped together people who had—at least as expressed in their choice of email lists—much in common (Donath 1995).

Visual Who did not impose a single, definitive picture of the community; instead, it allowed people to interactively explore the roles and relationships of its members by choosing different mailing lists as the visualization's anchors (see figures 1.1 and 1.2). People enjoyed using it. Seeing who

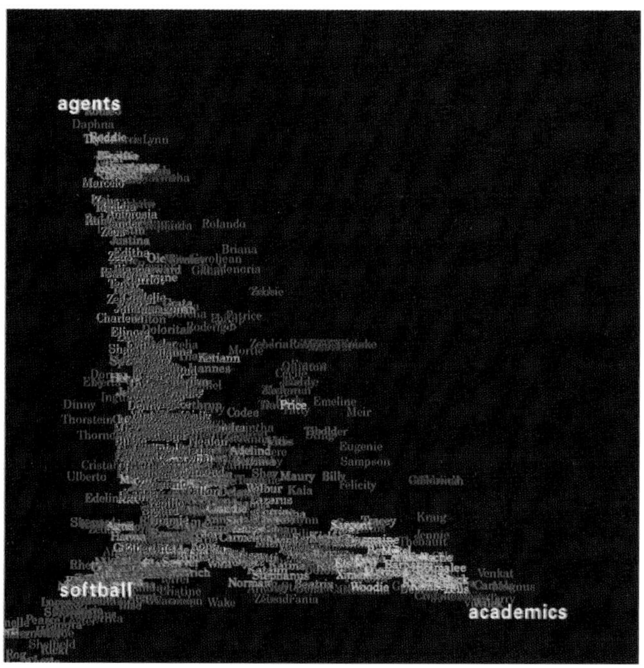

FIGURE 1.2
Judith Donath, *Visual Who* (1995). Roles and relationships mode, three anchors.

unexpectedly shared your interests was fun, as was learning more about newcomers and others you might otherwise know only as a username on a mass mailing.

Once you had found a satisfactory arrangement, you could use *Visual Who* as a window onto the community's activity (see figures 1.3 and 1.4). This mode showed only people who were logged in to media-lab, displaying their names brightly if they were active and dimly if they were idle. In the middle of the day, the "window" shimmered with people coming and going; late at night it was dark, with only the occasional user checking in.

In the physical world, we live amid an abundance of sensory detail. We are attuned to the appearance and behavior of other people, their facial expressions, changing fashions, and the ebb and flow of crowds. But online, these social patterns are harder to perceive. They are hidden in the abstract archives of data from activities, updates, and conversations. It is hard to sense the scale and composition of online groups and to form nuanced impressions of individual people.

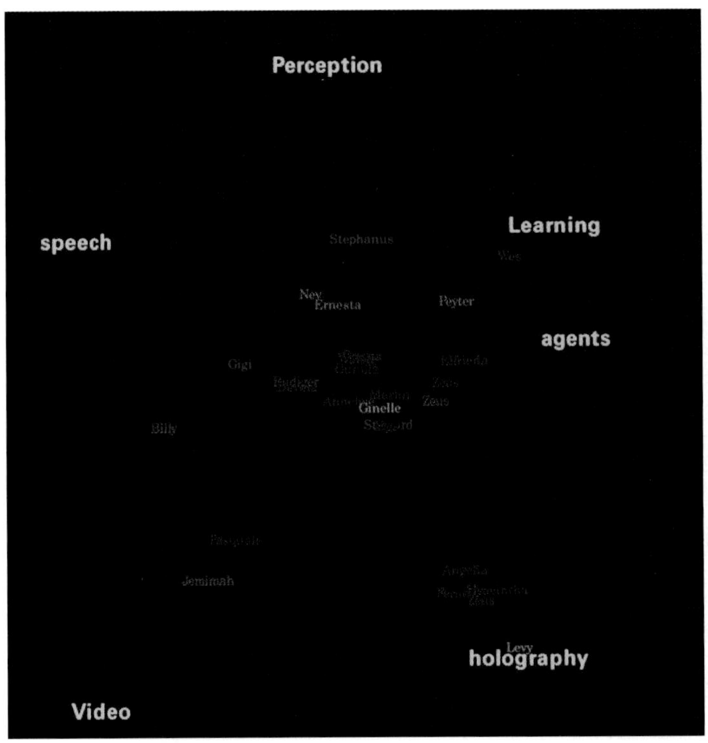

FIGURE 1.3
Judith Donath, *Visual Who* (1995). Activity mode, 4:00 a.m. This mode shows only members who are present. Brightness indicates recent activity.

Visual Who was compelling because it provided viewers the ability to see social patterns more easily online, such as who had similar interests and which topics appealed to different groups. It also provided a feeling of co-presence, revealing that the barren-seeming machine was actually a vibrant and inhabited space. The information that *Visual Who* used was always there in the computer, just not in a sensory form; the visualization transformed the abstract data into a visible, navigable scene.

This visualization is just the beginning. Using *Visual Who*, we can see that there is activity online, but not what it is; we can see names, but little about the people they represent. What ideas are discussed in the email lists, and what are the patterns of response and reputation that emerge within them? How can we use the histories of conversations and the data that accumulate about a person to create sensory and comprehensible online societies? What other ways are there of depicting the relationships within a large group of people?

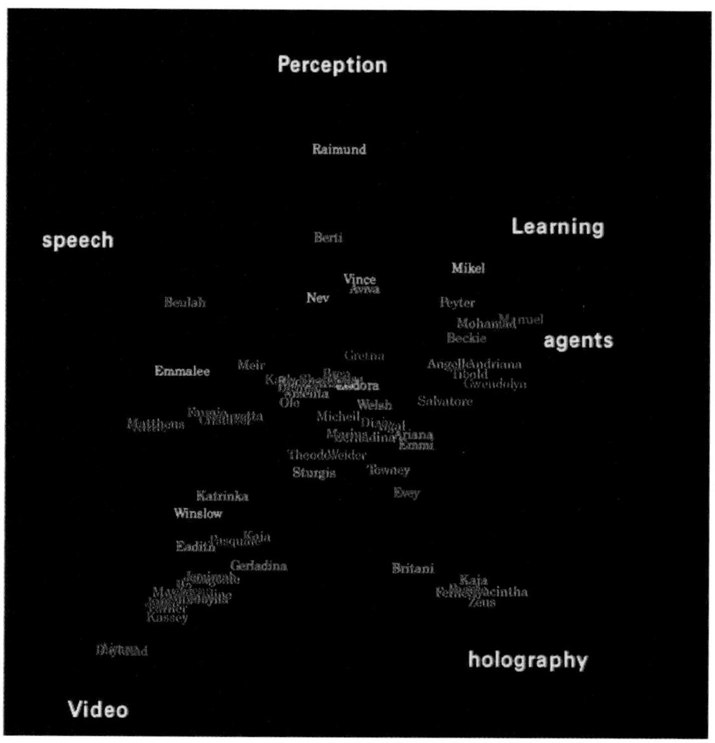

FIGURE 1.4
Judith Donath, *Visual Who* (1995). Activity mode, 1:00 p.m.

We are at the beginning of a revolution in human communication. The online world has the potential to connect each individual to millions, if not billions, of others. This is an unprecedented scale for forming communities, for meeting people, and for working together. Elements of this revolution are already part of daily life: people work and learn in distributed groups, with colleagues and fellow students scattered across the globe, their meetings taking place for the most part online. They rely increasingly on online people, many of them strangers, to be the gatekeepers to news, to help make decisions about everything from which toothpaste to buy to which laws to support.

Yet at this stage the social dimension of the Internet remains primitive. The interfaces are still clunky and our online social experience is visually dull, far from the vibrant and subtle richness of face-to-face interaction. Current interfaces for conversation and social navigation are awkward; they are designed around office work, with metaphors based on filing and typing. We have little sense of the presence of other people, their character and intentions, where they congregate and what they do.

The online world may evolve into an extraordinary new form of human society, where people make discoveries collectively, produce important works, and form friendships and other connections at a vastly unprecedented scale. But it is not there yet. Humans are fundamentally sensory and social beings: for the online world to achieve its promise, we need to design interfaces that work with how we see and respond to the world around us.

DESIGN GOALS FOR ONLINE SPACES

Designing online spaces requires balancing three fundamental goals:

Be innovative: Explore extraordinary possibilities.

Be legible: Bring clarity to a complex and abstract environment.

Be socially beneficial: Support the emergence of desirable social norms and cultures.

We want innovative designs that explore the potential of a densely populated world with immense troves of data but no physical bodies. At the same time, we want designs that make this world comprehensible to us; we are, after all, embodied creatures whose cognition is based on physical experience. Perhaps most importantly, we want designs that encourage people to contribute to their community, (usually) by participating, cooperating, and being honest.

Innovation: Exploring Extraordinary Possibilities

Science fiction versions of the distant future feature people projected as moving, speaking, 3D holograms, appearing just as if they were standing there, aside from some obligatory jitter and glitches.

> Robert squinted and shrugged, squinted again. And then suddenly he got it right: his visitor was standing in the middle of the bedroom. … It was his first real three-dimensional success. … Robert stood and stopped to the side, looking behind the visitor. The image was so solid, so complete. Hmm. And yet the visitor cast shadows contrary to the real lighting. I wonder whose fault that is? (Vernor Vinge, *Rainbow's End*, 106)

Physical limits shape our everyday, unmediated interactions. Most informal conversations are among six or seven people at most; beyond that size it is difficult to hear everyone. Larger gatherings, such as classes, meetings, and big rallies, need some form of amplification, whether modern megaphones or the ancient practice of the crowd chanting back the speaker's phrases.[2] Face-to-face discussions require the participants to be in the same place at the same time. If someone needs to be elsewhere, his or her role in the conversation ends.

Online, we can change this, by creating virtual spaces where hundreds of people can converse comfortably and conveniently. These interactions differ significantly from our face-to-face conversations. For example, online participants usually type rather than speak. In spoken conversation, words are ephemeral, disappearing into the past as soon as we utter them, but in text conversations, they exist indefinitely. This introduces new concerns about privacy, for a statement's meaning and impact change when someone reads it at a later time and in a different context. Most significantly, the medium is computational, allowing us to analyze text, visualize patterns, and in many other ways enrich and transform the communicative experience.

In an influential paper entitled "Beyond Being There," Jim Hollan and Scott Stornetta (1992) argue that the goal of new communication media should be to provide an experience different from, and potentially better than, face-to-face interaction. They contend that mediated interactions that attempt to mimic immediate presence will always be inferior to the real thing, whereas an innovative interface can provide unprecedented communicative abilities.

Technologists have put much effort into creating systems such as specially equipped videoconferencing rooms that attempt to mimic the experience of actually being with another person. Although there is something magical about seeing someone who is actually thousands of miles away appear in front of you, it is also mundane. Given the tremendous bandwidth and advanced technology necessary to create the illusion of presence, is the impression of ordinary "being there" the best we can do? My goal with this book is to go "beyond being there," to explore new types of interactions and situations that are possible only *because* they occur within a computational medium.

Online social interaction goes beyond being there when the amount and type of information we have about each other differs from ordinary life. Sometimes we get *less* information online. For example, lack of identity information is quite unusual in face-to-face social gatherings: it is only at masquerade balls that we do not see each other's faces. Online, however, anonymous interaction is common, and verified identity is the relatively rare and valuable condition. Other mediated interactions are different because there is *more* information. Unlike the ephemeral worlds of our face-to-face conversations, much of what we write online persists indefinitely in various electronic storehouses. We may at times want designs that highlight and emphasize information unavailable face to face, such as the histories of our conversations; at other times, we may want to omit things that ordinarily we can see, such as the race or gender of our conversational partners.

If we evaluate online interactions using face-to-face conversation as the ideal, they will inevitably come up short. Email, for example, has no gestures, no tone of voice, and no facial expressions. With those as criteria, it seems an impoverished medium. Yet email also enables anonymous interaction so we can converse without revealing our race, gender, or identity; it allows for asynchronous discussion, which frees us to read and respond at our convenience. Looking at how email *differs* from face-to-face experience shows how much it enriches our conversational repertoire.

Whether email's features make it preferable to in-person conversation depends on the situation. Anonymity is seldom desirable in ordinary social interactions, but it can be literally life-saving for whistle-blowers and political dissenters (Kling et al. 1999; Marx 1999), and whereas the immediate, nuanced back-and-forth of live conversation is better suited for complex negotiations, asynchronous media allow us to participate in many discussions, devoting time to each as we can. The goal in designing new social media is neither to imitate in-person encounters nor to replace them, but to complement them, to add new communicative options to suit our varying needs.

Legibility: Bringing Clarity to Abstract Worlds

As we create systems that explore the extraordinary possibilities of the online world, we also want to keep them legible, to aim for clarity as well as innovation.

We are embodied beings, who have evolved in the physical world; our thoughts and imagination are rooted in the sensory experience of our physical surroundings. Online, there is no body; there is only information. We comprehend abstract ideas by reframing them in metaphoric terms that ultimately derive from physical experience (Lakoff and Johnson 1980). A key role of interface design is to translate the abstract data of the computational domain into metaphors and sensory representations that we can understand.

The design needs to be based on an understanding of human cognition. Our minds create narratives out of sensory input. We see faces in the moon, mythical figures in the stars. We connect sequential events into stories and group similar objects into clusters. Presented with an interface, we interpret meaning from the color and shape of its lines, the rhythm of its interactions, and the juxtaposition of words and pictures. To ensure that the meaning we read is the intended one, the interface designer needs to understand the implicit meanings we find in shapes, colors, and interactions and use this knowledge in creating landscapes of words and bodies of data.

In the world of information, a rich trove of data is more valuable than a reference to gold and diamonds. To appreciate its value, though, we need the ability to perceive it. Visualizations that make data such as a good reputation or a history of insightful comments easily perceivable may use metaphors such as gold stars from the physical world to convey their meaning, but the actual value derives from the underlying data.

Interfaces and visualizations add an inescapable level of editorializing as well as making information understandable.[3] An interface that highlights "constructive" participants measures this quality with subjective metrics. It might use the number of posts someone made, the percentage of their posts that people responded to, or the tone—angry or supportive—of their writing. Each measure would yield different results and represent different values. Even something as innocuous as displaying conversations by threads rather than sequentially sends a subtle message, encouraging the introduction of new topics by prominently featuring the initial message. Designers need to be cognizant of the values they disseminate, and users need to recognize how design encodes subtle messages.

Social Benefits: Shaping Online Culture

Communication technologies can transform society for better or worse. One can optimistically envision a future in which the xenophobic barriers of racism and sexism collapse as people make contact with diverse groups, and in which an increasingly well-informed populace engages in democratic discourse and uses its collective intelligence to solve the great problems facing the twenty-first century. But one can also foresee dystopian scenarios in which a repressive government uses the trails of information we all leave behind to control dissent and intimidate citizens. Other predictions, less dire but still undesirable, show a future in which shallow virtual relationships overshadow real ties and real responsibilities, where a pale and puffy populace lives vicariously through their make-believe avatar alter egos. Although we cannot foresee all the social ramifications of this revolution in communication, we can make educated predictions and design accordingly.

Some of the forces that determine how closely the future resembles these scenarios lie outside of the technology itself: governments can enact legal safeguards or they can spy on their citizens; religious leaders can guide their followers toward tolerance or terrorism. However, the creators and users of technology can also have a tremendous impact on how the future unfolds.

To achieve a future in which online interaction breaks down cultural barriers and solves big problems, we need to design interfaces that encourage people to take responsibility for their words and to engage with each other more cooperatively—far too many of today's discussions descend into vicious acrimony. The requisite trust and cooperation depend on participants knowing more about each other, but we are understandably wary of the digital footprints we leave. The designer's challenge is to balance these competing values.

Good design is situation specific. You can make a romantic restaurant with candlelight and tablecloths, a place that serves multicourse meals that take many hours to consume, where people talk in quiet voices, display their best manners, and spend large amounts of money. You can also construct a family restaurant featuring bright lights, unbreakable crockery, easy-to-clean plastic menus, and food served quickly and cheaply. One is not better than the other; rather, their suitability depends on whether the customer is seeking a perfect evening with a date or an easy meal with young children.

Similarly, the design goals of online sites can vary widely. In the online world, cooperation is usually a virtue, but when designing games, inciting ruthless competition may be the goal. Many sites forbid anonymous participation because it enables irresponsible behavior, but anonymity is sometimes desirable: a forum for people to speak freely about dangerous topics without fear of reprisal must be able to assure them that their identity is secret. At the same time, if a site wants to encourage rash and outrageous behavior, enabling anonymous action can provide exactly the sort of disinhibition it wants to foster. This book generally assumes that encouraging social interaction and cooperation is the goal, but the examples also include sites and artworks deliberately designed to provoke disorder or discomfort.

To shape online culture, we must be able to identify elements and features that encourage or daunt particular behaviors and uses. The restaurateur chooses between bright lights or candles, washable surfaces or fine linen, open communal tables or hushed, quiet spaces. Online, we choose among features such as the availability of anonymity or long-term personas; whether people gain prominence for being funny, knowledgeable, or supportive; whether they can see with whom they are speaking or how their audience reacts. It is important also to note the word "encourage." The interface creates an environment that is conducive to certain types of experience and activity, but it does not control the users.

The users of social technologies are a diverse group, drawn from an increasingly large percentage of the population. They may be conservative church-going Americans, Iranian dissidents, radical militants, prankster teens, or sentimental grandmothers. They may be highly successful professionals or barely literate slum-dwellers. Their social goals, and the technologies that best suit them, are likewise quite diverse. People socialize online to bond with existing acquaintances as well as to meet new ones. They may be seeking fame, publicity, and attention, or looking for a low-key, efficient way to obtain advice. Their actions may be innocuous or criminal. Each individual, who might simultaneously be a spouse, coworker, boss, parent, sibling, friend, and customer, can single-handedly embody a multitude of goals and intentions.

"WHERE THE ACTION IS"[4]

The urban sociologist William Whyte spent years observing how people walk, sit, work, and live in the city. His fundamental observation was that "what attracts people most, in sum, is other people"; and he went on to say, "If I labor the point, it is because many urban spaces are being designed as though the opposite were true" (Whyte 1988, 10). We undervalue how much we like and need to be around other people, simply observing them and trying to make sense of the changing social world around us.

Our awareness of what the people around us are doing ranges from focused attention to peripheral awareness. When engaged in an intense discussion, we are acutely aware of the other's movements and words, possibly to the exclusion of much else. At other times, while working on a task or casually chatting, we are also tangentially aware of the people and movement around us. Places have a typical level of activity that ebbs and flows throughout the day, and we become accustomed to their ordinary rhythms, noticing any unusual disruptions or silences. Hearing a colleague's voice in the distance, we register her presence, perhaps subconsciously when we have no particular concern with her; however, if we would like to speak with her or her presence is unexpected, this distant awareness can shift to more focused attention.

Online, many sites provide little indication of the thousands of people who may be present. But some do make people and their activity visible, and this social information has been very useful for their users. For example, instant messaging applications show who among one's contacts is online and whether they are active or idle. A study of teen users found that they were quite sensitive to how their presence and absence registered to others, learned each other's activity patterns, and diligently provided reasons for unexpected moments of unavailability; here, social awareness shaped the evolution of the community's social mores (Grinter and Palen 2002). Streams of updates, such as one sees on Facebook and Twitter, also provide a vivid sense of activity, though the non-contributing readers remain invisible.

Yet, these interfaces are rudimentary, showing presence with a list of names or scrolling updates. Reading a list of names is fine when you have a goal in mind—for example, looking for someone to chat with—but it does not provide ongoing, lightweight social awareness. A more visual approach to depicting presence—a window onto a virtual world rather than a list of names—can give the viewer insight into a community's patterns at a glance.

A window, such as that created by *Visual Who*, provides awareness, but also separation; windows are for observation, not immersion. We want this sometimes—for instance, when we are working—for, though we like to see the comings and goings of our colleagues, we may also want silence in order to concentrate better, and to see but not be seen, the better to avoid distractions. But at other times, we want to participate, to be part of the conversation, to "reach out and touch someone." Ideally, an interface should make possible seamless transitions between being peripherally aware of ambient social information and becoming actively engaged with others in the virtual space.

THE SOCIAL MACHINE

People invent new social technologies for a variety of reasons. Their intention may be to improve society, to make a profit, or some combination of both. This book will focus on the social goals: creating mediated spaces for people to meet, play, work, and argue; designing tools to help people express themselves and make sense of others in the mediated world; and understanding the social impact of different design decisions. The fundamental goal is to benefit the individual and the community.

My hope is to inspire designers to be both more radical and more thoughtful in their creations—to push the technologies farther and create innovative forms of communication, but also to think more deeply and knowledgeably about the likely social impact of their designs. For users—that is, anyone who communicates online—I hope to clarify how technologies shape our impressions of people and influence our behavior. This knowledge will help us better navigate the online world, whether in deciding what information to make public or keep private, choosing what medium to use in a particular situation, or assessing the veracity of other people's stories and identity claims.

The online world is a synthetic universe—entirely human-made and designed. The design of the underlying system shapes how we appear and what we see of other people. It determines the structure of conversations and who has access to what information. Winston Churchill once said, "We shape our buildings; thereafter they shape us." Architects of physical cities determine the paths people will take and the vistas they will see. They affect people's mood by creating cathedrals that inspire awe, schools that encourage playfulness, and jails that evoke dread. Architects, however, do not control how the inhabitants of those buildings present themselves or see each other—but the designers of virtual spaces do, and they have far greater influence on the social experience of their users. They determine whether we see each other's faces or instead know each other only by name. They can reveal the size and makeup of an audience, or provide the impression that one is writing intimately to only a few, even if millions are in fact reading. They can make words ephemeral, disappearing forever once they leave the screen, or eternal, by permanently archiving them, amassing a history of a person's views and reactions.

This book is about the design of these interfaces, written for both the creators and users of new social technologies. It is a guide to understanding how existing systems influence behavior and a manifesto for designing radically new environments for social interaction.

2

VISUALIZING SOCIAL LANDSCAPES

Think of walking through a physical, populous city on a summery Saturday evening. Some streets are bright and full of people, others quiet and deserted. Some cafés have boisterous crowds; in others, groups of two or three gather for serious discussion. The situations and people are detailed and vivid.

Contrast this vivid, physical city with much of the mediated world. Though tremendous amounts of social activity take place online, it feels far less vibrant. Screens of text convey little vitality. Unlike in the physical world, where people's faces, hairstyles, clothing, and voices create memorable individual appearances, many people you encounter online create only a vague impression. A particularly outspoken or colorful writer may make a strong impact, and over time we do start to recognize and make sense of others; but in general our ability to perceive people and the subtleties of their relationships is relatively poor in online environments.

Visualization is one way to give online gatherings and conversations the vividness and legibility of the streets and cafés of the physical city. Visualizing an online conversation can help the participants better perceive each other's roles in the community; mapping the activity in a large virtual space can provide an intuitive impression of what the different "neighborhoods" are like; and depicting an individual's history of interaction can create a vivid portrait without necessarily revealing gender, race, or age. Visualizing social data can enliven an online space, filling it with rich detail about the inhabitants and its history, while also providing contextual cues about the tone and expectations of the setting.

Visualization is only one part of designing social interfaces—how we interact with each other via a new medium is certainly a fundamental issue—but it is an essential part of making meaning out of the vast amount of data that makes up the online world.

VISUALIZING SOCIAL DATA FOR SOCIAL PURPOSES

Social visualization is the sensory representation of social data for social purposes (Donath, Karahalios, and Viégas 1999). We call it "visualization" because the representation is usually graphical, but it can be auditory, haptic, or even olfactory. The key element is that the purpose of the visualization is social—it is meant to enhance the experience of the participants in the depicted community.

Visualizing a community can be useful to both the social scientists studying it and the people participating in it, but their goals differ significantly. The social scientists' primary concern is to thoroughly and accurately gather and analyze the relevant statistics; they need to see the data without bias, which the neutrality of box charts and bar graphs provides. The participants' concerns are more experiential: they want to gain an impression of their fellow participants, figure out the evolving mores of their situation, understand the social roles others are playing, and navigate the immense landscape of online social situations. Although some of the social visualizations we discuss in this book can be useful for analysis, it is not their main purpose, and the ones that feature more interpretive illustration are too subjective for social science research.

Like traditional data visualization, social visualizations highlight important patterns by turning abstract numbers and relationships into concrete images. But their use for social purposes means that they should be evocative as well as accurate: their meaning comes from the visceral impression they make, as well as from reading, say, the x- and y-axis and the labels. For example, to show which discussions on a site are active and lively, one could map the number of participants and their posting rates in several ways: line graphs, bubble charts, animations, and so on. The line chart is very clear and precise, and one can read the answer easily. But it evokes financial data or rainfall statistics more than a feeling of people and their activity. The bubble chart (whose little dots are vaguely anthropomorphic) reads more like a representation of population and presence; a deserted group makes a sparse chart, while a populous group yields a full one.

Social visualizations can be stand-alone depictions, but they are most transformative when integrated with the communication interface, such as an email program that includes visualizations of email patterns. These inhabited visualizations integrate the processes of creating the data and depicting it.

The Visualization Process

Visualization has two steps: choosing and analyzing the data and rendering it in a visible form. Both stages require special consideration for social application. Social data are often inexact or subjective: though we can accurately measure, for example, how many words someone used, whether the tone of his statement was angry or his answer helpful is more idiosyncratic. And, when visualizations represent individuals and social situations, we need to be aware of how highly attuned to subtle cues people are, and take care to avoid making misleading impressions.

The first step in any visualization is to choose meaningful data.[1] For example, say you want to depict a discussion group and show the participants' varied roles within the group. An initial thought might be to measure how often each person posts. This is an easily measured statistic, but seeing who posts prolifically and who posts rarely does not alone give much insight about people's standing in the group. The most active participant may be a leader, but he may also be a nuisance—either a benign one, such as an inveterate writer of banal follow-ups (someone who responds to every posting with a content-free "yes!" or "me too"), or a hostile spammer, filling the conversation space with irrelevant or provocative postings. No single measure alone indicates a person's role, but a well-chosen combination of statistics, such as the ratio of initial posts to responses plus how consistently others respond to the subject, can yield insightful patterns.

Some visualizations depict straightforward statistics: how many people are in a group, how many words are in an article, or what times of day have the most activity. But if you wish to assess the emotional tone of a message or discern the topic it addresses, you will need to further analyze the data.[2] These analyses inevitably introduce some bias. For example, in visualizing a conversation, we might want to highlight changes in the emotional tone, which requires assessing whether a message conveys anger, happiness, or is simply informative. Analyzing the sentiment of the messages is qualitative, and different algorithms (or human readers) will make different interpretations. Automatic recognition of emotion is far from a solved problem, and people's frequent use of irony and sarcasm in their everyday writing greatly complicates this task.

Indeed, even for human readers, recognizing irony and humor in brief textual messages, without the facial expressions and other cues that help us face to face, is notoriously difficult. Highly processed data can reveal fascinating patterns that would be impossible to discern in the raw statistics, but the processing can introduce errors and biases. Good design needs to assess the appropriate trade-off to make for a particular use; it also should help make the choice transparent to the viewer.

The second step in visualization is to represent the data: to find expressive forms that match meaning. Visualizations can use the lines and color of traditional graphs, and can incorporate text and images; they can also use sound, motion, and interactivity to illustrate the data.[3] (We will discuss these in greater depth in the next chapter, "Interfaces Make Meaning.") The goal for the rendering might be to be accurate, legible, beautiful, evocative, or persuasive. Throughout this book, we will explore the balance among these often conflicting goals.

Visualizations can range from neutrally objective to prescriptively subjective. Neutrality is important when the visualization will be used for varied situations. A site that hosts multiple forums whose topics range from serious health problems to campy TV shows might want to use a common design for all of them. Participants in the former may be mainly concerned with expressing empathy and being able to identify trustworthy information, while those in the latter might admire witty banter, full of in-jokes and in-character writing. Here, a straightforward visualization that highlights basic social patterns, such as activity level and responsiveness, allows the viewers to see the social dynamics more clearly, without imposing a preference about which discourse style is more desirable.

For example, *Loom2** is a conversation visualization that clusters messages and participants by thread (boyd et al. 2002). In designing it, we chose to show conversations as circles to reflect how people position themselves when they converse; this makes the visualization intuitive, without being prescriptive. Figure 2.1 shows a sociable and thriving group, with numerous ongoing conversations; figure 2.2 shows one where nearly all the messages are single posts, with no responses. (In this particular case, it is because the group has been overrun by spam, but there are other situations, such as announcement-only newsgroups, which similarly lack interaction yet are functioning as intended.) The visualization quickly conveys how sociable each discussion space is, while allowing the viewer to decide whether that level of sociability is desirable.

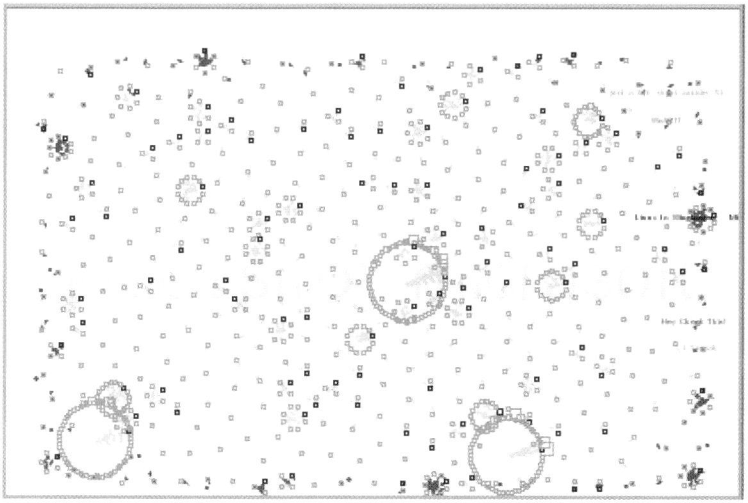

FIGURE 2.1
danah boyd, Hyun-Yeul Lee, Dan Ramage, and Judith Donath, *Loom 2* (2002). Visualization of a thriving, conversational group.

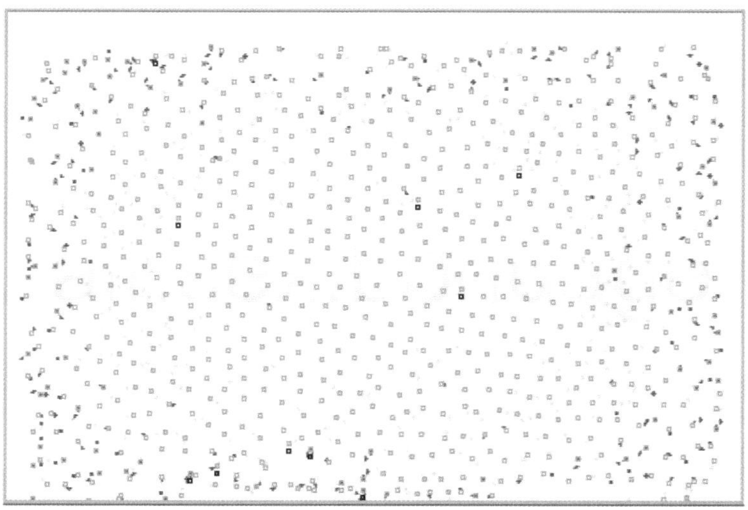

FIGURE 2.2
danah boyd, Hyun-Yeul Lee, Dan Ramage, and Judith Donath, *Loom 2* (2002). Visualization of a group that comprises mostly spam, seen here as single posts with no response.

A visualization designed for a specific context can be more prescriptive. Discussion hosts, whether the owners of large sites or the writers of personal blogs, often want to set a particular tone for their community. The desired tone can vary considerably: one host might want to encourage supportive conversations and community growth, while another might want to encourage piercing critiques and rigorous arguments. Each could specify visualizations that endorse their version of desirable behavior.

Illustrative rendering makes a depiction more vivid but also more subjective. A map of discussion spaces that shows angry exchanges as dark red and purple, and supportive ones as light blue and yellow, will be easy to interpret, but it also reflects the values—and analytic techniques—of the mapmaker. We can think of these as "semantic visualizations," conveying the designer's interpretation of the data, not just the data itself (Donath 2002). All renderings are to some extent semantic, but typically the goal with data visualization used for science is to be as unbiased and accurate as possible, whereas semantic visualizations strive for expressiveness.

Visualizations present the patterns; as viewers, our role is to think about what they mean and why. Figures 2.3 and 2.4 show two charts from *timeu.se*, an interactive project that lets the viewer explore when different words and phrases appear most frequently on Twitter (Golder and Macy 2011). Figure 2.3 shows how often people mention email, and the data are unsurprising: they mention it most frequently during the weekday working hours. The plot of the word "bored" is a bit more complicated. Its lowest frequency, early morning, is predictable: people are not bored when they wake up. But its peak use is Saturday night. Are most of us really bored on what is supposed to be the most fun night of the week? Are all those parties and movies really so dull? Here we need to distinguish the question "What do people do?" from "What do people do on Twitter?" My guess is that this result reflects a combination of societal expectations and technology use. People expect to go out and have a good time on Saturday night and are likely to be disappointed and bored when they instead find themselves sitting at home. Lots of people are indeed out, and many of them are having fun—caught up in experiencing it, rather than tweeting about it. Many who are on Twitter at 8:00 or 9:00 p.m. Saturday night are at home with their computers—and they are bored.

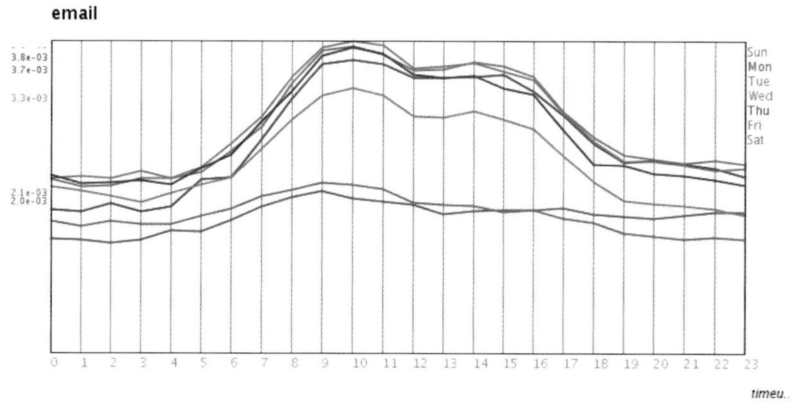

FIGURE 2.3
Scott Golder and Michael Macy, *timeu.se* (2011). Each line is a day of the week. For each day, the chart shows the frequency with which people mention the featured word over a twenty-four-hour period.

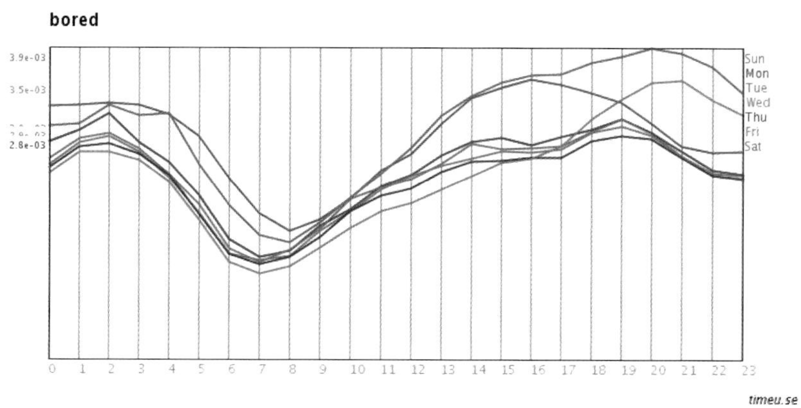

FIGURE 2.4
Scott Golder and Michael Macy, *timeu.se* (2011).

Seeing the World at Multiple Scales

We experience the world at multiple scales, moving fluidly among them. Standing on a high spot in a city, you see the urban landscape spread out in front of you: the neighborhoods, traffic flow, and the dance of lights at night. From this view you see overall patterns. Closer up, at street level, you notice groups of people and their interactions. You may want to know if an unfamiliar situation is safe: is that group of people just lively and boisterous, or are they aggressive and threatening? Or perhaps you are entering a party. You scan the room for familiar faces and look at the conversational groups, seeking one to join. Some are clearly talking about something light and funny, while others appear to be discussing more somber issues. One group of people is talking intimately, leaving no room for a newcomer, while another seems welcoming, the people making eye contact with you and shifting to make room. At a closer scale, you focus on an individual, perhaps a friend you are chatting with or a stranger who has caught your attention, and you study how he is dressed, his mannerisms, and so on, in order to understand more about who he is and what he is thinking.

In filmmaking, this multiscale perspective translates into the use of long shots, medium shots, and close-ups. Long shots, often called "establishing shots," show a wide perspective of the scene, giving the viewer a sense of the overall setting. Medium shots show a few people in their frame, allowing the viewer to see the relationships among them and follow the dynamics of a conversation. Close-ups portray an individual.

We can think of social visualizations in terms of these scales. One might want to depict an entire community, an ongoing conversation, or a specific individual. An overview of a community, the long shot, helps you find your way through a large and complex social landscape. This distant view is for observing patterns; users interact with it by manipulating the representation for their personal understanding. The medium shot, such as a visualization of a conversation, helps you make sense of relationships and roles. Here the viewer may be an active participant in the discussion. The close-up is a data portrait—a way of seeing and recognizing an individual based on her history and reputation, rather than her facial features.

In the physical world, moving between these scales is a matter of shifting focus, and the transition is typically smooth and continuous. Online, however, different interfaces handle different scales. Finding a way to smoothly transition between these scales online is a difficult challenge.[4] Zoomable interfaces allow you to go from a distant view to a close-up, but your role remains that of an observer (see figures 2.5 and 2.6). Designing an interface that smoothly shifts from observation to participation at the appropriate scales remains an open design challenge.

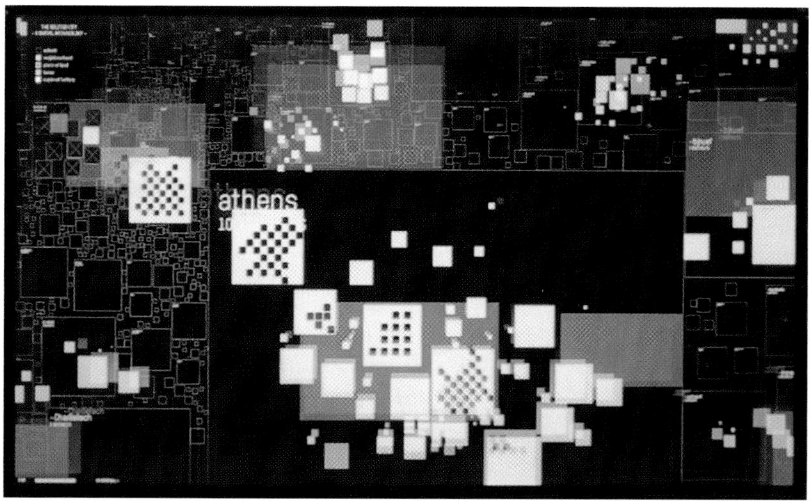

FIGURE 2.5
Richard Vijgen, *Deleted City* (2011). Overview. GeoCities was an early Web-based community site in which people created personal pages within various themed "neighborhoods." Designer Richard Vijgen visualized the archived content of the immense (over 38 million pages) but now defunct site as a zoomable map, which allowed viewers to move from an overview of the different areas to the individual pages. Although viewers could not interact with the content in this project, adding such functionality to a similar piece would not be difficult.

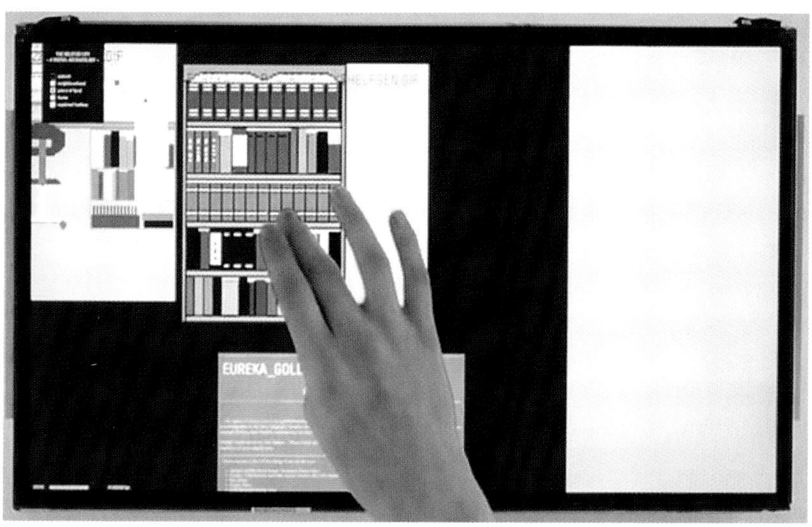

FIGURE 2.6
Richard Vijgen, *Deleted City* (2011). Closeup.

In the rest of this chapter, we will look at social landscapes, the equivalent of the establishing shot for online social spaces. Medium shots, focused on the interactions within a group, are featured in chapter 6, "Visible Conversations"; close-up individual portrayals are the topic of chapter 8, "Data Portraits."

In *Sophie and Bruno Concluded*, Lewis Carroll wrote about the futility of a truly accurate map:

> "That's another thing we've learned from your Nation," said Mein Herr, "map-making. But we've carried it much further than you. What do you consider the largest map that would be really useful?"
>
> "About six inches to the mile."
>
> "Only six inches!" exclaimed Mein Herr. "We very soon got to six yards to the mile. Then we tried a hundred yards to the mile. And then came the grandest idea of all! We actually made a map of the country, on the scale of a mile to the mile!"
>
> "Have you used it much?" I enquired.
>
> "It has never been spread out, yet," said Mein Herr: "the farmers objected: they said it would cover the whole country, and shut out the sunlight! So we now use the country itself, as its own map, and I assure you it does nearly as well." (Carroll 1893, 169)

A similar theme was explored by Jorge Luis Borges (1998) in a very short story entitled "On Exactitude in Science."

Abstracting and simplifying, not absolute verisimilitude, provide the value of the map.

VISUALIZING SOCIAL LANDSCAPES

As we have seen with *Visual Who*, often the most challenging part of depicting an online community is mapping its "landscape." *Visual Who* used the network of common interests as manifest in their mailing list subscriptions to create its interactive community map. This is but one of many possible approaches to mapping a community.

Another approach is a traditional geographic map, which places people and events in their physical locations; it is useful when those locations are especially meaningful (see figure 2.7). Often, however, data-centric mappings reveal more interesting patterns. Freed from the constraint of geographic location, such maps of social landscapes can use spatial features such as size and adjacency to convey relationships within a community.

The mutability of the online world presents a further challenge. Our familiar, physical surroundings are deeply rooted in the past; geological formations and historical events shape where roads are laid down and cities grow. Maps of physical space are anchored to this geography. Maps of virtual spaces, however, have no such firmament; it is a space with no geography.

Traditional maps are simplifications of geographic reality, highlighting different aspects of the terrain—streets, history, population, geology—depending on the purpose of the map. Their function is to abstract an orderly and comprehensible view from the immense and messy complexity of reality. Similarly, the makers of maps of virtual spaces must abstract key data from the messy complexity of vast archives.[5]

Here we will look at two approaches for mapping a large-scale virtual space, the handcrafted map and the algorithmic visualization. The first example, *Updated Map of Online Communities* by Randall Munroe, is a hand-drawn map of major online communities as of 2010. A handcrafted map can draw upon the artist's knowledge, humor, and opinions to create a witty and insightful depiction. However, it is difficult to generalize and must be (painstakingly) redone for new communities or even as an already-mapped one

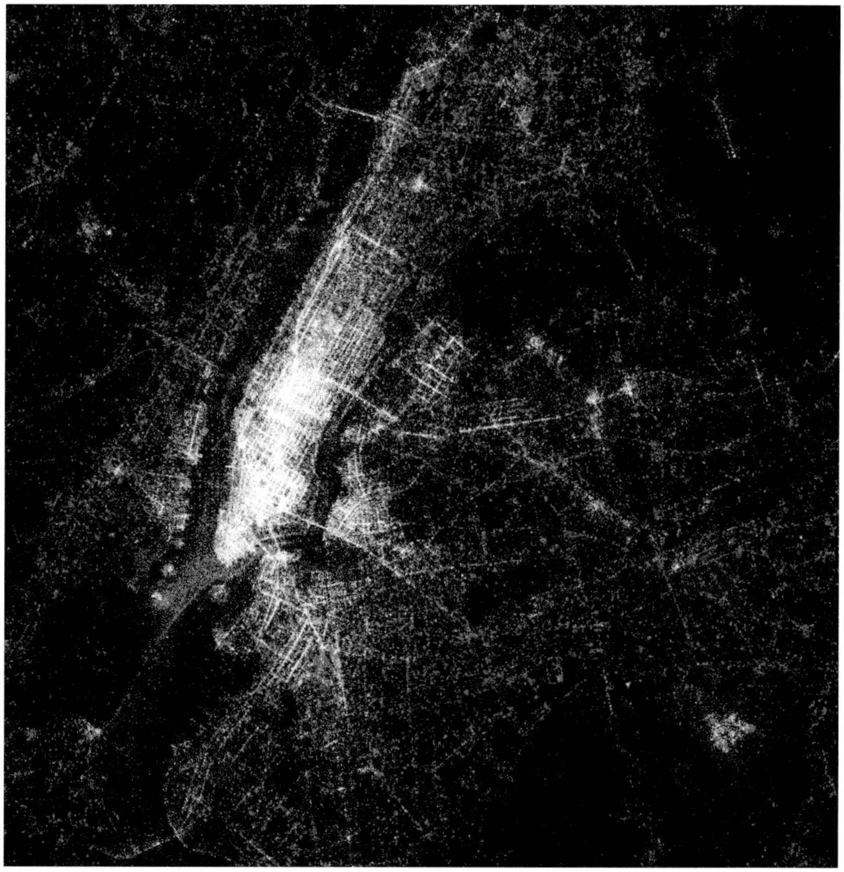

FIGURE 2.7
Eric Fischer, *See Something or Say Something* (2011). On this map of New York City, red dots mark places where people have uploaded a photo to Flickr, blue dots are the site of tweets, and white are places posted to both. We can see that Central Park, the Statue of Liberty, and the picturesque ferry route from southern Manhattan attract photographers, while many text tweets are sent from Kennedy Airport (lower right). Text also predominates in poorer neighborhoods. This seemingly simple mapping of two forms of quick broadcast communication reveals both aesthetic and economic geographies.

evolves. Often, hand-drawn maps are subjective; the artist's beliefs shape its world. This is an excellent quality when the goal is to editorialize or critique, but viewers seeking to observe the actual social patterns of a community need a more objective view.

The second, *Netscan* by Marc Smith, is an algorithmically generated map of discussions on Usenet circa 2004. Algorithmic maps are more generic, and often more objective, though the choice of data and display inevitably introduces some subjectivity—and possibly a lot (Gillespie 2012, 2013).[6] While an algorithmic map cannot match the idiosyncratic wit of the hand-drawn one, it can, once programmed, depict numerous communities and update them frequently. Algorithmic maps can incorporate immense amounts of data and show us interesting and sometimes surprising and anomalous patterns.

Our focus in this book is on designing computer generated depictions; the goal in looking at hand-drawn maps is to see what we can learn for that endeavor from the construction of a handmade one.

The Insight of a Hand-Drawn Map

Updated Map of Online Communities by Randall Munroe, the originator of the online cartoon *xkcd*, is a hand-drawn map of the major online communities as of 2010 (see figure 2.8). Sites are grouped thematically. For example, the mainland is made of social network sites, dominated by Facebook, and surrounded by geographical features such as the "Plains of Awkwardly Public Family Interactions" and the "Northern Wasteland of Unread Updates," while various technologies for real-time conversation—Google Talk, Skype, and ICQ—are islands off the "Sea of Protocol Confusion." The map is enjoyable to peruse because of the meaningful juxtapositions and distributions of its landmarks. Its insight, humor, and irony will be beyond the capabilities of computer-generated maps for quite some time.

Though the layout is witty, it is not entirely fanciful. Geographic size represents "total social activity in a community—that is, how much talking, playing, sharing, or other socializing happens there." For readers familiar with the online social sites of that era, the map is intuitively accurate. The designer, Randall Munroe, went beyond straightforward statistics in his assessment of "social activity." He points out that with the rapid rise and subsequent abandonment of social sites, membership numbers are not the most meaningful: one wants to measure vitality, a more salient, but also subjective, quantity.

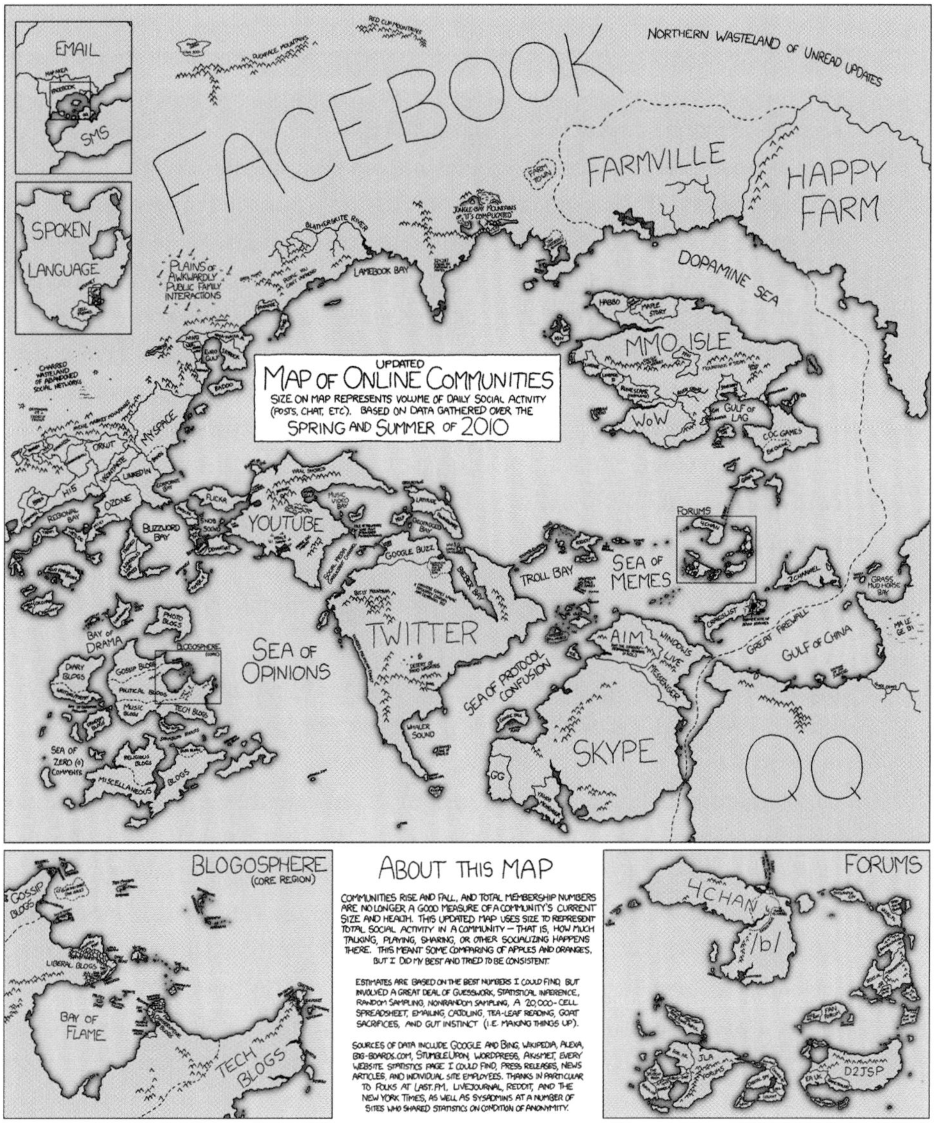

FIGURE 2.8
Randall Munroe, *xkcd's Updated Map of Online Communities* (2010).

"Estimates are based on the best numbers I could find, but involved a great deal of guesswork, statistical inference, random sampling, nonrandom sampling, a 200,000-cell spreadsheet, emailing, cajoling, tea-leaf reading, goat sacrifices, and gut instinct (i.e. making things up)."

A great deal of knowledge goes into making a map such as this one, beyond the multivariate assessment of "vitality." Munroe grouped communities by their technological underpinnings, their role in society (corporate communication versus game playing versus subversive meme generation), their national origin, and more. The layout makes no claim to satisfying all these criteria equally, and, indeed, there is no two-dimensional layout that could. It is, however, a meaningful layout, in which each adjacency depicts an interesting relationship. A key lesson from this is that layout is important, but imperfection is tolerable. There are inevitably other connections that, in any particular layout, are not shown. Each possible layout would yield different insights and comparisons.

The *Updated Map of Online Communities* presupposes that the viewer has considerable knowledge of these social spaces. For the uninitiated, "Duckface Mountains" and "Bieber Bay" are unremarkable, indeed meaningless, but for those in the know, they are little jewels of humor.[7] Much of the pleasure in viewing this map is in finding familiar sites and seeing how they have been depicted.

Perhaps the most important lesson to be learned from this map is that visualizations should be interesting to peruse. Monroe's map is both informative and funny. It includes many sites that the typical *xkcd* reader, though quite Internet savvy, may be unfamiliar with, such as Chinese and other non-Western social network sites. Its details reward careful viewing. For example, Facebook has been criticized for making it difficult for users to adjust their privacy settings, and in the Facebook subcontinent, beyond the foothills of "People You Can't Unfriend," is a small lava pool, with the island of privacy controls set unreachably in the middle.

Algorithmic Maps of Online Communities

Algorithmically generated maps of online communities take data about a community and render this information visually. The designers of such maps do not draw each line and detail; their craft is instead in choosing interesting

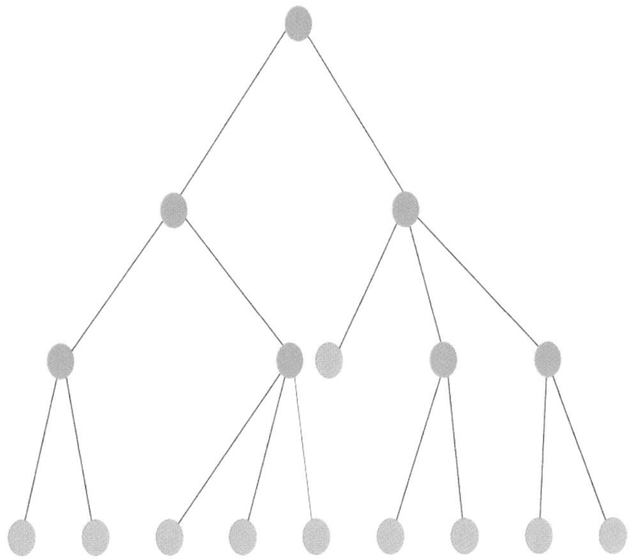

FIGURE 2.9
A tree graph. Tree graphs have traditionally been used to depict hierarchical data.

data, creating algorithms that reveal key patterns, and writing programs that render them clearly and engagingly.

Though we cannot computationally generate incisive wit, as in Munroe's *Online Communities* map, there are other ways to intrigue the viewer. We can add information, giving the viewer a glimpse of what each space is like; a map of a conversation space can allow the viewer to zoom into the actual text of a particular discussion. More generally, interactivity—letting the viewer explore the space, such as by varying the layout or delving more deeply into particular regions—helps people make sense of vast datasets and complex material, showing further detail or other dimensions of it. It encourages the viewer to spend more time examining the data, trying different combinations and seeing the relations that emerge (Donath 1995; Keim 2001; Shneiderman 1994; Yi et al. 2007).

Tree graphs (see figure 2.9) have traditionally been used to depict hierarchical data, but the graphs do not show comparative measurements such as size. Treemaps are a technique for depicting such data using nested rectangles (Balzer, Deussen, and Lewerentz 2005; Bederson, Shneiderman, and Wattenberg 2002; Shneiderman 1998–2009). The advantage of the treemap is that it can show very large datasets in a limited amount of space and make it possible to compare data about the different branches of the hierarchy at a quick glance. Marc Smith and colleagues' treemap visualization of Usenet is an example of this kind of algorithmic map (see figures 2.10, 2.11, and 2.12).

Usenet was a very large discussion site with thousands of hierarchically organized topical newsgroups (see chapter 7, "Contested Boundaries," for more on Usenet history). At the top level were divisions such as rec (for recreation), comp (for computers), sci (for science), and alt (alternative, things that did not fit elsewhere). "Comp" was then further subdivided into areas such as lang, comp.graphics*, and comp.theory*. (The asterisk is a placeholder for all the groups at the next lower level.) Specific groups would then be comp.theory.cell-automata and comp.theory.self-org-sys. Other hierarchies had groups such as rec.sport.soccer, rec.pets.cats, or alt.sex.bondage. The different discussion groups had distinct and varied personalities. Even ostensibly similar ones, such as two computer language groups, could be quite disparate: one might be rigorous and technical, while the other mixed social chitchat in with answers to beginners' questions. Some groups were quite civil, while others were plagued with hostile comments. (In chapter 6, "Visible Conversations," we will look at some approaches for depicting these differences.)

The major categories were also distinctive: comp.* and sci.* were home to the more serious research and technical discussions that were the original foundation of Usenet; soc.* and rec.* contained discussions and arguments ranging from politics and religion to the care of houseplants. Most of Usenet was governed by a set of strictly administered rules about who could add new discussion groups and on what topics. In contrast, in the alt.* hierarchy, which was created to provide for everything that did not fit the main groups, anyone could start a new group on any topic. Alt.* included such groups as alt.suicide.holiday, alt.tasteless, and alt.usenet.kooks.

To make a treemap from a hierarchy, the overall space is first divided up into smaller rectangles, one for each of the top levels of the hierarchy. The size of the rectangles is in proportion to some quality of the category. In figures 2.10 and 2.11, it is the number of postings; in figure 2.12, it is the number of replies. Then, each rectangle is similarly divided into smaller rectangles for each of its subcategories, and so on for as many subdivisions as there are levels of hierarchy. Thus, in figure 2.11, alt is the large top-level category on the left side, taking up more than half the main rectangle. Alt.binaries, outlined in yellow, is a big subcategory, which in turn includes individual groups

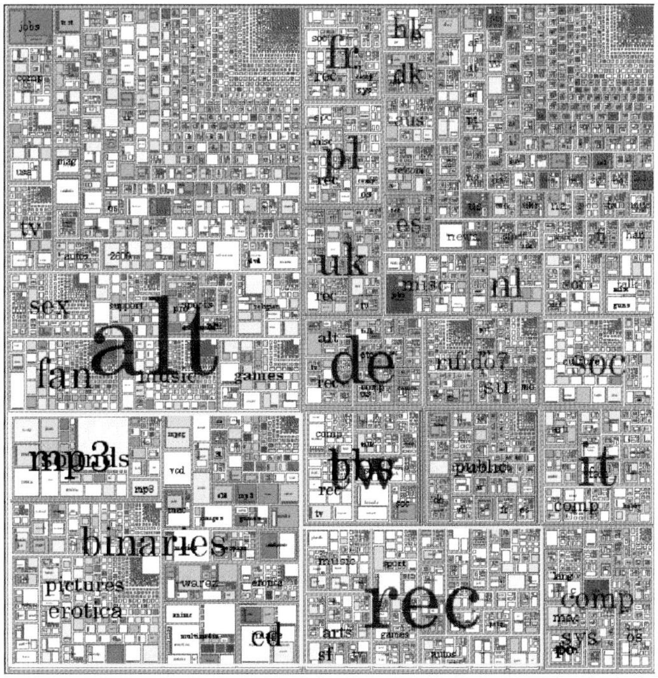

FIGURE 2.10
Marc Smith, *Netscan* map of Usenet postings (2000). In this figure and in figure 2.11, the number of postings to a group during the past month determines the size of the group's square. Color shows growth over that period: red groups are shrinking, green ones are growing. Yellow boxes outline the alt.binaries and rec hierarchies.

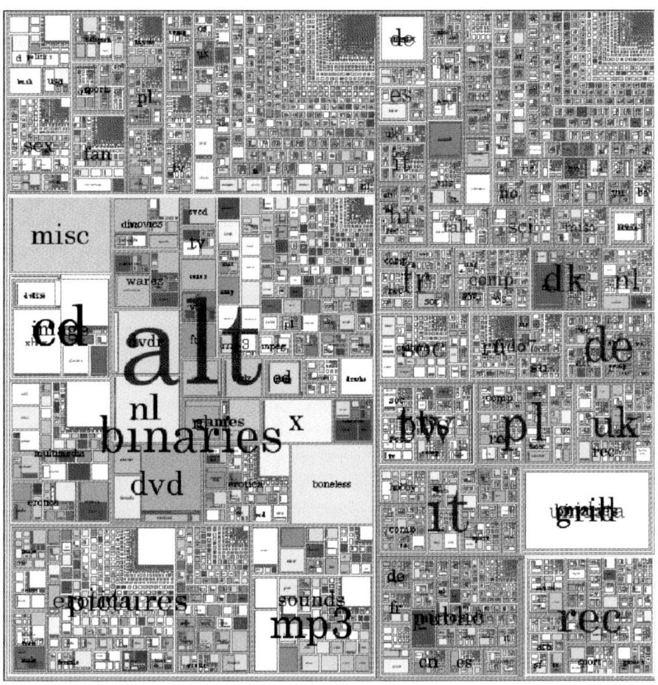

FIGURE 2.11
Marc Smith, *Netscan* map of Usenet postings (2004). The same information as in figure 2.10, but measured four years later.

such as alt.binaries.misc, and further subcategories such as alt.binaries.mp3, which includes alt.binaries.mp3.sounds.

Usenet was changing during the times these maps depict. In the 1990s, it was the major site for online conversation. By 2010, the *xkcd Updated Map of Online Communities* would show Usenet as a tiny island, labeled "Usenet, still there!" How do these maps tell that story?

At first glance, there seem to be no signs of Usenet's deterioration. In fact, it looks to be thriving. Green means growth, and the 2004 map is much greener than the 2000 one. But a closer look shows more troubling developments. In figures 2.10 and 2.11, the categories alt.binaries.* and rec.* have been outlined in yellow. Binaries are data files, meant to be read by machines, not humans. The binaries that are posted to Usenet are often illicit: pornography and pirated music, games, and movies. And it is alt.binaries, the non-conversational repository of this material, that shows the most vigorous growth in number of postings. Rec.* and the other original top-level hierarchies—once the site of lively conversations, exchanges of technical information, and social support—have become comparatively small. By 2004, over half of all postings to Usenet were in the alt.* hierarchy, and the majority of them were binaries. Although these maps cannot tell us *why* it happened, they do show that while the quantity of data uploaded to Usenet rose, its quality—at least in terms of sociability and human interaction—declined precipitously.

The question one wants answered determines which data are best to map. A count of the number of postings answers "Where is there the most activity?" It does not tell you what kind of activity it is, whether it is friendly discussion, political disagreements, blatant advertising, or illegal uploads. It does not tell you where the most resources are being used, that is, what group is using the most storage and bandwidth. But it does give you a general idea of the trends in what people are doing on the site: the maps in figures 2.10 and 2.11 show a Usenet in which people are uploading binaries more and talking about compilers less. Similarly, a street map, though a useful thing in its own right, provides only subtle hints about, say, the terrain or a neighborhood's economic status.

The person seeking a congenial conversation needs a different map, created from different data. Smith made another Usenet treemap, this one based on the number of replies, rather than all postings (see figure 2.12). Since spam and binary uploads tend to be stand-alone posts, this visualization provided a

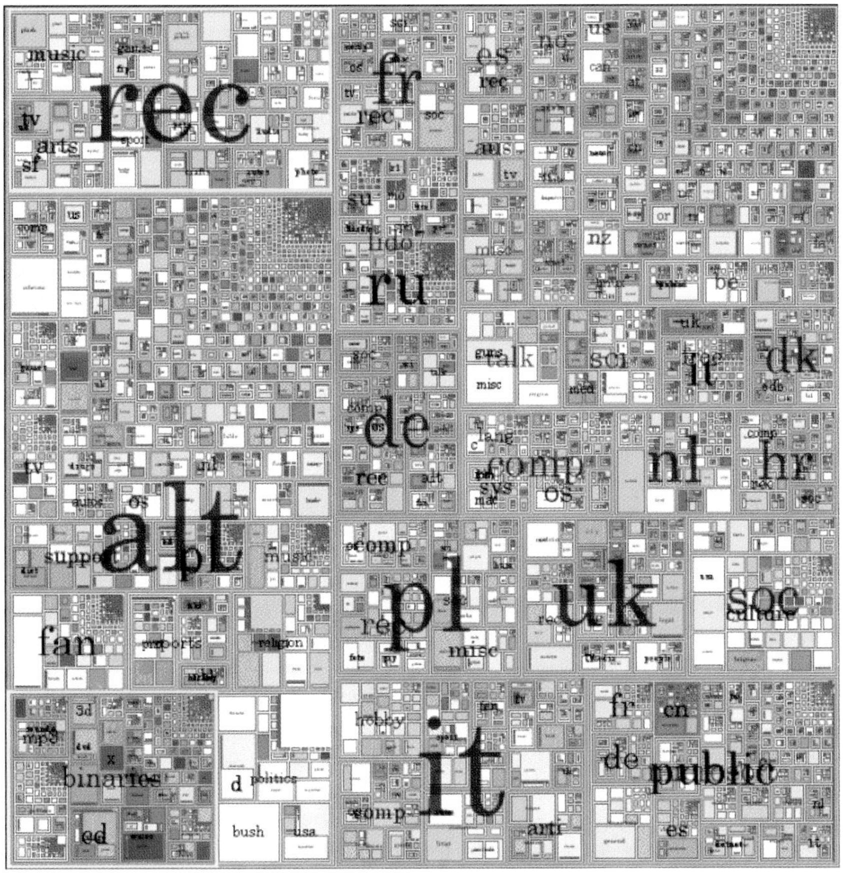

FIGURE 2.12
Marc Smith, *Netscan* map of Usenet replies (2004).

better indication of where social interaction was still occurring; in this map, alt.binaries appears relatively small, as few of its immense number of posts are part of a conversation.

Reply counts alone are insufficient to guide the viewer to a vibrant conversational space. A group might have many replies, but still many times more junk postings, which people do not want to be forced to sift through to find something useful. For this goal, mapping relationships such as the ratio of replies to postings or the average number of exchanges in a conversational thread would create a more informative image. Smith and colleagues used color to show whether a group was growing or shrinking, but one could create similar maps to depict almost anything: the size of the postings, the number of different posters, the predominant language, and so on. A version

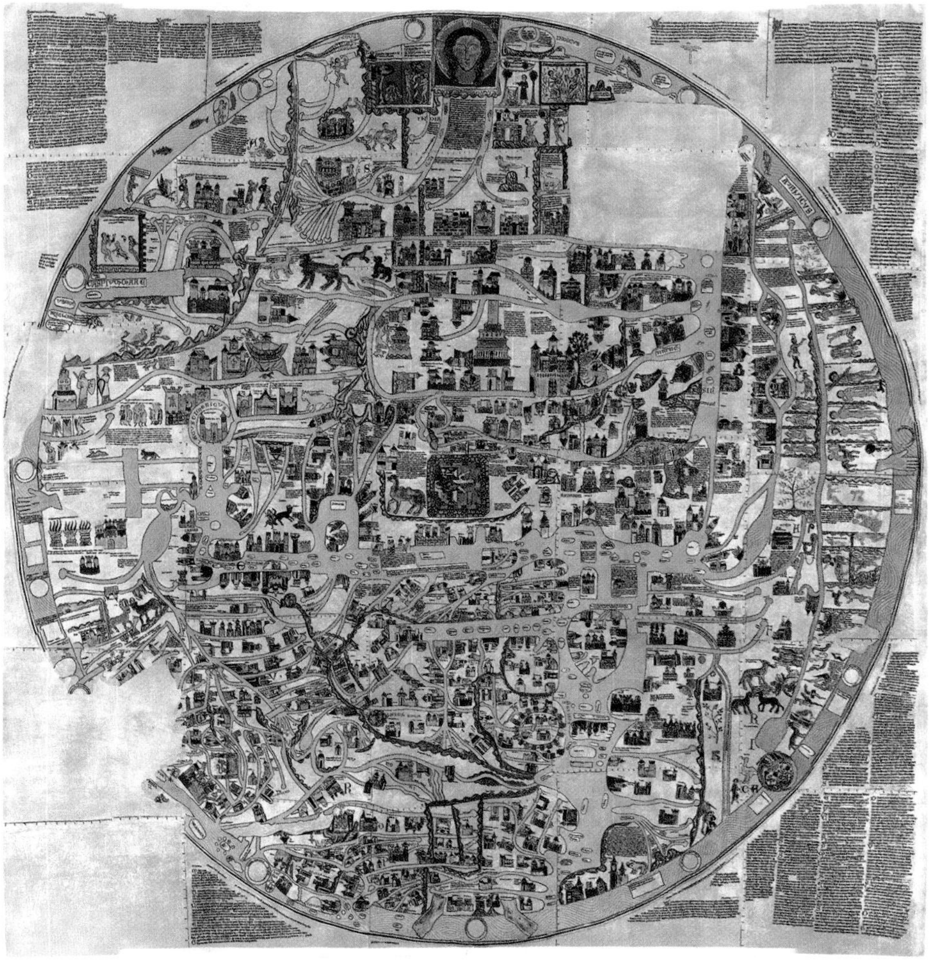

FIGURE 2.13
Gervase of Tilbury, *The Ebstorf mappamundi* (c. 1234). This map shows the known world of the thirteenth century. Jerusalem, "place of man's redemption," is at the center (Siebold 1998).

Cultural biases and political maneuverings reshape maps. We can see in the map shown above what critical cartographer John B. Harley called "omphalos syndrome," the tendency of mapmakers to place their homeland in the center of the world, as well as in ancient Mesopotamian maps that place Babylon in the center, Islamic ones that put Mecca there, Greek ones that set Delphi there, and so on. Some contemporary maps of the United States center the map on the US and shrink the Southern hemisphere to a fraction of its real scale (Harley 2008). See also *How to Lie with Maps* (Monmonier 1996).

of this map that allowed viewers to experiment with looking at different statistics would be fascinating to explore.

Algorithmic maps do not have the overt idiosyncrasy and editorial commentary that a hand-drawn map may feature, but they are still subjective: the designer's choices of data and depiction shape the message they convey. Sometimes the map's intent is to be objective, in which case its subjectivity is, like the distortions inherent to physical maps, inevitable yet regrettable. Sometimes, though, the exaggerations and highlights are deliberate: a map's purpose might be political, to persuade or take a position. Much as newspapers distinguish "news," which aims for objectivity, from "editorial," which is clearly labeled as subjective, a map should ideally make its purpose and biases clear to the viewer.[8]

The big question we are addressing here is how to navigate an immense virtual social space. Today, this question arises when one looks at Twitter and tries to decide whom to follow, out of the possible millions. It arises when looking at a newspaper such as the *New York Times* online, where many articles generate hundreds of comments. It arises when visiting any of the innumerable sites that are, like Usenet was, home to myriad conversational communities centered on diverse topics and with greatly varying levels of sociability. Even seemingly niche sites, such as "Digital Photography Review" (http://www.dpreview.com), host numerous forums, with some, such as "Canon EOS 7D/60D–10D Talk," comprising millions of messages on hundreds of thousands of topics.

Maps are an aid to navigation, an invitation to explore. The goal of mapping the social landscape is to help the viewer understand what is possible and where one might go—where to find a compatible community, a lively debate, an up-to-date source of news or gossip. Without a map, we can search to find a discussion of a particular topic, or follow the recommendations of writers we already read, but these approaches can be narrow. A map designed to highlight relevant social patterns helps the viewer find unfamiliar yet promising places.

A map that shows activity helps us see the vibrancy of the online world: it makes the virtual crowd come alive. Though many of the lively areas may not be relevant for you (e.g., fan sites for celebrities you don't care about, discussions about products you don't own or diseases you don't have), it is interesting to know where and what they are, to be aware of what fascinates your fellow participants.

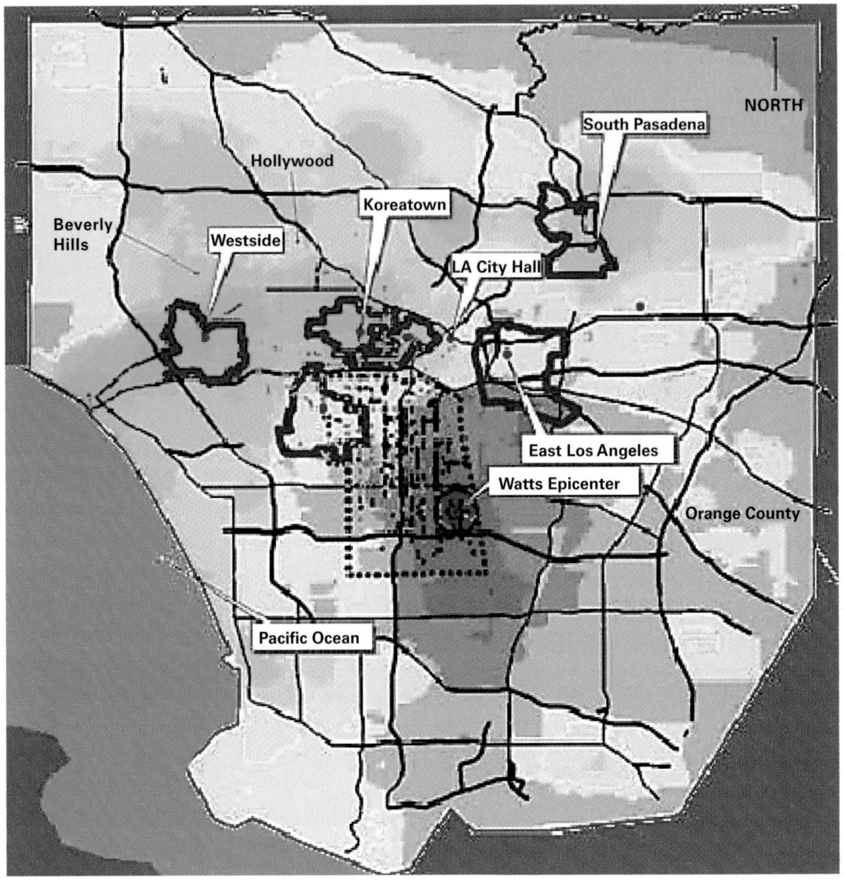

FIGURE 2.14
Sorin Matei and Sandra Ball-Rokeach, *Metamorphosis Affective Map* (2001). This map was created by combining the opinions of 215 residents of Los Angeles about which areas they think are dangerous (shown in red) and where they feel safe (in green) and superimposing these data on a map of the city (Matei, Ball-Rokeach, and Qiu 2001). It is a subjective map, but one that presents the community members' opinions rather than the mapmaker's. It is also interesting in the context of thinking about the questions people want a map to answer. Street maps typically show you where the roads are, but little about the advisability of taking them. This map tells you where you should and should not go, according to the surveyed residents.

Even without the set geography of the physical world, the map of a virtual space can still reflect its structure. A treemap suits a site with a fundamentally hierarchical structure, such as Usenet or a newspaper with topical sections. Other structures, such as networks, call for different depictions. The "Interactive Persian Blogosphere Map" depicts a network of blogs (see figure 2.15). This map also combines algorithmic and hand-drawn techniques: each dot is a blog, and an automated program places them algorithmically based on the interconnections between the blogs (their links to each other) and

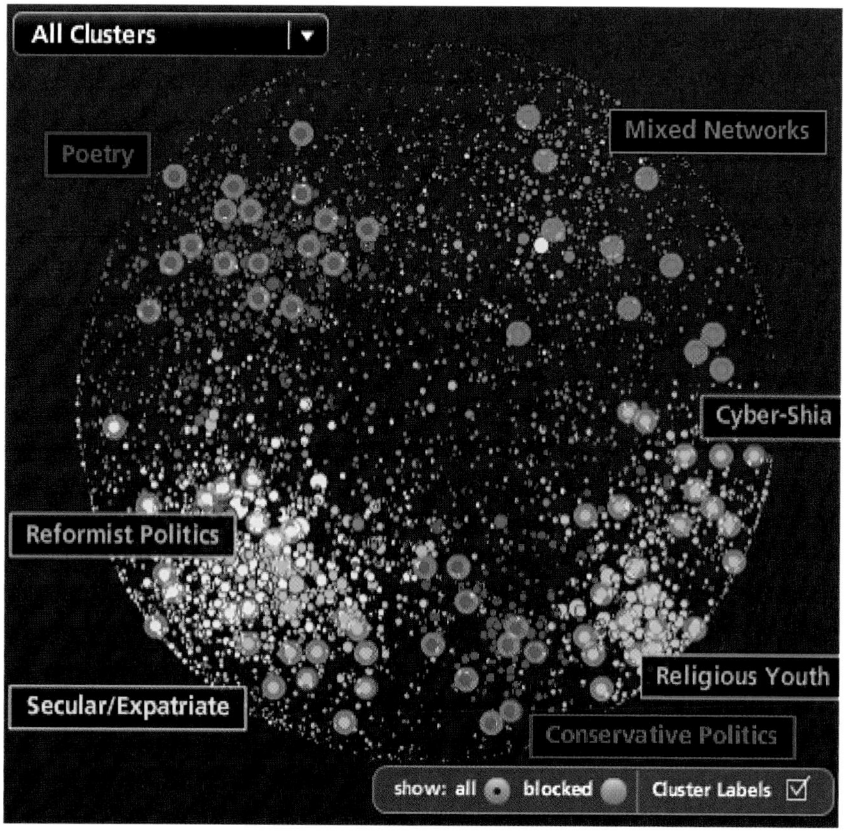

FIGURE 2.15
John Kelly and Bruce Etling, *Interactive Persian Blogosphere Map* (2008).

their common external links. The map designers labeled the clusters by hand and annotated both the clusters and the circled blogs with descriptions of their contents, putting them into the larger context of Iranian politics (Kelly and Etling 2008). Using a computer to make the algorithmic layout allowed them to locate a large number of blogs using fairly complex criteria, while the hand annotation adds a human interpreter's insight to the map. *Visual Who*, the project that opened this book, is another way to map a network; we shall look at others in chapter 4, "Mapping Social Networks."

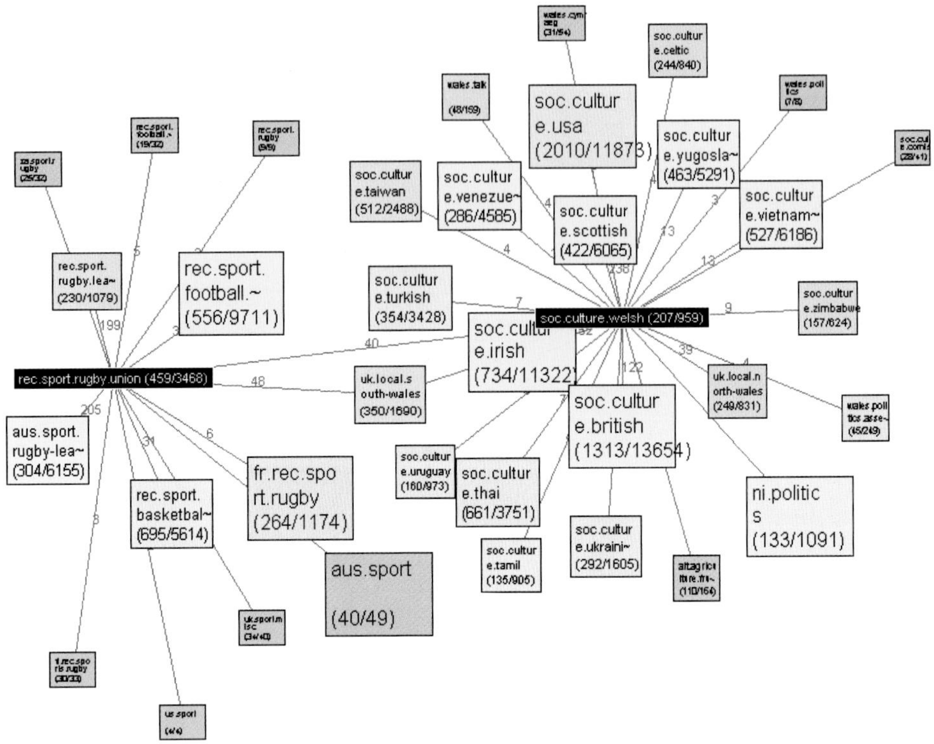

FIGURE 2.16
Marc Smith, *Netscan* network map of Usenet newsgroups (2004).

There are multiple ways to depict a single site. The treemaps we have been examining were part of a larger endeavor that explored different ways of mapping Usenet; a related map (see figure 2.16) showed the newsgroups as a network, where the number of cross-postings (postings addressed to two or more groups at the same time) was the measure of tie strength. The treemap and the network depiction are both "right"—they highlight different patterns.

The visualization's sensory quality is also important. Voronoi treemaps (figure 2.17), for example, present the same information as traditional treemaps, but are gracefully organic, appearing to have evolved naturally, rather than as if they were mechanically sliced (Balzer, Deussen, and Lewerentz 2005). One might prefer to use this approach for depicting a discussion space, because it gives the impression of a living, active community. In the next chapter, "Interfaces Make Meaning," we discuss the elements that contribute to the sensory qualities of online interfaces and how these, as well as metaphor and interactivity, produce the feel of an online experience.

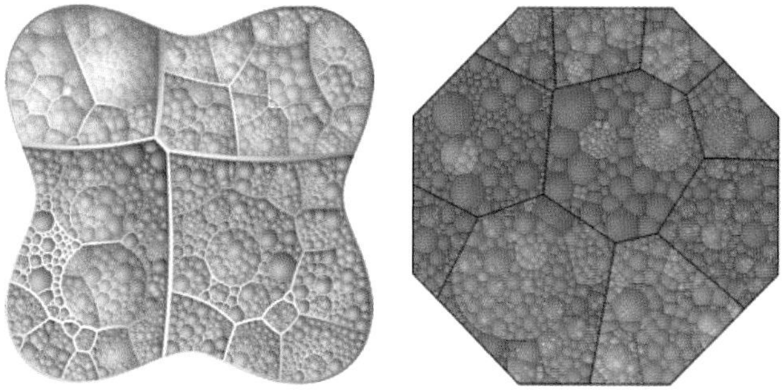

FIGURE 2.17
Michael Balzer and Oliver Deussen, Voronoi treemaps (2005). Voronoi treemaps are similar to rectangular treemaps, but use polygons of various shapes to represent nodes and levels (Balzer, Deussen, and Lewerentz 2005). The one on the left shows 4,075 nodes at 10 levels; the one on the right shows 16,288 nodes at 7 levels.

POSTSCRIPT: THE SOCIAL PARADOX OF MAPS

A history of eighteenth-century English road infrastructure makes an interesting point about the social change from wayfaring to map-reading (Guldi 2012). In earlier days, when maps were vague sketches, travelers needed to ask for assistance throughout their journey: what to do at the next turn, where to find a decent inn, were the roads passable? As infrastructure became more reliable and maps became more accurate (the detailed surveying that was needed to build the road also greatly improved mapmaking ability), people became more self-reliant in their travels. They no longer needed to engage their fellow travelers for information about the next turn to take or cultivate good will to get reliable news of the conditions. When we travel today, most of us rely on GPS, guidebooks, and maps, and as a result travel can be an isolated experience. It is only when we get lost or if there is an unexpected problem that we need to stop to talk with other people. Maps let us navigate asocially.

A parallel transformation happened in the early days of the Web. Before search engines existed, people relied on each other to find their way around the burgeoning set of Web pages. Users created home pages that, in addition to describing themselves and their interests, included a list of links to things they had found to be useful or funny on the Web. The most comprehensive or well-curated lists of recommended pages became themselves among the Web's most popular sites. Then search engines were developed. Today information seeking on the Web no longer requires that you find the individual people who create the best lists and guideposts; now algorithms compile this information for you.[9] You simply type a query.

It is easy to romanticize the wayfaring travel of the past. Being dependent on the kindness of not always well-meaning strangers can be uncomfortable, as well as dangerous. Relatively few people traveled then, and not for recreation. The advent of easily followed maps helped fuel an immense leisure tourism industry (Strickland 1998). Online social way-finding does not raise the specter of being robbed on a deserted country road. But relying on social connections to find information is far less efficient than performing a quick search of a fully indexed and massive trove of data. Few people would argue for a return to the days when web users relied on Yahoo, "Cool Site of the Day," "Justin's Links from the Underground," or other handcrafted lists to find interesting material. But in other cases, something valuable has been lost in the achievement of efficiency.

At its height, Usenet hosted thousands of active conversations and was a place people went to find stimulating discussions, social support, and, above all, useful information. Obtaining this information was a social process: you were expected to familiarize yourself with the past discussions and social mores, to be a part of the community, not simply an opportunistic answer-seeker. In the mid-1990s, Usenet's data was imported to the Web and it became much easier to search it (Brown 1999; Hauben 2002). Information seeking became divorced from relationship building, contributing to the collapse of community on this site.

Maps of communities allow us to see histories and relationships that would otherwise require extensive study to discern. As social visualizations, their purpose is to aid in social engagement. But do they have the paradoxical effect of making us less social, less dependent on building relationships to learn about the surrounding milieu? I would argue no, that they ultimately aid sociability; they make it easier for us to make initial contacts, to find the person we want to speak with, and to understand social nuances that might otherwise escape us. But we need to be cognizant of this tension, and use design to foster sociability, not supplant it.

3

INTERFACES MAKE MEANING

In July 2012, physicists at CERN discovered a subatomic particle they believe to be the long-sought Higgs boson, a key piece in confirming the Standard Model of theoretical physics. "Today we have witnessed a discovery which gives unique insight into our understanding of the universe and the origin of the masses of fundamental particles" (Professor Stefan Söldner-Rembold, Professor of Particle Physics at the University of Manchester, quoted in Davies 2012). The presentation announcing it was witnessed by a standing-room-only audience in Geneva, including many of the world's top physicists, as well as a large international audience online. Yet many people noted an incongruity: the presentation (see figure 3.1) was written in "Comic Sans," a cartoonish font that seems more suitable for elementary school bulletins than for groundbreaking discoveries in particle physics (Randall 2012). "CERN's Higgs presentation just added weight to the theory that Comic Sans is a terrible font," said popular Twitter user @Hal9000.

Part of what you say is how you say it, and in writing, fonts and color take the place that tone of voice has in speech. These paralinguistic (i.e., nonverbal) elements of communication convey emotion, level of seriousness, and cultural references. Features such as accent and aesthetic choices provide cues about the speaker's (or writer's) identity, which the listener (or reader) uses to decide whether to trust and believe the message.

So, why did the physicists at CERN choose Comic Sans for their presentation of such extraordinarily important experimental results? It is possible that although the choice seemed incongruous to viewers who expected the presentation to convey the significance of the event, the physicists had a different message. They were cautious about overstating claims, and the slides

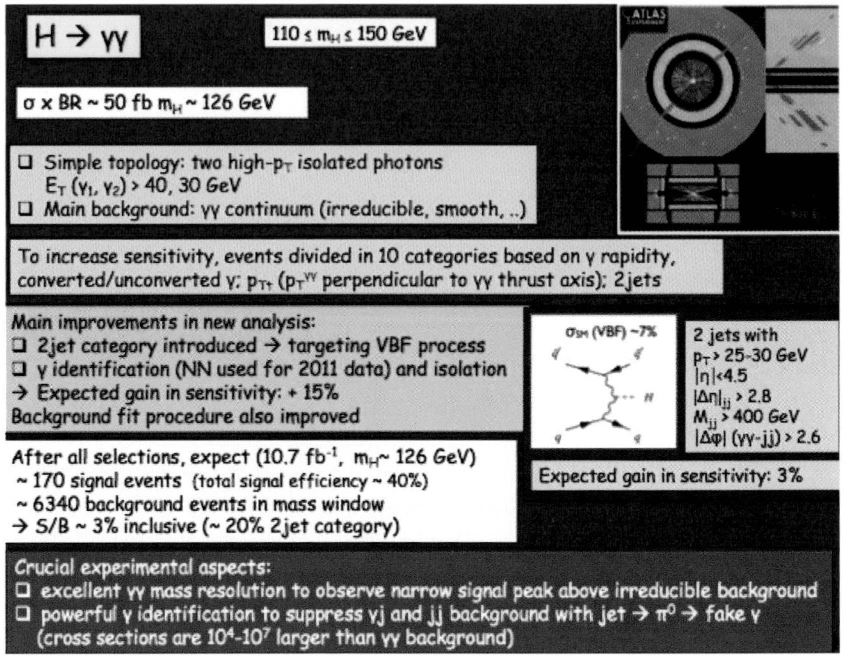

FIGURE 3.1
Fabiola Gianotti, slide from the Atlas presentation at CERN, July 4, 2012 (Gianotti 2012).

were meant to educate and explain the results, with the goal of making the complex mathematics as understandable as possible. Hence the choice of a friendly, school-like font. It is also possible that the inappropriate font and garish colors were the PowerPoint equivalent of the stereotypical physicist's rumpled clothes and uncombed hair: simply careless design, made by people focused on the content of the slides, with little concern—perhaps even disdain—for appearance.

Here we see how even the mere choice of a font can shape impressions. The design of an online interface involves many such choices. Its words present information, while its fonts, lines, and colors convey mood and provide a setting for the information. As a computational medium, online interfaces have the added complexity of interaction. Interactive interfaces can seem to be sentient; the scale and timing of their reactions can evoke a personality that may be sluggish or alert, businesslike or subtly humorous.

Understanding how an interface's design shapes the impression it conveys is useful for any application, but it is especially crucial for communication media. Interfaces set the scene for online sociability. The features of a social space not only facilitate discussion, they also set the tone for it, affecting how the users perceive each other and conveying cues about how to act. Representations of people, even if abstract, should portray the individual vividly and evocatively.

Metaphors are one way that interface design creates meaning. We use metaphors to give shape to the inherently and incomprehensibly abstract world of data. Some metaphors are subtle, almost unnoticeable; but they are also pervasive, occurring in all our thinking about nonphysical concepts. When we plot data so that positive values are shown as higher, we are using the metaphor of growth. Other metaphors are deliberate and literal, such as the recycling bin on the computer desktop where we dump unwanted files. Metaphors, whether subtle or conspicuous, shape how we think; in the case of interface design, they control what we can do. They provide legibility by letting us see abstract concepts in concrete terms. But they must be used skillfully, or they will constrain the electronic world unnecessarily to mimicking the physical one.

Another way that interfaces shape meaning is through sensory elements, including color and motion. We humans are physical beings, interacting with the outside world through our senses. In the physical world, we are surrounded by vibrant hues and shades, objects in motion, and responsive, animate beings. The world on today's computer screen is often comparatively lifeless; or, alternatively, it is excessively bright, with flashy ads and quizzes grabbing at your attention. A sensory interface need not be garish, but should instead contribute to our ability to communicate.

Interfaces also shape meaning through interactivity, the distinguishing feature of online (as opposed to traditional) media. This responsiveness adds a new dimension of expressivity: does it react fast or slow, in an expected or surprising way? Different response styles can give the impression of an entity that is alert and accommodating, or one that is shy or sly. Even simple activities, such as what happens when you move the mouse across a page, can be imbued with expression: imagine a page where words grew immense or disappeared when the mouse passed over them, or ones that seemed to be drawn to or repelled from it, as if magnetic. Though not appropriate for business memos, such expressive interactions can help set the tone of a game or social space, or enliven the experience of exploring a social dataset.

This chapter will examine how interfaces make meaning using metaphors, sensory elements, and interactivity. It is but an introduction: interfaces convey meaning in many other ways, including fonts, layout, sound, and the like; and of the topics we do cover, whole books can be (and are) devoted to each one.[1]

The goal here is not to provide in-depth instruction on how to use these elements in design, but to raise awareness of their use and capabilities. As designers, we are sometimes oblivious to the messages design choices carry, from graphical elements to the fundament metaphors that shape the interface; as users, too, we are often unaware of their effects, responding to them subconsciously.

METAPHOR

> But he that dares not grasp the thorn
> Should never crave the rose.
> —Anne Brontë

The world of information is inherently abstract, and we use metaphors drawn from our everyday physical experience to bring sense and structure to it. Metaphors ground our thinking, allowing us to understand novel and abstract concepts in familiar terms. They take the knowledge and beliefs we have about one thing and let us apply them to make sense of something new and unfamiliar. When a metaphor works well, this framing is enlightening. Comparing a lover to a rose evokes beauty, bright colors, and a sweet scent, yet also impermanence and hidden prickly thorns. This is a complex image, and when it is appropriate, the rose metaphor is a powerful shorthand way of communicating this intricate set of properties. Yet if some of the properties are not relevant—if you do not want to bring up the issue of thorns, for instance—that particular metaphor may not be right. No metaphor is perfect. The art of applying them comes from understanding which are good enough, as when the power of the image overcomes the inconsistencies or even when the inconsistencies are ironic and desirable.

Verbal metaphors help make our language more colorful and expressive. They influence how we think about something, but they do not change the thing itself. Interface metaphors play a more fundamental role in how we experience and interact with the technological world, affecting function as well as feeling. The metaphor that is chosen for an interface shapes how it can be used. When we put computer "files" into "folders," these metaphoric constructs help us think about the way information is organized in our machine, but they also constrain what we can do with it. Interface metaphors also influence the feel of the experience, the emotional and aesthetic response we have to our interactions with and via the machine. The desktop metaphor evokes office work: secretaries, bosses, quarterly plans, and cubicles. It was developed in the late 1970s and early 1980s, when office work was seen as the primary use for personal computers (Johnson et al. 1989; Perkins, Keller, and Ludolph 1997). The desktop image certainly is appropriate for that setting. However, it is less appropriate when we use the computer as an entertainment center or as the locus of our social life.[2] Interface metaphors need to fit both the feel and function of the application.

When the computer is a social medium, its primary purpose is not organizing documents. Instead, it is a machine for playing games, making friends, reading news, and watching movies amid a virtual crowd of other viewers. People use it to keep up with a wide range of acquaintances, to see what others are doing, to participate in discussions, and to present a particular view of themselves to close friends and distant strangers. Making an intuitively usable interface for this world requires making the information accessible and navigable, delineating public areas versus private space, and enabling various channels of communication. At the same time, it needs to capture the feeling of being in a social space, not a filing cabinet.

Metaphorically Thinking

In *Metaphors We Live By*, George Lakoff and Mark Johnson (1980) show how our abstract thoughts are built metaphorically on more concrete foundations (for example, this sentence uses the metaphor of thought as construction). These cognitive metaphors allow us to use what we know about an easily understood domain in order to comprehend a more abstract one. For example, we sometimes think about money by using the "money as liquid" metaphor: "his assets were frozen"; "they have good cash flow"; "it's like pouring money down the drain"; "their cash source dried up." Like water, money flows according to certain rules, and we like it to be plentiful. Metaphors can also build on each other, so that we think of one abstract concept in terms of another. Thus, money can be the basis for understanding time: "I like spending time with you"; "we are wasting time"; "this will save time."

The choice of metaphor influences our beliefs about abstract things. When we speak about arguments using the metaphor of war ("I lost that argument"; "he shot down all her points"; "you caught me off-guard in that discussion"), the goal is to win, to crush the opponent. Yet there are other metaphors for argument, such as construction ("his argument rests on a weak foundation") or fabrication ("she wove all the strands of the discussion together"). With these, the goal is to construct a solid and compelling position; such metaphors encompass working cooperatively together.

Metaphors help us understand the abstract, but it is an imperfect understanding—and we may find ourselves relying on other metaphors to figure out what went wrong. We often think about information as if it were a solid object: "I can grasp that idea"; "give me all the info about her"; "throw away that thought"; intellectual property law is the legal formalization of the information-as-object metaphor. Yet laws based on the information-as-object metaphor are difficult to enforce, as stories that "go viral" or "spread like wildfire" vividly illustrate with their metaphoric casting of information as contagion and conflagration.

When we are oblivious of the metaphors we use to make sense of the world, they simply seem like the way things naturally are. For people who think of argument as war, building consensus with others seems foolish; to them this appears to be an inherent feature of arguments, not an effect of their own conceptual framework. Metaphors help us grasp abstract ideas, but they also constrain how we think about them. By becoming more aware of the metaphors we use, we can better understand the assumptions we make about a topic or situation, and we can choose to try other conceptual frameworks, to see what insights may come from a fresh perspective.

Computer Interfaces Are Metaphors

Computer interfaces use metaphoric structures to shape and define the way we think about data, interactions, and computation; without them, it would be very difficult to understand these concepts. In fact, metaphors permeate our computer interactions. We put our email (a postal metaphor) into folders (a physical document metaphor), and we read stories on Web pages (physical documents again, mixed with a spidery biological metaphor).

Much of what you see on a typical computer screen is visual metaphor. There aren't really "buttons" or "scroll-bars" embedded there, but visual cues that remind you of these objects, and an interface that reacts consistently with that metaphor. A physical button is a familiar object. You know that when you press a button on a machine, something happens; you also know that it doesn't matter where on the button you put your finger, or for how long you hold it down. The screen button behaves in a similar way.

Because the screen button is a virtual object, the designers could have made it to have all kinds of behaviors: to respond differently when clicked in different spots, to cause something to increase the longer it is held, to disappear when you press it, or to grow or seem to explode. In general, however, screen buttons are made to act as much as possible like ordinary physical buttons. This makes them *legible*; we don't have to think very hard about how we expect them to behave, and they do what we expect.

One can, of course, make exploding or disappearing or otherwise bizarrely acting screen buttons for dramatic effect; viewers perceive these to be strange because they have preexisting expectations of normal behavior that are subverted in this situation. Cognitive metaphors can be (mis)used poetically.

While metaphors can borrow the cultural meaning of the thing that they reference, they do not import its full significance. A jewel-encrusted gold locket in the physical world has real properties of rarity and expense; but while decorating a picture of one's self (or avatar) with a rendering of such a locket may attest to your aspirations, the picture itself is no more valuable than any other carefully chosen array of pixels. The locket's meaning, deeply rooted in its physical state, becomes only a "cheap" reference when used online.

Metaphors help us make sense of abstractions, but they also limit what we do with them. Email is an example: organizing the formless stream of emails into folders makes us better able to organize them, but it also imposes the limits of physical folders on the more versatile electronic form. Whereas a physical letter can only be in one folder at a time, it is technically possible for electronic messages to be in more than one virtual folder at a time. However, since such multiplexed existence is inconsistent with the folder metaphor, most programs make email conform to paper's limits in order to maintain consistency. This makes email function less well than it could.[3] If you have a folder for email from friends and one that is for financial information, where should you put the note from a friend with useful investment information? People spend a lot of time trying to decide where to file a piece of email, and spend even more time in retrieval, searching through multiple plausible folders to find the one they chose some time ago (Mackay 1988a; Venolia et al. 2001; Whittaker and Sidner 1996).

We could build an interface that allows for filing a single email simultaneously within multiple folders, but doing so within the existing folder metaphor would be confusing. The users would not know whether a single email is somehow visible in many places at once or if there were multiple copies of the email. They would then be unable to predict whether deleting the email in one folder would delete all of them (as would happen if it were a single email) or if the other copies would remain (as would happen if there were multiple copies). This confusion arises from breaking the folder-as-container metaphor.

Instead, we need to take a fresh look at which metaphor is best suited to the problem. Rethinking the purpose of the folder makes it clear that what we really want is something else entirely, something like a label, many of which can apply to a single piece of email, rather than a container, only one of which can hold that mail.[4] With this interface metaphor, users no longer need to decide if a note with stock tips from a colleague who is also a friend goes under "work," "friends," or "finance." They can label it with all the relevant tags and would intuitively understand that it is a single item with multiple labels.[5]

Beyond understanding how to apply metaphors, the art of interface design requires knowing how to stretch them so that they are more useful. For instance, we can give electronic labels capabilities beyond those of ordinary physical ones, such as instantly searching for every message featuring a combination of one or more labels; although this cannot be done instantaneously in real life, it is not outside our established model of what it is possible to do with labels. It bends the metaphor but does not break it.

Interface metaphors shape people's understanding of online social situations, including their notion of how private or public is the space they are in. In the early days of "chat-rooms," many novice users were coming online. The "room" metaphor was a useful way to help people understand, with little visual assistance, that multiple separate conversational threads were available, that one could participate in only one at a time, and that only those who chose a particular one would be privy to it.

The downside of the metaphor is that features that are not typical of physical rooms break the metaphor. In a physical building with different rooms, walls block sound. Thus, calling a conversation interface a "chatroom" leads people to expect that others in that shared space can hear the discussions in it, but those outside cannot. This is good so long as the virtual experience stays close to the physical model. Yet, for example, keeping a publicly available archive of the conversation violates the privacy expectations set up by the room metaphor. The problem is not the existence of the archive itself, which may serve a useful purpose, but the mismatch between the permanence and openness of the discussion archive with the expectation of privacy established by the room metaphor (in chapter 11, "Privacy and Public Space," we will look more closely at how people understand privacy online).

Concrete metaphors make interfaces legible, but excessive use of them constricts functionality. Ted Nelson, one of the pioneers of computer interface design, noted: "We are using the computer as a paper simulator, which is like tearing the wings off a 747 and driving it as a bus on the highway" (quoted in Freiberger and Swaine 2000). Since metaphors limit as well as empower, it behooves the designer to choose them carefully. The challenge is to design interfaces that go beyond copying the everyday physical world, yet remain intuitively comprehensible.

More abstract metaphors are often more versatile. Instead of using a room, which is a physical structure with many well-defined properties, one might instead depict conversations occurring in different generic "containers," which could have different properties; for example, one could be anonymous, another could have archives, and another could be publicly broadcast. Visual cues, such as text, transparency and murkiness, and color and borders, could help users understand the properties of the different containers (Harry and Donath 2008). We are still using metaphors here, but they are less concrete. In general, using metaphors that are abstract and general, yet still convey the necessary meaning, provides the most flexibility to make interfaces that go beyond being there.

"Information Physics"

Metaphors such as the computer folder are deliberate and obvious, but interfaces can be more subtle and conceptual yet still legible. Ben Bederson and Jim Hollan used the term "information physics" to describe interfaces that were consistent and believable yet did not rely on high-level metaphors such as desktops and files (Bederson and Hollan 1994). This "physics" is still metaphorical, but it is much more abstract and ultimately flexible. Growing, shrinking, coming together, pushing apart—when an interface implements these behaviors consistently, the underlying model will seem invisible to the user: it will simply seem to work and make sense. Many familiar designs make use of such metaphors. For example, we are accustomed to things growing upward: saplings and children are small, whereas grown trees and people are tall. Thus, though it is possible for the axes in graphs to reach in any arbitrary direction, it is intuitive to put the origin at the bottom of the screen and have amounts rise as they get bigger.

The most fundamental and ubiquitous metaphors are spatial. They derive from our basic relationships with things around us: up and down, near and far, in and out, in front and behind. We conceive of time using spatial metaphors: "the holidays are approaching"; "I'm glad that week is behind us." We structure our own activities spatially: "I'm going to go ahead with that plan"; "I'm falling behind on my work." Spatial metaphors are inescapable and they ground our thinking about abstract concepts (indeed, being "grounded" is itself a spatial metaphor) and serve as building blocks for creating more complex concepts (Harnad 1990; Lakoff and Johnson 1980).[6]

Space is abstract but not necessarily neutral; we ascribe values to space. When we make a stock market graph, we put the bigger numbers up and the smaller ones down. This could be a direct representation of how things accumulate in piles: the more there is, the higher the pile. But height also connotes deeper meanings. Emotionally, up is happy (upbeat, rising spirits), whereas down is sad (low energy, depressed). When we feel happy, we stand taller; when we're sad, we slouch and look at the ground. I would rather feel upbeat than down on my luck; I would like to have the upper hand.

Our metaphoric interpretation of "up" also embodies ethics. Lakoff and Johnson note that we think of virtue as up, as in "an upstanding citizen" versus being "down and out." People are quicker to comprehend words representing power relations (e.g., professor–student) when the powerful one is shown on top (Schubert 2005). These metaphoric associations shade how we interpret the vertical location of data.

This is fine when up is good, strong, or powerful, but what about when more is bad? A chart in which everything is rising looks encouraging, even if the measured quantity is one we would prefer to see go down. For example, a chart showing how gas prices are rising has that optimistic upward slope; to make it visibly convey that this is an unfortunate trend one could instead graph an equivalent downward statistic, such as how much gas $10 will buy. Being aware of metaphoric meaning helps us ensure that the intuitive impression a graph makes matches the meaning of the data.

Metaphors have the power even to change how we perceive the physical world around us. For example, the spatial orientation on maps affects people's understanding of distance. Going uphill is harder than going downhill. Maps depict north as "up." Studies show that people perceive traveling north (which is "up" on a map, but not physically) to be harder than going south, even for short distances (Nelson and Simmons 2009). If metaphoric constructs can reshape our perception of the solid physical world around us, imagine how strongly they can influence our understanding of the abstract and inherently formless virtual world.

Spatial metaphors are so basic and common that often they are nearly invisible. Yet, like the poetic metaphor of the rose with its sweet scent and prickly thorns, spatial metaphors can encompass a complex mix of meanings that designers need to be cognizant of in order to create coherent and intuitive interfaces.

Let's look at the seemingly simple task of making a circle on the screen larger. The circle could become larger because the circle itself is growing (scaling), because the circle and viewer are moving closer to each other (translation), or because the viewer's eye, acting like a camera's lens, is changing its focal length (zooming). The result of each of these transformations is a larger circle, but each changes the scene in different ways.

If the object itself scales, then it will take up more space, while other things around it stay their original size. A pen that had originally been too thick to write inside the circle would then be proportionately smaller and able to do so. If the viewer moves closer to the object (translation), he will be able to see more detail on the circle than had been previously visible. His relationship to all other objects will also be different: some objects that had been in front of him might now be behind him, out of sight. Scaling and translation involved actual changes to the things in the scene. Zooming, on the other hand, is a change in perception only; things just appear larger to the viewer, and objects that had been in the periphery of his vision would now be out of sight.[7]

How is making circles grow and shrink part of designing sociable media? Later in this book, we will encounter problems such as how to explore the dense interconnections of social networks or interact with the vast archives of a large-scale, long-term conversation. To do so, we may want some parts of the interface to expand and reveal more information while other parts are still visible but less detailed. The designer needs to be aware of the different ways of doing this and their significance. We might want to scale some participants in a forum to be larger than others, because they have been active longer or more prolific. We might use translation to bring them closer, because the viewer is engaged in a direct discussion with them. We might use zooming to get a detailed view in order to be a neutral observer, looking more closely but not changing the underlying representation.

Turning Time into Space

In our everyday, unmediated existence, we live in the present. Our words and the activity around us are ephemeral, disappearing into the past as soon as they occur. Media, on the other hand, accumulate over time, allowing us to contemplate and analyze it at leisure. From the time that the first primitive people drew oxen on the walls of caves, we have been taming time by recording the events of a moment. Books record narratives that can span centuries, and photographs freeze a singular instant.

Online, there are vast stores of history: conversation archives, Web browsing records, and accumulated years of status updates. Yet in their raw form, these are of limited use. We seldom want to look at history at the rate that it occurred. Instead, we want to compress time, to see at a glance patterns that unfolded over days, months, or years (see figure 3.2).

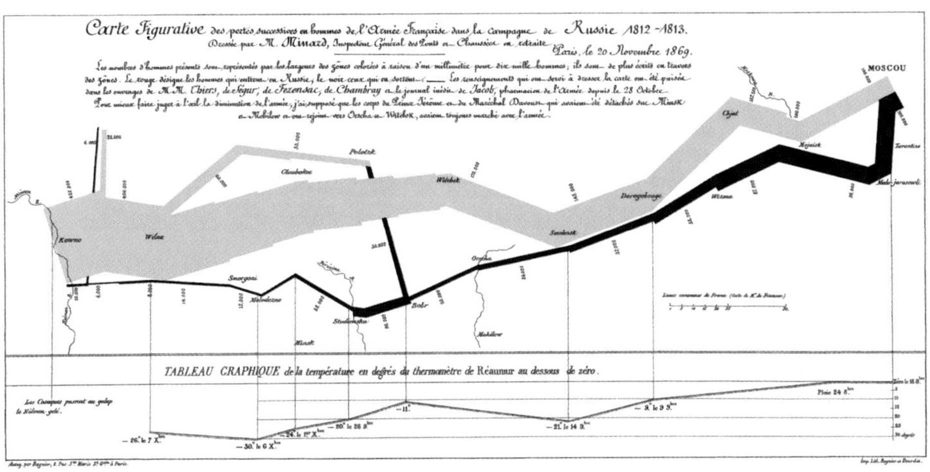

FIGURE 3.2
Charles Minard, *Carte figurative des pertes successives en hommes de l'Armée Française dans la campagne de Russie 1812–1813* (1869). Quintessential depiction of action over time. This graph shows Napoleon's losses in Russia from 1812 to 1813. The thickness of the band depicts the size of the army as they marched to Moscow (beige) and retreated (black) (Tufte 1982).

A key problem—and one that we will return to throughout this book—is how to represent history, how to show time as space. We cannot think of time without using metaphors (Lakoff and Johnson 1999). Mostly, we think of it as motion in space. We think of time as linear: the past stretches out behind us, the future is before us, and we are at an ever-changing present. We think of time as being extended in space ("the meeting took a long time"); we think of it as having boundaries ("he did it in the allotted time").

We may view ourselves as moving along this timeline ("we've passed the deadline") or we may perceive ourselves as static while the timeline is shifting ("the weekend flew by"). This makes phrases such as "let's move the meeting forward a week" ambiguous. If I think of myself as moving through time, moving a meeting ahead pushes it further into the future; if I think of time as coming toward me, moving it ahead brings it closer, that is, less far into the future (Boroditsky, Ramscar, and Frank 2001).[8]

There are visualizations of time in nature (see figure 3.3). One of our most familiar representations of time, the (analog) clock, comes from the pattern a stick's shadow makes as the sun makes its daily trip across the sky. Tree rings depict local conditions over the centuries. The accumulation of layers in the

FIGURE 3.3
Zuni Douglas fir, © Henri D. Grissino-Mayer, The University of Tennessee–Knoxville. Tree rings can be the inspiration for visualizing history. They show seasonal changes, so are appropriate for situations where there are variations in a repeating temporal cycle. They are directional, showing greater growth in one area or scars in another. What significance might you apply to different compass points of the ring?

geological record shows the passage of millennia. These are natural metaphors, and when the data fit, they can inspire intuitive and beautiful interfaces.

On the eve of their move to a new building, the Institute of Contemporary Art in Boston commissioned the Sociable Media Group to create an artwork to commemorate their original gallery space. Inspired by the geological accumulation visible in a canyon's wall, we designed an installation, *Artifacts of the Presence Era**, that built a growing wall of images of gallery activity (Viégas, Perry, Howe, and Donath 2004). Visitors were photographed as they entered the gallery and irregular slices of these images, algorithmically chosen according to the sound and activity level in the gallery (analogous to wind and rain shaping deposits in the natural world) became the new layers of video sediment (see figure 3.4). These layers told a story of past events; they revealed long-term patterns—the rhythm of night and day, periods of great activity or empty silence—while retaining occasionally serendipitous but often arbitrary and mundane samples of the passage of life. In addition, the growing accumulation of events weighed down and compressed the distant past. This visible distortion referred both to metamorphic rocks in the geological metaphor and to the distortion of the distant past in human memory.

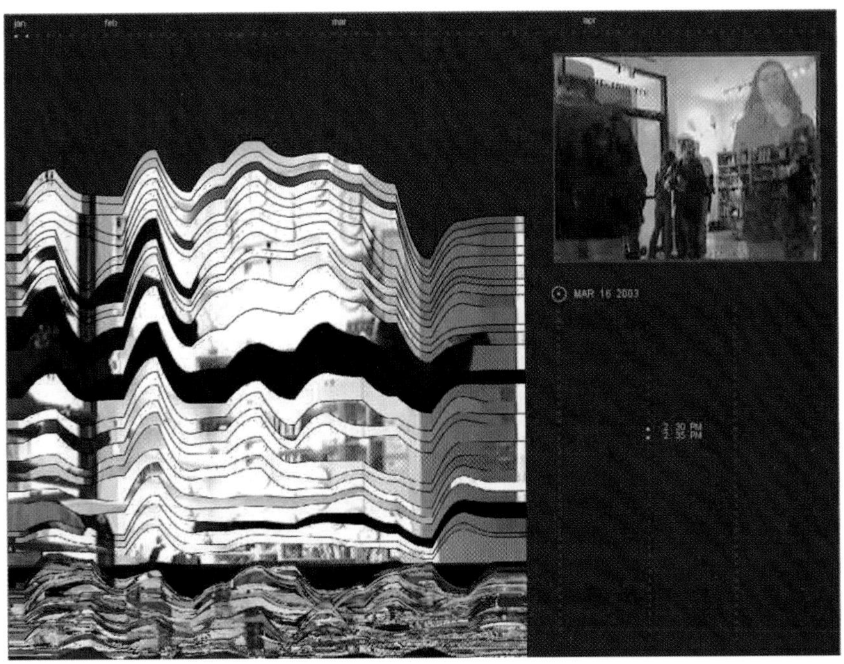

FIGURE 3.4
Judith Donath, Fernanda Viégas, Ethan Perry, and Ethan Howe, *Artifacts of the Presence Era* (2004).

A still image can encompass activity occurring over a period of time or capture an instant. In a single panel, ancient reliefs told tales of complex battles (see figure 3.5) and medieval altarpieces depicted people and events from disparate places and times (see figure 8.1). It was not until the Renaissance, with its emerging scientific mindset, that reproducing the experience of seeing—to depict what something looked like at a given moment—became the goal of painting. Today, both approaches are common. At one extreme, stroboscopic photography shows us events too fleeting for our eyes to perceive, reminding us that what we do see most of the time is a mental construct, a canonical view of a world in constant motion.[9] At the other, graphs that show data such as housing prices, birthrates, or the Earth's temperature depict patterns that occurred over weeks, decades, or eons in a single image.

In addition to representing the passage of time, design can help us manage time. How we talk about time and coordinate with others profoundly effects social organization and the development of industry, travel, and worldwide communication. Until the mid-nineteenth century, most interactions took place with neighbors, and local events—a church bell, the rising of

THE BATTLE OF TULLÎZ.
Drawn by Boudier, from a photograph of the original in the British Museum.

FIGURE 3.5
The Battle of Tullîz. Assyrian. Drawn by Boudier after original in British Museum (Maspero 2005).

the moon over a landmark—could coordinate action. Even the most industrialized cities still ran on local solar time (mechanical clocks were set by the sun's meridian), and time varied significantly from one neighboring town to another. With the advent of trains, telephones, and other transportation and communication technologies, interactions occurred over greater distances—and timekeeping needed to be standardized and coordinated at a global scale.[10]

Today we take for granted the ability to coordinate time with distant people. We can schedule a conference call for a specific time on a particular date, and all the participants will share an understanding of exactly when the call is to take place. Yet meshing local and global time still presents challenges. Time has social meaning, and scheduling involves negotiating among different participants' customs and convenience. A group may decide to hold their weekly conference call at 3:00 p.m. Eastern time; for the participant in Japan, this is an inconvenient 4:00 a.m. Designs that bring people from distant places together online may find it useful to establish a common time, or to highlight awareness of participants' local times.

Time unfolds in a series of rhythms: there are days and nights, the seasons, the year. Most days we sleep, eat breakfast, make use of some kind of transportation, go in and out of a door. Time is marked by events and anomalies. You get older, the mountains get older, the bread on the counter gets older. A tree grows, a species evolves. Depicting time and the accumulation of history requires distinguishing among repeated cycles, progressions, accumulations, and discrete events, and highlighting those that trigger a change in normal growth and cycles. Depicting time is an intrinsic part of social media design, whether facilitating communication across time zones, showing the temporal patterns in a conversation, or making visible the persistence of information into the unknowable future.

SENSORY DESIGN

We are sensory creatures, living in a world with colors, movement, sounds, tastes, and smells. In our face-to-face social world, we are very aware of how other people look, the sound of their voices, and the smell of their perfume. We enjoy sensory experiences with other people; we go out to dinner or for a walk on the beach. We may participate in rallies with colorful posters and anthemic music, cheer with the crowd at a baseball game, or talk quietly with a friend, listening not only to her words but to the tone of her voice. When we are with others, both the people and the surroundings engage our senses and shape the meaning of our experience.

Our surroundings also provide cues about the sort of social situation we are in. A dark smoky bar and a sunny health-food restaurant are conducive to different conversations; we relate differently to people dressed in business suits versus bathing suits. Social visualizations can provide these sorts of contextual cues for online encounters. Yet many online social interfaces have the warmth and sensuality of a financial report. They may have some decorative elements, but these tend to serve as background graphics that are not incorporated into the interaction space. Design aesthetics should be a fundamental part of conveying meaning, for the style and appearance of a setting shapes our impression of the people in it.

Color

> Yellow, if steadily gazed at in any geometrical form, has a disturbing influence and reveals in the color an insistent, aggressive character. … Blue is the typical heavenly color. The ultimate feeling it creates is rest. When it sinks almost to black, it echoes a grief that is hardly human.
>
> —Wassily Kandinsky, *Concerning the Spiritual in Art* (2009)

Color is everywhere we look. Ordinary in its ubiquity, it has also puzzled and fascinated philosophers, scientists, and artists throughout history. What is the relationship of one color to another? How can we systematically understand how two colors combine to produce a third? Why do they appear different in different lights, and do they appear different to different people (Land 1977; Sloane 1989)?

Colors have had symbolic significance since prehistoric times, perhaps the earliest example of this being the use of red ochre in burials 92,000 years ago during Middle Paleolithic era (Hovers et al. 2003). In American culture today, red can stand for attention and danger (stop signs, alarms, and fire trucks), for sexuality (red lipstick, "red-hot mama"), and for allegiance to particular teams (Republicans, the Boston Red Sox). We associate blue with calmness, the cold, and Democrats; green with the environment, safety, and Ireland. Colors derive these meanings from the biology of the human visual system, from our experience of nature, and from cultural use. The meanings that derive from our biology are universal, whereas those that arise from cultural use vary greatly from place to place and time to time.

Our perception of color is a function of both the spectral quality of light—the color that is "out there," its wavelength measurable by a spectrometer—and the response of our visual system to these different wavelengths. We notice reds and yellows much more than blue because our visual anatomy causes us to see them more vividly: we have numerous cones in the fovea, our central vision, that are receptive to reds, yellows, and greens, while the few blue receiving cones are more peripheral.[11]

Although any account of why our vision evolved as it did is necessarily speculative, many scientists believe that primate color vision evolved at least in part because it was helpful in foraging for brightly colored fruit and/or fresh young leaves. Once primate vision evolved to perceive these colors, color-based signals could then evolve, such as the red tinge that is a sexual signal in baboons and chimpanzees. These biologically established correlations would subsequently be the basis for the human cultural evolution of symbolic color meaning, such as the use of red lipstick and blush (Surridge, Osorio, and Mundy 2003).

The biology of our vision and our natural surroundings intertwine in their shaping of our reactions to colors. This helps us understand why a red mark is so attention grabbing, whereas a blue one is not. Red stands out: our visual system is highly attuned to it. The associations we have with red are intense and varied. It is the color of many fruits and berries (which may be the genesis of our evolved ability to see it so well) and thus associated with celebration and plenty, but also, in a culture that is suspicious of bodily pleasure, with temptation. Red is the color of blood, associating it with danger. Red cosmetics and body paint, symbolizing sexual availability and power, decorate the faces and hands of people in cultures ranging from hunter-gatherers to contemporary jet-setters. Blue, on the other hand, is the color of the sky and ocean. We see them, but we need not pay the same attention to these distant backgrounds as to our activities. Blue is a calming color—but on the face or body it evokes cold and illness.

Although biological and environmentally based color associations are universal, there are significant differences between cultures in the meanings they ascribe to different hues and shades. White symbolizes purity in American and many European cultures, but is associated with death in Eastern ones. We can see natural roots for both: a light object shows stains easily, so

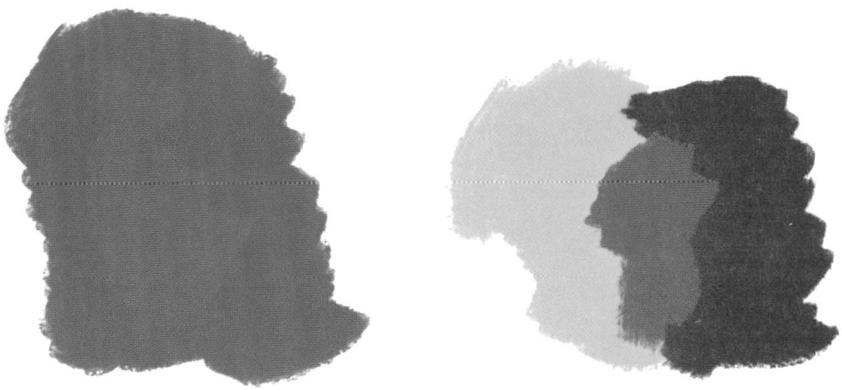

FIGURES 3.6, 3.7
Adjacent colors change the way we see a color. The centers of these squares are an identical shade of gray; the centers of the blotches are identical purples. (Adapted from Albers 1975.)

one that is all white must be pure and clean; our hair turns white in old age and white snow blankets the world in winter, the season of death and hunger. The symbolic interpretation of a color depends on its metaphoric context. Yellow hair turns white as it ages (white as symbol of death), but white paper yellows as it ages.[12]

Colors interact with each other. The way we see a color changes as the colors around it change. Although we cannot distinguish between two very similar colors when viewed separately, when they are adjacent to each other not only do we see the difference between them, but we perceive a line drawn between them. The interaction among colors also changes their emotional impact. Purple can seem neutral against a gray background, but can look harsh and glaring in a field of yellow and red. Every color that is added to a composition changes its overall feel (see figures 3.6, 3.7).

A common error in visualization design is to use hue to represent a sequence. The visible spectrum and the computer's representation of color treat hue as a linear series of values, but it is not so perceptually.[13] Rather, we see the hues as different categories, with red, blue, yellow, and green as the major ones and then branching out to orange, purple, and cyan. Hue thus is best at demarcating a small number of categories. For representing a sequence, using a range of lightness values is better, as is a progression along the saturation/brightness scale from black or white to a solid color. Saturation can also provide an intuitive depiction of activity: the brightness of and contrast among richly saturated colors looks lively, whereas dull, gray colors appear inactive.

In designing an interface, legibility is often the primary concern, especially with text and charts. Black text on a light background is legible; bright orange text on a bright blue background is not. To achieve greatest clarity and readability, colors should be muted and information presented in a dark color against a light background. Bright colors can highlight key points, but are not good for long blocks of text. In general, high luminance (brightness) contrast between text and background makes things more legible, and low color saturation is good for long blocks of text (Hall and Hanna 2004; Jacobson and Bender 1996; MacDonald 1999; Tufte 1990).

Yet legibility is not always the primary concern. Sociable media design is as much about creating the feel of a place as it is about conveying information. Ensuring that a design is legible is important, but creating the right experience is also essential. Sometimes this means minimizing the use of color to remain neutral. Or, a site may choose to be less legible but more edgy if that better conveys its message. Breaking the rules of legibility should be done only for a reason.

Motion

> Motion is the strongest visual appeal to attention. … It is understandable that a strong and automatic response to motion should have developed in animal and man. Motion implies a change in the conditions of the environment and change may require reaction. It may mean the approach of danger, the appearance of a friend or of desirable prey.
>
> —Rudolf Arnheim, *Art and Visual Perception* (1974)

Nouveau praxinoscope à projection de M. Reynaud.

FIGURE 3.8
A praxinoscope, 1879. Experiments with "persistence of vision"-based technologies, the precursors to film, were increasingly common in the nineteenth century. The zoetrope, originally invented in China (approx. 180 AD) and its refined version, the praxinoscope (invented 1877), showed a sequence of images on a spinning cylinder (Needham and Wang 1972; Turner 1983).

Artists have been using color since the days of cave painting, but the ability to use motion easily as a design element is much more recent.

Motion in the interface can grab attention, alerting you to some event that you must attend to immediately. This is helpful in some cases: a message you have been waiting for, a caller you had hoped to hear from, an emergency weather bulletin, a notice that you need to leave now for an important meeting, or a flight update. Yet the attention-grabbing flashes of animated advertisements make many sites clamorously distracting. When you are attempting to concentrate, a constant stream of popping alerts is annoying and unhelpful.

Motion can also be more subtle. Animation on the desktop can make the "objects" seem more real, though this stylistic realism need not conform to physical reality. For example, clicking on a button at the bottom of the screen opens a file. As this occurs, a very quick animation shows the "file" expanding out of the button. We do not notice this animation because it is fast, almost to the point of being subliminal. The animation helps us connect the button at the bottom of the screen to the expanded file; it makes the action more legible, even though in our everyday experience, files do not magically emerge from buttons.[14]

Motion in the interface can create the impression of vitality: living things are never completely still. Even when one is sleeping, the gentle rhythm of breathing is a visible sign of life. For interfaces that represent people and presence, we can incorporate subtle movements that invoke a living metabolism. Such motions can depict a functioning, changing online social world—not the sudden motions of pop-up notifications, but a constant, smooth growing and shrinking, a slow change of color and brightness. These movements indicate vitality and dynamism, without demanding an instant response.

For example, I may have many sources of frequently updated information—my email accounts, some news organizations, a few online discussions, and the like. Without a visual representation, I have no visceral sense of this lively activity when I look at my computer. Notifications that demand attention create a distracting interface; what I would like instead is a design that provides awareness of change without inciting reaction. Here we want neither the clamor of pop-ups, nor the sterile stillness of typical desktop interfaces.

One approach is to use ambient motion.[15] This is different from the narrative motion that shows progression through time. Leaves rustling on a tree or waves lapping at the shore do occur over time, but what we see as most salient is not the progression of a story but the rhythm of repetition. We can convey information using ambient motion by changing the frequency, rhythm, and duration of the pattern (Lam and Donath 2005). Many patterns can be the basis for such animation, the key being that they are slow but rhythmic. Repetitive motions such as ocean waves, a fire flickering in a fireplace, or the flow of traffic as seen from many stories above can inspire interfaces that inform without distracting. A pattern can pulse slowly from dark to light, or waves can smoothly ripple across it. The fundamental rhythm can be set to reflect, for instance, the typical number of messages and updates one receives over a certain period; and current variations from the normal pattern can be represented as changes in that rhythm. Multiple rhythms can concurrently show patterns at different timescales, such as what is typical for a day and what is typical for an hour.[16]

Aesthetics

When representing social information, the look and feel of the interface—the subtextual messages that its visual style conveys—can be as influential as the actual data. In designing visualizations, legibility, accuracy, and aesthetics are all important. Traditional scientific visualization has focused primarily on the first two, legibility and accuracy. I will argue here that aesthetics, particularly for social visualizations, is also important.[17]

Aesthetic judgment is a combination of cultural taste and personal response. It is a subjective assessment, drawing from both our sensory responses and our learned interpretations. Let's take the example of a page with a border of intertwined flowers. Part of our sensory response comes from our biological reactions to colors: if they are blue and purple, they will seem calmer than a border of bright reds and yellows; this is inherent to the structure of our visual system. Personal taste determines whether they seem delightfully bright or unattractively garish. The meaning we ascribe to the border comes from both its innate properties—living flowers are signs of life and of pleasant weather—and from learned cultural associations. If I see a flowery-bordered Web page, my immediate guess is that it belongs to an older woman who is interested in homey crafts, possibly religious and conservative, and probably not very technical. Whether I find the design attractive depends on whether I find the associated traits appealing. Aesthetic judgment often has a class component: things we associate with higher status and admired social affiliations appear attractive. The unattractive appearance of things associated with social affiliations we disdain or dislike feels like an inherent property of the thing, and we thus see those who like them as having poor taste, without recognizing the extent to which our aesthetic judgment is a learned and cultural response.

Aesthetics affects the impression that a visualization makes about the social phenomenon it depicts, and it influences the social behavior an interface promotes. In the physical world, noteworthy buildings are more than just functional; their architecture and interior provide us with cues about the tone and purpose of the space. We see this in restaurants, where the lighting, colors, and materials tell us whether an establishment is formal, romantic, or a great place to bring small children. People communicate this way in their homes, consciously or not, conveying not only an impression of who they are or aspire to be, but also of their expectations for visitors. How your guests sit, stand, and what they discuss with you may be different when in a room with formally arranged antiques versus brightly colored beanbag chairs. Magazines' layouts and fonts provide us with clues about their content and editorial policy.

Art historian E. H. Gombrich writes:

> The geometrical structure of a visual design can never, by itself, allow us to predict the effect it will have on the beholder. … [In addition to perceptual elements such as scale and color] the visual effect of any design must also depend on such factors as familiarity or taste. … It is this subjective element in the visual effect of pattern which seems to me largely to vitiate the attempts to establish the aesthetics of design on a psychological basis. (Gombrich 1981, 117)

FIGURES 3.9, 3.10, 3.11, 3.12
Vitaly Komar and Alex Melamid, *People's Choice* (1995). Which fonts, colors, shapes, and motions are attractive, and what they signify, varies from culture to culture and from person to person. The artists Vitaly Komar and Alex Melamid, in their "Most and Least Favorite Painting" project, surveyed hundreds of people around the world about what they liked in a painting—colors, sizes, subject, and so on—and painted the results, country by country. The results show intriguing differences in national taste: Americans, overall, like traditional paintings with a historical figure in an outdoor scene, whereas the majority of Dutch people surveyed preferred abstract art with blended colors. "Most and Least Favorite Paintings" is a brilliant critique of opinion-survey-driven design, and a celebration of the power of visualization. Whereas reading the survey results, country by country, is dull and meaningless, seeing them rendered as paintings is fascinating (Komar and Melamid 2011; Komar, Wypijewski, and Melamid 1997).

3.9
USA's Most Wanted
(dishwasher size).

3.10
USA's Least Wanted
(paperback size).

3.11
Holland's Most Wanted
(magazine size).

3.12
Holland's Least Wanted
(wall size).

Aesthetics also affects the visitor's or viewer's emotional response and enjoyment of an experience. Around 2010, Apple's iPhone became the most popular cell phone in the United States. People found the way it looked and responded so enjoyable that they preferred using it over a phone that had better service. Viewers will spend time with a visualization that they find attractive (calm, soothing images attract some, whereas bright animation appeals to others). When something seems dull or irritating, it is not easy, even if you are quite motivated, to look at it for very long. A dry graph may be accurate, but if the viewer's eyes glaze over, the information will not be conveyed. Yet when something is appealing, you can look at it for quite a while. You can take your time and think about the patterns you see; you can watch it long enough to formulate impressions, to wonder about certain anomalies or correlations. The aesthetic appeal of the visualization is important in motivating people to spend time with the material, to contemplate it, and to think deeply about it.

In 2005, Martin Wattenberg launched the NameVoyager, a Web applet that lets people explore the popularity, since 1900, of about 6,000 names. It was immediately popular, with over 500,000 visitors the first two weeks and still heavily visited years later. It is a graceful and enticing visualization. You can type a name to see the arc of its popularity. As you type, it instantly shows the graphs for all names beginning with the letters you have entered (figure 3.13 shows names beginning with "N," with "Nicole" highlighted). Expectant

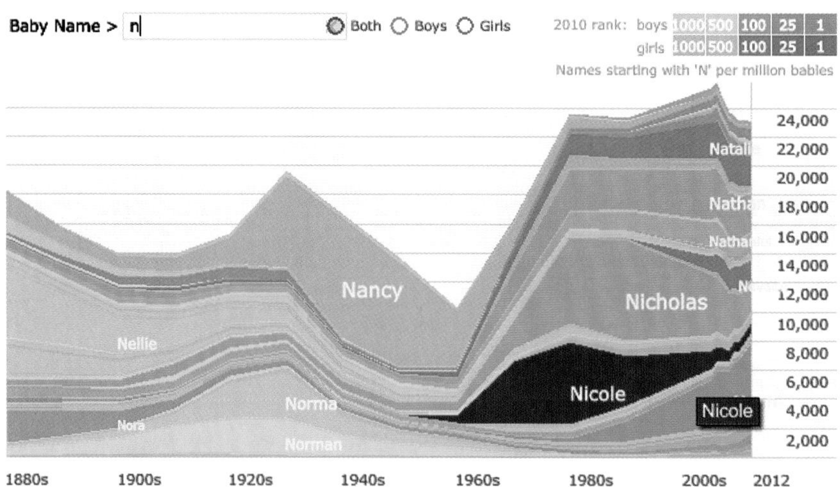

FIGURE 3.13
Martin and Laura Wattenberg, *Name Voyager* (2005).

parents are interested in baby names, but this site attracts a broad audience, many of whom spend quite a bit of time delving into a dataset that would normally be of only passing interest. People discussed it on blogs and discussion sites, commenting on the changing fashions in names, speculating why a name had a peak of popularity at a particular time, and looking for ethnic and cultural patterns in the names. The intriguing graphical form and intuitive interface inspired hundreds of thousands of people to explore this data (Wattenberg and Kriss 2006; Wattenberg 2005).[18]

There is no sharp division between legibility and aesthetics, between form and function. A casual and curvy chair that reveals itself, when actually sat on, to be uncomfortable has a (lack of) functionality that belies its initial appeal. An attractive visualization whose meaning is hard to decipher will eventually prove more frustrating than fascinating.

The influential graphic designer and writer Edward Tufte strongly advocates a minimalist approach to visualization. He has waged battle against what he calls "chart-junk"—embellishments and decorations that do not convey the focal statistics—and recommends a high "data-ink ratio." Tufte's work features graphs that he has made sparely elegant by removing outlines, extra markers, and even pieces of bars from bar graphs (Tufte 1986, 1990).

Yet, decorative graphs can be more memorable than simpler ones, and are often as legible (Bateman et al. 2010). They may draw the viewer's attention and keep it longer. A graph's style can provide cues about the objectivity and completeness of the data. Minimalist statistical graphs convey seriousness and exactitude. They imply that the data are solid and significant. Decorated graphs usually convey some editorial position about the data, which can also draw viewers' attention; they present an argument, take a stand, rather than just offering dry statistics. Deciding on the right approach depends on the type of data and the goal for the depiction.

Ambiguity

For a visualization to be accurate, it should appropriately display the degree of exactness of the data it renders. In many cases, the ideal depiction is a rendering of ambiguity.

Social data are often inexact, and rendering them too clearly can misleadingly imply accurate precision. For example, one can make social network diagrams that show the connections among a group of people, as inferred by their common interests. Different ways of depicting these connections give viewers different impressions of how solid each tie is. Drawing a line connecting two people implies there is a palpable connection, that they know each other personally. But their tie may be weaker; the connection between two people may only be that they have used many words in common in their postings or expressed interest in the same movies, books, and music. Tenuous connections should be drawn with the appropriate ambiguity—for example, by putting the people near each other, but not connecting them with an unambiguous line. (The next chapter, "Mapping Social Networks," looks more closely at how to depict the often complex relationships between people.)

There are many ways to visually render inexactness and ambiguity, including oscillation, blending, blurring, and waviness (Pang, Wittenbrink, and Lodha 1997; Zuk and Carpendale 2006). *Visual Who* (which was discussed more fully in chapter 1) showed connections among people inferred from common mailing-list membership. As it animated the clusters, rather than snapping each new configuration decisively into position, it rendered them as if invisible rubber bands attached the names, which thus oscillated indefinitely, only slowly settling into place. This conveyed the imprecision of the associations (Donath 1995).

INTERACTIVITY

Interactivity sets computational media apart from others. With interactivity, the viewer provides input and the interface responds; it is a dialogue between person and machine. The designer defines the machine's role in the human–computer dialogue. That role may be simply to be a tool: click on this button and a picture appears; click on that button and the cursor looks like a pen, and now moving it around leaves marks on an image. Seemingly simple and straightforward, this human–computer dialogue is carefully crafted to seem intuitive (Card, Moran, and Newell 1983; Preece, Rogers, and Sharp 2002).

When we interact with something online, we expect it to react. *How* it reacts provides our impression of what it is and shows the effect of our action. Interaction may be exploratory, where what changes is the user's perspective; the underlying data remain intact. Or interaction may change something in the online space. Interface objects such as the button that maximizes and minimizes a window have the power to act on other things. Part of the design challenge is helping the user understand what these powers are.

When something reacts to our actions as we expected, we perceive it to be working; if it does so in an unexpected way, it may seem broken; or, if cleverly designed, funny or thought provoking. Many online interactions are metaphoric constructions drawn from familiar objects, like the buttons that I mentioned earlier. Most of the time, they behave as a physical button does: press or click anywhere on it and it will set some other action in motion. We are not surprised if they change in some way to show the mode they are in; physical buttons do this when they stay depressed or light up. However, we do not expect buttons to do different things depending on where on the button we press them. Like their physical model, we expect the online button to be a solid object; but online, that solidity is a design choice rather than a physical constraint. The cursor usually moves freely across the screen, floating above the interface objects—buttons, file icons, and the like. Yet we can make interfaces where things push against each other, deform their shapes, or attract and repel each other like magnets. Used carefully, interactions can convey a wide range of expressions.

The Illusion of Sentience

When we interact with something that behaves in a very simple and predictable way, we think of it as a mechanistic object, something that we can manipulate, that may in turn cause something else to happen; a switch turns on a light, for example. If it behaves in a more complex way, perhaps with unexpected responses, we start to see it as sentient. The new car that starts up flawlessly with the turn of a key is a machine; the old one that must be coaxed with just the right amount of pedal pumping and rest between tries seems to have a will and personality.

An important distinction exists between interactions that give the impression that a sentient being is responding to you and those that feel as if you are controlling a puppet. Many experiments with interactive portraits (Cleland 2004) and other artworks, intended to create a sense of dialogue, instead feel as if one is controlling an object. The cause is often an overly simple script: if I move closer, it does X; if I move away, it does Y; if I speak, it does Z. The setup may be complex and the visuals elaborate, but the actual interaction is made up of a series of discrete actions with predictable responses.

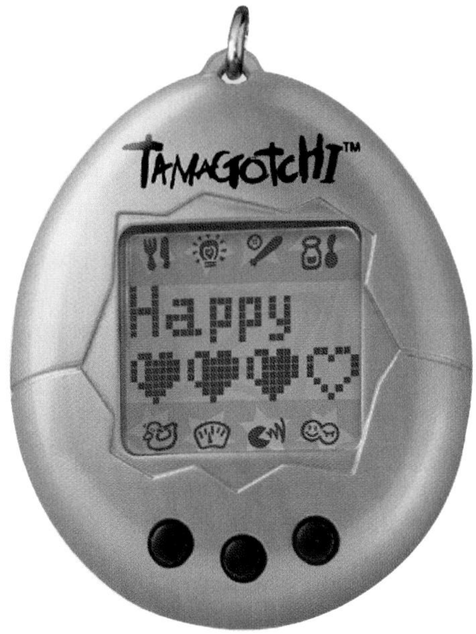

FIGURE 3.14
Tamagotchi, Bandai Corporation. This virtual pet requires continual care in order to thrive.

"Keychain pets" show how a very simple interactive object can still provide a strong impression of sentience (see figure 3.14). These interactive toys were first released in Japan in the mid-1990s. The owner's job is to keep the pet happy and healthy by feeding it, playing with it, disciplining it, cleaning up after it, and so on. If the owner assiduously attends to its needs, the pet will thrive and behave well; if ignored, the pet will sicken and die. All these actions are carried out through an interface of a few buttons and simple screen graphics; they are metaphorical creatures, created out of hints and references to real animals. They are interesting because the design of the interaction between owner and "pet," through a combination of autonomous behavior, dependency, intensive interaction, and ongoing development, engenders deep devotion to them (Donath 2004a; Kaplan 2000).

An artificial pet acts—or, more precisely, appears to act—autonomously. Its actions seem to be internally motivated; it appears to have its own goals, feelings, and desires. It does not necessarily obey human commands but instead makes its own demands on its owner. When machines work exactly as we expect them to and do what we request of them, we think of them as simply machines. It is when they do not work as expected that they appear to have a will of their own and we ascribe intelligence to them. Most artificial pets start as "infants." This elicits nurturing and affection: we instinctively take care of the young. The pets are designed to require their owner's help throughout their life span in order to thrive and survive. If the owner does not "feed" or "entertain" them, they become ill or even die. The pet's dependence makes the owner feel responsible for it. Feeding, cleaning, and playing with the pet all involve interacting with it, and the pet becomes integrated into the owner's daily routine. Having spent a considerable amount of time and energy on the pet, the owner is invested in its well-being, a feeling that is enhanced by the way the artificial pets are designed to develop in response to the owner's treatment of them: a pet that is well cared for will be healthier and more tractable. The owner is thus encouraged to take pride in his or her pet's well-being.

Artificial pets also demonstrate how metaphorical thinking influences our sense of ethics. If we think of them as games, the time spent playing with them is entertainment and somewhat self-indulgent; if we think of them as animals, time spent playing with them is caretaking, an act of responsibility and altruism. It is obsessive to leave a meeting or dinner because a game requires attention, but it is reasonable to do so if a pet is in need; indeed, it is heartless not to. This is a vivid example of the power of metaphor: the metaphor we use to think about something can change how we interpret it, act toward it, and judge how others behave toward similar things (Donath 2004a).

The metaphors that we use to think about other people online similarly affect our sense of responsibility toward them. If I ask a question of a search engine I am pleased if I get a useful answer, annoyed if I do not. But I (correctly) do not feel thankful to the search engine for the time and effort it has put into helping me; it is an information machine, not a sentient being. If I ask the same question of an online forum, the process of typing words into a box is quite similar. Yet the person who answers me has donated time and effort. Ideally, I recognize this work and acknowledge the person behind it. Yet online interactions can suffer from "depersonalization," where we fail to think of the others truly as people, which lowers the barrier to responding angrily and other antisocial behavior. A social interface should promote the view of the other participants as human, creating a sense of community and responsibility.[19] Understanding phenomena such as the nurturing response that artificial pets trigger helps us see the complex ways that interface and interaction shape our perception of others.

AFFORDANCES AND PERCEIVED AFFORDANCES

The psychologist James J. Gibson coined the word "affordance" to describe the properties of the environment relative to a particular animal. "The *affordances* of the environment are what it *offers* the animal, what it *provides* or *furnishes*, either for good or ill" (Gibson 1986, 127). For a human (and other animals), the ground, for example, affords support. For a lightweight insect, so does the surface of a pond—but not for heavier creatures; we sink. For a small child, a toddler's tiny chair affords sitting, but not for a stiff and heavy older person. A book affords reading, but only to someone who is literate in its language. Affordances describe our potential relationship with any external entity, from the basic elements of water and air to the social interactions we have with other people.

> The other animals afford, above all, a rich and complex set of interactions, sexual, predatory, nurturing, fighting, playing, cooperating, and communicating. What other persons afford comprises the whole realm of social significance for human beings. (Gibson 1986, 128)

An affordance is something you can actually do with a given element of your world. A perceived affordance is what you believe you can do with it.[20] One can perceive an affordance that is not there: I can walk across what I think is solid ground that affords support, but if it is actually thin ice and I fall into the wintery pond, then it did not, for me, have the actual affordance of support.

Gibson notes that one might not always be aware of an affordance, but stresses the independence of affordances from the concerns or goals of the animal: "The observer may or may not perceive or attend to the affordance, according to his needs, but the affordance, being invariant, is always there to be perceived" (Gibson 1986, 139).

An affordance is different from a function because the latter implies an intended purpose. A fallen tree and a chair both afford sitting (for people), but it is the intended function only of the chair. Affordances are about what someone actually can do with some other thing or being; they are independent of intention. For a thief, a tourist with a wallet in his back pocket affords pickpocketing, but that is not the tourist's intention. Gibson's point, that affordances are invariant, means that the pocket affords picking for all of us with dexterous hands, though few of us are inclined to do so.

Designers fashion cities, houses, furniture, and interfaces with an intended function in mind. Yet people often use them in ways very different from those the designers had envisioned. We put matchbooks under a leg of a tippy table and store paintbrushes in old coffee cans. Houses are turned into schools and schools into houses. The artist David Byrne created visual poetry using the corporate presentation software PowerPoint (Byrne 2003; see figure 3.15). Homemaking magazines offer tips to thrifty readers about using rain gutters to keep computer cables in order and turning egg cartons into jewelry boxes. In West Africa, plastic-fiber rice sacks are unwoven and then rebraided into strong new ropes (Steen, Komissar, and Birkeland). Such repurposing is about discovering the affordances of the item beyond its stated uses.

Some designers work very hard to maintain control of their creations, making them specialized and difficult to convert to other uses.[21] Others intentionally create flexible systems. For social communication, more flexible, adaptable technologies are generally the most successful. An interface that enforces a strict protocol of behavior is not only more limited in its uses than a general-purpose one, it also provides fewer opportunities for a group

FIGURE 3.15
David Byrne, *Sea of Possibilities* (2003). PowerPoint presentation software repurposed as art medium.

to develop its own communication mores (Sproull and Kiesler 1991 a,b). For example, if you are trying to schedule a dinner party, you could discuss possible dates with several friends via email, a general-purpose tool, or you could ask them to check off possible dates using a scheduling tool. One is not better than the other; but we should be cognizant of the trade-off between sociability and efficiency. The scheduler makes gathering the information easy and organized, but you do not get the stories about where one unavailable friend will be for the month, nor the social cues that people exchange about the importance of the event, and so on.

Most environments contain innumerable affordances, potential relations that a being in that space could have with the other things in it. We become aware of them only when we have some need, simple or complex as it may be, or when we are faced with a novel goal. If there is a sudden leak, for instance, we may look around for things that afford catching water. Stories of unexpected affordances fascinate people. A recent news article about a woman who fended off a ferocious black bear by throwing a zucchini at it made headlines around the world. With that story in mind, I see my coffee cup—which I usually think of as simply a container for hot beverages—and all the other small yet heavy objects in reach as potential projectiles, a stash of desktop weapons.

Lost affordances also capture our attention. The nightmarish edge of surrealism is a place where objects appear nearly normal, but some distortion has eradicated their common and expected function: Meret Oppenheim's *Object*, a fur-lined coffee cup, or Man Ray's *Gift*, an iron with a tidy line of spikes on the bottom. The Sociable Media Group's *Cheiro** chair was designed as a physical avatar standing in for a distant person (see figure 3.16 and the discussion in chapter 12, "Social Catalysts"). The chair itself is a surrealistic object, a chair that does not afford sitting. It was sculpted to capture a moment in a chair's transition from furniture to sentient object, its arms changing from rests to limbs, lying in its lap. And while the arms that make it impossible to sit subvert the customary purpose of a chair, in this case, that serves a deliberate and useful purpose, for *Cheiro* is an art object, and we wanted people to look at it, but not sit on it.

A legible object is one whose affordances are clearly perceivable. Some basic ones are instinctive—air affords breathing, unless you are a fish—but most of our understanding of what we can do with the world around us comes from learning. Babies crawl, taste, and touch their way into understanding that flat surfaces afford support and that blocks afford stacking,

FIGURE 3.16
Francis Lam, Scott Weaver, and Judith Donath, *Cheiro* (2006).

whereas balls do not. Much of our social communication is about providing cues to each other about our "social affordances." We do this with words: "Call me any time, I'd really like to help you"; "I'd love to, but I'm terribly busy." And we do it with gestures, with how long we hold eye contact, how close we stand to another.

In designing social media, a key issue in legibility is how others will see someone else's actions. Communicating via computer media takes a leap of faith. You trust that the words or images you wish to send out will go to the people you want them to (and only to them) and in the form you intend. With an unfamiliar medium, you may not know if your typing is instantly visible to your correspondent, or if it appears only after you type a carriage return, press a send button, or perform some other action. It may be unclear who will see your writing, where it will appear in the context of an ongoing discussion, and whether you can subsequently withdraw it. The role of design is to make the perceived affordances match the real ones.

4

MAPPING SOCIAL NETWORKS

You live in a network, a complex web of relationships that connects you with your family, your friends, your coworkers, and your classmates from your early school days. Some of these people you know within a close group, connected to you in a dense network in which everyone knows everyone else. Others, such as a friend you met by chance while on vacation, connect to you only loosely; she has close networks of her own, but you do not know them. We learn from early childhood how to navigate these relationships, figuring out to whom we must speak formally and with whom we can relax, who knows the best jokes and who needs our help. This network of relationships is the fundamental structure of society (Wellman 1999).[1] Understanding these networks is essential for social scientists, who seek to better model how society functions; for activists, who want to change it; and for individuals, who need to navigate a rapidly changing and fragmented social world in which our network structures are becoming both larger and more diffuse than in the past.

If we could see a map of all these connections, stretching around the globe, we would see that a giant network of acquaintances links almost the entire world. Hundreds of years ago, this was not true; there were many isolated tribes and villages.[2] But a century of mass migrations, missionaries, airplanes, road-building, and telecommunications have woven the world into a single social web. Today, with the possible exception of undiscovered remote tribes, these chains of acquaintanceship connect the entire human population. A series of historical social network maps would show us a profound change in how society is structured.

One reason to map social networks is to help us understand the implications of such a change. Is bigger better? Do technologically enhanced networks lessen the social network differences between urban and rural dwellers or exacerbate them? Mapping these changing networks helps the social scientist understand how the changes in society affect the way people form groups, receive support, and get information.

But network maps are not just a tool for social scientists and policy makers. They can be a guide for the members of this expanding society, helping them keep track of the increasingly numerous and complex connections among their acquaintances. Many people today live very mobile lives, changing cities and jobs frequently. Each move requires starting over in a new community, learning the relationships among new acquaintances from scratch. What sort of map would make these transitions easier? As the structure of our society moves to a scale "beyond being there," network maps are an invaluable tool for making sense of our complex and diffuse web of connections.

Social network maps can potentially be part of the interface people use for communicating with each other. If I have 20 close friends, 200 acquaintances, an extended network of 1,200, and another few thousand very loose ties, how do I pick the subset of people I want to say something to, or who I would like to hear from at a particular time? Laboriously going through alphabetical lists of names is not useful; instead, I would prefer to be able to create groups around meaningful network clusters.

Another reason to map social networks is to create a data portrait; the map of your personal network is itself a portrait of you as a social being. Upon meeting a new person, a common conversational topic is "do you know so-and-so?," as we try to place each other within our personal social world of friends and colleagues. Would seeing a network portrait of people we meet help us get to know them better? How would we manage such a map: what information is private or public? What should the map immediately display or slowly reveal?

In this chapter, we will examine conceptual issues in mapping social networks. This chapter is not a technical guide for producing these maps,[3] but we will discuss the problem of who should be included and where should they placed. Legibility is a key issue in designing network maps, for a visualization of their interwoven connections can quickly become an unintelligible tangle. We will look at what meaning one can infer from the basic map and then explore approaches to depicting the information and support that flows through the network. We will talk about where the data come from, particularly online sources, and the challenges with this, such as incompleteness and maintaining privacy.

A PERSONAL NETWORK MAP

In theory, it is possible to draw a map of the network connecting all the people on earth. What would such a map actually look like? With a node for every person and a line connecting all acquaintances, it would be a hopelessly tangled mess. In fact, even when we reduce the scale quite a bit—say to the network consisting of you, your ties, and all of their ties—it is still a big and complex structure. Yet at this scale we can think about some practical questions. How do we decide where each person should go on the map? How do we want to define a connection: Is it everyone we've ever met over a lifetime? People we've been in contact with in the last five years? People to whom we would send a holiday card? You can sketch out a map of your own connections as a way to think about these problems. Take a piece of paper and sketch a social map of 50 or 100 or 400 of your friends, family, coworkers, and acquaintances. How did you cluster people? Whom did you put nearest yourself?

You may have started with your immediate family. It may be a cohesive group or fractured by feuds, divorce, and death. You may be very close to some members, while other relatives are emotionally distant. You may have included people you have worked with. Some jobs engender strong relationships, such as those between a student and mentor, company cofounders, and employees bonding in an exciting new venture or in an unhappy workplace. Or maybe work is just a place, and your coworkers only slight acquaintances. You may have worked at the same business for decades, or your social map may have several clusters of friends from various past positions. Some relationships span multiple parts of your life, such as a high-school classmate who is also in your running club and married to your cousin; this is someone you see at reunions, family get-togethers, and every other morning at 6:00 a.m. Other relationships are more tenuous, such as the people you are tied to via a single common connection, such as in-laws or a coworker's friends. Some friends on your map you may see daily; others are far away and, though you feel attached to them, you may not have seen them for years. You may have included people who are neither friends nor family, but who have had a big impact on you, for example someone who caused an accident or saved a life. This social map is an autobiography. You know the stories of how you met each of these people and of your relationship with them, and how it has ebbed and flowed over time.

A hand-drawn map like this is idiosyncratic. Not only does it show your social world, it shows how you think about it. You may or may not have shown the relationships your acquaintances have with each other. You may have indicated different types of relationships: family versus work, romantic versus platonic. The categories you chose are part of your subjective view.

The metaphor of relationships as distance also shapes many social network maps: "He is a very close friend"; "I haven't seen him for a long time"; "She's a distant cousin." Putting people who are close socially near each other on the map makes intuitive sense. If the depiction shows only your relationship with the other individuals, the map is possible to draw; you could, for example, make concentric circles of increasing intimacy. But once relationships among all the people are factored in, there are too many dimensions to place everyone ideally.

In drawing this map, you are likely to have encountered some of the difficulties that beset any attempt to depict social space. If you used distance to show the closeness of all the ties among the people, you probably quickly noticed that a two-dimensional graph cannot accurately depict the multiple constraints. You probably put people into groups, based on the context in which you know them, where they are, or their role in your life. But many people belong to multiple groups, so how do you show this?

The structure you are likely to have used is called an "egocentric" map. In the world of social network mapping, "egocentric" does not imply narcissism; it simply means a map that shows the connections of a single person. The map you drew consists of only your knowledge about certain people and their relationships. There may be friendships among them that you are unaware of. Other people, even a close friend who knows many of the same people, would depict these relationships differently.

The structure of the nodes and links in a network map highlights some interesting things. For example, if you draw people so that they are close to the others they know, you may see that there are "bridge figures," people who connect otherwise separate groups (see figure 4.1). Bridge figures are conduits for information to flow from one group to another (Burt 2002;

Granovetter 1973; Lin 2002). Because this is a map of your social world drawn from your perspective, you are the bridge between all the separate groups in it. Your network might be such that you are never the sole bridge between groups; if you live in the same town you grew up in, and socialize with friends from work, you will see mostly overlapping groups with multiple interconnections. But if you have moved around a lot, and have acquaintances from very separate social arenas (you may work in a law firm by day, practice salsa dancing at night, and do volunteer teaching for a month each summer in remote Australia), you will see a number of disconnected groups, linked only through you (see figure 4.2).

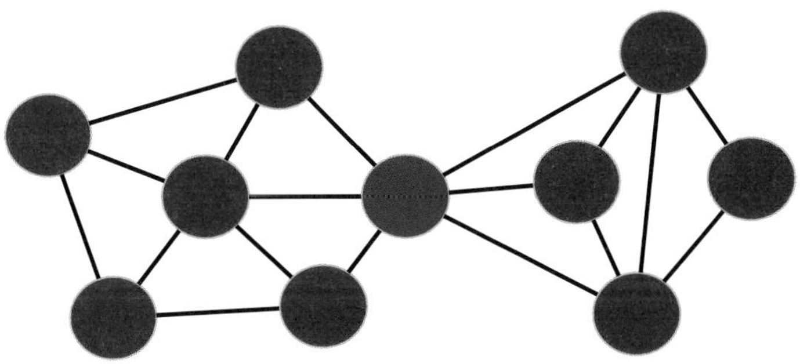

FIGURE 4.1
The blue circle is the bridge between the two groups.

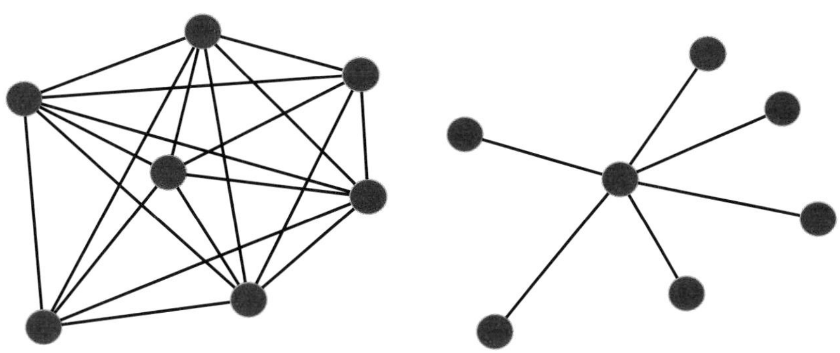

FIGURE 4.2
Left: a dense network. Right: a sparse network, connected through a single hub.

Since you know all the people in this sketch, you know that there is much more to the story of their connections. Some are truly close friends who would do anything for each other. Some share many of the same interests and beliefs, while others have conflicting ones. A gay rights activist and a religious fundamentalist may know each other, but they may never speak to each other. Or perhaps they are connected through some other dimension—maybe they are siblings or coworkers—and manage a cordial relationship through careful editing of what they discuss. You also know more about the individual personalities, such as who is gossipy, generous, or needy.

The network sketch of your acquaintances is a subjective view of a tiny piece of the vast network of human society. It includes only people you know, remember, and choose to include. It includes only a fraction of the information you have about the people and their relationships. This subjectivity is inherent to any social network depiction (Wellman and Wortley 1990). Whether the data come from exhaustive interviews by trained sociologists or from analyzing email records or social network sites, it will inevitably have many omissions. The sources' perspectives will shape it, and the way "connection" is defined will limit it arbitrarily. Even so, social network maps are a very useful tool for making sense of people as social beings and for understanding the connections that shape society.

SOURCES OF NETWORK DATA

The map you drew used your memory of your acquaintances as its data source. It is an egocentric map, showing your extended network as seen from your perspective. Sociologists studying social networks collect this information by administering surveys and interviewing people.[4] One challenge with this work is standardizing the information gathered from multiple people. Asked to name our "closest ties," you might think of the one or two people you have relied on the most and for the longest time, whereas I might enumerate everyone I discuss anything personal with; our networks might actually be quite similar, but to such a survey they would seem quite different because of our different interpretations of the question (Bernard et al. 1990).

Researchers address this by asking more specific questions, such as to list everyone to whom they sent a Christmas card (Hill and Dunbar 2003) or from whom they would borrow $100. The boundaries of one's network are always fuzzy. It's clear that you know your sister and your best friend, and that the person who just walked past is a stranger. But what about the dry-cleaner whose shop you've visited every week for years? The sociologists' questions and definitions create the boundaries of the networks they depict.

Another approach looks at "sociocentric" rather than "egocentric" networks. Instead of defining the network as the people connected to an individual, the sociocentric approach focuses on a limited populace—all the people who live in a neighborhood, work at a company, or publish in a field—and attempts to enumerate all the connections among the people in that group. Here the goal is to map the overall network structure, measuring density, finding key bridge figures, and so on (see, e.g., Wellman and Wortley 1990; Barabasi et al. 2002). For example, one might map the social networks of several departments in a company to understand how they access information and allocate responsibilities (Krackhardt and Brass 1994; Krackhardt 1990).

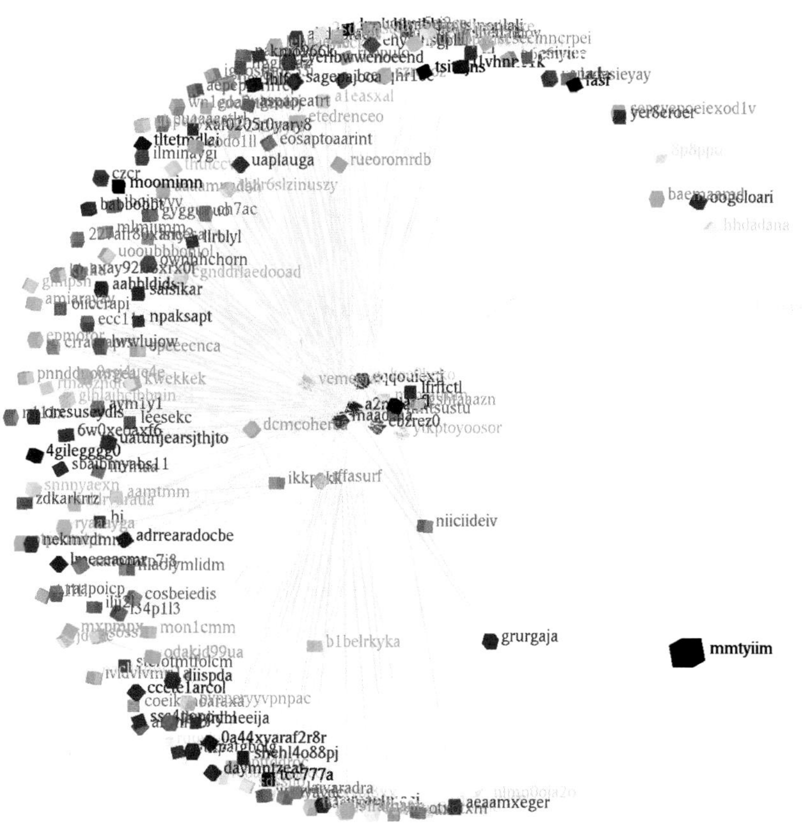

FIGURE 4.3
Adam D'Angelo, *BuddyZoo* (2003). *BuddyZoo* visualized one's network of SMS contacts. People posted these as self-portraits that showed their popularity and social reach (D'Angelo 2003).

These days much information about social networks comes from online sources, such as email and social networking sites. The advantage here is that there is a great deal of easy-to-obtain data. One can write a program that goes through all of someone's email (Adamic and Adar 2005) or SMS buddy lists (see figure 4.3; D'Angelo 2003), traces connections between blogs (see figure 4.4; Adamic and Glance 2005) or on a social network site (Ellison, Steinfield, and Lampe 2007; Heer and Boyd 2005), or monitors phone calls (Eagle, Pentland, and Lazer 2009) and extracts a network of relationships. Unlike interviews, which favor depth of information about a few contacts, electronic analysis generally provides a little information about a lot of contacts.[5]

The key problem here is in understanding the significance of the material. Electronic data mining measures a set of communicative acts, rather than emotions and impressions. It measures it impartially, but the data may be incomplete and unrepresentative. For example, a woman may be very close to her husband but email him infrequently, since they live in the same house. She may have the most email contact with her assistant at work, but

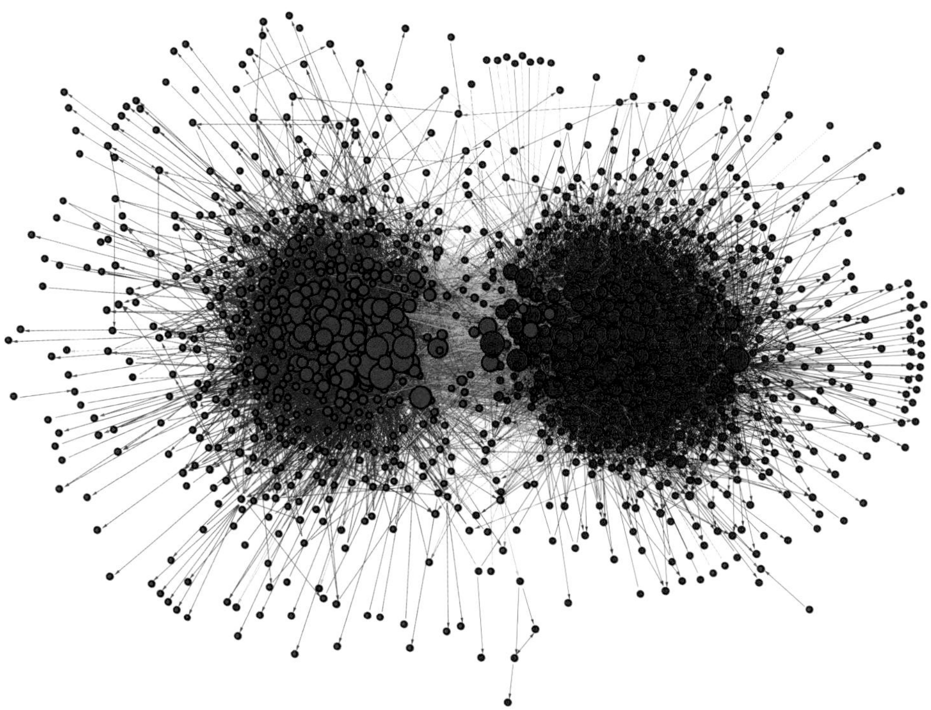

FIGURE 4.4
Lada Adamic and Natalie Glance, *The Political Blogosphere and the 2004 U.S. Election: Divided They Blog* (2005). Red dots are conservative blogs, blue are liberal. Links from liberal to conservative are orange and from conservative to liberal are purple (Adamic and Glance 2005).

that does not mean they have a strong tie, either personally or professionally. Even looking at the content of the messages can be misleading; the few emails she exchanges with her husband may be terse and factual, not because they are at odds, but because they use that medium mainly for logistical planning.

Some very social people send few emails because they prefer talking on the phone or sending text messages; other infrequent email users may be solitary loners who communicate little in any medium. Similarly, people use social network sites differently; some connect to only a few colleagues, others to thousands of strangers. Online communication provides a rich set of data for analyzing and mapping social networks, but it is important to keep in mind that each dataset provides only a partial and probably skewed view of its subjects' social connections.

USES OF NETWORK MAPS

From private record keeping to political provocation, a social network map has many possible uses. With personal maps, the audience is familiar with the network; it is his or her own set of acquaintances. Here the goal may be to reveal unexpected connections or to provide a useful tool for navigating one's social world. With other maps, the goal is to make the audience care about and understand the relationships in the depicted community. A map also makes it easier to explore a new territory. We can easily understand this in terms of physical travel; without a map, our progress is slow and tentative. Social maps have an analogous function. They can help us navigate new social territories quickly and they can help us manage an unprecedented number of social connections.

Personal Navigation

A personal network map can help people understand the relationships among their own acquaintances. Figure 4.5 shows all the people connected to one person (me) in the social network site Facebook in the summer of 2009. Any observer can quickly see the network's size and basic clusters and structure.[6]

To me, it is a familiar landscape that I recognize and understand, though I had not previously seen it laid out in two dimensions. It is very much like looking at a map of a well-known neighborhood: it is a top-down abstraction

FIGURE 4.5
My connections on Facebook in 2009. Made with TouchGraph.

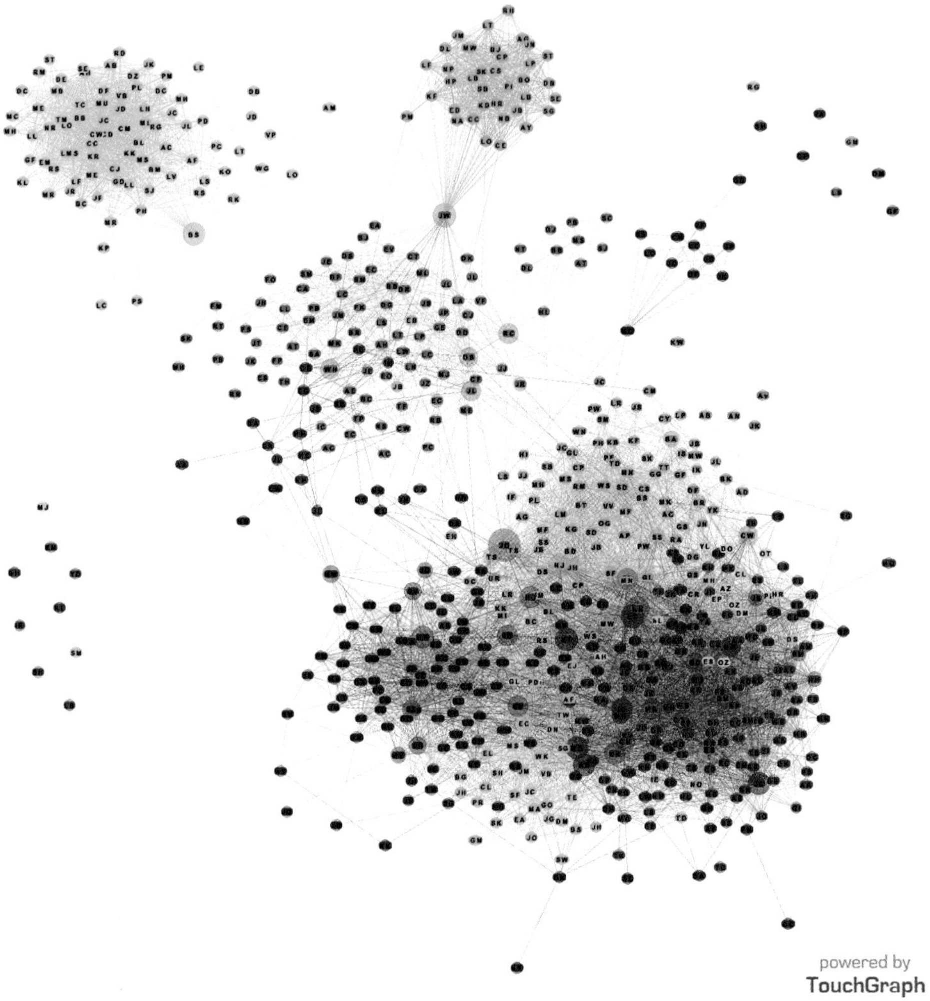

that clarifies how everything fits together. I can easily recognize and interpret the clusters; the disconnected group at the upper right consists of friends from high school, the other small, tight cluster is a close-knit email group of women who had babies in August 1997.

This is an egocentric map; everyone depicted in it is connected to me. But it also includes information beyond my personal knowledge. Facebook allows you (usually) to see the connections of people with whom you are connected. This map includes that data—information that I am privy to on that site, but may not be aware of—and thus I can discover unknown connections. For example, I see that a European colleague knows the mother of one of my daughter's friends; it turns out they are friends from their college days.

The map is interactive: clicking on a node shows the name of that person and highlights his or her connections within this network. As I write this, Facebook's interface for browsing one's friend list is a clunky alphabetical list, which shows nothing of the relationships among people and is dull to peruse. The network map is a far more beguiling way to look through one's social neighborhood. A map like this could easily function as an interface, where clicking on a name would bring you to the person's profile. Since it is situated in a site where people send messages, comment on each other's updates and photos, play games, and so on, there is a wealth of social data that could be depicted in such a map.

In a world of small, tightly knit communities, you would not need these kinds of maps. Your social world would be limited enough, and repeated interactions frequent enough, that you could keep identities and relationships clear in your mind. Today, our social networks are expanding, owing to physical and socioeconomic mobility and to new communication technologies. In the past, we shed acquaintances as well as added them, but new social tools make this shedding less of an inevitability. Previously, keeping in touch was costlier, and fading weak ties—elementary schoolmates, acquaintances met at distant conferences, a friend's cousin met at a wedding—would have dissolved entirely. Technologies such as Facebook make it easy to stay in casual contact with large numbers of people, and one of the primary attractions of social network sites has been to revivify such dormant ties (Smith 2011). The combination of mobile lifestyles that give us the opportunity to meet many people and social technologies that make it easy for us to stay in touch is creating enormous active personal networks, too big to manage without assistance. They are social landscapes in need of a map.

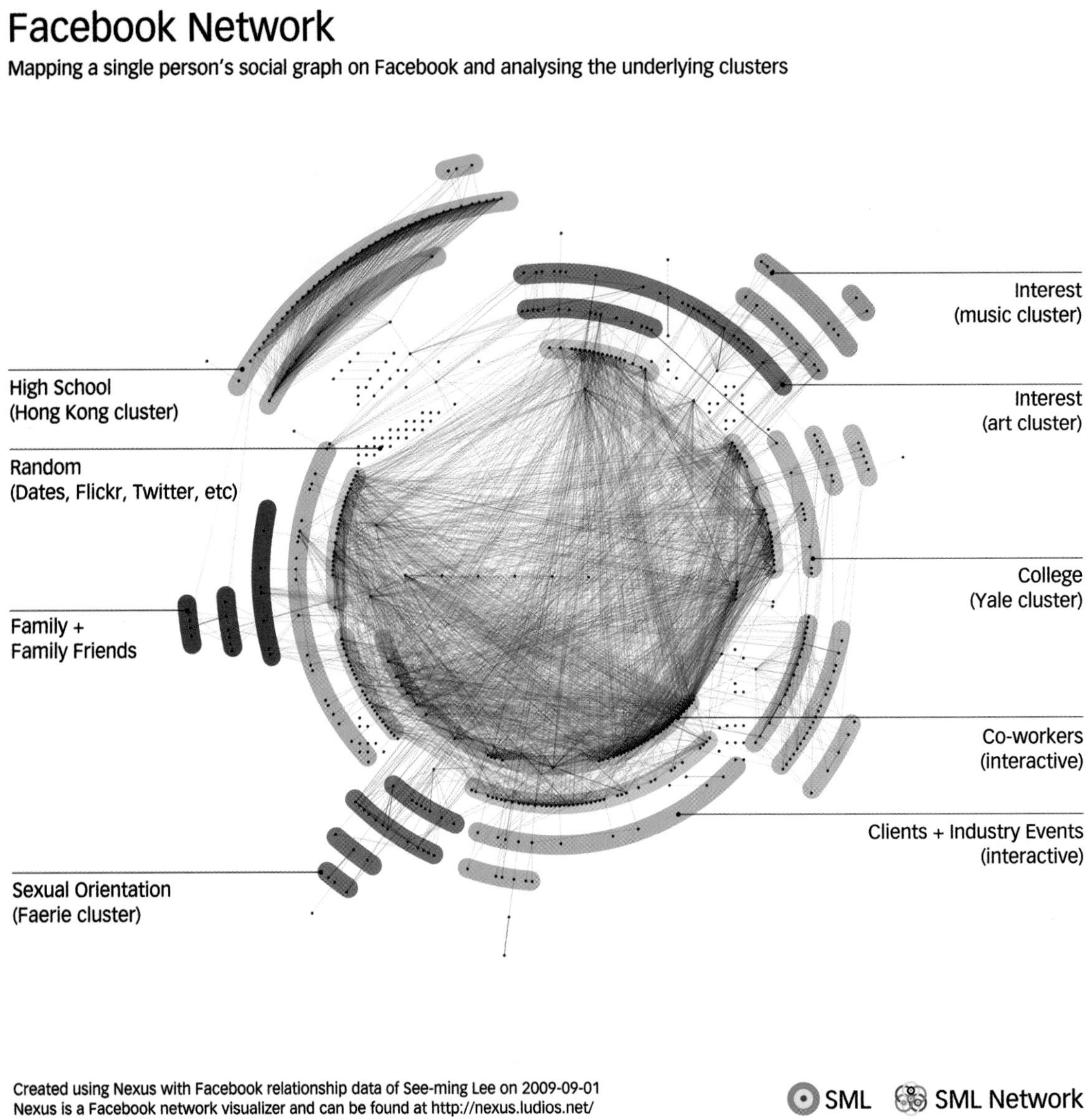

FIGURE 4.6
See-ming Lee, *Annotated Facebook Social Graph* (2009).

Maps as Portraits

A map of one's personal social network can function as a portrait.

People post maps of their own networks to photo-sharing sites, much as they post photographs of themselves and their friends at various events; the point is to show who you are, what you do, and whom you know (see figure 4.3). Some are annotated, explaining the significance of the clusters to others (see figure 4.6).

Like any portrait, the network map shows only one perspective of its subject. Although the map of my network in figure 4.5 includes many people, it is far from a complete—or even representative—sample of the people I know. It shows the people I know who happened to be on Facebook back in 2009 and who had chosen to connect to me and vice versa. It does not include some of my closest friends, my children, my neighbors, or my dentist, and it does include some people I have a very tenuous relationship with: vaguely remembered high-school classmates and colleagues met at a long-ago conference. Furthermore, many of the people who appear to have only a few connections actually have very large networks of friends on the site, but I am not friends with their friends so they do not appear on this map.[7]

The selection of who is included in any network depiction is somewhat arbitrary. The Facebook networks vary by how people use the technology: some connect only to close friends, a subset of the people they would send holiday cards to; some connect to anyone who asks; and many gather thousands of on-site ties, few of whom they would recognize if they ran into them on the street. The visualization accurately portrays how the subject uses that particular technology. But one must be careful in making broader assumptions about the subject's sociability or personality since his use of a particular technology may not be typical of his overall behavior.

The map of a friend's network can be fascinating to peruse. The names are familiar, and thus exploring the relationships is interesting (see figure 4.7). A similar map of a stranger's connections provides some, but limited, insight. One can see if that community is unusually large or small, and whether it is a dense network of interconnected ties or a loose network of many separate groups. If it is a map of a community, rather than an egocentric map of an individual's connections, one can see the individual's role: Does she have many connections? How well connected are her connections? Are they densely connected among themselves, or is she the bridge between diverse groups? (See this chapter's appendix for more on bridge figures and network structure.)

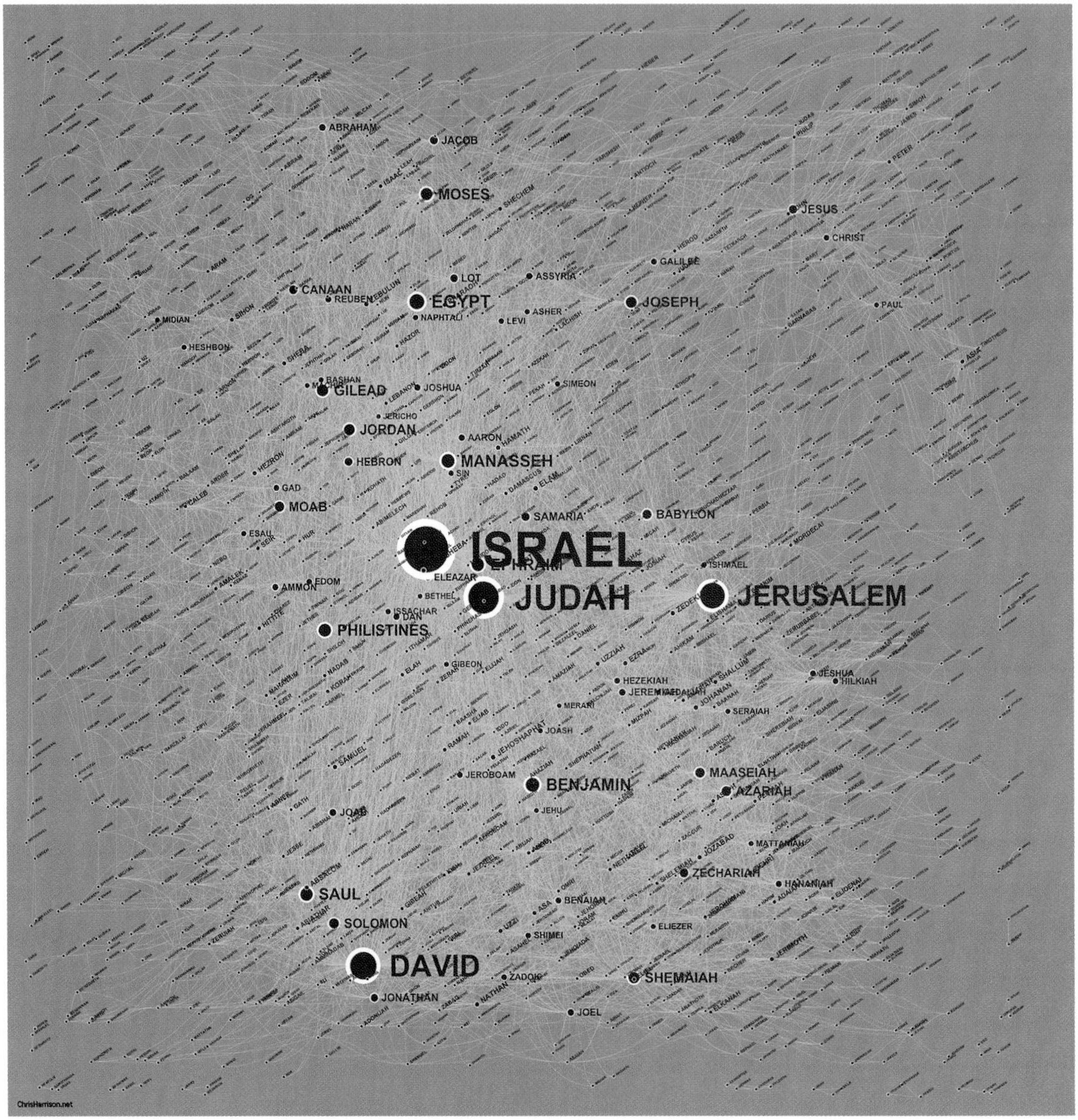

FIGURE 4.7
Chris Harrison, *Biblical Social Networks* (2008). Familiar networks need not be personal ones: Chris Harrison's social network map of people and places in the Bible is interesting to peruse for both known and obscure names. Here, connection is defined as "appears in the same verse."

A social network map has the potential to be a vivid and evocative portrait, but the information must be more than just the skeleton shape of the network. Most contemporary network maps are just nodes and generic connections. To tell a story, we need more information than that. Which are the close connections? What brought these people together? What is surprising about finding this person next to that one?

Telling Stories

A network map can be a narrative device, providing the framework for a detailed annotation of people and their relationships.

Dramatis Personae (see figure 4.8) is a map of the social connections among the guests at a wedding. It is a hand-drawn map that describes itself as "a useful (if inexhaustive) visual taxonomy of the binding ties … between the characters gathered here today." The purpose of this map was to introduce the guests at a wedding, providing them with some background about the various relationships to help start conversations. Had it simply connected names with lines like a typical network map does, it would be a nice image, but hardly a compelling conversation starter. However, the mapmakers annotated each line with a pithy comment about the relationship between the two connected people: "Mick, father of the bride learned to play bridge from the mother of Bill." "Andy nearly died of sunburn after swimming in the Elk River with Chrissy." Here, the network map functions as the foundation for telling stories. While a few of the annotations provide basic relationship information—"*June* is the proud mother of *Officiant Ellen*"—most are notes about intriguing exploits or quirky facts: "Kay makes the favorite strawberry jam of Andy." It is network map as humorous ice-breaker.

Any organization—a club, a corporate or academic department—could collectively create a similar map as a way to capture its social history. One can imagine this being especially helpful to newcomers as they attempt to learn the often taken-for-granted and unspoken structure of the community.

Other social network maps tell stories to critique society. Mark Lombardi made hand-drawn network maps that depicted the relationships among people and corporations in a variety of complex scandals: the relationship between big oil companies and terrorists, the collapse of the Vatican bank, and so on (see figure 4.9). The data they depict, though newsworthy, could make for a dense and dry textual narrative. But drawn as elegant maps, they have been exhibited, reprinted, and widely discussed.

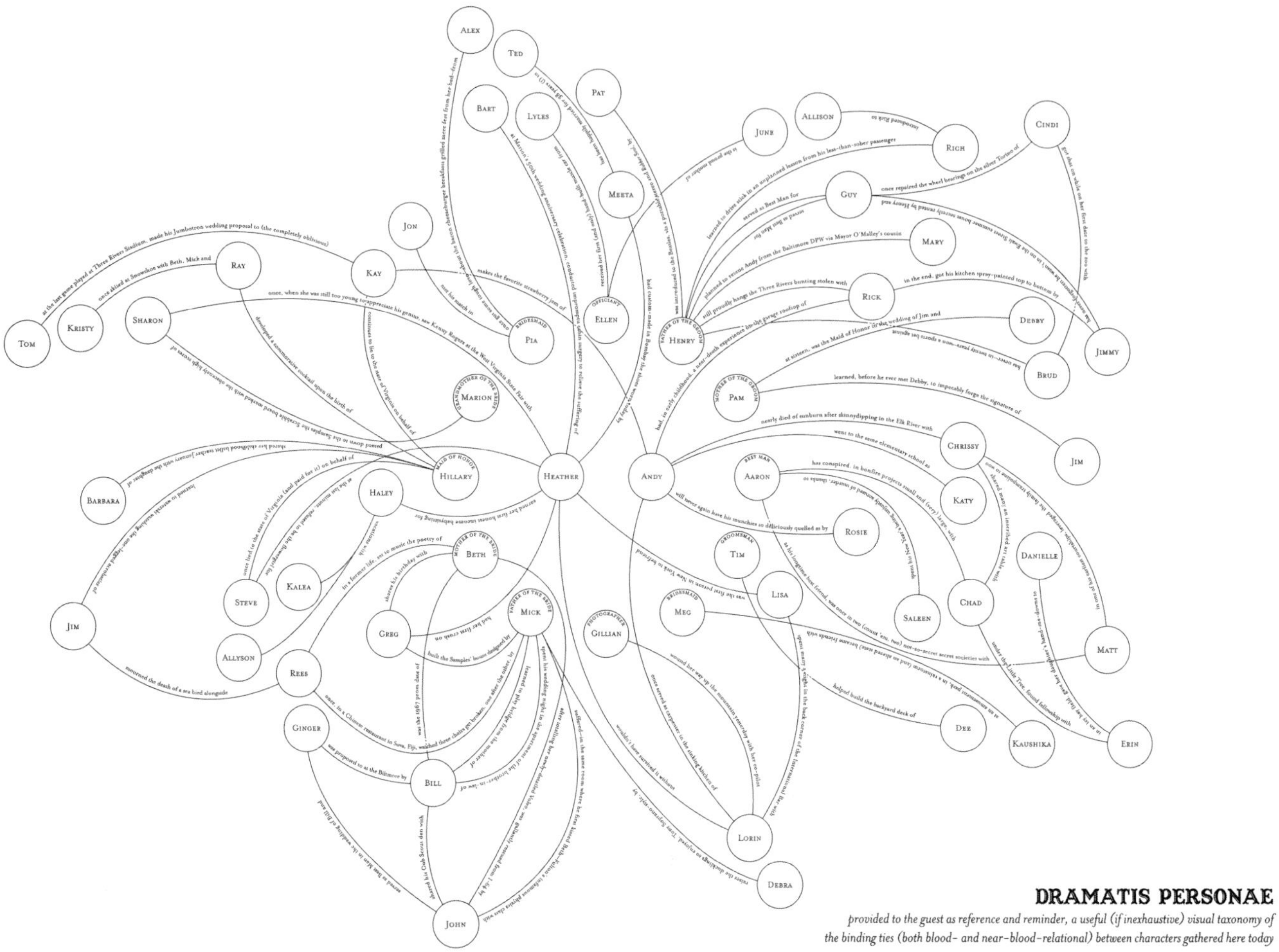

FIGURE 4.8
Andrew Coulter Enright and Heather Samples, *Dramatis Personae* (2006).

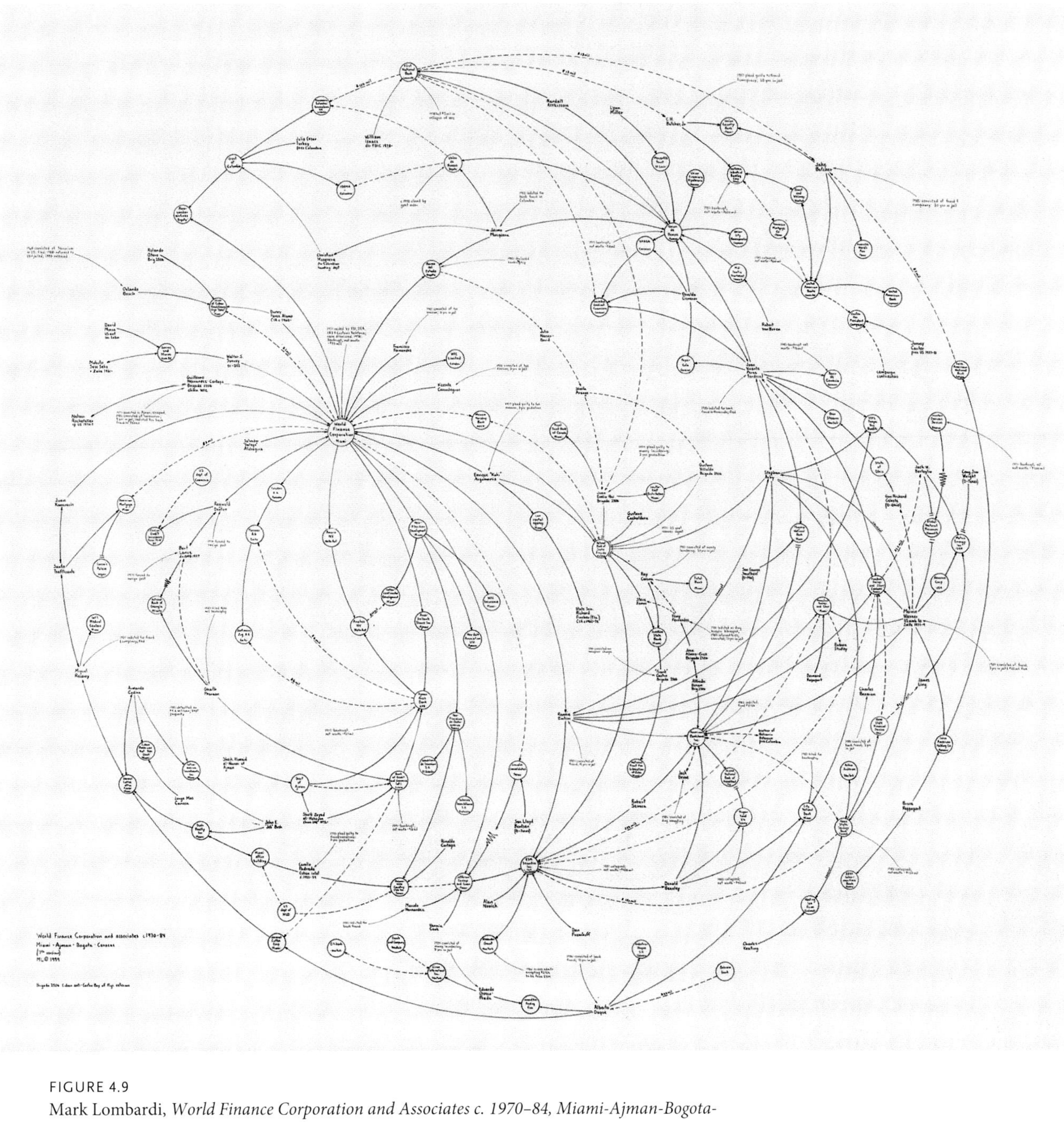

FIGURE 4.9
Mark Lombardi, *World Finance Corporation and Associates c. 1970–84, Miami-Ajman-Bogota-Caracas (7th version)* (1999). Graphite and colored pencil on paper, 60 × 78 inches.

Lombardi's drawings are activist maps, telling stories of undue influence and compromising relationships. Here, the hand-drawn quality conveys subjectivity; it reminds the viewer that an artist is behind the map, and the map shows the world through his eyes.

Drawing a social map by hand provides freedom that an automated map does not have. Computer-rendered maps are limited to the expressive range of the rendering software (which can be quite limited or very powerful), whereas making a map by hand can provide greater flexibility in how a line is drawn or which symbols are used. Lombardi depicted the nuances of social structure using arrows, circles, and scribbles. His diagrams still greatly simplify complex relationships, but they are more informative than simple line-and-node network maps (Tufte 2006).

Hand-drawn maps can be subjective, even propagandistic. Computer-generated maps generally depict some mathematical relationship derived from a dataset, and although one can certainly use biased or fictional data as the basis, the map is a faithful depiction of that data. The hand-drawn map is more easily skewed; here, where each node and link is individually marked, accuracy is harder and drawing by feel and intuition easier. That said, the hand-drawn map conveys to the viewer that it is a personal expression, whereas the computer-rendered one appears more objective, "data-driven," and authoritative, whether or not it actually is.

Density

Unlike hand-drawn maps, where the process of individually marking each node and link limits the size of the network it is practical to depict, computers can render immense datasets of connections. Here the challenge is to make the densely complex image legible to the human viewer.

Figure 4.10 shows Jeffrey Heer's map of three degrees of his connections (his friends, their friends, and the friends of those friends) on Friendster, an early social network site. It has 47,471 nodes with 432,430 connections among them. Brightness represents degree: Heer himself is the brightest node (0 degree), followed by his connections, and so on. The image is striking, but also illegible.

The impenetrable denseness of this image, however, is part of its message.[8] Friendster and several other early social networking sites were designed around the idea that if you could follow a chain of connections to someone, a

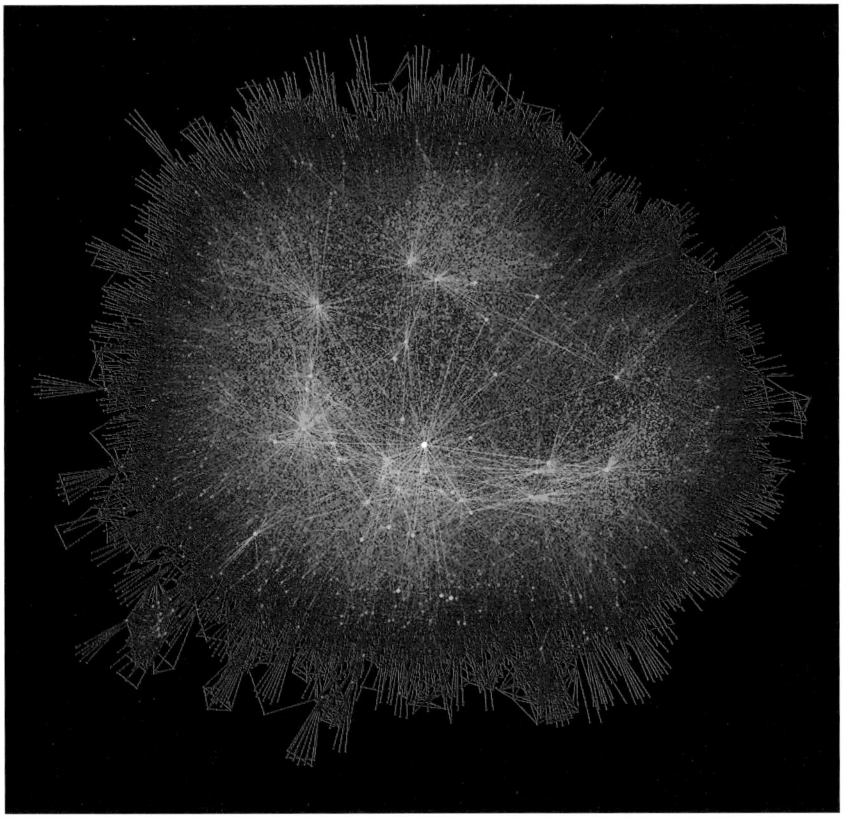

FIGURE 4.10
Jeff Heer, *Vizster Social Network Map* (2004).

chain of a length that sounds small, like three, four, or five hops, you had a real connection to that person. In reality, that is a big social distance. You are probably at most four hops from everyone in your city (and less than that in a smaller town), but that does not mean the stranger you just passed is nearly an acquaintance. The tangle of Heer's map makes the immensity of the three-degree distance palpable.

We usually, however, want something more comprehensible. One of the most powerful ways of bringing legibility to a dense dataset is to make the visualization interactive (Ahlberg, Williamson, and Shneiderman 1992; Becker, Eick, and Wilks 1995; Heer, Bostock, and Ogievetsky 2010; Keim 2001; Shneiderman and Aris 2006; Yee et al. 2001). This allows the viewer to explore the data, uncovering different patterns. With network visualizations, a common simplification is to remove nodes—either before the layout is made (thus simplifying the dataset that is shown) or after (thus removing some of the clutter from the image, but leaving the remaining nodes as they were located within the full dataset of connections). By alternating between the full view, which shows overall structure and clusters, and the filtered view, which reveals details such as individual connections, the viewer gains a fuller picture of the structure (Ahlberg and Shneiderman 1994; Jia et al. 2008; Kumar and Garland 2006).

Visual Who, which we discussed in chapter 1, used both interactivity and filtering. The viewer explored the community's relationships by adding and removing anchors (representing foci of interest) to attract different names of community members, based on their affinities. The names of people with strong ties to the current anchors would be brighter and layered on top of those with a weaker affiliation, effectively filtering the display (see figures 1.1 and 1.2).

The lines in a social network map represent relationships ranging from vague acquaintances to the closest of relatives. Information may flow symmetrically between them, or only one way. The next stage in designing social network maps involves looking more closely at what flows through the network.

HOW INFORMATION FLOWS THROUGH THE NETWORK

The basic network of nodes and links is the skeleton of society, setting its fundamental shape. Mapping the flow of information (or money, services, social support, etc.) through this network gives us a much fuller picture of the significance of the connections.

A map that shows nodes and links is a map of potential flow—of support, gossip, germs, or the like. However, because something *can* flow through a connection does not mean that it necessarily does—a road map shows where you may drive, but it does not tell you where traffic flows lightly or is jammed up with bumper-to-bumper traffic (Zuckerman 2008). In a social network, information can potentially flow from any person who possesses it to anyone with whom they connect; but in practice, of course, we do not tell everything we know to everyone we know. The network maps we have looked at so far show people and their connections as generic nodes and links. But, in terms of information flow, people are filters, modifiers, amplifiers, and sources. We do not share all the information we have with everyone we know, and when we do, we change it from the form in which we received it. We add commentary and omit details. Sometimes we attenuate it because the story is unimportant or inappropriate to pass on. Sometimes we amplify it, adding remarks or credibility that will make it more likely that others too will pass it on. Even if Beth repeats verbatim to Charlie something she heard from Alex, the message is different because the source is different: Alex may be more believable than Beth, or something that sounds ordinary coming from Alex is quite surprising to hear from Beth. Moving through the network transforms information.

Trust and Interest Shape Information Flow

Breaking bin Laden (see figure 4.11) by Gilad Lotan is a visualization of the spread on the Twitter network of the news that Osama bin Laden had been killed. This image and Lotan's discussion of the event illustrate the complex relationship between connections, trust, and value in determining how information flows through a network (Lotan 2011).

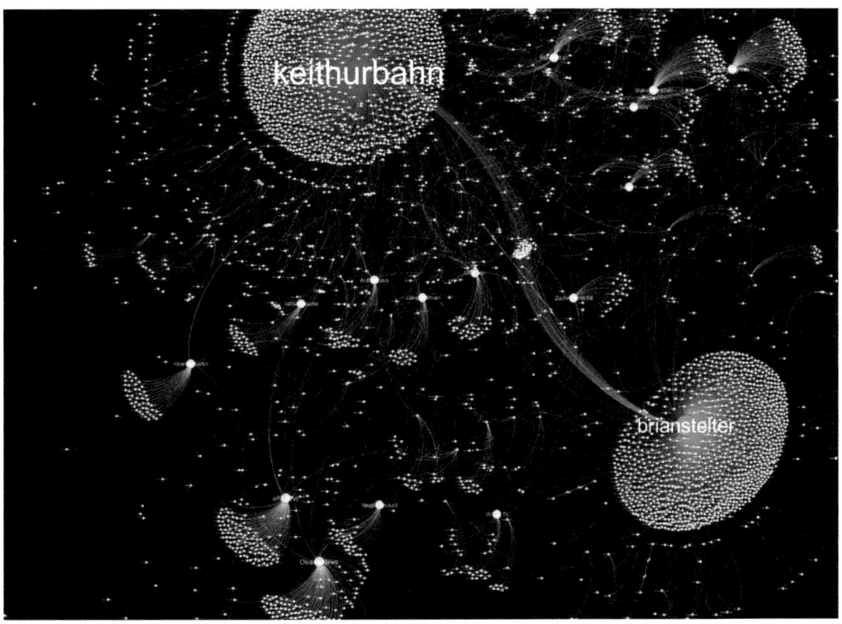

FIGURE 4.11
Gilad Lotan, *Breaking bin Laden* (2011).

On Sunday evening, May 1, 2011, the White House announced that President Obama would be making a special address to the nation later that night. This prompted much speculation on Twitter about what the subject might be, with guesses ranging from news about Libya's Gaddafi to various jokes. Although some speculated that it involved the death or capture of bin Laden, none of these tweets had a big impact until Keith Urbahn, a Twitter user with a relatively modest following, posted "So I'm told by a reputable person they have killed Osama bin Laden. Hot damn." Hundreds of people almost immediately reposted or responded to this tweet.

Urbahn was not the first to mention bin Laden in this context. There was other speculation, but those postings did not spread. What was different about Urbahn's? For one, Urbahn was a trustworthy source: he had been Chief of Staff for former Defense Secretary Rumsfeld, a fact that most repostings of his message mentioned. People saw this source information as significant, for on Twitter, where each post is limited to 140 characters, such identifying information is included only when essential.[9] Furthermore, his post was declarative and decisive sounding. Others had made similar predictions, but more tentatively. For example, a security expert with a larger following than Urbahn's had written, "I'm saying OBL is dead—I want to be the first on Twitter to engage in complete speculation that might be correct." Although this writer had expertise and connections, he presented only a guess and his posting made little impact (Lotan 2011). Urbahn's post, citing a "reputable person," was worded as fact.[10] Network position also helped. Among Urbahn's relatively small following were some influential people. Brian Stelter of the *New York Times* wrote to his more than 50,000 followers: "Chief of staff for former defense sec. Rumsfeld, @keithurbahn, tweets: 'I'm told by a reputable person they have killed Osama bin Laden.'" And finally, it was exciting yet believable news. Other predictions were less attention getting (the announcement will be about the death toll in recent storms) or too far-fetched (the president will announce that a comet is heading toward Earth) (US Political Madness Forum 2011). Here we see how in a social network, the role and reputation of the people, the network's structure, and the content of a message shape information flow.

Why spread such a story? Part of the dynamic was social support. People were intrigued and concerned about the mysterious announcement. Chatting on Twitter or other forums was a way to share the anxiety and try to find out some news as quickly as possible. But there is also an element of status competition. In the information-based world of Twitter, being at the forefront of a new story—being one of the earliest posters of a story that becomes big—confers prestige. And on Twitter, prestige immediately translates into increased influence: if more people follow you, your subsequent postings reach a bigger audience. Urbahn's list of followers went from about 300 to over 5,000 in the twelve hours following his bin Laden posting (Gavin 2011) and rose to 8,000 in the following days.

Being the first to convey a piece of information is valuable. If you hear something novel and fascinating from me, that raises my standing in your opinion. But being at the forefront is also risky. Announcing a story before it is verified makes you a leader, but if you turn out to be wrong, you lose credibility; do so often enough, and no one will listen to anything you say. Yet if you wait to say anything until the information you are passing on is well established, you gain little prestige, and indeed risk boring your listeners. The tension between the rewards of being first and the risk of being inaccurate is one of the key forces shaping the dynamics of public, information-based social networks.

Having a public voice has only recently, with the rise of mass online communication, become commonplace. Forums such as Twitter, blogs, and other social network sites form a middle ground between personal communication and large-scale broadcast, such as TV and newspapers. They have the personal connections of traditional conversation—I am likely to be more influenced by something a friend tells me than a stranger—but their reach, and the speed at which news travels through a network, is far greater. Mapping how information flows through these new channels can help us understand how these technologies are changing society.[11]

Mapping Information Flow for a Community Mirror

Although networks of personal connections form the basis of our communities, their structure can be hard to see even in familiar circumstances. Mapping how information flows in our everyday life lets us perceive the dynamics that shape our communities.

An elementary school, with its grades, classes, and ever-changing friendships, is a small but complex social world. To help students see the intricate web of their relationships and understand how this affected who learned what from whom, Rick Borovoy and his colleagues created *i-balls*, simple animations and games played on small keychain devices. Children could create, play, and—most interestingly—pass these games on to others by linking their devices together. The goal of the project was to recreate, in a form that could be recorded and visualized, the richly innovative and sociable world of children's folklore, where stories and traditions are invented, refined, and spread from person to person (Borovoy et al. 2001).

In one version, the designers gave out the devices to the students and staff at a public elementary school. The project was very popular, and over the course of a few weeks they designed and disseminated hundreds of i-balls. The students were fascinated by maps showing how the i-balls traveled (see figure 4.12). They could see which ones had circulated mainly within a single grade, and which had spread beyond a limited group, and who was the bridge making that connection. They could see who shared which game or picture widely, and who received it but chose not to pass it on. "There was a sense of

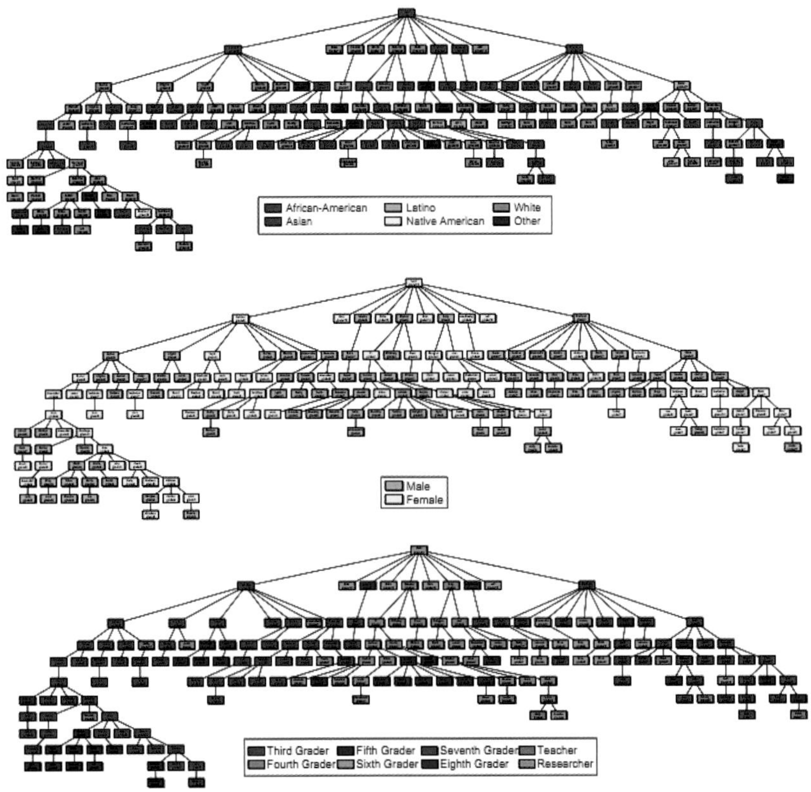

FIGURE 4.12
Rick Borovoy, *Spread of the Romance i-ball* (2001). Charts are colored by ethnicity (top), gender (middle), and grade (bottom).

excitement around this privileged view these students were getting of a geometry they always sensed, but could never before directly apprehend" (Borovoy et al. 2001, 470).

Mapping the Flow of Personal Conversations

The bin Laden Twitter visualization and the i-ball maps show how information—a rumor, a game—spread throughout a community. Sometimes, however, the act of communication itself is what is interesting, and thus we want to see which links in a network are active or dormant.

In the mid- to late 2000s, the most popular social network site was MySpace, with well over 100 million users. It was a bustling, diverse, and sometimes gritty virtual city, populated with regular users keeping in touch with friends, bands and celebrities promoting their new projects, as well as spammers and other undesirable accounts.

One problem users faced was forming an impression of strangers they encountered on the site. Unlike Facebook, which discouraged people from linking to strangers (and ultimately greatly surpassed MySpace in size and influence), MySpace encouraged people to add connections, and it was quite common to get numerous friend requests from strangers. Some might be intriguing—someone with common interests or who had posted interesting content. But not every friend request was desirable. Some were from "collectors"—people trying to accumulate as many "friends" as possible, who often used automated programs to solicit connections. Worse, an attractive-looking profile might be a front for a spam account that would fill one's profile with unwelcome advertising (Zinman and Donath 2007).

Another problem was simply making sense of the activity on the site. Which of your friends was active? Whom were they communicating with? Like other early social network sites, MySpace had no news feed (a feature Facebook introduced in 2006, which gave users a continuous stream showing what their friends were posting)—one had to visit each individual profile to see what, if anything, was new.

*Comment Flow** by Dietmar Offenhuber is a network map annotated with snippets of conversation, designed to bring social legibility to such sites (see figure 4.13). It shows the rhythm and volume of interchanges between people and provides a glimpse of their content, using as source data the public comments people posted on their connections' profiles. By showing a bit about a

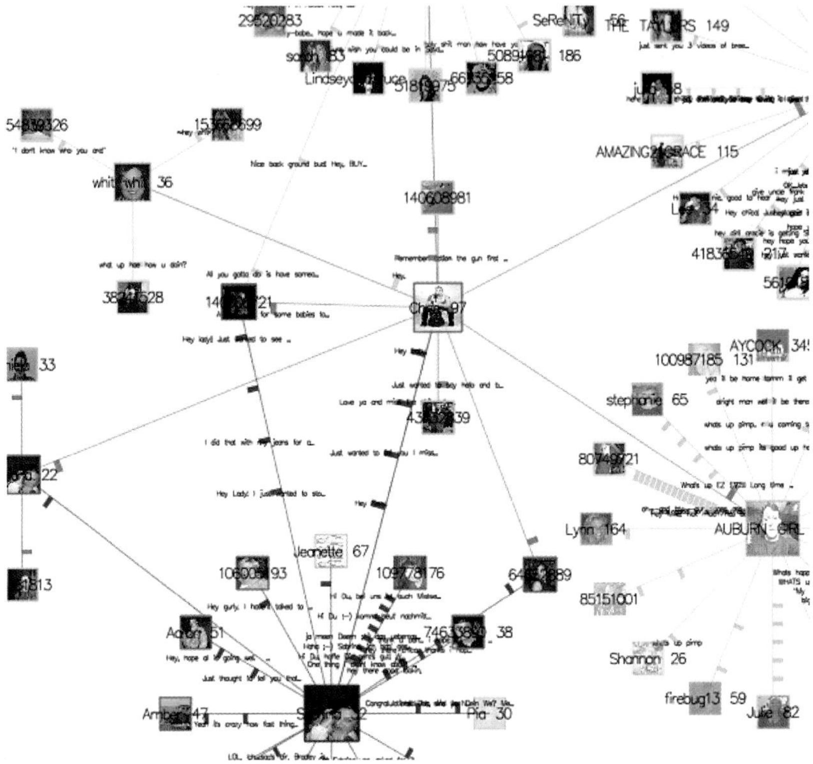

FIGURE 4.13
Dietmar Offenhuber, *Comment Flow* (2007).

person's relationships with his various connections, this annotated social network diagram creates a more nuanced data portrait (Offenhuber and Donath 2008). One gets a very different impression from seeing a person with numerous friends, most of whom appear to be other people, all having various sorts of social conversations, than one gets from seeing a person with an equivalent number of connections, most of whom are promotional entities, their "conversation" a one-way stream of press releases and announcements.

Data Caveats

Mapping information flow and revealing hidden patterns can make for a vivid portrait or community mirror; it can also violate the privacy of the depicted individuals. We need to be cognizant, when designing or displaying these renderings, of people's expectations of what is public or private. The display of data visualizations should reflect the publicness of the underlying data.

Email, for instance, is generally private. Different levels of information can be derived from it: a network map may simply show a person's contacts; it may show how much communication occurs through the different connections; or it can show what the people are saying to each other. I may feel comfortable allowing other people to see a map of who my contacts are, but not one that shows what we discuss. And, though you may think that one would never want to make the content of email public, there are situations where it could be appropriate. For example, a group of people working on a project, who know from the start that their communication is public, at least among themselves, could find such depictions useful.

Omitting identifying information, limiting words, and otherwise abstracting the data can make a visualization derived from private material appropriate to a public setting. The data used in *Comment Flow* were semipublic, more visible than a private email, but certainly meant for a smaller audience than the general public. For public settings, it could omit the message text and show just boxes to indicate the quantity and frequency of messages.

It is important to keep in mind that the data about a community may be unrepresentative of the actual relationships among the people. My closest friend may not be on the map at all if she does not use the site, or if I am linked to her, it may show no communication, though in fact we are in frequent contact—just via other media and in person. It may show lots of communication with someone who is not at all a close tie, but who is a prolific writer. Some of this information is outside the designer's knowledge, such as how much do a pair of people communicate elsewhere. To clarify and provide context of the picture, additional data may be incorporated. Am I one of five ties Bob has, or one of seven hundred? Are Sue's five messages to me typical of her correspondence rate, or am I the only person to whom she has written?

Much flows through a network besides information: social support, money, and so on. Sociologists gathering network data often ask questions designed to elicit information about the strength and function of each tie (Hogan, Carrasco, and Wellman 2007; Roberts et al. 2009). How often do you speak with this person? Is this a relative, a coworker, a lover? Would you confide in him or her about a relationship problem? Would you ask to borrow money from him or her, or vice versa? This is fascinating information, and certainly can turn the dry outlines of the network into a much more colorful narrative. When can these data be part of a community map? The surveying sociologist works on the condition of anonymity; his subjects appear in

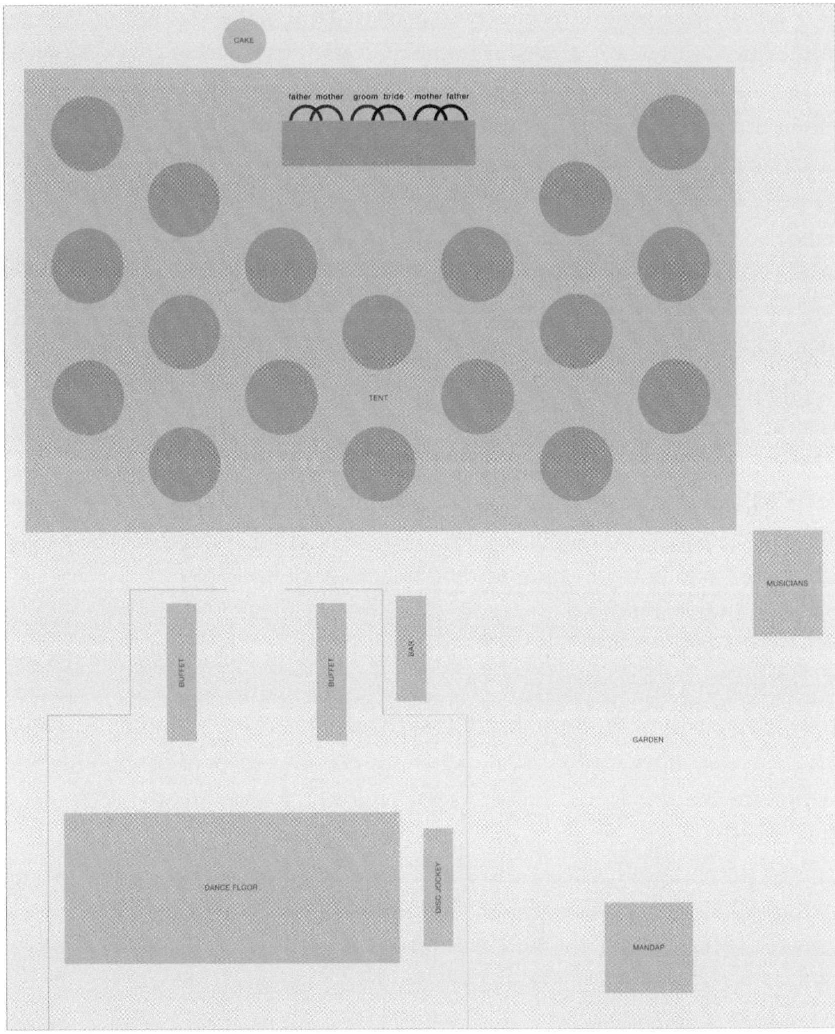

FIGURE 4.14
Kelly Sherman, *Seating Plans (Brooklyn Society for Ethical Culture, Brooklyn, NY—June 8, 2006)* (2006). Courtesy: Artist and Barbara Krakow Gallery.

reports identified by pseudonyms: their friends do not see that they've been judged to be only a casual acquaintance, or an unreliable person to confide in. One display approach for these data is to aggregate and anonymize them to create community mirrors that do not identify specific individuals, but can still show us the types of communities that form in different parts of our country and how our peers live.

The artist Kelly Sherman used wedding reception seating plans to create a series of family portraits (see figures 4.14, 4.15). In these spare, stylized, and

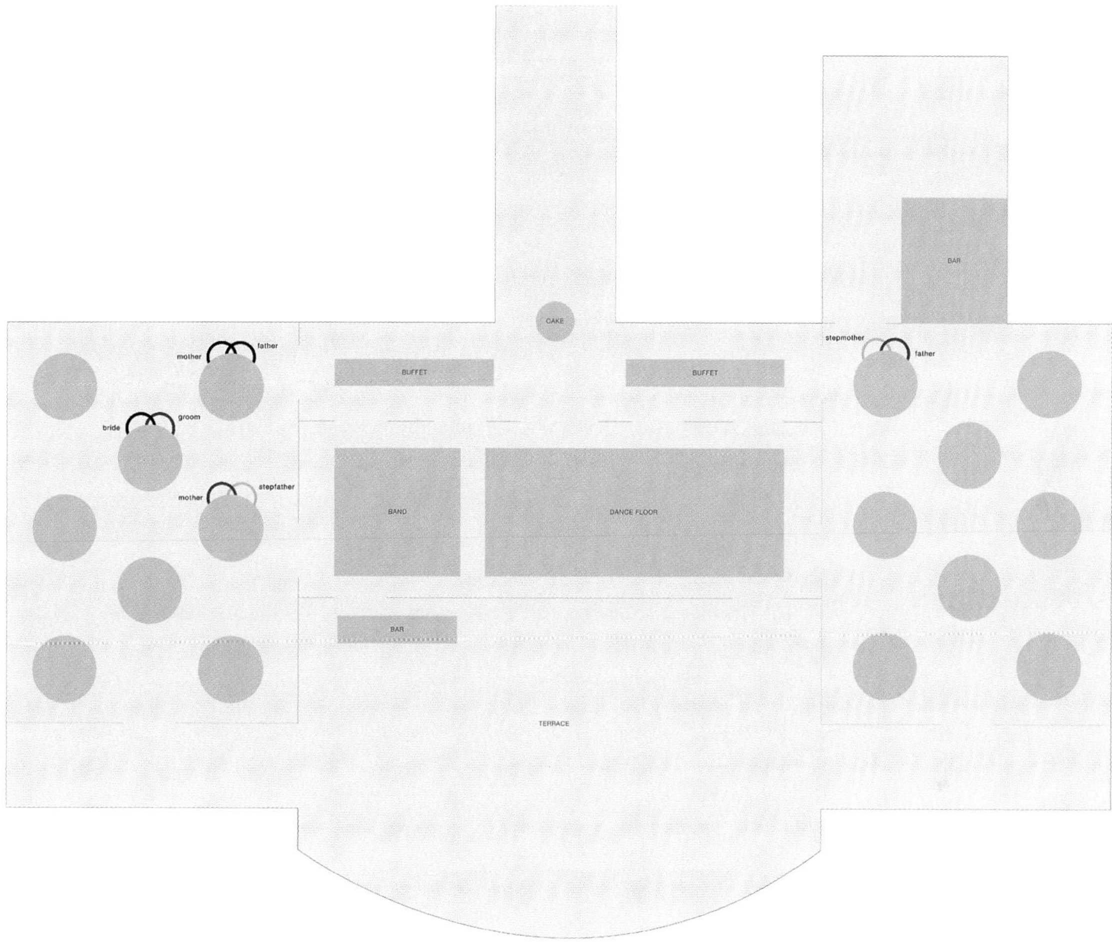

FIGURE 4.15
Kelly Sherman, *Seating Plans (Wadsworth Mansion, Longhill Estate, Middletown, CT—August 6, 2004)* (2006). Courtesy: Artist and Barbara Krakow Gallery.

mostly gray graphics, the location of the bride and her parents is marked in red and that of the groom and his parents in yellow; these simple charts hint at complex family histories and dynamics. The tales are told in divergence from the norm. In most of the arrangements, the bride and groom sit at a table near, but not with, their parents, but in figure 4.14, they are together on a dais, evoking a close-knit family with strong ties between generations. In figure 4.15, the bride and groom are near the bride's parents and the groom's mother and stepfather, but the groom's father and stepmother have been relegated to the other side of the room, separated by the wide expanse of band, buffet, and dance floor.

While these are not network maps, they are abstract—yet vivid—depictions of people's relationships. As the viewer, we try to understand what makes some families diverge from the expected arrangement. Similarly, one goal in designing network maps is to help a community evolve its understanding of norms in order to see anomalies; this is what makes a network map truly legible.

TECHNOLOGY CHANGES INFORMATION FLOW

Unlike the impression given by a network diagram's uniform nodes and simple links, real social networks are composed of diverse individuals with complex motivations. They choose what to pass on and to whom, shaping the dynamics of flow in the network. And they continuously reshape the network itself. Sharing gossip and providing support to another makes a tie stronger. (Or, it usually does. Sharing highly critical opinions or political views another finds offensive can sever ties.)

Technology changes these dynamics. It makes communication easier, while also altering people's motivations for communicating.

In our face-to-face conversations, we are selective about what we tell and to whom. If you hear a rumor that your boss is going to be replaced by someone from another department, to whom do you tell this? Not to everyone you know, because most would not care. You tell one colleague at work because she is a good friend and this change will affect her; but you don't tell others there because you are unsure if it is true and do not want to be the source of misinformation. You have lunch with a friend from outside work and tell him, not because he is deeply interested, but because you are chatting about your day and how things are going at work. Throughout the day, you are constantly taking all the news you are privy to and knowledge you have accumulated and deciding whom to tell and why. You may have a new kitten, but you only tell funny kitten stories to other cat lovers. You may have heard an off-color joke; who else will find it funny? You do not insert your entire store of knowledge at random into conversations, but as the topics in a discussion change, you bring up related facts and anecdotes.

Publication media such as blogs and Twitter make it more efficient for us to communicate with many people at once, but they make it hard to tailor our communication for specific relationships. Thus, many of the things we read on such sites are of little interest; but we also become privy to stories that we

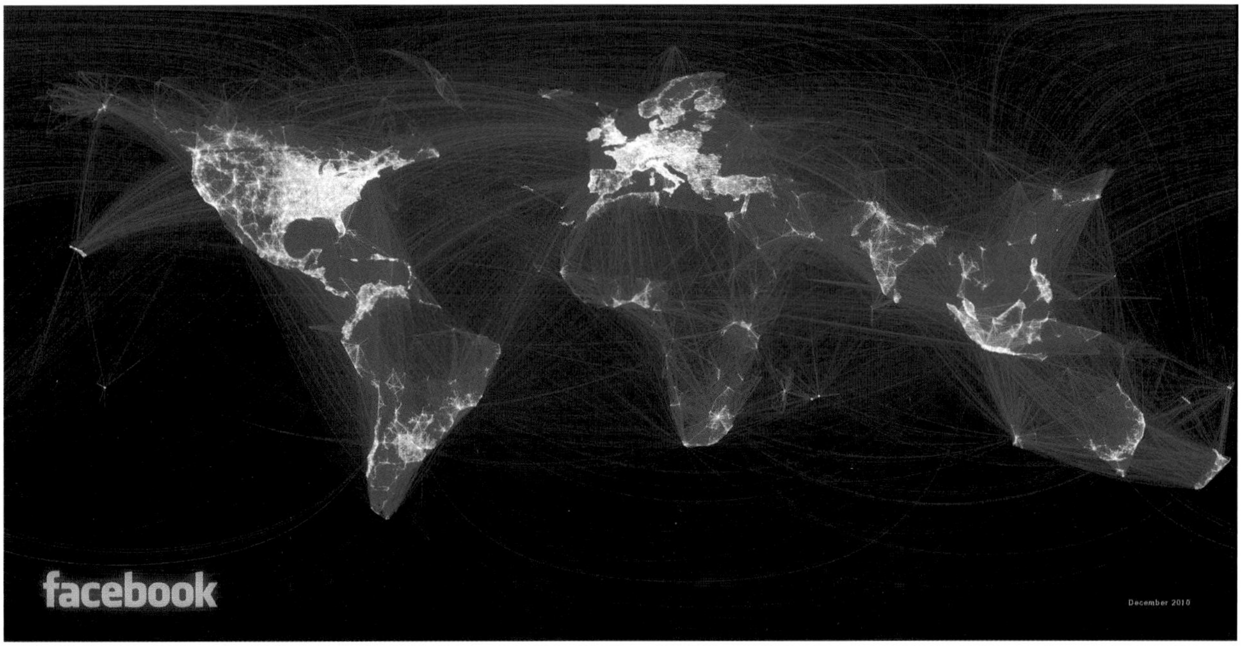

FIGURE 4.16
Paul Butler, *Facebook Map of Global Connections* (2010).

otherwise would not have heard. At its worst, the overly wide audience is a privacy failure (we discuss the effect of such social context collapses in chapter 11, "Privacy and Public Space"). At its best, this new form of serendipitous learning can strengthen relationships, as when we come to see more aspects of a person we had known only in a limited context (which we discuss further in the next chapter, "Our Evolving Super-Networks").

Figure 4.16 is a map of the world drawn entirely from data about the Facebook connections between people. Lines connect cities, and their brightness represents the number of Facebook ties between the two locations as of 2010. The map has no drawn geographic outlines; the recognizable world map emerges from the connection data alone. We began the previous chapter by noting that, were it possible to map all the connections among everyone on Earth, a historical series of such maps would reveal profound changes in society's structure. The *Facebook Map of Global Connections* is one of the closest approximations we have to such a map.

This map shows a recognizable world, its geography resembling—but far from identical with—the familiar outlines of continents. It is similar to a population map—but with some interesting exceptions. Connections in

Europe stop abruptly as it meets the Russian border, and the massive population of China produces barely a light. In Russia, a local site dominates social network activity, and China had blocked access to Facebook the year before the map was made. It is a map not of connections in general, but one that shows how communication flows—or not—through one increasingly influential medium.[12]

At another level, we can read many stories into this map: it shows the ties emigrants maintain with their families at home, college friendships kept long after the students graduate and scatter to distant jobs—the global web of relationships spun by a highly mobile population (Zuckerman 2013). It is not a route map: technically, any two places where there are Facebook users link as easily as any other pair. Instead, it shows the social relationship between places. Although figure 4.16 shows geographical contours, it actually depicts the collapse of distance.[13]

It also hints at the future. The development of any new channel—whether roads and air routes to travel on or new media to communicate with—affects the social structure of the linked communities. In the next chapter, we will look at how increased mobility—both social and geographical—changes the form and function of our social networks.

APPENDIX

Centrality: One Measure of Significance in Social Networks

The basic graph of a social network, with the people as nodes and their connections as the edges between them, is an abstract and minimalist representation of the complexities of human social structures. Yet we can still glean insight about the roles and relationships in a community by analyzing a simple map of their connections.

One of the basic attributes of the nodes in a network is centrality. Centrality is a way of measuring a person's role in a network—how likely is it that she will be aware of what is going on with the others? Does she control access to information? One can make a basic assessment of centrality with only the graph of a network, without knowing details of the characteristics of the ties.

Figure 4.17 is a simple social network, designed by network analyst David Krackhardt, to explain the network concept of "centrality" (Krackhardt 1990; Krebs 2004). There are several ways to measure how central a node is in a

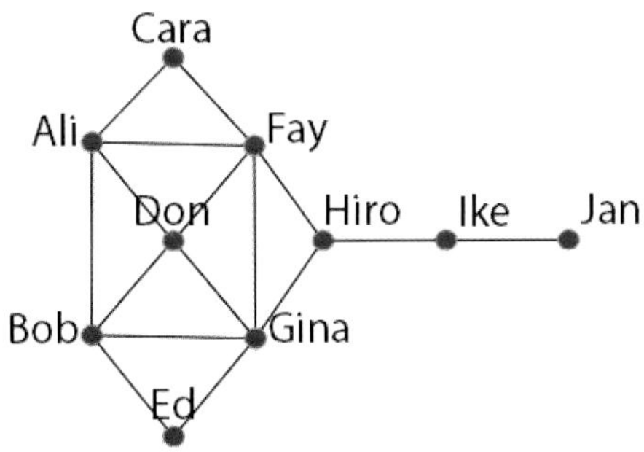

FIGURE 4.17
Centrality in a simple network. After David Krackhardt.

network; we will look at three of them: degree, betweenness, and closeness centrality.

Degree centrality is the most straightforward. It measures how many direct connections a node has. Someone with high degree centrality knows a lot of people, and someone with low degree centrality might be a newcomer, a loner, or someone peripheral to the group. In the network shown in figure 4.17, Don, who has the most connections, six out of a possible nine, has the highest degree centrality, whereas Jan has the lowest, with only one.

However, although having many connections can make one privy to much information, it is also important to measure how disparate one's sources are. Although Don has the most connections, they are all within a tight cluster. Hiro, who has only three connections compared to Don's six, has more diversity in his network; he thus has a higher *betweenness centrality*. Like Don, he has access to the information in the tight cluster on the left, but also to the separate world of Ike's knowledge. Furthermore, Hiro is what is known as a *bridge figure*. He is the sole link between two (or more) groups. He controls what information moves between them, and were he to leave, they would be disconnected.

Another form of centrality is *closeness*, which measures how far you are, on average, to other members of the network. As ties become increasingly indirect, their value quickly fades. Here, Fay and Gina have the highest closeness centrality; Jan, off at a distance, has the lowest.

In this mini-network, we can compute these measures by hand, but once the network becomes more complex, it is easiest to do so computationally. Degree centrality is the number of connections someone has divided by the number of total possible connections. This network contains a total of ten people, so the most connections one could have is nine. Jan, with one connection, has a degree of 1/9, while Hiro, with three connections, has a degree of 3/9. Closeness centrality is measured by summing how far someone is from each member of the network (what is the shortest path between them) and dividing the total number of connections by that sum. Fay needs fourteen hops to reach each person in the network, giving her a closeness centrality of 0.643, whereas Jan, who is quite distant from most, has a closeness of 9/29 or 0.310. Betweenness centrality is measured by determining the shortest path between all the nodes and counting the number of times a node is in the midst of one of these paths. Here, Cara, Ed, and Jan are never part of a shortest path, so their centrality is zero.

In mapping social networks, we can use these measures to help viewers understand the community. We can highlight key figures, such as the popular member with high degree centrality, or the important bridge figures. We can use variations on these measures, depending on what story we want to tell: some take into account the varied strength of different ties, whereas others are optimized to understand a particular problem, such as how catastrophic for the community would it be to lose a particular member of the network.

There are numerous other network features to explore. Networks can be densely or loosely connected. The ties between people can be strong or weak, narrowly focused or diversely multiplexed; a tie might represent a formal work relationship within a clear hierarchy, a warmly supportive friendship, or a wary truce between ex-partners. Some of these features (such as density) can be represented with a minimal graph, whereas others require more nuanced information than the sparse node and connection model. A full overview of social network analysis techniques is outside the scope of this book; to learn more, see Borgatti et al. 2009; Garton, Haythornthwaite, and Wellman 1997; Girvan and Newman 2002; and for a history of the research field, see Freeman 2004.

5

OUR EVOLVING SUPER-NETWORKS

The previous chapter closed with the image of the world drawn entirely with Facebook connections. Such global connectedness is a modern phenomenon, made possible only with communication and transportation technologies. We will start by looking at the questions—and designs—it has inspired.

Global travel and increasing social mobility have made our personal acquaintance networks larger and more diverse. At the same time, many of the needs these networks traditionally fulfilled have been outsourced to the market: we still value friendships, but no longer have to rely on them to build our homes, watch our children, or even recommend movies to see. What then is the function of the social network in contemporary life? In this chapter we will look more closely at how social networks are evolving and how our need for them is changing too.

A SMALLER WORLD?

In a short story by the Hungarian writer Frigyes Karinthy, the narrator recounts his friend's suggestion that they "select any person from the 1.5 billion inhabitants of the Earth—anyone, anywhere at all. He bet us that, using no more than five individuals, one of whom is a personal acquaintance, he could contact the selected individual using nothing except the network of personal acquaintances" (Karinthy 1929, 2). The characters easily imagine a social chain linking themselves to a Swedish novelist or, with a bit more difficulty, to an obscure riveter working at the Ford Motor company.

The point of this thought experiment was "to prove that the population of the Earth is closer together now than they have ever been before." The year was 1929. By then, telephones were commonplace and the first trans-Atlantic phone calls had been made. Millions of cars were on the road, explorers had reached the poles, and traders and travelers were establishing contact with the remaining isolated tribes and remote communities. For the first time in history, it seemed plausible that every person on Earth could be reached through a finite—and perhaps even rather small—number of personal connections.

Such games and the promise they held of a world united through continuous links of acquaintance resonated with many people.[1] In *Life and Death of Great American Cities*, pioneering urbanist Jane Jacobs recounts playing a similar game with her sister: "The idea was to pick two wildly dissimilar individuals—say a head hunter in the Solomon Islands and a cobbler in Rock Island, Illinois—and assume that one had to get a message to the other by word of mouth; then we would each silently figure out a plausible, or at least possible, chain of persons through which the message could go" (Jacobs 1992, 134). These games were entertaining, but the connections made in them were conjectural. Would it be possible to actually make them?

In the mid-1960s, social psychologist Stanley Milgram conducted a series of experiments to study "the small world problem" in the real world, to see how people would actually create paths of personal connections to a distant, unknown person. He picked a target person in one community and distributed letters to participants in another community with the instructions to give the letter to the target if they knew him (or her) personally and if not, to give it to some other person whom they believed would be closer to the target. Milgram found that the average number of steps needed to make the connection was 5.5. The popular magazine *Psychology Today* published his findings (Milgram 1967; see also Travers and Milgram 1969), the story caught people's imagination, and "six degrees of separation"—the idea that we are now, at most, six links of personal relationships away from any other person on Earth—became a popular truism, inspiring TV shows, parlor games, a Broadway play, and a Hollywood movie.

Why was there such interest in this social psychology experiment? One reason was the change in society it marked. Advances in travel and communication had made the world smaller, making such universal connections conceivable. As Karinthy (1929) had written: "Planet Earth has never been as *tiny* as it is now. It shrunk—relatively speaking of course—due to the quickening pulse of both physical and verbal communication."

But the fascination with this experiment was also a response to the ways the world was becoming larger, both in the number of people and the distance between them. Population growth was rapidly accelerating: in just the decade and a half following 1960, more than a billion more people were added.[2] Jane Jacobs noted that she and her sister had felt rather isolated, having just moved to a big city from a smaller town—their game, she said, made them feel less alone.

And, by the mid-twentieth century, many people were experiencing life in what Marshall McLuhan termed the "global village," a deceptively cozy term for a world in which you are governed by distant, inaccessible politicians and far-off CEOs, one in which you no longer know about your neighbors, but instead are enthralled by the marriages, scandals, and babies of celebrities you see on TV. In this world of one way mass-media experiences, where you can look but cannot touch, the promise that a small chain—just six people or fewer!—of personal, real connections bridges the gap between you and any other person makes the vast impersonal world seem close and comfortable.

Milgram's work was quoted, repeated, and believed. But his actual results were rather different from the myth that grew up around them. We will look more closely at his experiments because (a) their failures tell us a lot about the function of—and friction among—the connections in social networks and (b) the mythologized version influenced the design of early social network sites.

Navigation in Social Space

Milgram's "small-world problem" showed how people navigate the social space between themselves and a distant person. Milgram gave the searchers the target's name, town, and occupation. One strategy was to get the letter physically closer: searchers who did not know the target would often give the letter to a resident of or someone from the target's city or state. Another strategy was to get it professionally closer. One target was a stock broker, and the path that reached him led through a series of bankers and brokers. The viability of this strategy depends on the target's career. If you are trying to find, for example, a physicist, there is an international community that knows each other via publications and global academic conferences; finding someone in that community can help you reach the person, even if the intermediary is physically farther away. But if your subject is, say, a cashier, there is no network or trade association of cashiers.

The notion that a small-sounding number of links connects us all has fascinated many people. In John Guare's play *Six Degrees of Separation*, the character Ouisa says:

> I read somewhere that everybody on this planet is separated by only six other people. Six degrees of separation between us and everybody else on this planet. The president of the United States. A gondolier in Venice. Fill in the names. I find that A) tremendously comforting that we're so close and B) like Chinese water torture that we're so close. (Guare 1994, 81)

The information provided about the targets shaped the searchers' strategies. Different data would change the paths: imagine that Milgram had given, instead of occupation, the target's favorite hobby, religious organization membership, or children's ages. Each of these would provide access to a network that would lead, via a different route, to some of the targets. Not all data are useful for way-finding in a network. Birthdate, for example, though it helps to uniquely identify people, is not much use for finding them. Sociologist Scott Feld used the termed "foci" to encompass the range of interests and situations that bring people together—the forces that create our personal networks:

> Foci may be many different things, including person, places, social positions, activities, and group. They may actively bring people together or passively constrain them to act. … For foci where everyone is forced to interact much and often (e.g. families), all of the individuals associated with that focus will be tied to each other; but for foci that are less constraining on interaction (e.g. city neighborhoods), only a slightly higher proportion of individuals will be tied than would be tied in the general population. (Feld 1981, 1018)

Our social networks are not composed of random connections, but are structured around the interests and activities through which we meet and spend time with people.

With casual acquaintances we often know only about the part of their lives related to the focus that drew us together. One might be quite friendly with people at a gym or evening class without knowing what they do for a living. The searchers in Milgram's experiment—like all of us—were "blind" not only to the world beyond their immediate network, but also to many aspects of the people they personally knew.

Often, the most useful thing to know about a person was not their specific interests but their social role. The strategy that many successful searchers in Milgram's small-world experiment used was to find "bridge figures"—people who connect otherwise separate groups. If the target is in Boston and you not only don't know him, you don't know anyone in Boston—you're not even sure you know anyone who definitely knows people in Boston—what do you do? You look for someone who has a wide circle of diverse acquaintances, what Milgram terms "a sociometric star" (Milgram 1967, 271). If, as was the case with some of the initial participants in the experiment, you live amid an insular, dense network of close family and friends, you seek the least confined person: someone who travels, or whose work means she meets people from different places and social circles.

Milgram's small-world problem did not, and was not intended to, measure the actual distance between source and target. Each person was acting somewhat blindly: if he didn't know the target, he was to give the letter to someone he thought would bring it closer. But there could well be unrecognized, more direct, connections: unknown to you, your second cousin might be best friends with the target's daughter, and so on. Many short paths exist that are unlikely to be discovered by blind social way-finding: a full network path would reveal them.

In the 1960s, such a map seemed like a fascinating but unrealizable idea. But with the advent of computer-based communication—and specifically, social network sites[3]—this changed.

THE MYTH OF FRICTIONLESS CONNECTION

The line from Stanley Milgram to the early social network sites is easy to draw: the first one was named sixdegrees.com. Created in 1997, it attracted users but was a few years too early: most participants had only a few friends who were also online, which limited its appeal. Five years later Friendster appeared; it was the first social network site to become widely known and, at least for a short while, wildly successful, signing up a million users in a few months.

Friendster's founder, Jonathan Abrams, envisioned it as the next wave in online dating. Although dating sites, such as Match.com, were among the most popular commercial websites (and at the time, they were almost alone in their ability to get people to pay for access), they did not appeal to everyone. Typical dating sites are places to meet strangers—the nameless profiles are unverified self-descriptions, modeled after the personal ads in the classified section of the traditional newspaper. The potential dates are unmoored from any common context and the safety of community. By contrast, meeting people through friends is comforting; it provides the sense that the person has been vetted and can thus be trusted. If a friend introduces me to a new person, I assume she thinks that we would like each other—or at least, not be a harmful combination. Yet most people are not inveterate matchmakers, assiduously introducing their niece to their jeweler and their downstairs neighbor to their best friend's cousin. Abrams saw a world full of unmade introductions and built Friendster to automate the process of meeting friends of friends.

The site rapidly became very popular. People made profiles and connected to friends, distant acquaintances, people they barely knew, and complete strangers. Friendster soon had millions of users. Yet by 2005, it was failing. What happened?

The problem was not a lack of interest in online social networking. MySpace, launched in 2003, was quickly overtaking Friendster (much as Facebook would a few years later overtake it—but in 2004 Facebook was a small site, accessible only to students on a limited number of campuses). Friendster attracted its millions of registered users because the concept of connecting to others in such a network is very appealing. But several key design flaws doomed it.

Abrams cited Milgram and the idea of "six degrees of separation" as one of his inspirations in designing the site (Calacanis 2012; Chafkin 2007).[4] Here, finally, would be a piece of software that, once everyone joined, would allow us to see the global web of connections between people.

Perhaps the fundamental mistake was thinking that distant connections are meaningful. When you logged in to Friendster, you would see a note about the size of your network, measured not in direct connections, or even friends of friends, but by several degrees out. This could quickly grow to an astronomical number. If I connect with only ten people, but some of them connect to hundreds of others and so do some of those connections, I could effortlessly acquire an extended network of hundreds of thousands of people. One view of this is that it is an exciting indicator of the computer's ability to expand our social networks. What more could the lonely engineer, shy and awkward in person, but craving a richer social life, want?

At first, exploring this network was intriguing. Whenever you added a new person to your network, novel sections of the overall network become visible to you. But, the excitement of this wore off. The people beyond second degree are really just strangers, and reading their profiles—which on Friendster were fairly minimal—was not deeply interesting.[5] Once you had made your profile, found some old friends, and poked around a bit, there was not that much to do there.

And, in reality, the immense network was rather meaningless. Logging in and seeing that your twenty or forty connections gave you a network of hundreds of thousands did not really put you in touch with multitudes—the distant "connections" were still strangers. Moreover, since the site encouraged growing your network, people added connections indiscriminately. The connections you had to those hundreds of thousands were via some extremely weak links (boyd 2004).

But, because Abrams had initially found the idea of delineating one's extended network so compelling, it became the central motif of the site. Not only were the numbers featured on your page, but enormous amounts of computing power were expended calculating it in as close to real time as possible. This slowed the site down, so that a page might take thirty or forty seconds to load—a very long time for an audience increasingly used to instant results. In an effort to speed it up, the company spent enormous amounts on bigger, faster computers—which ultimately were not big and fast enough for the network rendering challenge, but were a big enough drain on its finances that they accelerated its downfall (Chafkin 2007).

The delineated social network is an intriguing concept. The ability to see the path of connections to distant people makes the world seem a bit smaller, cozier—more connected. But that is an illusion. In practice, even second-degree relationships are tenuous.

Milgram (1969, 274) himself noted:

> Almost anyone in the United States is but a few removes from the President, or from Nelson Rockefeller, but this is only as seen from a particular mathematical slant and does not, in practical sense, integrate our lives with that of Nelson Rockefeller. Thus, when we speak of five intermediaries we are talking about an enormous psychological distance between the starting and target point, a distance which only seems small because we customarily regard 5 as a small manageable quantity.

THE COMPLICATION OF NETWORK FLOW

To talk about society as "connections" in a "network" is to use a simplifying metaphor to refer to a tangled web of complex relationships. One flaw that results from this simplification is the impression that once a connection exists, anything can flow through it. In fact, the existence of the connection is only the most basic requirement; the specifics of each situation—the nature of the relationship and of the thing to be transferred (money, support, ideas, a psychology experiment's letters)—add friction to the flow.

A closer look at Milgram's experiments shows that smooth flow of the s letter from source to target was the exception, not the rule. Unpublished data reveal that in Milgram's initial experiment only 5 percent of the letters made it through at all (Kleinfeld 2002). Yet, the failures are as interesting as the successes, for they show us the complications of moving things through a network.

Although popular imagination claims that Milgram's experiments proved that everyone in the world, no matter how distant, is at most six degrees apart, in fact his seekers and targets were already quite close. They were socially similar—middle-class, English-speaking Americans. Milgram's notion of "distant" communities is almost comical: "We thought it best to draw our starting people from some distant city such as Wichita, Kansas or Omaha, Nebraska (from Cambridge, these cities seem vaguely 'out there' on the Great Plains or somewhere)" (Milgram 1967, 265).[6]

The closeness of seekers and target suggests that lack of a path did not cause the high failure rate; subjects chose to drop out.[7] Perhaps the person who got the package intended to pass it on, but forgot it in a welter of other responsibilities. Or perhaps he or she was being socially frugal. Milgram noted that the best people to pass this task onto were what he termed "sociometric stars": bridge figures with many and diverse ties. But such people are also valuable connections, and participants might be leery of using up their social capital with a well-connected acquaintance for this purpose.

Varied goals and perceptions motivated those who did pass on the letter and affected their choice of to whom to give it. Some may have participated because they felt an obligation (the "letter" was ornately designed, and prominently mentioned Harvard as its source). Those who saw it as an intriguing experiment may have felt that passing it on was a favor to their acquaintance, providing an opportunity to be part of an interesting project. Some may have chosen to give the letter not to the best person they could think of for the task, but to someone whom they did not mind embroiling in this slightly odd activity.

The path something (an idea, object, support, etc.) takes through a network depends both on how individuals value it and on the dynamics of their relationships. Think about who you would turn to for help with a technical problem, to borrow $1,000, or for advice about a romantic relationship. Both your friend who started a software company and your thirteen-year-old niece might have the knowledge to solve your technical problem, but the former is not happy to be tasked with people's computer problems whereas the latter is thrilled to have knowledge and abilities for which adults seeks her assistance. A close, generous friend might willingly lend $1,000, but you know it would be difficult for her. Our choices of from whom to seek support (or to whom to provide it) depend on the nature of the support, how close we are to the person, and their personality and circumstances.

Many of Milgram's letters failed to reach their destination not because of a lack of a path—especially given how close his searchers and target were—but because of friction at the individual level. Milgram noted, "The subject operates under the restriction that he can send the folder on only to one other person. Thus, the efficiency with which the chain is completed depends in part on the wisdom of his choice in this matter" (Milgram 1967, 265). For the numerous chains that did not complete, someone gave the letter to the wrong person—to someone too busy, uninterested, or shy to pass it on. Many chains broke not because of a lack of knowledge about the network structure, but because of a lack of knowledge about the interests and circumstances of one's immediate acquaintances. The challenge for designing social technologies is not just to connect people, but to help them learn more about each other. We will next look at how technologies are changing and expanding our social networks and then at how technology can help deepen our connections.

SOCIAL SUPER-NETWORKS

Changes in communication and transportation have indeed made the world smaller, and there is now a chain of connections (or many chains) between nearly any two people anywhere.[8] The structure of our immediate, personal networks has also changed. We will now look at the nature of that change.

Social networks are notoriously difficult to measure precisely, for the boundaries and definitions of categories such as "close friend" or "acquaintance" are subjective and shifting. But a number of studies seem to agree that, regardless of exactly how you define them, there is a trend toward larger networks of weaker ties (Hampton, Sessions, and Her 2011). Why is that? What does it imply for daily life—and how can we design technology to most usefully support the society we are moving toward?

In traditional societies, people lived in small villages among other lifelong residents, with densely connected networks in which everyone knew almost everyone else. People relied on their personal networks for assistance with major tasks, such as raising children, building a home, and harvesting crops. Their relationships were primarily strong ties. These are the ties that bind family members and close friends; they are the ties between people who share many interests, are emotionally invested in the relationship, spend much time together, and can be relied on for assistance.

A network of strong ties works well in a traditional setting, where social and material support is the most important function of community. However, this social structure is inherently insular: the network is densely connected (everyone knows everyone else) and the time it takes to maintain these ties precludes cultivating a wider world. People in these homogeneous, close-knit groups quickly share among themselves the information they have, and they have limited access to other sources of news and opportunities.

In much of the Westernized, urbanized world, things are now very different.[9] It is increasingly common for people to frequently move and change jobs, and to meet new acquaintances through activities outside of work and family. They build loosely connected personal networks, with numerous ties scattered among disconnected groups. Furthermore, tasks that people had exchanged with close friends and family are now outsourced to the market: babysitters watch the children, contractors build and repair the houses, and psychologists dispense comfort and advice (Hochschild 2012).[10]

In today's world, access to information and the ability to adapt to change are increasingly important. The old model of lifetime employment is quickly shifting to one of rapid turnover and short-term contracting—where keeping food on the table and a roof over your head requires frequent searches for leads on jobs. It is a world where people regularly uproot themselves, moving for college or for work, often needing to start over in a strange new place. With each move and job change, they need to acquire vast amounts of new information: where to find housing, schools, groceries; who among the new neighbors and coworkers is trustworthy and of whom to be careful. They need reputational information to navigate the marketplace that offers everything from household services to a dazzling and confusing array of new devices.

It is a world in which people strive to stay in style—in the clothes they wear, the slang they use, the cars they drive—following a subtle but ever-present trail of innovation information. In this world, where people hunt for trends and data rather than foraging for nuts and berries, there is tremendous benefit to having a wide and varied circle of acquaintances. Being in touch with a lot of people keeps you in touch with the changing zeitgeist. You learn quickly about new technologies, new ideas, and new places to go.

In contrast with the traditional society's dense network of strong ties, the large, diffuse network that epitomizes contemporary mobile society includes a large number of weak ties. These are ties that connect distant acquaintances: people who do not rely on each other and who may have only one or two interests in common.

Imagine someone whose job moves him frequently from one metropolis to another. He knows many people around the world: colleagues met at trade shows, squash partners from the gyms he joins in each new locale, fellow players of online games and participants in online forums—but none are intimate friends, and many are unknown to each other. This large network of weak but varied ties works well for this prototypical mobile lifestyle. The network of professional colleagues helps him keep up with the rapid changes in his industry, and when he moves to a new city there is a good chance he already knows someone there or certainly can obtain introductions from his extensive network. Depending on the value you place on deep, strong relationships, this may seem to be an easy, efficient way of life—or an empty and lonely existence.

The Internet has made it easy to amass very big networks of weak ties. There is considerable evidence that new social technologies can expand their users' social networks, providing them with a larger and more diverse set of weak ties and helping to maintain connections with people over time.[11] They vastly extend the individual's voice, making it possible for people to broadcast to thousands anything from the mundane details of what they had for breakfast to their impassioned pleas for political engagement. (Broadcasting something does not mean that huge crowds are actually listening. Whereas celebrities can command a vast audience, the average person's acquaintance network is their audience.)

These technologies are enabling the development of social "super-networks": personal social networks of a scale far beyond what we could maintain unaided. The core of these networks—composed of the strongest ties—is not bigger; the growth is primarily in weak ties, in relationships with people with whom we have less in common and on which we expend relatively little time or resources.

Many popular articles decry this development. "The Internet allows only ersatz intimacy," says one (Marche 2012). Yet in some ways a social life that consists primarily of weak ties, of numerous diverse but distant acquaintances, is very suitable for contemporary mobile life with its constant change and the insistent necessity of keeping up to date, of being a consummate information forager. And our mobile life itself creates this sort of social structure, with our short-term jobs and restlessly changing domiciles. Yet taken to an extreme it is a lonely way of life, where most relationships remain at the surface, where you know most people through a single context—the guy from the online football club, the excellent doubles partner, the sales rep who knows the best new restaurants in town. To assess the advantages and drawbacks of this emerging social structure, we need to look more closely at weak ties, diverse networks, and ultimately at the question of what our social networks are for.

Sociologists characterize the relationships, or ties, between individuals that collectively compose a social network along several dimensions. Tie strength is measured by a number of factors, including how often the individuals are in contact, how long they have known each other, whether they are related, and whether they provide mutual support and confide in each other (Granovetter 1973; Wellman, Garton, and Haythornthwaite 1997). Strong ties are often also multiplex—the individuals have multiple interests in common and know each other in various contexts. Weak ties are the relationships between acquaintances who do not know each other well; they are usually are connected through a single context.

Networks of Weak Ties

"The Strength of Weak Ties" is the title of an influential paper that argued that for gaining access to information, weak ties are valuable (Granovetter 1973, 1983).[12] Its thesis is that if you know many people through a variety of contexts who are themselves members of disparate communities, you become privy to a wide range of information from different sources.

However, it is important to recognize that it is not the weakness of the ties that is valuable, but rather their heterogeneity.[13] Knowing people from different communities and with different values, interests, and experiences gives you access to a wide range of information and a broad audience for your ideas.

The weakness of the ties is a drawback, but arguably it is necessary if you are to have a large number of heterogeneous ties. Such ties come from disparate backgrounds and are unlikely to know each other; one maintains these ties individually or in small separate groups. Maintaining a large network of diverse acquaintances from different walks of life necessitates expending relatively little time on each individual relationship.[14]

Yet, even for information access, weak ties may suffer from their weakness. If I have something I want to promote (whether I'm a marketer selling chocolates, an evangelist seeking converts, or anyone seeking status and attention), I am happy to spread that information broadly—here a big diverse network that connects me to many communities is ideal. But if the information I have is very valuable but would lose its worth if broadcast, then I will be much more selective with whom I share it. We may get—and spread—a broad range of information via weak ties, but not the most valuable information.

Granovetter's paper on "the strength of weak ties" used the example of finding a job and argued that weak, heterogeneous ties were better because they would have a more diverse pool of knowledge. This assumes that the cost of providing the information about the job was low enough that a weak tie would be the best channel. However, in an economy where jobs are scarce and knowledge of upcoming openings rare, those who have this valuable information will use it carefully. They are more likely to give it to a strong tie, someone whose success they care deeply about. Alternatively, in a field where information about job openings is widely publicized and hiring done via exams or other formal procedures, people do not need information or influence from their personal network to obtain employment; here the market replaces social networks (Putnam 1995).[15]

Furthermore, we may not trust weak ties or the information we receive from them. For some types of information, trust is less important: for example, news we are reading casually, a mild joke. Sometimes it is useful just to have a sense of what lots of diverse people are talking about—what events are people concerned about? What new products, fashions, and ideas are generating excitement? However, once we are ready to act on information—whether for deciding something as casual as what movie to see, as serious as who to vote for, or as consequential as determining whether a particular route is safe in a warzone, snowstorm, or on a steep mountain—we need to trust its source.

Trust comes from two main sources: either we know the person well ourselves, or we know their reputation among others whom we trust. In situations of frequent change (such as the increasingly project-based nature of contemporary work), which require us to frequently evaluate unfamiliar people and ideas, we rely on our networks to establish trust and convey sensitive information about reputation (Feld 1981). What sort of network is best for this?

In a close-knit group, maintaining a good reputation is essential. If someone treats another member of the group badly, everyone soon learns about it and the group can sanction the culprit. This creates a high level of trust among tightly connected groups, allowing, for example, diamond-traders who are members of close Orthodox communities to exchange millions of dollars of gems on simply a handshake (Ruffle and Sosis 2007). A dense network of strong ties is trustworthy, but provides relatively little information. Furthermore, the safety of the dense, homogeneous network comes at the cost of personal freedom, for such groups also put greater constraints on members' activities, enforcing compliance with the group's norms: the close-knit religious groups whose members can trust each other deeply relinquish much freedom in return (Sosis 2005).

There is less trust in a social network made of numerous weak, disconnected ties, but it provides a wider range of information and greater autonomy.[16] (Of course, this also means that an untrustworthy person with weak and disconnected ties has greater freedom to reinvent herself than one enmeshed in a dense network.) Among unconnected ties, however, reputation has little force. If a weak tie has repeatedly exploited people whom you do not know, you are unlikely to be forewarned.

Salaff, Fong, and Siu-lun (1999) observed how Hong Kong residents of varying social class used network connections to emigrate. Working-class émigrés relied on strong ties because they needed material assistance—financial help, a place to live—that is costly for the giver and thus provided only by close ties. Members of the upper class maintained and used larger networks of weak ties—they needed access to information about jobs, schools, and housing—but not material aid; the help they needed was less costly for the giver, and thus could be obtained from weaker ties.

Bian (1997, 1999) studied job seekers in 1980s China and noted that they relied on strong ties for job information, in contrast with the weaker ties that characterize Western job searches. The difference, he said, comes down to the need for trust:

> Strong ties tend to act as bridges when an exchange of resources or favors between social actors (individual or organizations) is unauthorized or when mechanism for their operation are unavailable in the formal social structure. Thus, mutual trust is required to link these actors in order to reduce the uncertainties and potential risks that are likely to occur otherwise. (Bian 1999, 272)

Residents threatened by the 2007 southern California wildfires had a great need for local, immediate, and trustworthy information—they would be making life-and-death decisions based on it. They found that broadcast information sources such as television news were not updated frequently enough or had poor—and thus potentially dangerous—information. Social media let them communicate with others in their neighborhood, people whom they might not know personally, but with whom they shared the significant commonality of locale. One resident wrote: "What we learned in the Cedar fire [in 2003] is that there is no 'they.' 'They' won't tell us if there is danger, 'they' aren't coming to help, and 'they' won't correct bad information. We (regular folks) have to do that among ourselves." They developed websites that featured rapid updates and used other publicly accessible media to keep each other informed. This process relied on the community's ability to converge on the most reliable sources, including some with advanced information, such as one with a press pass who went into the fire zone and sent updates to neighbors (Sutton, Palen, and Shklovski 2008).

For our rapidly changing, mobile, and diverse society, we can argue that the ideal network is what we will call a super-network: large and densely connected, yet consisting of heterogeneous (and thus relatively weak) links (Hampton, Sessions, and Her 2011). There should be enough awareness of what others are doing, so that the desire to maintain a good reputation motivates people to behave responsibly, but enough diversity that there is not an enveloping and repressive standard for thought and behavior (Donath 2007). We shall next look at how to create and maintain such networks.

Network Size: Natural Constraints and Technological Augmentation

If costs were no issue, bigger networks would be better. Having many close friends (strong ties) is good because it provides a great deal of material support in the form of people willing to supply time, energy, and social capital to help you. Having numerous and diverse acquaintances (weak ties) is also good: it exposes you to new and varied information and makes it possible for you to disseminate information broadly, whether to further a cause about which you are passionate or to enhance your status and reputation.

But big networks are costly. They require time and energy to maintain—we not only receive support from our friends and family, but are also obligated to reciprocate. Although much of our "supporting" may be outsourced to the market, we still visit friends and family when they are sick, attend their recitals, graduations, and weddings, help them move to new homes, and so on. Social activities such as talking, visiting, sending notes, and going out may be quite enjoyable, but they still take time. At work—do you finish that report or chat with your colleague? Even a casual chat with a neighbor uses several minutes. Moreover, there is a cognitive limit to how many people we can keep track of—not only their names and faces, but also their relationships, beliefs, and changing life situations. The size of the social network we can maintain is limited by both our available time[17] and our cognitive abilities.[18]

Unaided, our network size is limited. To cultivate a larger network, we need to find ways to nurture our relationships more efficiently. Much as the hammer extended the human hand and the car extended the human leg, we seek tools that extend human social abilities.

Designs to Foster Multiplex Relationships

Is there a way that technology can help us maintain large, heterogeneous networks of *stronger* ties?

One strength of weak ties is that they are potentially stronger ties. Weak ties are by definition narrow; they are relationships between people who know only one or two aspects about each other. They are, for example, work colleagues one knows only in their professional role, the neighbor known only as an avid gardener or punctual dog-walker, the fellow participants in an online forum seen only through the lens of their knowledge of Linux or their dexterity at games. However, we might, in fact, have much more in common than we know.

We all have innumerable beliefs, concerns, interests, needs, experiences, hobbies, and so on, each of which can be a relationship-binding thread (what Feld [1981] called "foci"). We do not continuously display and advertise everything that concerns and intrigues us; thus, many such foci-in-common—and thus potentially multiplex relationships—go undiscovered. For example, many people face taking care of an elderly and failing relative. It is a very difficult task, requiring much new information (about medicines, disease progression, insurance, care facilities, etc.) and support for the caregivers, whose role is emotionally (and often physically) exhausting. Two acquaintances who discover that they are both in this role might bond over their shared plight, finding an opportunity to both share knowledge and commiserate. Yet people can know each other superficially for years, without realizing they share this concern.

Anything from illness to an intensive new hobby, even simply a new friendship, changes how we spend our time and with whom we want to—or can—spend it. We all experience friendships that grow and wane: the officemate you once chatted with daily becomes someone you have an occasional lunch with after you move to another division; a neighbor you vaguely recognized becomes a closer confidant when you discover you are each caring for far-off, aging parents. People entering new romantic relationships lose touch with many of their existing friends: the time devoted to the new relationship takes away from the time available for other acquaintances. After having a baby, people often become closer with their family, make friends with other parents, and spend less time with childless friends.

The anthropologist Robin Dunbar argues that hundreds of thousands of years ago, the emergence of language in humans provided an early jump in this sort of efficiency, enabling our comparatively large scale society (Dunbar 1996, 1998). In the wild, apes groom each other to remove parasitic bugs. Besides being pleasant, relaxing and hygienic, this behavior establishes social bonds: apes who groom each other are more likely to help each other and not fight. But long grooming sessions are time consuming and since the ape must also find food, sleep, etc., grooming can sustain only a limited number of relationships (evolutionary biologists Dorothy Cheney and Robert Seyfarth note that apes also use vocalizations to communicate social information [response to Dunbar 1993]).

In human societies, language, especially gossip, has taken over the social function of grooming. Instead of removing lice from each other's hair, we check in with friends and colleagues and chat about common acquaintances, the news, or local sports (Ellison, Steinfield, and Lampe 2007; Fischer 1994; Wellman and Gulia 1999). Language is much more efficient than physical grooming, for one can talk to several people at once. And language makes reputation possible—individuals benefit from the experience of others in determining who is nice, who does good work, and who to shun for their dishonest ways. By using language to maintain ties and manage trust, people can form more complex and extensive social networks.

Exactly how big and complex is this network is a difficult question to answer. Popular literature often cites 150 (sometimes called "the Dunbar number") as the standard group size among humans, but even Dunbar's own research shows a range of group sizes, from below 100 to well over 200 (Dunbar 1993). Dunbar's notion of group is exemplified by the Hutterites, who limited their communities to 150; Dunbar argues that 150 was the maximum group size that can be controlled by social pressure rather than an authoritarian police force. But "group" is not a well-defined concept—depending on what one calls a group, their size is even more variable.

Sociologist Linton Freeman points out that there is an important distinction between "group size" and one's personal network, which is what cognition limits (response to Dunbar 1993). Personal network is in theory precisely definable and measurable, but in practice, measuring the size and structure of an individual's network of close ties and casual acquaintances has difficulties both definitional (when does a close friend who has moved away cease to be a "strong tie"? Is a store clerk you see and greet frequently a familiar stranger or an acquaintance?) and empirical (how do you get people to reliably count how many people they know?). (See, e.g., Fu 2005; Hill and Dunbar 2003; Marsden 2005; Marsden 1990; Roberts et al. 2009 for a variety of approaches to taking these measures. See Castells 2000 and Rainie and Wellman 2012 for an extensive discussion on the history of the rise of networks as the primary structure of society, rather than groups.)

People seek to extend their social network when changes to their lives create new needs. But the process of finding and making acquaintances can be hard. Although a new stage in life—moving to a new city, having a baby, developing an illness, even becoming passionately interested in a new topic—creates a need for compatible companions, it does not automatically produce them.

In our immediate, face-to-face community, the pool of possibilities is limited. One of the big promises of the Internet was that it would hugely expand this pool—which it has done, to some extent. There are many online support groups and communities devoted to parenting, religion, surfing, dieting, programming, game playing, and so on. People do indeed find support and make friends online (Boase et al. 2006; McKenna, Green, and Gleason 2002; Rheingold 1993; Wellman and Gulia 1999).

Yet not all online discussions create strong bonds; many sites feature some desultory exchanges, but nothing that one would call a community. One reason is that the cues to the identity of the participants are so sparse. In a face-to-face setting, if you ask a stranger what time it is, you see also his face and clothing, you hear his voice when he answers—in other words, you are privy to innumerable identity cues about him, hints of other potential areas of common interest beyond simply the words of the exchange. In most online forums, one sees far less. The strong bonds that do form online are between people who interact extensively, whether playing games or participating in a wide-ranging discussion—people who, over time, see multiple dimensions of each other.[19]

Over time, our connections change us. You may, for example, become friendly with a work colleague who is a devoted salsa dancer. Though you've never done any formal dancing, she persuades you to join her; you enjoy it and begin taking lessons. People may become friends through a common focus, but over time, they influence each other, introducing new ideas and interests.[20] In this way, a weak tie based on a single shared focus grows into a stronger, multiplex relationship.

An ideal network for today's world is large, with many diverse yet not very weak ties—the super-network. Yet such a network requires tools to support it, for its scale and diversity place it beyond the ability of the unaided human to easily develop and maintain. These tools must go beyond amassing an extensive collection of disconnected, weak ties. Such ties may bring us a wider range of information—but how do we know whether to trust it? And, if the information is valuable, what would motivate a tenuous connection to share it with us? A more important role for social technology is to help us strengthen weak ties. An excellent party host is one who introduces her guests to others they might like and helps them discover their common interests. Similarly, social technology can function as such a host: by facilitating connections among them, it helps strengthen their relationships and makes their network denser (Ellison, Steinfield, and Lampe 2007; Hampton, Sessions, and Her 2011).

Friendster was eclipsed by other social network sites. Of these, Facebook quickly became the most successful.[21] Facebook's network is much more private. There is no exhortation to grow your network; rather, the site emphasizes connecting only to people you know in real life and tries to ensure that people use the site in the guise of their everyday identity. Facebook's salient feature is its news feed, where users see the updates that their connections post. Each person's friends can comment on his or her updates, thus turning the profile into a combination of personal performance and hosted salon. I see the updates my existing ties make; this helps me keep up with what is new with them. I also see the comments their friends make, which can give me a new perspective on what my ties are like around other people. And, these exchanges with friends of friends introduce me to people in the context of a mutual acquaintance.

Earlier we discussed how one characteristic of stronger ties is that they are multiplex—you know a variety of things about a person that help you see them as a multidimensional individual. The Facebook model of social networks supports this by expanding the audience of our small-scale statements. It provides a forum where one can publish one's thoughts on topics great and small, from your take on world politics to the blister on your toe. The key role of technology in supporting social super-networks is to help us turn weaker ties into richer relationships by helping us discover more about each other.

POSTSCRIPT: WHAT ARE SOCIAL NETWORKS FOR TODAY?

Our expanding social networks present a paradox. At the same time that our networks are growing, nourished both by our highly mobile lives (we meet a lot of people) and our new communication technologies (we can keep track of and maintain connection with more of them, with greater ease), our actual need for connections has arguably diminished.

To
Aldrm: John Johnson
Merch.tt
Newyorke

FIGURE 5.1
Letter to Alderman John Johnson (1718). A letter addressed with only the recipient's name and "New York" to guide its delivery. Courtesy Siegel Auction Galleries, Inc.

Many years ago, the person-to-person letter delivery chain of Milgram's experiment would have been not the artificial construct of a sociology experiment, but a common method of getting letters to a distant person. Letters were typically addressed with no further identification than name and town (figure 5.1). When a ship arrived in a colonial port, for example, people came by to claim not only letters that were addressed to themselves and their family members, but also for any other people they knew. Unclaimed letters would be left at a popular tavern, and those going to distant recipients would, eventually, be given to a minister or other official (i.e., a bridge figure) from that area to deliver (Gavin 2009). The delivery of a letter was a social process.

Over the last few centuries, street addresses became commonplace in most areas except for the most rural, making it possible for postal services to deliver mail without any further knowledge about the recipient or community. Today, we are hyper-reachable, with email addresses and cell phone numbers that stay with us wherever we go. At the start of the twenty-first century, Duncan Watts and colleagues replicated Milgram's experiment, using email messages rather than letters (Dodds, Muhamad, and Watts 2003; Watts, Dodds, and Newman 2002). But the experiment felt oddly forced; in the intervening decades, Google had profoundly changed the way we searched for unknown information—and people.

Although our network reach is becoming greater, our reliance on networks is diminishing. We still like to have friends, perhaps more than ever. We like having an audience and sources for all kinds of information. But, much as the need for strong ties and their material support has been outsourced to the market, is much of our need for weak ties and their diverse information being outsourced to an ever faster and broader world of digitized knowledge, sophisticated searching, and democratized publishing?

It has been clear for a while that our need for strong ties is diminishing. For a growing number of people, the market, not family and friends, provides the means of obtaining shelter, food, childcare, and the like.

But we also see a diminishing reliance on connections to provide information, the resource most resonant with contemporary, online, networked living—the one that big networks of diverse ties are deemed so useful in obtaining. Today, we are more likely to search the Web rather than ask a friend.

For example, let's look at changing strategies for finding childcare.[22] People living in tight-knit communities could rely on the close ties of extended family to help raise their children. But as society became more geographically mobile, frequent moves and other social changes disrupted these close networks. A history of childcare says of the post–World War II migration to the suburbs, "The scarcity of grandparents and 'maiden aunts' posed a [childcare] problem that few young suburbanites had considered in their flight from the extended family ties that many had found both 'stultifying and oppressive'" (Forman-Brunell 2009, 94).[23] For parents without nearby family or close friends (or whose close ties were increasingly busy with their own jobs and lives), hiring strangers to take care of their children became increasingly common.[24]

Strangers, however, are not always reliable—unlike family, they have no personal stake in the well-being of the child—so the big challenge with sitters is finding one who will be trustworthy and attentive. A family newly arrived in town would need to befriend their neighbors to learn who was a good babysitter (and a host of other clues about life in their new location). While people may have ceased relying on close ties to take care of their children, they still needed acquaintances to provide introductions to and recommendations about those they would hire to do so—that is, they relied on personal ties for information. But today, even that need has commercial solutions, such as the website sittercity.com, which provides, for a monthly fee, listings of babysitters, rated by previous clients. The new parents in town no longer need to develop friendships in order to access local information.

We can now access all kinds of advice online, without needing to ask anyone. Yelp.com tells us where to dine, whether we want a four-course French meal or a quick breakfast to go; it can also recommend hair salons, church services, tattoo parlors, hardware stores, and so on. We can get book recommendations that are algorithmically generated from the reading habits of anonymous strangers who are reading the same novels we are, and they are likely more suitable than the suggestions of a good friend with different taste.

Almost anything we can think of for which we have relied on our friends and acquaintances we can now find online or hire someone to do (Hochschild 2012). We no longer need to ask friends to help us find romance—dating services are a $2 billion industry in the United States alone (Marketdata Enterprises, Inc. 2012); nor do we need them to help us work out our emotional problems—we can hire therapists or find online support groups for that. Services such as TaskRabbit provide a market for the sorts of favors once exchanged among friends—such as helping to lift an air conditioner to the window, or advising you on which clothes to keep and which to discard as you do your spring cleaning.[25]

The concern here is that without the acute need for networks, they can seem optional—and wither away, dispensable in the search for a more efficient life. Yet, we are still social beings. We still deeply enjoy the company of friends, the excitement of being out at a party as well as the warmth of being home with family. Dunbar's metaphor of gossip as grooming has strong resonance. It's not just that grooming maintains ties—but that maintaining ties is pleasurable. Even at a distance, much of what is compelling about participating online is making a comment and receiving a response—we exchange information for the pleasure of contact. The contact is an end in itself. In the next chapter, we will look at designs that foster online conversations, the fundamental form of mediated contact.

6

VISIBLE CONVERSATIONS: SEEING MEANING BEYOND WORDS

People participate in many social activities online: they post pictures and videos, write long, impassioned articles, and battle each other in multiplayer games. The predominant social activity, however, is conversation in its many forms: email; chat; discussion postings; status updates; comments exchanged about photos, games, and articles; and so on. Though the form may vary, all share the fundamental quality of being exchanges of words among two or more people.[1] Conversation is much more than a means for exchanging information. It is a form of social grooming: it is how we form and maintain ties, hold our community together, and establish social norms (Dunbar 1996).[2]

Like face-to-face speech, online conversation is an exchange of words among people. Yet there are significant differences. Most spoken conversations are ephemeral: the words disappear into the past as soon as they are said. Many online conversations are persistent, their text permanently preserved in an archive. Spoken conversations occur in real time: you hear what I say as I say it and can respond immediately. In contrast, many online conversations are asynchronous: I write a message, and you might not read and respond to it until hours, days, or more have passed. Asynchrony adds convenience, for I can maintain a long discussion with you, even if we are never free to meet at the same time, but it also drastically changes the rhythm of discourse.

In this chapter, we will explore visualizing the social patterns in online conversations. These visualizations are the "medium shot," showing the participants in their situational context and highlighting their relationships and reactions. Our focus will be on visualizing text conversation, the ubiquitous medium of online comments, email, discussion boards, and so on. We will also look at how visualization can supplement even face-to-face discussion, bringing our attention to the nuances and behaviors of which we are often unaware.

TEXT AS CONVERSATIONAL MEDIUM

The primary medium of online interaction is text. Text conversations are interactions stripped of almost everything but the words, a simplicity that yields many advantages. They are easy to implement; pioneering programmers developed the earliest systems in the mid-1960s to send messages among users of time-sharing mainframe computers (Van Vleck 2001). They are also easy to participate in, requiring only a keyboard. The sparseness of text conversations focuses attention on the words themselves, without the distraction of the speaker's appearance. No one can dominate the conversation simply because he or she is bigger and has a louder, deeper voice. In discussions where the participants are strangers to each other, text interactions make it possible to converse without being swayed by knowing the others' age, race, or gender.

Simple as they are, text conversations are an example of a design that goes "beyond being there." The writer of a message can carefully edit it before sending. Recipients can read a complex text slowly and repeatedly, yet quickly skim routine communications or dull sections. They can save messages, forward them, or send them to a computer for analysis and visualization. Text conversations are frequently asynchronous, so one can read and write at one's convenience. Text conversations can be dialogues between two people or a mass discussion involving hundreds or more. Text is flexible. You can use it to write a formal document or to toss off a slang-encoded message. It's easy to quote someone else's words to respond to a particular point. Text requires only a keyboard to produce. Reading text is fast; experienced readers can skim paragraphs quickly.

Yet the sparseness of text conversations has disadvantages, too. Face-to-face conversations convey subtle but important social information nonverbally, such as the speaker's emotions and the participants' relationship with each other; these are hard to discern through text alone. In person, we gather much identity information simply by seeing each other—even when talking to a stranger, you can infer gender, age, race, and the myriad cultural affiliations we advertise with our clothes, hair, and the like. When strangers converse via online text, they remain ciphers, lacking the identity information that provides essential context for understanding each other's meaning.

Text conversations have little of the rich nonverbal communication that face-to-face conversation offers. Gestures, facial expressions, gaze, accent, and tone of voice all contribute to the social meaning of an exchange. We look at other people's facial expression to judge their sincerity, to assess whether we are holding their attention (and if not, to see what has drawn their gaze). We add meaning to our words with tone of voice; we can make a "thank you" heartfelt, perfunctory, or ironic, simply by changing the way in which we say it. Furthermore, these numerous and subtle forms of nonverbal communication exist within a set of cultural norms for their performance: we assess others in terms of how they conform to expected behavior. Gaze alone has an enormous number of rules: how long do you hold someone's eye when you speak to him, when is looking away "shifty," when is looking at someone paying attention, and when is it rudely staring? Where on a person may you look? Deviating from the norm may make the impression that one is aggressive, shy, lying, and so on. A vast amount of subtle interpersonal communication occurs outside the realm of the words themselves and is simply missing from the abstract space of text-based communication.

VISUALIZING TEXT CONVERSATIONS

Visualizing text conversations can bring richness and subtlety to this medium by making visible the existing but hard-to-discern social patterns within them.

Although social cues are sparse in individual interactions, many social patterns exist in the history of the interactions. Visualizations compress this history, making it immediately accessible in the context of the ongoing conversation. We can design visualizations that trace the patterns in, for example, individual participants' actions, the changing topics of conversation, and the temporal rhythms. The challenge is both to identify which are the meaningful patterns and to represent them in a form that is both intuitively readable and yields a more nuanced understanding of the conversation's social dynamics.

Visualizing text can help convey the emotions behind the words or the ebb and flow of excitement in the discussion. The overall appearance of a screen full of comments angrily arguing about mandatory vaccinations or Israeli settlements is not very different from one full of readers' funny pet

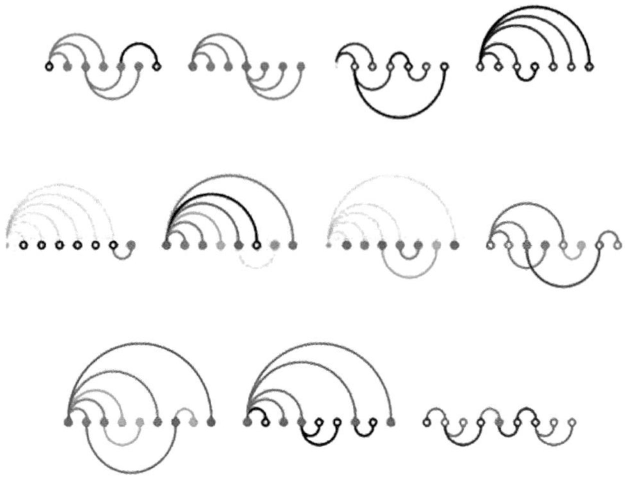

FIGURE 6.1
Bernard Kerr, *ThreadArcs* (2003). *ThreadArcs* is a compact and graceful depiction of an email conversation's threading structure. Each dot is a message and the arcs show replies. One can quickly see the characteristics of each conversation—in some, discussion focuses around a single message, whereas others consist of independent comments with occasional responses (Kerr 2003).

stories. By highlighting the rhythms and emotions in a discussion, visualizations create a vivid and legible social space.

Participants in online discussions come and go, making it hard for a newcomer to grasp the relationships and dynamics within the group. And even regular participants may have trouble picking up the local social mores because subtle expressions of encouragement or disapproval are hard to see. Visualizations that show the participants, their roles, and the patterns of their interactions can make the social information that is embedded in online discussions easier to perceive.[3]

The archives of a conversation are a rich source of information, not only for finding specific facts (which search interfaces enable), but for seeing the development of a decision and the structure of the community. But wading through this material can be tedious. An interface that makes the archives more interesting and that highlights key information encourages people to read and understand the context before joining in.

Here we will examine three examples of conversation visualization. *Newsgroup Crowds* depicts the tenor of a discussion space by analyzing the basic social roles its participants play. It is designed to help participants more easily see the social groupings and mores of a large-scale conversation. *Themail* analyzes email exchanges to create a portrait of a relationship; it makes it easy to explore one's personal archives. Finally, *History Flow* depicts the evolution of a collaborative production, revealing the controversies and social dynamics that lead to the final text.[4]

These examples were made as stand-alone visualizations, but it would be easy to integrate them into a live conversation space. One could display *History Flow*, which shows changes in Wikipedia articles, at the top of an article's history page; *Themail* could be part of an email interface. As supplements, the role of the visualization is to add context, clarity, and vividness, without taking away from the simplicity and versatility of the medium.[5]

Newsgroup Crowds

From the late 1970s through the 1990s, Usenet newsgroups were the most popular form of online conversation (Hauben and Hauben 1997; Whittaker et al. 1998). These large-scale, public discussions covered an immense range of topics, from technical discussions of computer systems to political arguments and child-rearing advice. Although all the groups shared a common technology—plain text threaded discussion—the tone and interaction patterns varied greatly between groups. Some were lively, sociable discussions that flowed freely from topic to topic. Others were more cut-and-dried question-and-answer forums, where people went for advice on a specific problem. Some had been taken over by "flame wars," in which a few participants argued furiously and endlessly. Some were vibrant and populous, with numerous messages appearing every hour, while others were withering away.

As is typical with many large discussion sites, if you were seeking something specific—if you had a question about writing compilers for the computer language C or verb forms in Serbian—you could probably find the right newsgroup to ask. But finding a congenial community—a place you could return to day after day, not just to ask questions but also to answer them, and to enjoy the banter among people who shared some interest or outlook with you—could be harder.

The *Newsgroup Crowds* visualization depicts the interactions within individual groups, making it possible to see their ambience at a glance (Turner et al. 2005; Viégas and Smith 2004). It is a simple bubble chart, a form of statistical graph often used for financial projections and other business statistics. But in this case, it creates an evocative view of the discussions. Its strength is in its careful choice of what data to depict.

Each circle represents an individual. Size shows the overall number of posts the person made, and brightness shows how recently he or she participated. The visualization's expressive power is in the circles' placement.

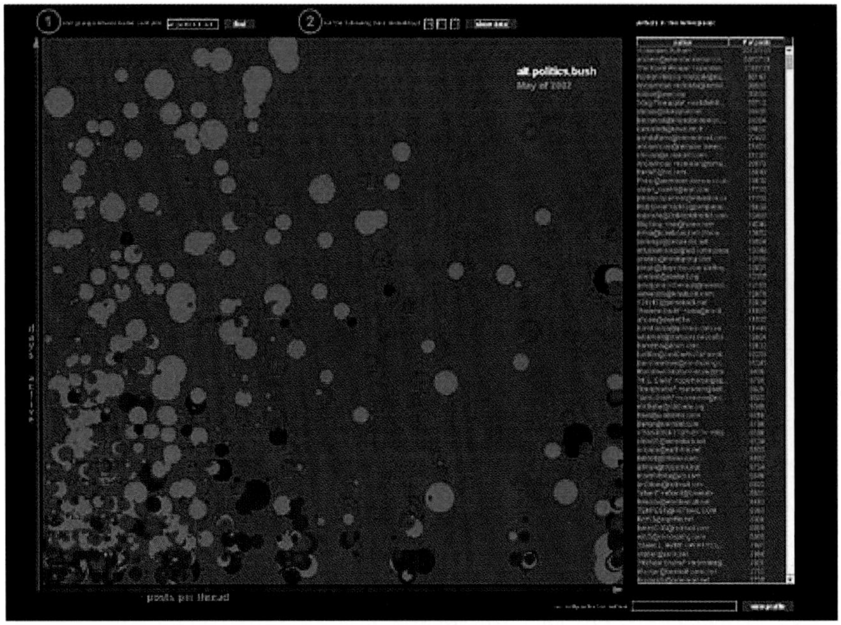

FIGURE 6.2
Fernanda Viégas and Marc Smith, *Newsgroup Crowds* (2004). A popular and lively group, with both deeply engaged participants and occasional visitors (alt.politics.bush).

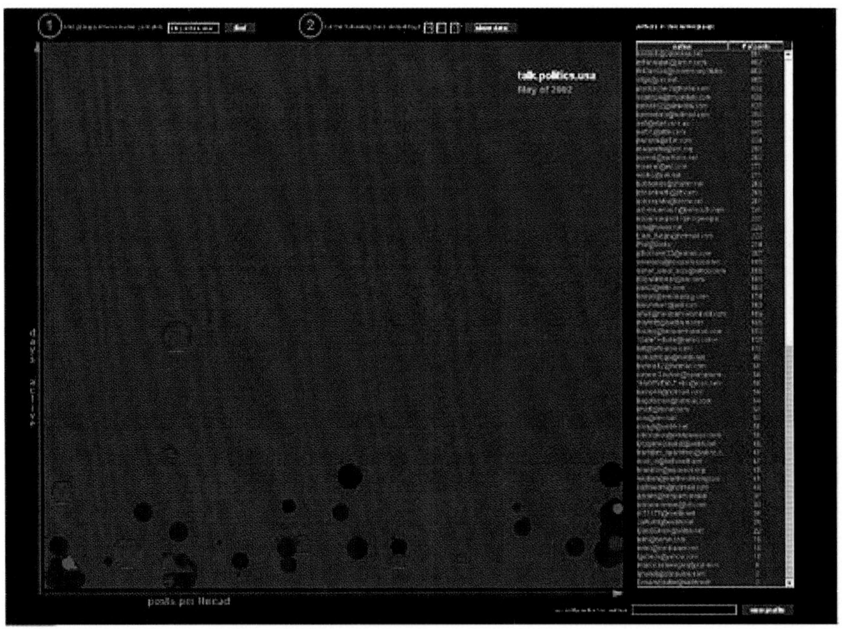

FIGURE 6.3
This group seems moribund, with no recent posts and mostly short-term visitors (talk.politics.usa).

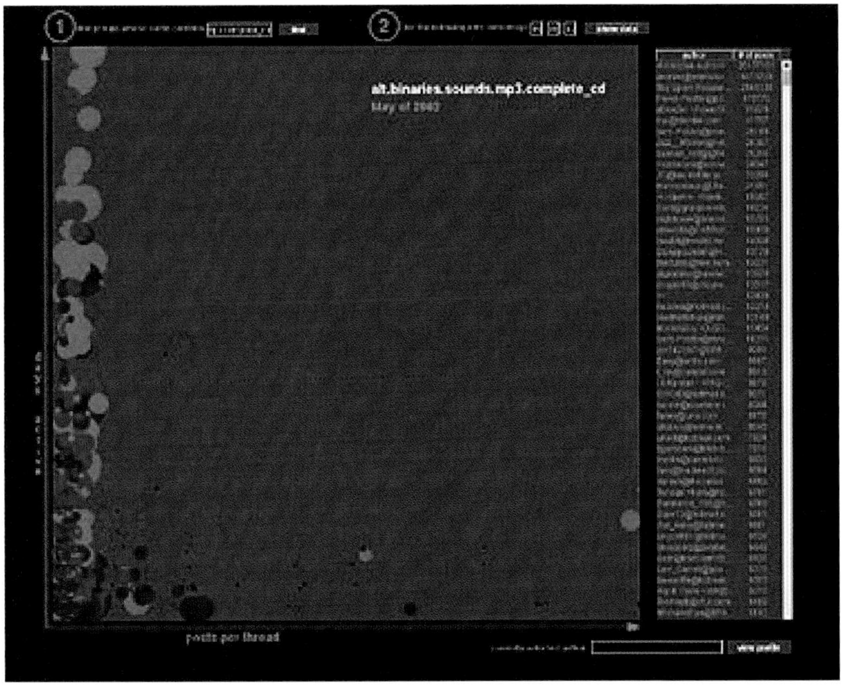

FIGURE 6.4
The clustering of all participants to the right shows that this is not a conversational group: people post only once in a thread And, in fact, it is a binaries group, a place to upload media, not converse (alt.binaries.sounds.mp3.complete_cd).

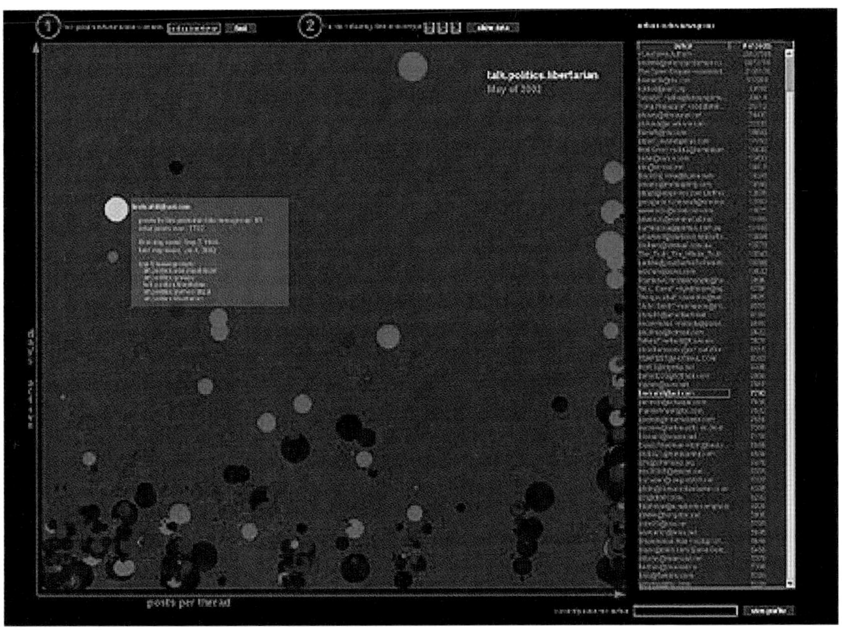

FIGURE.6.5
A group dominated by an inner circle of very active participants—quite likely an argumentative group. Other people do participate, but more occasionally (talk.politics.libertarian).

Location on the y-axis shows the number of days the person has been active in the group over a chosen time period. The x-axis location shows the average number of posts he or she contributes per thread, a statistic that provides an interesting measure of conversational participation: the amount of back-and-forth discussion in which the person engages.[6]

The *Newsgroup Crowds* visualization forms clusters of participants based on their characteristic behaviors. Occasional visitors, those who come to ask a question and then are gone, are in the lower left. People who answer questions are typically in the upper left; they return habitually, but contribute few posts per discussion. Engaged participants are further toward the right, with more messages per thread, for they participate in back-and-forth conversational exchanges. However, among the most engaged are the flamers, people who argue viciously and destructively. Nonconversational—and indeed, not necessarily human—contributions appear at the extremes near either axis: these are postings of binaries,[7] newsfeeds, and other automatic scripts.

Understanding the social roles the participants play in a discussion helps you know what to expect from them and provides context for interpreting their words and behavior. Seeing the distribution of roles within a group—leaders, supportive people, cranks—can help you understand its social dynamics. A group with two or three strongly opinionated leaders will have lively, but possibly constructive, disagreements. One with too many cranks and other irritating participants is likely to quickly lose members.

The distribution of these different types creates a group's ambiance. As with diet, variety is best. A diverse set of participants—some devoted, engaged participants, some quieter but pithy answerers, and newcomers for fresh ideas—makes for a vibrant conversational setting (figure 6.2). One where few people are posting and not much has been added recently is probably dying off (figure 6.3). One that has many postings but few ongoing threads is not a social space; this is the signature of a group that functions mainly as a repository for binaries (figure 6.4) A group dominated by a few debaters may be an interesting discussion between a few experts or, more likely on Usenet, a flame war (figure 6.5).

This visualization is simple but clear. It is easy to grasp that a chart with a few faded bubbles is moribund, and that a crowded, bright one is lively. Viewers need to learn the meaning of the axes, but once they understand that, the depictions of different conversation environments are legible and expressive.

Themail

People save a lot of email—not just important messages, but also seemingly inconsequential exchanges, the ones in which you reschedule lunch from noon to 12:30, the quick thanks for a useful reference, and so on. Do we keep these out of laziness because it's too much effort to clean out the inbox, or do they have some value?

We designed *Themail**, a visualization of one's email archives, with the belief that that people keep email not just to have a record of key facts and agreements, but also to maintain a history of their work and personal life (Viégas, Golder, and Donath 2006).[8] Though there are some significant individual messages, much of the value of this correspondence is in the cumulative social patterns. Existing tools for managing these big personal archives focus on search, which addresses the problem of finding specific messages, such as those that contain a particular phrase. But many of the messages that people keep are unlikely to ever be specifically recalled. Their value is not in their isolated content, but rather their contribution to the record of the relationship.

Themail's approach is different. It is designed to allow a person, its subject, to view the changing relationships they have with their contacts. It creates portraits of how the subject's relationships with other people change over time by featuring the words that characterize their email correspondence (Viégas, Golder, and Donath 2006). Each *Themail* portrait highlights words that the subject and correspondent use with each other more frequently than

FIGURE 6.6
Fernanda Viégas, Scott Golder, and Judith Donath, *Themail* (2006).

both with the subject's other correspondents and is common in general English usage (see figure 6.6).[9] The columns of yellow words show the words that typify a month's correspondence. The height of the columns shows the volume of email exchanged that month, creating a histogram of the frequency of their correspondence. The circles represent individual messages; their color indicates whether they were received, sent, or came via a list, and their size indicates the length of the message. The green words in the background are words that typified the subject and correspondent's exchanges over the course of a year.

A quick glance shows the extent of the relationship: whether correspondence has continued over years or was a brief flurry over the course of a few weeks, whether it is regular or intermittent. The background words give a basic picture of the content of their discussion. But a closer look at the words in the timeline really makes it come to life. These lists sketch the outlines of a personal narrative. Some are banal, such as the many columns dominated by "meeting," "schedule," "time," and "room" in one's correspondence with the departmental secretary. Others recollect travels, with distant cities and foreign money units, or events such as weddings, with words like "invitation," "seating," and "honeymoon."

We use photographic images to record our shared experiences in the physical world. *Themail* visualizes our shared interactions in the online world, an increasingly significant part of our lives.

Users of *Themail* found the portraits recognizable and evocative, mentioning that the depicted histories reminded them of forgotten events or captured incisively what makes a particular relationship special.

> The most unexpected thing for me was simply the amazing feeling of launching this visualization and seeing, for instance, the exchanges with [my wife]. There were words like "love," "hope," "marriage," "change ..." It was great! It managed to sum up in a few words a lot of what was being said at that time.[10]

Others noted that it helped them see how their relationships evolved:

> I was really interested to see this one. During the past five years Ray has gone from being an acquaintance to a very good friend. Looking at it actually takes a while for the words to be dominated by things like bar names, beer and

> cinema! There are a couple of things that come out of the visualization, like a holiday when we all went to Sri Lanka and when Ray went to work in another town for a few months.

People usually think of their email as private, and indeed *Themail* was designed to be a personal visualization for perusing one's own email. But as with photographs, many of the users of *Themail* wanted to display the portraits and share them with others. *Themail* skirts the boundary between public and private; by using only single words, it depicts the essence of a conversation without revealing the specific meaning. It creates displayable virtual snapshots that reveal enough of the relationship to be interesting to an outside viewer, but which also maintain the privacy of the subjects' correspondence.

> To be honest, I shared stories that I discovered in the archive with family members and with a few colleagues. I was moved to talk about the content of some of the messages, much like someone would be moved to share a memory sparked by an old letter or photograph.

Themail depicts personal history, reminding the user of forgotten events and previously unnoticed patterns. The next visualization, *History Flow*, depicts the public history of Wikipedia edits, showing the social interactions that shape an article's evolution.

History Flow

Wikipedia is a collaboratively written encyclopedia: hundreds of thousands of individuals write, edit, and revise its articles (Suh et al. 2009). It is a fascinating and highly functional model of collective work. There are no barriers to participation: anyone can edit it. Some contributions are poorly written, others are badly researched or express personal opinion rather encyclopedia-style fact; some are deliberately and maliciously wrong. Yet over time, the collective editing process hones the articles to high standards that are arguably equivalent to *Encyclopedia Britannica* (Giles 2005).

We can think of the articles themselves as discussions in which participants communicate through both additions and deletions. (There are also traditional discussions on the Wikipedia site. Each article has a discussion page where contributors can explain the reasons behind their edits.) Wikipedia articles include a link to their history of editorial exchanges, but in raw form these are far from compelling reading. A contributor involved in a heated edit war might be motivated to delve into this material, but few ordinary readers would. Yet this "conversational" history is rich with detail about how the article came to be. Is it primarily the work of a single person, or has a broad community created it? Are sections of it controversial? What have the arguments been over? Is the controversy between two or more sincere though conflicting views, or has the article attracted malicious vandals?

History Flow visualizes the edits that have produced a Wikipedia article (Viégas, Wattenberg, and Kushal 2004).[11] Each contributor is represented by a color, with anonymous ones shown in white and gray. Vertical slices show the state of the article at a particular time, and text that persists between versions is connected between slices. We can thus easily see whether an article has a few authors or many, and whether they are named or anonymous. We can also see periods of growth. Most interestingly, we can see areas of controversy, where prose has been repeatedly added and deleted, as well as instances of vandalism—and the speed at which they are repaired.

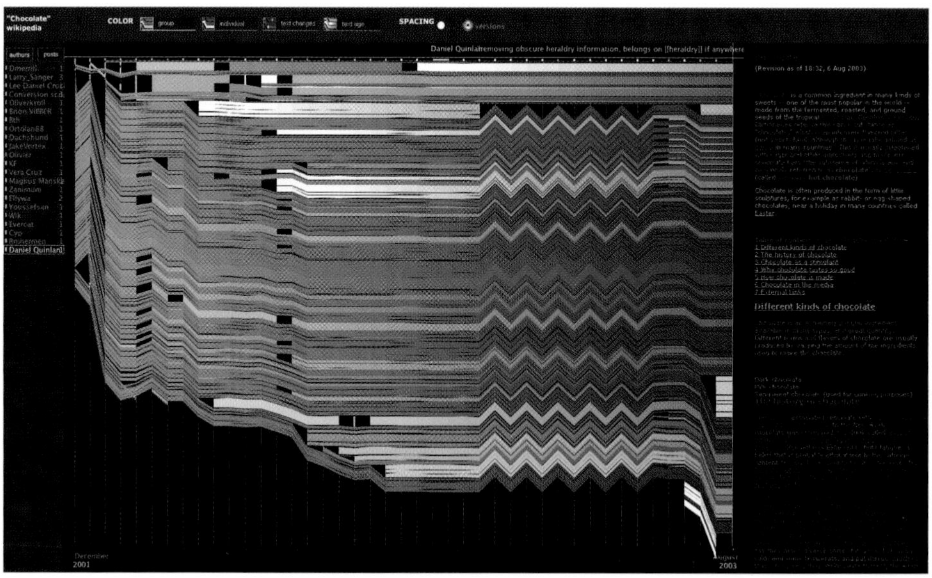

FIGURE 6.7
Fernanda Viégas and Martin Wattenberg, *History Flow*, "Chocolate" (every edit) (2004). This figure and figure 6.8 show the history of edits to the article about chocolate. This version shows the state of the article each time there is a new version. On the right, you can see the characteristic zigzag pattern of "edit wars," where a change is made and then repeatedly removed.

History Flow illustrates how an article changes over time in two ways. One shows all the edits that have been made (see figure 6.7); when there is an "edit war"—repeated edits and reversions—the first mode displays a characteristic zigzag pattern. The other mode shows a snapshot of the article at equal time intervals and a blank column where a page's content has been deleted (see figure 6.8). This version presents a much smoother picture of the history. Here, the edit wars are often invisible, since the reversions are made so quickly that we do not see them in these time slices.

This vividly demonstrates how a simple design change can tell a different story; both versions are useful, for each depict Wikipedia from a different perspective. The first version, which shows all revisions, no matter how briefly they were up, tells us about the writing experience: where was there controversy, how many authors have worked on the article, and so on. The second, temporal view tells us about the readers' experience. If vandalized pages are found and corrected quickly enough, few if any people will see them (Priedhorsky et al. 2007); this view shows which versions have been online long enough to have been read.[12]

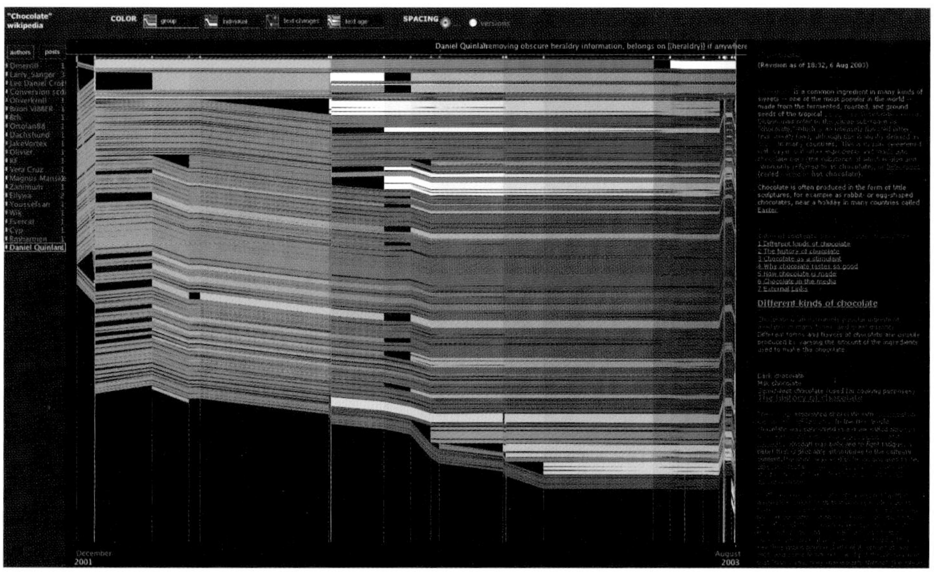

FIGURE 6.8
Fernanda Viégas and Martin Wattenberg, *History Flow*, "Chocolate" (temporal sample) (2004). This version shows the article's state at measured time intervals. It demonstrates that viewers are unlikely to have noticed the edit war: sampled over time, the article appears far more stable.

Wikipedia's transparency is one of its great benefits. We usually see finished products, whether articles, movies, or car designs, with little idea of the process that created them or the controversial decisions made along the way. Wikipedia's archives let us delve into the making of an article. At first, the idea that one might want to peruse the editing history of an encyclopedia article might seem unlikely, but *History Flow* helps you immediately see where interesting things have taken place, and it easy to imagine the viewer of this visualization becoming intrigued about what occurred. Making the history of creating an encyclopedia article into an interesting narrative encourages readers to investigate its reliability. With a tool such as *History Flow* they can quickly see what statements are controversial; they can see if an article was written by a couple of people or by hundreds: the highest-quality articles have had extensive editing by many people (Wilkinson and Huberman 2007). The visualization shows the importance of seeing the social process that created the finished article.

VISIBLE SPEECH AND PRESCRIPTIVE DEPICTIONS

The value of visualization with online text discussions is clear: it can make typically hard-to-perceive social patterns visible, thus providing additional social cues to an otherwise sparse medium. But can visualization add anything to the already rich experience of face to face encounters?

The most useful visualizations show us patterns beyond what we typically observe. Try this design exercise: Follow two conversations, one online and the other among people meeting face to face, and sketch them in any way that seems meaningful. When I assigned this to my students, the differences between the two sketches were striking (Donath 2004b). Almost invariably, the sketches that they made of the online conversation focused on the discourse, delineating the ebb and flow of topics. The sketches they made of face-to-face conversations focused on the people, with the individual participants' and their words each occupying a defined space (see figures 6.9 and 6.10).

The sketches reflect what we typically observe. Online, we primarily see streams of words, and the people are not immediately perceived as distinct individuals. This suggests that a key role for conversation visualizations is to portray the participants more vividly, in order to help the viewer see the conversation space as populated by unique individuals. We will look at several approaches to doing this in chapter 8, "Data Portraits."

FIGURE 6.9
Francis Lam, face-to-face conversation sketch (2004). Each colored circle represents a person; it is pink when they are speaking, and the circle grows larger the longer they talk. The white circle moves to show where the person's attention is focused.

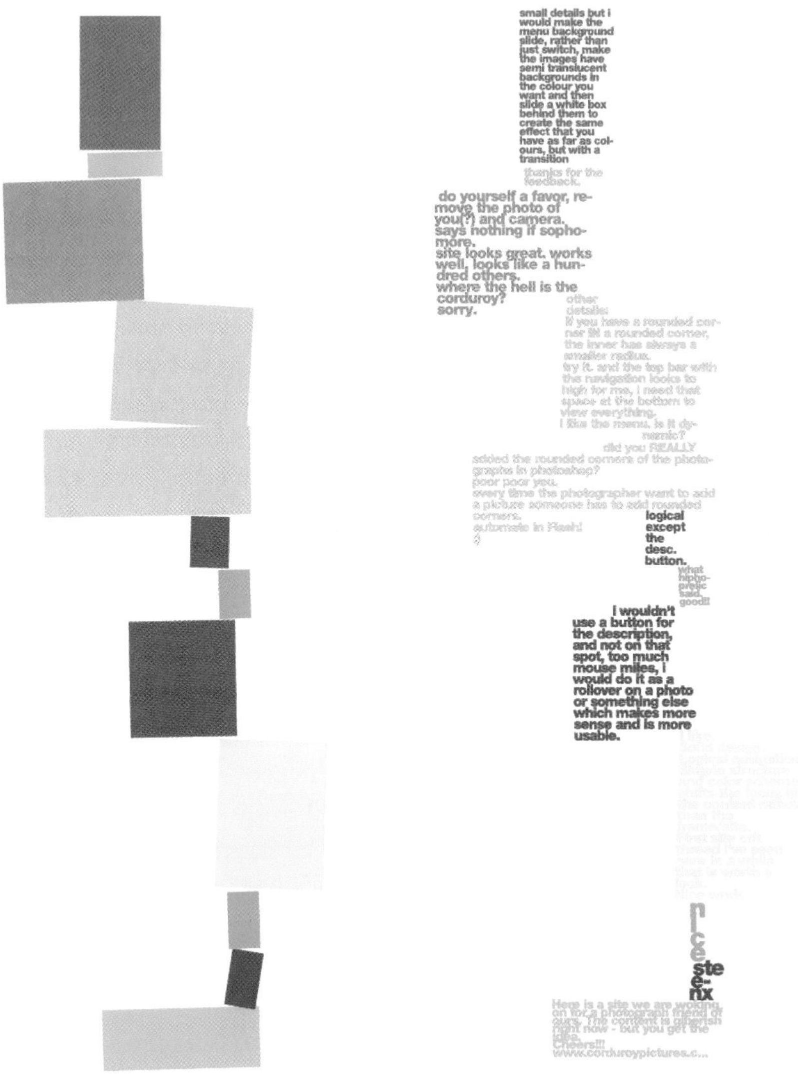

FIGURE 6.10
Francis Lam, online conversation sketch (2004). Here the focus is on the flow of words, rather than the people. Each box is a message, its size corresponding to the message length and its color indicating the author. Boxes stacked to the right are supportive notes; those on the left are more critical. It has a subtly prescriptive air, for one wants to make the tower of messages well balanced.

On the other hand, in face-to-face discussions we are typically aware of the other individuals but often have less of a sense of the conversational dynamics, especially our own contributions. Do I speak more or less than most other people? Do I interrupt others, or are people excessively aggressive in interrupting me? Visualizing spoken conversation to show topic flow or interruptions can reveal surprising insights into how a conversation is controlled and the roles different participants play.

One scenario where visualizing speech would be quite useful is listening to archived discussions, such as a missed meeting or class discussion. Here, visualization can provide a useful way to find key moments. As with the text visualizations we have seen, such a depiction can show where there are moments of excitement and controversy or highlight the roles different participants take in the discussion. For spoken discussions, however, we would use different data: rather than edits and response counts, we have the rhythm and volume of voices, the overlap of interruptions, and the like.

Beyond enlivening the task of listening to discussion archives, visualizations can enhance ongoing conversation, both mediated and face-to-face ones. Here the visualization may play a more activist role: by making otherwise hidden patterns visible, it can influence the participants' behavior (e.g., Bachour, Kaplan, and Dillenbourg 2010; Bergstrom and Karahalios 2007; Brandon et al. 2011; DiMicco et al. 2007). Even when we are present in a face-to-face conversation, we can miss key social patterns and cues. Someone may monopolize the conversation without being aware of it; men may be unaware of how frequently they interrupt women, for example. One goal for making these patterns visible is to provide a catalyst for more equitable interaction.

My students and I were once asked to make a device for "the kitchen of the future." We decided to make a social interface for keeping company with distant friends while cooking or cleaning up. The telephone does this, but we felt that audio alone is not ideal. We wanted to connect the spaces, not just individuals, so that if there were multiple people in one or both spaces, the virtual conversation would include them as well. A speakerphone does this, but a speakerphone left on indefinitely feels like surveillance; it is easy to forget that you are in a connected space in which your words travel beyond the people physically with you. Though videophones have long been a staple of futuristic domestic scenes, we felt they were poorly suited to this scenario. They work best when the users look into the camera, which is impossible when you are chopping vegetables or washing plates. We felt that a visual yet abstract interface would improve the experience in several ways.

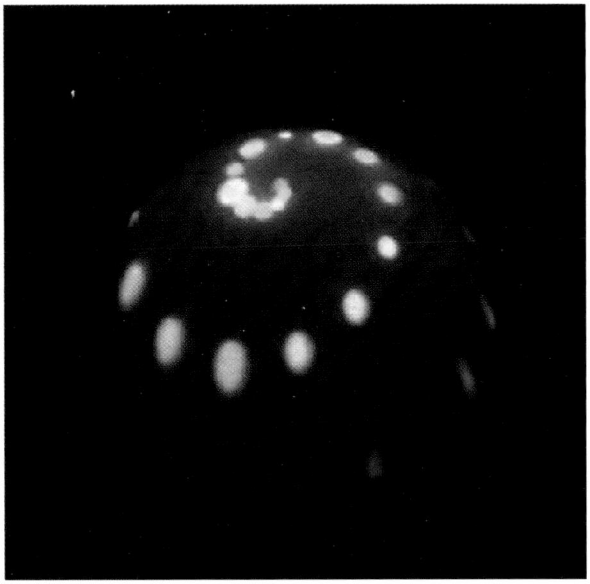

FIGURE 6.11
Judith Donath, Karrie Karahalios, and Fernanda Viégas, *Visiphone* (2000).

Our solution, the *Visiphone** (see figure 6.11), was a dome with an abstract design that showed the state of the connection (Donath, Karahalios, and Viégas 2000). The circle at the top represents the current audio condition: colored circles indicate that there is sound, with blue meaning local and orange meaning from the other location. The size of the circle represents volume and moments of silence appear as small gray dots. If two people speak at once, the circles are superimposed. The dots spiral down from the top, so the whole spiral is a visualization of the patterns of alternating speech for the past few minutes.

Our goal in designing the *Visiphone* had been to create a visual focus for and reminder of an otherwise invisible audio connection between two spaces. But when we showed this project publicly, many people were especially interested in the overlapping circles, explaining that they welcomed the ability to show overbearing companions how frequently they interrupt.

Karrie Karahalios, one of *Visiphone*'s creators, subsequently created the *Conversation Clock* (Bergstrom and Karahalios 2007), a table-top conversation visualization designed specifically to give participants in a small face-to-face discussion real-time feedback about "turn-taking, domination, interruption, and activity." Each ring is one minute, with a colored tick representing each person who was talking at a given time (see figure 6.12). At the

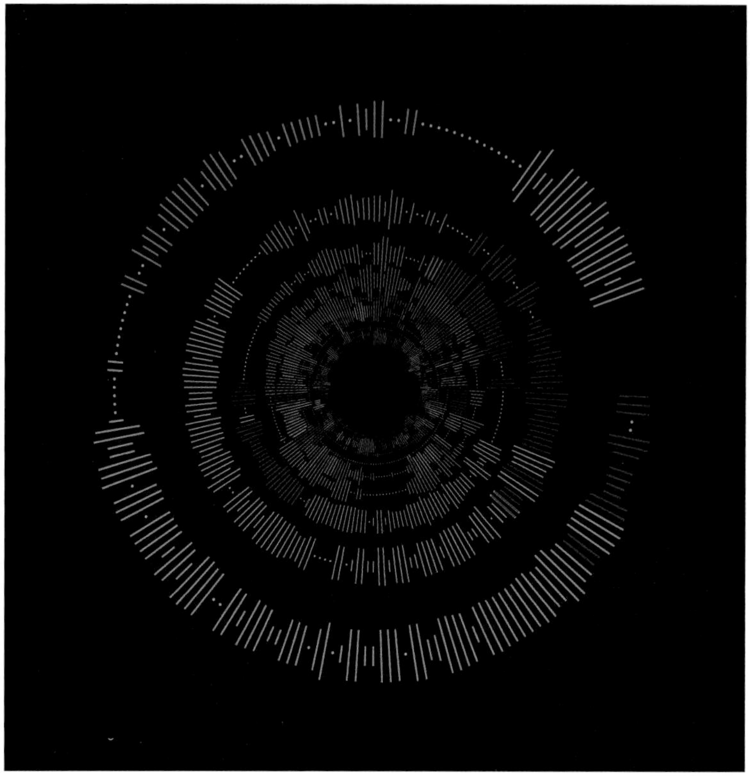

FIGURE 6.12
Tony Bergstrom and Karrie Karahalios, *Conversation Clock* (2007).

end of the minute, the circle shrinks toward the center and a new circle begins. It is easy to see at a glance who dominates the conversation, who interrupts, where there is excitement, and when there is silence.

Although the design is intended to be prescriptive and to influence people to adjust their behavior, it does not explicitly say what the ideal behavior is. The participants must already have the knowledge that, for example, interrupting is impolite.[13] The visualization simply makes the existing behavior patterns visible and clear; it is aimed particularly at improving self-awareness: I may know not to interrupt, but be unaware that I do so frequently, or that I talk much longer than others do. With no explicit labels of how one ought to behave, it allows for people with different roles or personalities to determine their own participation goals. Someone who is junior or who prefers minimal, concise contributions may be quite content to speak less than others do.

Other designs make their notion of desirable behavior clear. *Second Messenger* created histograms of spoken participation and labeled levels as over- or underparticipating, with the goal of equalizing participation (DiMicco et al. 2007; DiMicco, Pandolfo, and Bender 2004). The results were mixed: those who spoke more than most without the visualization reduced their contribution, but in some cases those who spoke little without it also spoke little with it. Sometimes the more equitable distribution of speaking time was beneficial for the group, but there were also examples where a group's ability to achieve the experimental task was better without feedback about their discourse style.

> Awareness applications do influence our behavior, because they provide a guide where there was not one before. … Providing any automated awareness feedback to groups will cause them to adapt their behavior to accommodate to the normative pressure implied by the feedback. (DiMicco et al. 2007)

Such results are vividly apparent with visualizations of live speech, but the same benefits and caveats hold for visualizations of written conversation, when the visualization is integrated with the user interface.

Visualizations can emphasize or diminish authority, welcome or discourage contributions, and otherwise influence behavior. The choice of what interface to use—or indeed, whether to meet face to face or online—requires first knowing what social structure and interactions one desires.

In face to face meetings, high status members dominate the conversation. Lower-status members participate less and are likely to offer opinions gauged to agree with those higher up, rather than presenting their own assessment. Online, the power of these hierarchies is flattened (Dubrovsky, Kiesler, and Sethna 1991; Sproull and Kiesler 1991a,b). Text discussions generally see greater participation from members at lower ranks—at least in part because the visible reminders of status and identity are greatly reduced.

Is this desirable? It depends. If the lower-status members have useful contributions and critiques to make, then yes, the more open participation of an online discussion can be very valuable. And certainly if the hierarchy is based on unfair or irrelevant properties, flattening it is beneficial (though those at the top are unlikely to see flattening the existing structure as a better order of things).

However, hierarchies sometimes reflect expertise differences that are useful to preserve: when those at the top are the most knowledgeable, the discussion may work best with contributions coming mostly from the higher-status members while the others primarily listen and learn. Having many people chiming in who know little about a problem may be far less productive than having the most authoritative voices dominate.

Furthermore, getting input may not be the point of the discussion. The goal of some meetings is to convince the attendees to all buy into something; though some may have reservations, for better or worse the goal of the gathering is not to air them.

If you want to elicit a broad range of ideas from lots of people, an online forum may be more productive than a face-to-face meeting, where people are more likely to defer to the ideas expressed by more senior individual. But if you want to get a group of people excited about something—defects and all—then an in-person meeting, where leadership is more powerful, is likely to be more successful.[14]

A social visualization used in the context of interaction will affect the participants' behavior. It will do so if it advocates a particular behavior—but also if it simply reflects the group's behavior back to it. Exactly how individuals will react depends on the ideals explicitly or implicitly advocated by the display, the group's norms, and their own personality and role in the group.

TOWARD MORE INSIGHTFUL ANALYSIS

A social interaction generates an enormous amount of information that one could potentially visualize. Some is useless for social purposes, such as counting the distribution of letters in the words that people used (though a linguist or cryptographer might find something to study here). Some is socially relevant and easy to measure, such as how many postings each participant contributed. Some is relevant, but is much harder to assess computationally, such as who is supportive or has the best sense of humor.

The visualizations we have discussed so far have depicted activity and word-use patterns, but have not attempted to analyze meaning or sentiment. As participants in a conversation, we try to understand what is going on—what are people talking about? Are they happy about something? Critical? Is a particular person warm and supportive or frequently sarcastic? Answering these questions, particularly in the sparse environment of a text conversation, can be difficult even for a human reader.

FIGURE 6.13
Alex Dragulescu, *Spam Plants: Untitled I* (2006). Good designs use form and metaphor to convey the meaning of the data, making an image that gives the viewer an intuitive feel for its significance. But visualizations are inherently arbitrary: one can pick any data to show and render it in any form. Alex Dragulescu subverts the usual goal of visualization to create beautiful flowers from statistical analyses of spam email and computer viruses.

FIGURE 6.14
Alex Dragulescu, *Spam Plants: Untitled VII* (2006).

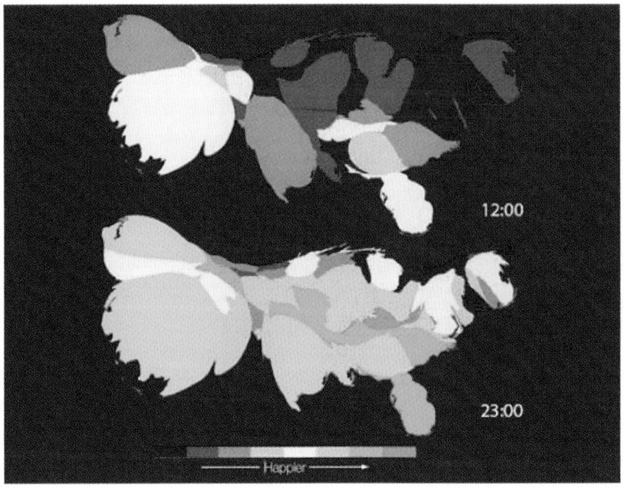

FIGURE 6.15
Alan Mislove, Sune Lehmann, Yong-Yeol Ahn, Jukka-Pekka Onnela, and J. Niels Rosenquist, *Pulse of the Nation* (2010). These cartograms (maps in which the geographic area is distorted to show some other variable, in this case number of postings), show the mood in different regions in the United States at various times of the day, as inferred by analyzing Twitter postings. Though reliably assessing the mood of any single posting is beyond current computational (and, sometimes, human) ability, given a large collection of postings, it is possible to make a good assessment of overall tone (Mislove et al. 2010).

For a computer, such understanding is a work in progress. Analyzing text to assess social and psychological characteristics and the like is an area of active research.[15] It is especially important to be aware of how accurate (or not) such an analysis is, and not to highlight misleading or erroneous data. For example, we might want to create a visualization that depicts emotion, to help us determine whether a community is upbeat or negative, or whether a writer is in an unusually good mood (see figure 6.15). To do this analysis, one might create a lexicon of positive and negative words, and score writings based on the presence or absence of these words. Yet, as this example from an article on sentiment analysis (Pang and Lee 2008, 22) shows, such counts can be misleading: "This film should be *brilliant*. It sounds like a *great* plot, the actors are *first grade*, and the supporting cast is *good* as well, and Stallone is attempting to deliver a *good* performance. However, it can't hold up." Though it has multiple positive words, it is a negative review. And just looking for negation at the end will not help; had it ended, "In fact, it couldn't be better," it would be positive. Quantity helps: a large dataset of comments will in the aggregate have more positive words if the overall reaction is positive, though any one comment may, like the example above, be misinterpreted.

Newsgroup Crowds mapped a rough assessment of participants' roles using the straightforward measures of total postings, postings per thread, total days present, and recency; these data are easy to track and socially relevant. Their clustering was useful and intuitive. But human readers, closely studying the interactions in the group, would distinguish among a somewhat different and more subtle set of roles.

"Celebrities" in online communities post frequently.[16] However, it is the quality of their writing, and not only its quantity, that makes them central figures. They are adept at the type of communication favored by the group, whether humorous repartee or rigorous scientific reportage. Furthermore, they are famous within the community: people talk about them. These influential participants shape the tone of the group, not only through their high level of participation, but also because their high status motivates others to emulate them.

"Ranters" also post frequently. And people talk about them, too. But these irritating participants have low status within the community. Unlike the celebrity, the ranter's tone or topics are outside of the group's norms: the atheist in the Christian worship group, the fundamentalist in the evolutionary biology group, the bottle-feeder in the breast-feeding mother's group, and the like. The distinction is as much one of tone as of topic: a gracious dissenter could be a valued member of the group, though the eloquence needed to sustain such a position in the volatile world of text discussions makes this rare.

A human reader familiar with the group would be able to identify these two (and many other) roles. The problem for visualization design is that statistically, the high-status celebrity and the low-status ranter look quite similar: both post and are mentioned frequently. The key distinguishing element—the esteem in which they are held by their community—is harder to measure. Ideally, the computational analysis should be able to distinguish, as the human reader can, between respect and rebuke; though not impossible, this is far from trivial.[17]

Adding another data element can help. Looking again at *Newsgroup Crowds*, some types might be more distinct if, for example, the visualization also indicated how many responses a user's posts received. Well-regarded participants often generate more responses, especially in a mature community that has established the norm of ignoring annoying or provocative postings. That said, while this simple statistic makes some additional differentiation, alone it is not an accurate role detector: unwelcome and provocative postings can also generate a flurry of reactions. A good approach is for the visualization to remain neutral about the desirability of having few or many responses; its role is to make the patterns clear, and the human viewer interprets them.[18]

VISUALIZATIONS SET THE SCENE

The setting of a conversation influences how the participants feel about each other. In person, we arrange the seating in our living rooms to be comfortable and go to restaurants to talk over cocktails; these settings enhance enjoyment and dispose us to be sociable. The physical setting—classroom, church, beach, elevator—also provides cues about how to behave. At a formal presentation, it is normal for some participants to only listen and not speak, whereas during a social dinner such silent non-interaction would seem strange. We learn how to act in certain settings and apply this knowledge to novel experiences: walking into a new classroom with chairs and desks organized in a familiar way tells us that the behavioral protocols we have learned in similar spaces are likely to apply in the new space.

Online, social visualizations can help establish the setting. Long-term discussions that share a common interface look the same, even though over time they have evolves quite different standards of conduct—ideas about what is funny, on-topic, acceptable, and so on. Visualizations of their individual histories can highlight the distinguishing social patterns.

We learn the mores of a setting by observing others and by noting their reactions to what we say and do. When we are face to face, others' reactions provide cues that tell us that we have been talking too long or using the wrong vocabulary: they start to fidget, look away, or appear displeased. But online, you don't hear any laughter if you amuse everyone and you don't see any raised eyebrows if people are offended, at least not until someone is sufficiently entertained or affronted to respond in writing. The difficulty of making subtle responses is the source of many angry online exchanges: offending behavior continues until it is truly egregious, and then meets with an infuriated response. Both the asynchrony of online conversations and the difficulty of conveying subtle hints via text make it difficult for newcomers to pick up the social mores of an online situation. Visualizations that highlight response patterns can help convey these social cues.

Common ground—the participants' shared beliefs and information—is essential to communication (Clark and Brennan 1991). When people communicate cooperatively (that is, when they are not deceiving each other[19]), they increase their common ground. Imagine asking someone on the street for directions. At first, you have little common ground. The initial task is to get the other's attention; you now have the common ground of agreeing to participate in some interaction. Next, you establish that you have a language in common. If they do not understand your initial query, you may try another language you know or write down the address you're trying to find. Once you've established a common understanding of your question, you then establish whether the stranger can help you. If so, they may say something like "Walk down this street until you get to that big tree, then turn right at the next street." These directions assume you share a common physical setting. You might spend some time working out that the tree you are looking at is indeed the tree the other person is referring to.

Throughout this experience, how you speak refers to and helps establish your common understanding of the social situation. If the two participants are college students on campus, even if they are strangers, they recognize each other as part of a larger community whose members easily provide this sort of information to each other. Though polite, they need not be elaborate; they need not explicitly establish the basic common ground of a cooperative relationship. Strangers in a high-crime area, however, might make more of an effort at the beginning of the interaction to establish their good intentions; for them, creating the common understanding of a harmless interaction takes more work. The common ground of a communication has numerous components: common surroundings (being in the same physical space or sharing a virtual space), cultural beliefs, language, and a growing understanding of each other's needs and abilities.

Cultivating cooperation is a form of common ground; it establishes your shared goals. Though the rituals of politeness may decrease common ground in factual knowledge (if you graciously convince me that you liked a gift that in fact you did not, my belief about your liking will be at odds with your actual feeling) they increase the feeling of shared good will—the mutual understanding that this interaction and relationship are moving in a cooperative direction. Rituals such as greetings, gift giving, thanking, and so on establish the social grounding of an interaction.

Creating common ground is a key issue in designing spaces for the physically distant and often temporally separated participants in online conversations. In text-based interactions, the participants' primary common ground is the conversation itself. For example, people quote previous messages in their replies to create a shared context for their remarks. But, beyond automatically inserting the replied-to message, contemporary interfaces provide little support for building common ground out of the conversational record.[20]

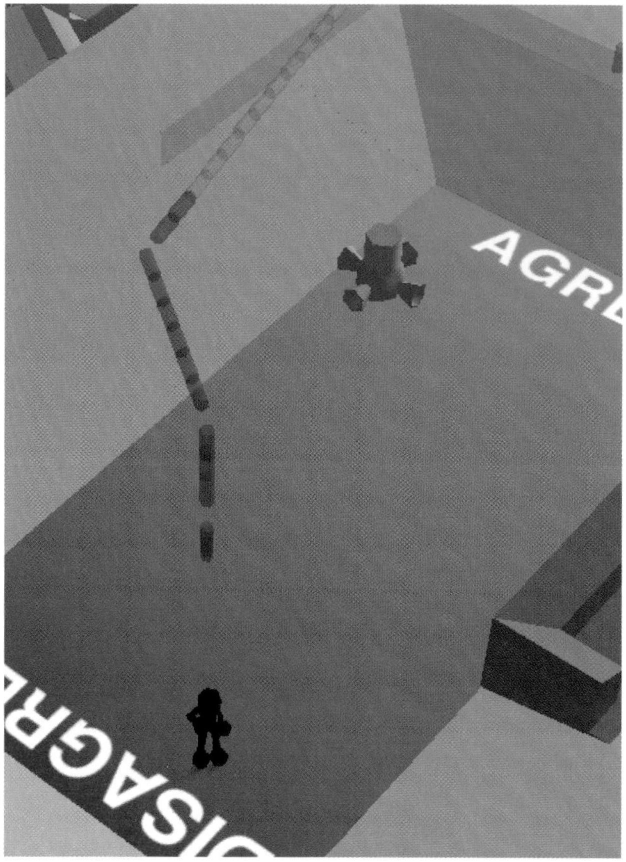

FIGURE 6.16
Drew Harry and Judith Donath, *Information Spaces* (2008). We designed *Information Spaces** to be a virtual space that makes social content physical. Conversations linger in the air—boxes that represent a person's contributions to the conversation rise over his avatar's head. In this interface, movement conveys meaning—in the scene in this picture, standing in the green area indicates agreement with a proposed idea, standing in the red, disagreement. Comments are correspondingly colored based on where the speaker was standing when making each remark. It is a virtual space composed of conversational context (Harry and Donath 2008).

Visualizing the history of a conversation—Who said what? What topics have gained much or little attention? What has been the typical rhythm of the interaction?—creates a setting that provides common ground for the ongoing conversation (see figure 6.16).

Settings are bounded; they are particular places (literally, in the physical world, and metaphorically, online). Who is privy to a particular conversation and how mores are enforced are issues of defining and defending boundaries: the repair records we saw in *History Flow* are in many cases the virtual archaeology of a skirmish over boundaries, over who defines a concept and who represents the truth. In the next chapter, we will introduce the history of contested boundaries in online discussion spaces and discuss various design approaches for maintaining strong yet also porous virtual bounds.

7

CONTESTED BOUNDARIES

In the face-to-face world, one of the primary jobs of any architect or planner is to create boundaries. Physical barriers, such as buildings and walls, along with social and legal norms, determine who can gain admittance at each door. The exterior walls of a home separate a family's private space from the external public world; its interior rooms bound different functions. Doors allow passage between one space and another, while locks on doors ensure that unwelcome visitors do not enter, yet permit the key-holders to come and go at will. Invited guests can enter at specific times; once in the house, they abide by other rules about which rooms they are welcome to visit and which are private, out of their view. The guest who is rifling through the upstairs bathroom's medicine cabinet or a bedside table is out of bounds. The boundaries of the home also keep people in: small children are forbidden to venture forth on their own; freedom to come and go is part of the passage toward adulthood. The boundaries vary with time: a cat-sitter may let herself in at certain times, but would be an illegal invader if she entered at others.

Our sense of comfort and belonging within our society depends on whether we feel our home—our basic personal space—is safe from intrusion. If only the inhabitants and invited guests enter, we have sovereignty over our space. If others are likely to intrude, whether burglars or police armed with complaints or warrants, we live on edge. Barred windows and heavily dead-bolted doors signal society's failure to maintain order. And to live in fear that authorities will enter one's home, whether because one is a dissident in a repressive society or a criminal in a lawful one, is to be alienated from that society.

Hi, I really don't mean to inconvenience you right now but i made a quick trip to London,UK this past weekend and had my bag stolen from me in which contains my passport and credit cards. It happened real fast leaving me document less & penniless right now. I've been to the US embassy and they're willing to help me fly without passport but I just have to pay for the ticket and settle the Hotel bills i resided at. Right now I'm out of cash plus i can't access my bank without my credit card here, I've made contact with them but they need more verification which could take more time for me wait. I was thinking of asking you to lend me some funds now and I'll give back as soon as I get home. I need to get on the next available flight.

Please reply as soon as you can if you are alright with this so i can forward the details as to where to send the funds. You can reach me via email or May field hotel's desk phone, the numbers are, 011447024043675 or 011447024051751 or instant msg me: jane_doe@yahoo.com

I await your response…

Infrastructural boundaries such as walls and doors neatly divide inside from outside, while complex and often unspoken norms create the social boundaries. Once at home, we are exempt from some (but not all) the laws and mores of the public sphere. One may not walk naked down the street, but can do so at home—yet not when casual acquaintances are visiting, especially children. One may look to the government to provide order in public, but see it as an intrusion when it reaches into the home. Our daily interactions involve negotiating many invisible social boundaries. Some are constructed through politeness. In a restaurant, we act as if there were walls around the other tables, neither making eye contact with people seated elsewhere nor interjecting comments into their conversation. Here there is no physical wall, but a boundary nonetheless. These invisible boundaries govern our public spaces, regulating how we move, speak, and look. Everyone is allowed to be out in public, with the caveat that you know how to behave; those who transgress may be placed in jail, putting a physical boundary between them and the public world. Boundaries protect us, but they also impede us.

Where are the boundaries online, and what are they made of? Although the online world is not physical, it also has both infrastructure boundaries and socially constructed boundaries.[1] The infrastructure boundaries, its gates and doors, are firewalls, encryption, and private sites. Passwords are the keys to the doors of cyberspace. Like doors, passwords vary from flimsy to fanatically secure. Also like doors, if what they are protecting is interesting enough, or the thieves are skillful enough, there will be break-ins. There is a continuous stream of news stories about corporate break-ins, malicious hacks, and secrets stolen from military networks. "Cyber war" threatens to be the next battle frontier. On the more mundane side, many of us have gotten emails purporting to be from friends, but which turn out to be spam; the friend's account was broken into and the identity-thief sent email to lure unsuspecting acquaintances (see sidebar).

In the physical realm, some boundaries have a person who checks each potential entrant. Guarding boundaries is the primary responsibility of many jobs: border patrollers, airport security agents, ticket takers, club bouncers, and receptionists in offices, schools, and libraries. Almost any semipublic space has people whose job is to maintain boundaries. Police do this at parades, in public squares, and for motorcades. One way of looking at communities is the extent to which their members feel entitled to and/or responsible for maintaining boundaries. Closed neighborhoods—from a trailer park to a gated suburb—can make outsiders wandering through feel very uncomfortable. The appeal of diverse urban neighborhoods, but occasionally their problem, is that no one feels entitled to turn others away.

Online, there are moderators. They are the doormen of discussions, vetting each comment to ensure that it is appropriate. Like the doormen of uptown apartment buildings, they are expensive. If a group that requires a moderator cannot find one, it may close. If the moderator is busy, the discussion flow might be halted as everyone waits days for their postings to pass through.

In general, the Net is a very open place. What makes it exciting—and often teetering at the edge of chaos—is that it connects a truly extraordinary number of people. An open discussion site can have participants from all over the globe, of different political, ethical, religious, and cultural beliefs, and with varied educational experiences. Some are seeking to learn, others to be entertained, still others to advance a cause. Some enjoy a constructive debate, some just want light humor, and some find fun in pulling pranks and upending discussions. There are also vast numbers of spammers, disruption professionals who will fill any unprotected space—email account, comment forum, or the like—with ads for cheap drugs and sexual aids, or worse, with stealth programs designed to infect one's computer and turn it into an unwitting spam server itself.

Any discussion needs multiple levels of boundaries. First, there are the boundaries that protect against spam. But once these clearly unwanted bits are kept out (and that itself is a constantly evolving battle), there are still the boundaries of behavior: the ability to keep out individuals and messages that are outside the boundaries of the group's norms. A group's culture evolves as it defines these norms and develops strategies to maintain them. In an online community, the key issues are determining whether someone should have access to a space and preventing problem users from repeatedly appearing.

The history of online conversation is a history of changing boundaries. It is useful to know, because it turns out that finding the right balance between public and private, being open yet not anarchic, is very important. The history of Usenet in particular provides a dramatic example of how societal and technological changes affected the boundaries in one very large community. Online, boundaries are not a matter of putting up fencing, but of defining how we recognize who can participate, what material is acceptable, and how openly available it should be. Today, there are various approaches to this issue: some sites focus on content, employing teams of moderators to vet contributions; others endeavor to establish a reliable community by rewarding highly regarded participants. Some are self-governed; others are managed by the site operators. There are sites whose goal is to create a definitive knowledge repository, to motivate renegade activists, or to be a supportive healing environment. We will look at what constitutes boundaries online, and how the choice of different types of bounds shapes the community. Ultimately, the key to a thriving community is maintaining boundaries that allow new people and ideas in while maintaining a sustainable scale and focus.

BOUNDARIES ONLINE: THE RISE AND FALL OF USENET

Computers were invented to be calculating machines for performing mathematical feats. Yet, when people started sharing computers in the 1960s, they also started using them as a social medium, leaving notes and messages to each other on the shared file system. Time-shared computing resources became the social focus for groups of researchers who otherwise might not have met (Licklider and Taylor 1968). The fundamental boundary to online interaction is simply access to resources. Conflicts over who should have access to scarce computer time and file space, and what they should be permitted to do with it, shaped the early days of online mass communication.

The Defense Department's ARPANET, the precursor to today's Internet, was created in 1969 to make more widely available the scarce computing resources found at major research hubs such as MIT and Stanford. Although ARPANET was intended for resource sharing, communication quickly became its primary use. By the early 1970s, programmers had adapted FTP, the system for sending files from one site to another, into an email-like messaging system. A 1973 study of network resource usage found that three-quarters of all ARPANET traffic consisted in email, and this was at a time when only the most basic mail exchange software had been developed. There was no message handling, so the stream of mail had to be read linearly; there was no reply function and no addressing tools, so each user needed to figure out the complex path from his computer to the recipient's (Hafner and Lyon 2000). Over the next few years, programmers added new features, such as the ability to read messages in any order, save them, and automatically address a reply message. By 1975, they had developed the key elements of the email interface that we still use today (Leiner et al. 2009).

Although using ARPANET for communication was controversial, the programmers who created email had the support of J. C. R. Licklider, an influential director at ARPA. In 1968, as ARPANET was still under construction, Licklider had set forth a vision for a universally networked communication system that covered the technical challenges, expressed tremendous optimism about the benefits of connectivity, and raised questions about access that resonate today. He wrote: "In a few years, men will be able to communicate more effectively through a machine than face to face" (Licklider and Taylor 1968, 21). Even more radically, he predicted that discussions would have images, information, and interactive models as their medium. He foresaw the development of geographically distributed online communities that would be united by interest rather than location.

Licklider was one of the original cyber-utopians: "Life will be happier for the on-line individual because the people with whom one interacts most strongly will be selected more by commonality of interests and goals than by accidents of proximity" (Licklider and Taylor, 1968, 40). But he also cautioned that universal access was essential: "For the society, the impact will be good or bad, depending mainly on the question: Will 'to be on line' be a privilege or a right? If only a favored segment of the population gets a chance to enjoy the advantage of 'intelligence amplification,' the network may exaggerate the discontinuity in the spectrum of intellectual opportunity" (ibid.).[2]

Soon after email was developed, ARPANET was hosting a variety of group email lists—the earliest online discussion groups. But access to ARPANET was limited: only research laboratories with Defense Department funding were connected. The content, too, was restricted. Although Licklider envisioned universally accessible, wide-ranging interest groups, he alone did not shape the ARPANET, which also had many other more conservative administrators whose focus was on ARPA's military and defense missions. They saw personal communication as frivolous, getting in the way or affecting the security of the central mission of the network.

Arguably, the first widespread incarnation of an open community like the one Licklider envisioned was Usenet, a system of distributed news postings developed in 1979 by graduate students at Duke University. Usenet was created to be an open service to which any site with a Unix machine could connect, with users at that site able to read—and most importantly, respond to—news postings that others on the network had uploaded (Hauben and Hauben 1997). Comparing Usenet and ARPANET discussions illustrates how the goals for a system shape its technology, which in turn shapes the resulting social boundaries.

ARPANET's mailing lists were centrally controlled and most were moderated, meaning that posts were not published until they were vetted for appropriate content, and users were warned about "non-official" use. ARPANET's boundaries were guarded both to prevent outsiders from participating in their discussions and to ensure that information from their discussions did not seep out; in addition to the obvious concerns about securing sensitive technological and strategic data and avoiding copyright problems, they were also concerned about the reputation of the agency if news of frivolous conversations on this Defense Department–supported service became public. An ARPANET user at MIT recalled:

> There is always the threat of official or public accusations of misuse of the network for certain mailing lists. This actually happened with a list called WINE-LOVERS and Datamation. … The fiasco nearly resulted in MIT being removed from the network, and cost us several months of research time while we fought legal battles to show why our machines should not be removed from the ARPAnet.[3]

Usenet, on the other hand, was designed by graduate students unhappy with being left out of the ARPANET community. The system they created was decentralized. Each machine kept a copy of the news database, and thus, while an individual system administrator could choose not to handle a particular newsgroup, no one could control the overall distribution. In practice, it was generally up to the reader to decide what to peruse. There was no central authority, and in the first years, no moderated groups. Posting was self-policed—if you had an account, you could post to any group. The discussions were far more free-wheeling than on ARPANET, where even discussions of science-fiction films pressed against the boundary of acceptable content.[4] Within a year of its creation, Usenet included net.gdead (for Grateful Dead fans), net.rec.birds (for birdwatchers), net.vwrabbit (for all the owners of that car), and net.suicide (for those contemplating ending it all).

In the early 1980s, the two networks began to merge. At first, communication was one way: Usenet users could read the ARPANET messages, but could not respond to them. Even once replies were permitted, the ARPANET users could be unwelcoming to the Usenet-based outsiders. One early Usenet user recalls:

> Adding the ARPANET lists to Usenet initially contributed to the sense of being poor cousins. It was initially very hard to contribute to those lists, and when you did you were more likely to get a response to your return address than to the content of your letter. It definitely felt second class to be in read-only mode on human-nets and sf-lovers.[5]

This clash, of an existing community feeling that it was being intruded upon by less knowledgeable and less well-disciplined outsiders, would subsequently be repeated several times in Usenet's evolution, notably in 1993 when America Online, a popular Internet service provider marketed toward computer neophytes, gave Usenet access to its subscribers, and in 1997 when DejaNews provided an easy-to-use, Web-based interface to Usenet. Indeed, it is one of the fundamental design problems in the online world: when do we want a closed community, with carefully vetted membership, versus a more open environment, welcoming to newcomers and engaging a larger population?

In this case, the feeling among ARPANET users was mixed. One said:

> I am beginning to wonder about USENET. I thought it was supposed to represent electronic mail and bulletins among a group of professionals with a common interest, thus representing fast communications about important technical topics. Instead it appears to be mutating into electronic graffiti. If the system did not cost anything, that would be fine, but for us here at Tektronix, at least, it is costing us better than $200 a month for 300-baud long distance to copy lists of people's favorite movies, and recipes for goulash, and arguments about metaphysics and so on. Is this really appropriate to this type of system?[6]

Indeed, since ARPANET was a closed and tightly controlled system, the question is what motivated them to provide access to Usenet at all?

Some ARPANET users believed that opening up their network would provide access to valuable information and relationships: Usenet at the time was still an elite community, limited to researchers and graduate students in established universities and laboratories; it was far from the massive public system it would become later. Others felt that an open network was itself a worthwhile experiment. In practice, it simply came down to a few individual system administrators, first at Berkeley and then at other ARPA sites, who chose to create the

The early Usenet group Human Nets focused on the unprecedented experience of being part of a vast communicative network. This post, written by the group's moderator in response to a complaint that the discussion had gone off topic, both articulates the novelty of this enterprise and demonstrates the tension between maintaining the strict boundaries of a tightly focused group or the loose ones of a group that shifts in response to participants' changing interests.

> Even if we have shifted away from discussing human networks, we are getting a first hand EXPERIENCE of what they are through this mailing list. No amount of `a priori' theorizing of their nature has as much explanatory power as personal experience. By observing what happens when connectivity is provided to a large mass of people in which they can FREELY voice their ideas, doubts, and opinions, a lot of insight is obtained into very important issues of mass intercommunication.
> The fact that ... dissimilar ... topics have been discussed in our own instance of a human network says a lot about its nature and the interests and nature of its members and should not be considered as detracting from the quality of the discussion. A human network is a springboard for human interaction and thus for human action. Let's view it as such and keep repression and censorship at a minimum. (Jorge Phillips to Human Nets Mailing List (ARPANET/Usenet), June 3, 1981: "administrivia"; quoted in Hauben and Hauben 1997, chapter 10)

ARPA/Usenet gateways. Although they were not representative of most ARPANET members, these gatekeepers' belief in openness was enough to establish the flow of information, tenuous as it may have been at times.

A fundamental difference between ARPANET and Usenet was their approaches to internal policing—keeping the discussion on topic and preventing abuse. Within ARPANET, a rigid infrastructure of moderators who determined whether each posting was suitable for publication patrolled the conversational boundaries. The open groups of Usenet had no such authority; a loose and evolving set of social norms and sanctions maintained conversational bounds. As the Usenet community expanded, the issue of how to maintain civility and order became a growing problem. As early as 1981, Usenet system administrators were grappling with the problem of protecting open discussions from disruption. In a discussion about the problem of "flames," Mark Horton, the programmer who first connected Usenet and ARPANET at Berkeley, wrote that "peer pressure via direct electronic mail will, hopefully, prevent any further distasteful or offensive articles. Repeated violations can be grounds for removing a user or site from the network."[7]

Usenet's open design was based on the assumption that people would, on the whole, behave responsibly. One could post freely to existing newsgroups and, with little central coordination, create new ones.[8] Inherent to this assumption was the fact that Usenet's initial users were clearly identified (Donath 1998), not only with their name, but also with their work or university affiliation; these affiliations provided the computer accounts and network access. People also volunteered additional identifying information. Although the posting software automatically included one's email address at the head of the message, many people also closed their postings with elaborate signatures that included their name, affiliation, interests, and humor.

This did not guarantee that all postings would be on-topic and civil. One problem was simply ignorance; the newsgroups had developed their own culture and rules of behavior (for example, don't post content with nothing more than "me too," and read past discussions to make sure that your question has not already been answered in earlier exchanges), but newcomers didn't know these rules. Usenet was growing rapidly and there were a lot of newcomers, particularly each fall when the new students arrived on campus and got their first computer accounts. The main repercussion for poor behavior was social sanctioning from within the community: people would send emails or write angry responses to offending users. Institutional monitoring

Some examples of Usenet signatures from the mid-1990s. See Donath 1998 for more on the social meanings encoded in Usenet signatures.

Signature of an anonymous remailer user:

```
Matou can be reached at anon-3458@anon.twwells.com, or atan97241@anon.penet.
fi, if you prefer to send your email on vacation to Scandinavia.
```

The following are signatures from rec.motorcycles. The DoD number is a signal of membership in the online, and somewhat parodic, motorcycle club, "Denizens of Doom":

```
"Tuba" (Irwin) "I honk therefore I am" CompuTrac-Richardson,Tx
irwin@cmptrc.lonestar.org  DoD #0826(R75/6) (Ducati 900GTS)
```

```
=-=-=-=-=-=-=-=-=-=-=-=-=-=-=-=-=-=-=-=-=-=-=-=-=-=-=-=-=-=-=-=-=-=-=-=-=-=-=-
Ged          |   You talking at me? Are you talkin'
DoD #5088    |   to me? Who are you talking to?
-=-=-=-=-=-=-=-=-=-=-=-=-=-=-=-=-=-=-=-=-=-=-=-=-=-=-=-=-=-=-=-=-=-=-=-=-=-=-=-
```

This signature, from comp.security.unix, is a joke accessible only to other advanced C (a computer language) coders:

```
main(v,c)char**c;{for(v[c++]="Rick Tait <rickt@gnu.ai.mit.edu>\n)";(!!c)
[*c]&&(v—||—c&&execlp(*c,*c,c[!!c]+!!c,!c));**c=!c)write(!!*c,*c,!!**c);}
```

varied. Employees of conservative corporations or military centers were more constrained; their supervisors were likely to be intolerant of wasting time and resources, let alone poor behavior. Most universities, however, did not closely monitor students' online activity, and did not act unless an offense was egregious enough to generate serious complaints; poor etiquette and hostile postings passed unnoticed.

Limited access to the requisite computers and the network put a hard, infrastructural boundary around Usenet. In the early days, it excluded everyone except for researchers at select institutions. Increasingly, though, people gained access to Usenet via commercial accounts—network connections that they paid for independently, unattached to a valued affiliation. Customers of the first such services[9] were still a technologically oriented group: personal computers in the early 1980s were a hobbyist's specialty. But, the significance for the Usenet community was that they were participating via services that, so long as they broke no laws, did not care how upstanding they were and that at most might terminate their account, but would not jeopardize their job or degree.

The phrase "Endless September" described the change in Usenet culture once novice consumer users gained access. The Jargon File, an open collection of hacker slang, defined it as follows:

> All time since September 1993. One of the seasonal rhythms of the Usenet used to be the annual September influx of clueless newbies who, lacking any sense of netiquette, made a general nuisance of themselves. This coincided with people starting college, getting their first internet accounts, and plunging in without bothering to learn what was acceptable. These relatively small drafts of newbies could be assimilated within a few months. But in September 1993, AOL users became able to post to Usenet, nearly overwhelming the old-timers' capacity to acculturate them; to those who nostalgically recall the period before, this triggered an inexorable decline in the quality of discussions on newsgroups. Syn. eternal September. See also AOL! (Raymond 2003)

In the 1980s and early 1990s, Usenet was thriving.[10] There were hundreds of topics and lively discussions. There were heated flame wars, but it was a very viable interaction space. At the same time, the user base was changing, from a small community of people with much in common to a heterogeneous crowd divided into a quickly multiplying set of subcultures. The technical users still dominated, and the most popular topics included computer languages, network properties, and science fiction. But as the population diversified, so did the range of topics and style of discourse.

Several developments in the early 1990s radically changed Usenet. The biggest immediate effect was when the large consumer network services—first CompuServe, then Prodigy, then AOL—gave access to Usenet to their customers. As with other commercial network providers, people who accessed Usenet via these services were coming in with an account unaffiliated with their livelihood. These companies marketed themselves to novices, to people who weren't interested in the computer as a machine, but simply wanted the services that it could provide. They were even more dissimilar to the computer professionals and researchers who dominated the early days.

Furthermore, they—especially AOL users—arrived with their own chat-room culture, in which identity was fluid. The AOL chat-rooms were often fantasy spaces, where users with sexy or silly names played games with each other, using an online patois filled with emoticons and abbreviations. AOL users were accustomed to fanciful and disposable screen-names: "sexymama69" and "BigGuyNumber1." Embarrass yourself or offend too many people using one such guise? It was easy to simply take on another name, a clean new identity.[11]

This population made a big impact when it arrived in the Usenet discussion space. Usenet had a culture of expertise: people were expected to take time and learn a group's mores before posting to it. The consumer services were marketed to newcomers and made their money by signing up more and more novice subscribers. To encourage inexperienced users, they created an environment where to be a naive user was fine; just try stuff, join in, say anything. Many users from these services saw Usenet as just a big continuation of their familiar, informal chat-rooms, and they brought with them their smiley faces, cheap identities, and naive ignorance of the conventions and mores of the established Usenet groups (Coates et al. 1994). The infrastructural boundaries of institution-based access and professional reputation dissolved into the much looser bounds of personal computer ownership and an inexpensive monthly subscription.

A second development at the same time—the creation of a public anonymous server, anon.penet.fi, by a Finnish programmer named Julf Helsingius—had a smaller immediate effect but was symbolically important. Usenet worked much like email: when you posted something, your username, including the service that provided your Internet access, was automatically included in the header. Even if your username had no resemblance to your real name, if someone wanted to know who you were, it would generally not be too difficult to trace your real identity. An anonymous server changed this. By routing your message through this server, it would appear under any name you chose there, and tracing it back to you would be beyond other users' ordinary means. Thus, if you wished to harass someone, or post neo-Nazi propaganda, or otherwise behave in a way that was disruptive and likely to inspire others to want to retaliate against you, the shield of an anonymous account could be quite useful.

Many of the users of anon.penet.fi were not, in fact, engaging in antisocial behavior. Many were committed to the principle that anonymity had an important role in online life. Anonymity protects someone when he or she is doing something that invites reprisal, which might be malicious behavior, but could also be dissent in an oppressive regime or whistleblowing in a corrupt corporation. The conundrum of anonymity is that whereas it protects those resisting an oppressive ruling group, it also protects those who are destructively disruptive.

Anon.penet.fi was actually a pseudonymous rather than an anonymous service. Helsingius kept a database that connected the users' anonymous accounts to their regular email addresses. One could thus receive mail via an anon.penet.fi account and establish a long-term history for a particular identity. But it also meant that Helsingius could be (and was) forced to reveal these identities.[12] Though anon.penet.fi turned out to be insecure, it was not long before other more secure remailers were set up. Some routed mail through multiple servers in different countries, making it much more difficult for someone to secure all the legal subpoenas needed for tracing identity. Others were true anonymous servers, where each post you sent would appear under a different name, with no records tied to you. Though you could not receive incoming mail via an anonymous remailer, they would suit someone who simply wanted to send off disruptive missives.

Soon there were floods of anonymous and untraceable postings to Usenet. Spam became a growing problem.[13] It became clear that the concept of Usenet as an open public community had worked only because in the beginning, "public" had not been very public. Admittance had required having already passed the admissions barriers to a high-end university or elite technical job. It had meant being a named person responsible for and protective of one's own reputation. Though Usenet had appeared to be an open public space, it had in fact been a protected garden set behind the walls of network access in the 1980s.

A third development eventually ended Usenet as a functioning community. In 1995 DejaNews, a Web-based archive and searchable index of Usenet postings, was started. It made it easy to search for messages by key word or author, but it also removed the postings from their original social context. Previously, you followed a discussion because you were interested in the general topic; conversations were the basic units, rather than individual postings. With the advent of a searchable Web interface, people started replying to posts with no idea of what came before or after. Easy searchability broke down the boundaries that kept newsgroups as coherent and semiprivate conversational spaces. Today, Usenet still exists, but it is an unsociable morass of spam, porn, and pirated software.

But elsewhere, online discussions are thriving. Some have strict boundaries: private mailing lists or discussions among pundits that the public is invited to read but not contribute to. Others are moderated by a trusted leader or through a system of meta-moderation, in which community members are given incentives for writing well and moderating fairly. Some require participants to use their real name and identify themselves within some community, such as their network of acquaintances. Because of the prevalence of spam, there are almost no wholly open sites; even the notorious anonymous boards of 4chan have moderators.[14]

BOUNDARIES OF ONLINE DISCUSSIONS

In the mid-1990s, when Usenet was an enormous but still thriving site, sociologists Peter Kollock and Marc Smith wrote a paper about it entitled "Managing the Virtual Commons." A commons is a resource shared by a population. The challenge of the commons is to provide open access while preventing destructive exploitation. For a commons to survive its users must take care of it; they cannot overexploit it or neglect it. Kollock and Smith drew on ecological and political theories of managing such communally shared resources to examine the rich possibilities—and looming difficulties—of a massive, online conversation space (Kollock and Smith 1996).

The notion of a commons, free and open to all, has great appeal.[15] But is it sustainable? In "The Tragedy of the Commons," ecologist Garrett Hardin (1968) argued that exploitation to the point of destruction is the inevitable fate of a publicly shared resource, since individuals acting in their own self-interest will use more and more of it, until it is ruined. For example, a village may have a common pasture on which all inhabitants may graze their sheep. So long as the pasture is healthy, everyone benefits. Yet since people individually accrue the benefit from feeding their animals there, while the whole community shares the cost of resources they consume, people will keep adding more and more animals until the pasture is overgrazed and barren, at which point everyone loses.[16]

Is Hardin right? Are common resources inevitably overgrazed, overrun, and overused? Hardin claimed that only strict, external governance could salvage these resources. When we look at the many ecological disasters of the last century, his pessimism seems well founded. Yet there are counterexamples. Elinor Ostrom won the Nobel Prize in Economics for her studies of economic governance, particularly of commons. She showed that there are many examples of communities that have successfully self-managed common resources. Central to their success are well-maintained boundaries, defining the extent of the resource and identifying the population of legitimate users. Also essential are locally adapted rules about sharing, collective decision making, and monitoring and sanctioning those who break the rules.

Both Hardin and Ostrom agree, and history demonstrates, that poorly governed commons will be overexploited. They differ in the solutions they propose and the enthusiasm with which they assess the likelihood of success. Hardin claims that only private property and centralized, external government can save common resources (and his overall assessment is quite pessimistic). Ostrom champions self-governance. While she readily concedes that self-governance does not always work, she points out that external force has fundamental problems in compliance and a poor record of adapting to local circumstances. She emphasizes the importance of local and evolving rules: there is no universal recipe for successful self-management, and changing circumstances, such as a growing population, new demands, or new technologies, require adaptability.

Elinor Ostrom's design rules for successful community management of the commons are:

1. Group boundaries are clearly defined.
2. Rules about use of collective goods are adapted to local needs and conditions.
3. Most people affected by the rules can participate in modifying the rules.
4. External monitors that help reinforce the group's rules are also accountable to the group.
5. Sanctions in proportion to the offense are assessed by other members (or other authorities they authorize) on individuals who violate the rules.
6. There are accessible and quick conflict resolution mechanisms.
7. External authorities respect the group's right to self-govern. (Ostrom 1999)

This chart shows the rough breakdown of goods according to whether they are ex-cludable (whether others can be prevented from using/obtaining) and rivalrous (whether one person's use diminish another's). Few examples are clean cut: a polluting factory makes air rivalrous, and the air in a scuba diver's tank is a private good.

	Excludable	Nonexcludable
Rivalrous	Private goods—cars, clothing	Common goods—public pastures, fishing grounds
Non-rivalrous	Club goods—satellite TV, private parks	Public goods—broadcast TV, air, knowledge

Thinking about public online conversations as a commons is useful for several reasons. It forces us to think about the resources that the participants use and the value they create, for themselves or others. Ostrom's model of what makes a commons sustainable provides a guide for designing better interfaces for these interactions. Economists who study commons and their resources classify them along two axes (see sidebar). One is "excludability," or how easy it is to limit access to the resource. Physical objects are excludable: storeowners hold onto cars, shoes, books, and so on until the customer pays for them, at which point ownership is transferred. Broadcast television is nonexcludable: once you send the signal into the air, anyone with the right receiver can view it. Technology can manage exclusion: if we encode the television signal so that you need to pay to get the key to decode it, we have turned it into an excludable good. The other axis is "rivalry": does one person's consumption of the good diminish what is available to others? A pie is rivalrous; television signals, whether free and over the air or limited by encoding and subscription, are not.

The "commons" in the "tragedy of the commons" refers to resources that are nonexcludable and rivalrous, meaning that it is hard to limit access to them and that one person's consumption reduces what is available for the others. But it is important to note (and many sources on goods and commons omit this) that often the resources in a commons are renewable. Grass grows, fish spawn. If they are ruthlessly exploited, they will disappear, but if managed well, they are sustainable.

When we look at a commons such as a pasture for cows, it is easy to see what the resource is that needs protection: the grass. But what is it in a conversation? Kollock and Smith (1996) identify the virtual resource in danger of overexploitation as "bandwidth."[17] People have limited time and attention. A public online conversation provides a platform for expression; anyone can write, at any length and on any topic. Repetitive, off-topic, or offensive postings waste bandwidth. If many postings are dull, uninformative, or irrelevant, people will give up. If we see bandwidth as a rivalrous resource, where one person's posting takes away from the attention available for another's, then boundaries need to limit who can post, and some form of rules and repercussions need to enforce these bounds. Yet it is important to keep in mind that the real goal is not fewer postings—indeed, too few is as much a problem as too many—but more high-quality contributions.

A different approach is to focus on conversation spaces as places where public goods in the form of informative or entertaining contributions are produced rather than as a commons of bandwidth to be preserved. Joseph Stiglitz, another Nobel Prize winner, referred to knowledge as a "global public good," and also good in the normative sense: something that benefits all. Public goods are nonrivalrous and nonexcludable. Being nonrivalrous, the key problem with public goods is not consumption (in the case of knowledge, my learning something does not impede your acquisition of that knowledge[18]) but in motivating their production. Much of Stiglitz's writing is about finding ways to finance research. Here, in the realm of online conversation, the challenge is to find the social motivations for knowledge production. What motivates people to answer questions, share knowledge, and organize information, usually without pay, in the context of an online social space?

The relationship between consumers and producers is quite different in a discussion space than in a pasture or fishery. In the domain of cows and fish, other herders and fishermen are, for the most part, tolerated but not desired. One would be happy to have the whole pasture or pond to oneself (though the sustenance of community is also a valuable thing). But the ecology of a conversation is different. Reading and writing are symbiotic: writing has no value without readers, and reading is not possible if no one writes. Most participants take both roles. Only spammers, the least welcome of writers, write without reading. Conversations are diverse ecosystems: the motivation of different people—or the same people, at different times—varies. Some are primarily readers seeking entertainment or enlightenment. Some are primarily writers seeking to promote a cause. Some write to ask a question, hoping to generate useful responses. Some people seek community and support; they want a back-and-forth exchange of ideas.

How people perceive this ecosystem has a big impact on the type of activity they will want to promote, and thus the designs they will prefer. Kollock and Smith (1996) referred to people who read but do not write as lurkers, a common though somewhat pejorative-sounding term frequently used within the online community (Nonnecke and Preece 2003). Their disapproval of this behavior was clear; they listed lurking as a form of free-riding. It is true that the lurker is not producing more knowledge or other valued content. Yet the quiet reader is not using up bandwidth; most importantly, he is an audience, without which the writers' efforts would be in vain.

The social ecosystem is in delicate balance. High-quality content needs to be encouraged, but poor-quality content is more harmful than nothing at all. Readers are valuable, and their presence motivates writing; but if the reader writes nothing, the writer has no way of knowing her work has been read.

Quality is contextual. Writing without adding significant content (the "me too" posting) is often considered to be poor-quality writing; it uses up bandwidth without adding information. Yet in conversations that are personal and supportive, phatic communications—messages that have purely social content, such as "you're so right," "we're thinking of you"—are essential for expressing sympathy and understanding. And, such social discourse is important even in technical discussions that rely far less on social bonds, for it is through such commentary that people form reputations and learn mores within a community context; it is key to motivating them to be productive participants.

Ostrom emphasized that commons need boundaries in order to survive. Usenet began as a bounded community; though ostensibly open to anyone with a computer account, it was effectively a small bounded community of researchers and professionals. As computers became more widespread, the community grew. Some growth was good; it went from a limited community of very like-minded users to an unprecedentedly immense social space in which enormous numbers of diverse participants engaged in a wide variety of discussions. But then it grew too big and too open. Its loosened boundaries allowed in too many exploitative users (spammers), and new technologies (search) further broke down the boundaries that had sustained ongoing discussions. In a world of anonymous accounts, sophisticated bots, and massive search engines, how can we design boundaries to sustain community?

Identifying Who (or What) Is In or Out

Personal identity is essential for most boundaries. Without it, history cannot accrue and a reputation cannot be established. Should the individual break the community's rules, identity enables social sanctioning and, if necessary, banning that person from using the community's resources. This identity might be tied to one's real name, or to a persistent pseudonym; these are discussed in detail in chapter 11, "Privacy and Public Space."

Social identity, or type, can also be the bounding delimiter. Some resources or communities are open to people only of certain type—those over age thirteen or eighteen, or those who are experts in particle physics. "Type" can refer to any number of characteristics: big social categories of age, gender, and race; institutional ones such as "employee of company X"; situational ones such as "sufferers of migraines"; and so on. Much of the controversy around exclusionary practices is about type-based boundaries; a society can find some boundaries to be quite acceptable, even imperative, while others are forbidden. Designing the boundaries for a closed group of known and identified individuals is a relatively straightforward issue of security (Harper 2006; Schneier 2011), but providing access to a whole class of people, without knowing in advance who the individuals are, can be more complex, socially if not technically. Social identity is the focus of chapter 9, "Constructing Identity."

In closed communities, individuals are vetted to ensure that they are of an accepted type to participate. They subsequently need only verify their identity (whether with an ID card to gain access to a physical space, or an email, username, and password in a virtual one) to enter. A closed mailing list works this way; once you are accepted as a participant, your individual email address is your key.[19] The list rejects mail sent from other addresses. Yet the great vitality and promise of online discussions is that they are open, providing support and camaraderie to and drawing from the knowledge of people from all over. The design problem is to figure out how tight or porous to make the boundary, how to protect the community while keeping it open to new people and new ideas.

The disadvantage of tighter boundaries is decreased access. If I greatly limit the number of people I hear from, I get less information; defining boundaries too narrowly or thoughtlessly loses valuable perspectives. Hearing differing viewpoints is difficult. We often like to hear only what reaffirms our preexisting beliefs. But much of the benefit of being in dialogue is learning about what people different from us think, and perhaps changing our own views or influencing theirs. Heterogeneity can be a valuable, though unpopular, goal.

Boundaries protect against two different types of outsiders. Aspirants to the group want to be part of it, to have access to its resources and the status it confers. In an open and mobile society, today's aspirant may well be tomorrow's insider. The country club membership, once denied, is granted when the applicant becomes partner at her firm; the newcomer to the city is invited to underground parties once he learns the nuances of how to dress and talk.

The other type, predators to the group, such as thieves, rival street gangs, or spammers, do not want acceptance by its legitimate members; they seek its resources or benefit by harming it. Many of the most visible barriers—from the barred windows and steel doors on houses in poor neighborhoods (and celebrities' mansions) to the requirement that comments be held until a moderator approves them in an online forum—are there to protect against predatory outsiders.

Malignant outsiders, whether deliberately malicious or simply in pursuit of their own incompatible goals, destroy the common resource. There may be plenty of fish in the pond, but not if a factory sets up on the shore and dumps toxic sludge into the water. On Usenet, spam was the equivalent of pollution, and the technologies that let it cross the boundaries of the discussion space were anonymous access, automated scripts, and computer viruses. One of the first widely disruptive spam campaigns on Usenet appeared in 1994. In numerous newsgroups, any mention of Turkey was answered by a user who called himself "Serdar Argic" and whose postings consisted of long diatribes denying the Armenian genocide committed by the Turks, and claiming instead that Turks were slaughtered by the Armenians. Argic posted prolifically, averaging one hundred posts a day.

Eventually, many people came to believe that "Serdar Argic" was actually a bot, a scripting program that automatically generated the messages; in this case, one that searched newsgroups for mentions of Turkey or Armenia and then pieced together a response by grabbing a line or two from the original letter and appending its typical tirade. This suspicion was strengthened by the poster's indifference to whether a mention of Turkey referred to the country or to Thanksgiving turkeys and other culinary, avian, and nonpolitical uses of the word.

Serdar Argic's histrionic messages were designed to provoke, using strategies such as taking the original poster's name, adding an Armenian ending to it and referring to the writer's "criminal Armenian grandparents" (DeVoto 1994). The reflexive response to an offensive post is to respond, whether calmly explaining why it was inappropriate or angrily demanding an apology. In a newsgroup, numerous people may respond this way. If the offending writer intends to be a participant in the discussion, he or she may learn from this response; it is a way of articulating and enforcing the group's social norms, and although it temporarily distracts from the main discussion, it serves a useful purpose. But posters deliberately inciting discord are only encouraged by such responses. Serdar Argic—and, over time, many other "trolls"[20]—was able to thoroughly disrupt several groups by hijacking the conversation to be about him; rather than the ostensible topic of the group, most posts would be Argic's rants, responses to his rants, or people telling others not to respond to him. Social sanctions work only when the person being sanctioned cares about being in good standing with the group (and is actually a person). People who intend to be disruptive cannot be stopped by sanctioning; they don't care if their reputation in the group is lowered.

Concern about unwanted intrusion influences design. In a safe neighborhood in carefree times, there may be many open windows and doors, few obvious locks, and building designs that maximize sunlight and views. In a high-crime neighborhood, the houses look like fortresses, with heavy steel doors and bars on the windows. Online, the barriers are complex registration processes and tests to prove that you are human, not a bot.

Knowledge Borders

In the physical world, access based on social type is often determined by physical characteristics, since they are easy for us to assess. A nightclub's doorman admits only stylishly dressed patrons; customers can try on clothing in the ladies dressing room if they appear to be female; decades of civil rights legislation still struggles against the legacy of racial segregation. Such boundaries can be essential to society or highly destructive, depending on who they admit and why. Online, where we have information, not bodies, potential entrants can be assessed based on their knowledge (or lack of it). Such knowledge boundaries have everyday precedents, such as the tests of knowledge that must be passed to gain admittance to college, to the police academy, or to obtain a driver's license.

A simple but good example has been in use since the early days of personal homepages. Someone puts up a collection of family photographs. They want their friends to be able to see them, but not the general public. They also do not want to enumerate everyone who should have access; it is too much work and they may omit someone. Instead, they protect the page with a password, and provide the clue that it is, say, the name of their middle son or the family dog. People who are close enough friends will know this information and be granted access to the photographs. And, unless they are famous or have posted this information elsewhere, it is the sort of data that online

FIGURE 7.1
A text CAPTCHA, circa 2012. (See http://captcha.net/.)

research will not find (at least not for now). Such "group knowledge" identifiers work best for small communities, whose members share knowledge that is obscure to outsiders. Sconex, an early social network site aimed at high school students, used a series of questions such as "What floor is the library on?" or "Who is the substitute gym teacher?" to assess whether applicants actually attended the schools they claimed to (Laraqui 2007). Some online sites for ultra-Orthodox Jews limit membership to followers of a particular rabbi; the organizer asks potential participants to name the topics discussed at recent gatherings (Campbell and Golan 2011). While the biggest design challenge is devising a test that works, other considerations further complicate design. A lengthy examination will be too onerous for most sites; it could discourage the legitimate users, too. So any "test" needs to be lightweight: the effort to gain access must be in proportion to the participants' desire to enter.

Since the days of Serdar Argic, arguably the most important boundary online is the one distinguishing humans from machines. The vast quantities of spam that clog mailboxes and message sites are machine generated, sent by programs of ever increasing sophistication. What is needed is a test that humans can pass and computers cannot, so that sites can grant access to the former while barring the latter. A CAPTCHA is a "completely automated public Turing test to tell computers and humans apart" (von Ahn et al. 2003). The challenge in making a CAPTCHA is not only to devise a test that only humans can pass, but also to make it so that both judging and generating new instances of it can be done automatically. A popular version today (circa 2012) uses pictures of distorted letters (see figure 7.1). Computers can generate these images algorithmically so that an endless quantity of them can be created as needed, and they can easily assess the correctness of an answer, which is simply a string of letters. Contemporary computers have difficulty deciphering them, whereas people can do so with relative ease. But computers are getting better at this task, and will soon be able to pass it. Other CAPTCHAs, perhaps also harder for humans to solve, will be needed.[21]

Moderated Borders

A different approach to bounding discussion focuses on the content of messages, rather than or in addition to identity-based boundaries. Moderated groups, in which a single person or small group of people read each message before it is posted, date back to the earliest days of ARPANET. Moderation ensures that only messages of sufficiently high quality become part of the discussion. But they are limited by size; if the discussion is too popular the moderators will be overwhelmed, resulting in long delays before messages are posted. They are also subject to the whims of the moderators, who may censor views contrary to their own.

Distributed moderation, in which many or all of the participants act as moderators, alleviates these problems. Commonly, participants can vote on the postings, and ones that receive higher ratings are given greater prominence; often there is a connected reputation system, and participants whose posts are highly rated receive corresponding reputation points. One of the earliest sites to successfully use distributed moderation is Slashdot.org (Lampe and Resnick 2004). It is a news discussion site focused on technological topics, where the discussions occur via comments on individual stories. The stories are suggested by the community, but the editorial staff decides which ones to feature on the site. The participants comment on them, and they also rate the comments according to a series of criteria including funny, insightful, redundant, flamebait, and so on. Not everyone can moderate all the time; it is a privilege that is granted at random for a limited amount of time. Slashdot also features meta-moderation; the ratings are themselves moderated by a rotating group of participants with more established accounts. The moderator's ratings on a comment raise or lower its score, which affects how prominently it is displayed. Ratings also affect the karma (Slashdot's version of reputation) of the users who wrote the comment. With higher karma, one is more likely to be chosen to moderate; thus, over time, the people whose contributions to the site align with the community's tastes gain greater influence over the site. Slashdot does allow for anonymous participation (see sidebar), though it encourages people to establish an identity; only logged-in users can moderate and contributions from identified users start with a score of one, whereas anonymous contributions start with zero. Anonymous commenters must solve a CAPTCHA to prove that they are at least human.

From the Slashdot Q&A:

> Most of the trolls and useless stuff comes from "Anonymous Coward" posters. Why not eliminate anonymous posting? We've thought about it. We think the ability to post anonymously is important, though. Sometimes people have important information they want to post, but wouldn't do so if they could be linked to it. Anonymous posting will continue for the foreseeable future. (Miscellaneous—FAQ—Slashdot: http://slashdot.org/faq/misc.shtml)

Slashdot's multilayered boundary sustains a robustly active (as of 2012) news-gathering and discussion site. The boundary includes the infrastructural layer of the CAPTCHA, keeping out vast quantities of automated spam. It includes the community itself, moderating and meta-moderating the content, a constant distributed sorting process that highlights the most important stories and comments and conveys increasing influence to its most respected members. And it includes the staff—the gatekeepers who determine which stories to feature, which moderators to reward, and which names or IP addresses to ban.

There are now a number of sites that use a variation of this multilayered boundary and incentive system to give prominence to high-quality content, filter out spam, and create a community of known users while still allowing pseudonymous and even anonymous participation. They differ in their technical implementation: Do users rate others? Re-edit their words? What are the privileges granted to trusted participants, and how does one gain them? They also differ considerably in their overall goals. Slashdot is used to quickly publish breaking news stories. Other moderated sites include Wikipedia, for collaboratively creating neutral, authoritative encyclopedia entries; the Stack Exchange network, for questions and answers on focused topics; and 4chan/b/, for the fast exchange of outrageous images.[22]

Stack Overflow is a site devoted to questions and answers about programming. It has a carefully planned economy of reputation points. You lose points if your postings are down-voted; you gain 5 points if your question is up-voted and 10 points if an answer you give is up-voted. All constructive (as defined by the community) participation is rewarded, but the more generous act of helping to solve someone else's problem is rewarded more highly; question askers, presumably, are sufficiently rewarded by the possibility of receiving a solution to their problem. Privileges are intricately engineered, with 15 levels of permissions: to create a post, you need one reputation point; 15 points will allow you to vote a comment up, but you need 125 to down-vote (and down-voting costs you a bit in reputation points, too); with 20,000 points you become a trusted user, with numerous privileges, including the ability to delete answers that have negative scores. As with Slashdot, you can participate anonymously, but with reduced capabilities.

Like the blueprints for an empire of carefully planned suburban developments, Stack Overflow's code has been reproduced to create the Stack Exchange network of Q&A sites, each of which have a different topical focus, though all share the same social infrastructure. One's identity works across sites, and experienced users with a high reputation on one site start off with 100 points on any new site they join. The designers emphasize that each site is designed to eventually be fully self-governing, though they are launched with moderators picked by the Stack Exchange staff.

Conversation on the Stack Exchange sites is tightly controlled. Clear directives stipulate exactly what sort of question is appropriate, and each site has parallel spaces for discussing issues of site governance, and what precisely is a prototypical question for that topic. Reputation and social approbation are central, but their operation has been made almost entirely infrastructural; the Stack Exchange model provides a prefabricated social structure for topical discussion. Indeed, even the concept of "discussion" is denigrated: when one answers a question, a note pops up saying: "Please make sure you answer the question; this is a Q&A site, not a discussion forum. Provide details and share your research. Avoid statements based solely on opinion; only make statements you can back up with an appropriate reference, or personal experiences."

This focus makes the Stack Exchange technical sites exceptionally useful. In the fast-moving world of programming languages and system administration, it provides a place to get help for problems like: "I bumped into this strange macro code in /usr/include/linux/kernel.h [paragraphs of code] … What does:-!! do?" A related site, MathOverflow, focuses on concrete, research-level math questions with definite answers;[23] it has attracted a remarkable community ranging from graduate students to Field Medalists. But definitive questions and answers are only one of the myriad forms that social interactions can take. For other topics addressed in the Stack Exchange network, such as science fiction or parenting tips, the regimented rigor that brings clarity to the technical discussion may be too stiffly reserved for these more inherently social discussions.

At the opposite end of the discursive spectrum from Stack Exchange's constructive regulation is 4chan. It is an image board site, where participants, usually anonymous, post and comment on pictures. It consists of various boards, some devoted to topics such as anime or food and cooking. The most popular and infamous is the random board, /b/. Obscene and destructive, it is popularly described as "the id of the Internet." At first glance, /b/ seems anarchic. Images are posted so quickly—4chan gets 1,000,000 posts a day[24]—that each screen refresh yields a new crop of raunchy, puerile, and offensive

FIGURES 7.2–7.6

Lolcats are pictures of cats with added captions. The captions themselves are in-jokes. They are easy to make, but one must understand the swiftly evolving idiom to create one that fits. Figure 7.2 and 7.3, for example, are plays on the phrase “im in ur base killin ur d00dz,” a popular gaming meme. Such in-jokes can function as cultural boundaries when only people who know the underlying pattern can understand the joke. A picture of the economist Adam Smith captioned with his famous phrase, “invisible hand,” does not seem funny at first glance. But in context with other “invisible [noun]” images (figures 7.4 and 7.5), it becomes humorous.

7.2

7.3

7.4

7.5

7.6

postings. The comments are unintelligible to a newcomer, filled with repeated references to "ponies," "newfags," "rolling," "bumping," and other in-jokes. Yet out of this chaos have emerged numerous memes that spread widely across the Internet, such as lolcats (pictures of cats with funny captions—see figures 7.2–7.6) and rickrolling (tricking readers to clicking on what they think is a relevant link only to get, instead, a video of Rick Astley singing "Never Gonna Give You Up"). It has also launched anonymous activist actions including cyber-attacks on the Church of Scientology. Users of the board have participated in large distributed denial of service attacks (DDOS), taking down websites of organizations, including antipiracy sites and news media sites that criticize them.[25] Though it has no formal organization or recognized leaders, the sheer size of the anonymous crowd that assembles on /b/ gives it power. Understanding the order in its seeming chaos can help us understand the source of its incisive creativity.

Almost all postings on 4chan are anonymous, including on the more innocuous boards, such as paper-crafting or science and math. Even if you do post with a name, anyone else can use that name, too. Though unique identities can be created using a technique called tripcodes (see figures 7.7 and 7.8), in this looking-glass discussion world creating an identity is perceived as unpleasantly attention-seeking.[26] On 4chan, although anonymity lowers inhibitions and allows more flaming and antisocial behavior, it can also foster stronger communal identity and encourage equity in participation (Bernstein et al. 2011).

Though anonymous, 4chan still has boundaries. To keep out automated spam, you must solve a CAPTCHA for every posting.[27] There are moderators and "janitors," hand-picked from the participant community; they are also anonymous, and forbidden to reveal their role on the boards. The moderators can delete postings and ban users; though participation is anonymous, users who break the rules have their IP address banned from the site for an arbitrary time. Rules vary from board to board—some are meant to be "worksafe," while /b/ is a (nearly) anything-goes board—but posting material that is illegal in the United States, being under eighteen, posting personal information, or calls to invasion will still get you banned from it.[28] Underlying the free-wheeling chaos of 4chan is a cryptic and sometimes arbitrary autocracy. For all boards except /b/, Rule 8 is "Complaining about 4chan (its policies, moderation, etc.) on the imageboards can result in post deletion and banishment." Many rules do not apply in /b/—and its own first rule is "ZOMG

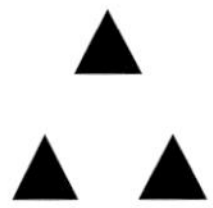

FIGURE 7.7
Correctly formed triforce.

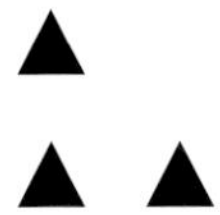

FIGURE 7.8
Incorrect triforce. One way of displaying status on 4chan is through the display of esoteric knowledge, such as knowing how to display a "triforce," a triangle of composed of three smaller triangles. If you copy and paste one that someone else has posted, it will appear incorrectly (see figure 7.8); only if you know the correct ASCII code will yours appear properly formed (see figure 7.7). A poster may challenge another to make this picture, and if he cannot, he is derided as a newcomer (http://knowyourmeme.com/memes/newfags-cant-triforce).

NONE!!!" (i.e., "Oh My God, None!!!"), with a note stating that this anarchic freedom applies to the moderators also.

For the first-time visitor, /b/ can be nearly unintelligible, filled with in-jokes, obscure references, and games whose goals and rules seem impenetrable. Such jokes and rules are emergent, bubbling up from the community; like the latest fashion, once too many people are familiar with them, they cease to be of use to the insiders. This is a knowledge boundary, separating the insiders from newcomers and curious observers. Status is signaled through complex codes and one needs to participate for a while to gain the knowledge—the communicative competence—required to compose an insider's well-received contribution.

Although reputation does not exist in this anonymous space, the dynamics of up-voting interesting posts still do. The board is designed so that the threads with the newest content are displayed at the top of the screen. Only a limited number of threads are kept on the board: once a thread slips below a certain position it is pruned, permanently deleted. This ephemerality—a rarity online, where permanent archiving is the norm—helps hone the community's ability to create imaginative and contagious memes. Given how quickly new postings appear on /b/, participants must keep actively commenting on a thread they like in order to keep it alive; a comment that is itself witty or provocative will help inspire more people to keep it going.[29]

Its ephemerality also gives this written space some similarity to oral narratives, with their memory-aiding repeated formulaic themes.[30] Because written texts do not rely on memory, they can discuss complex, abstract themes; their characters and details can be more subtle and mundane than the archetypes of oral narrative. They can be rewritten and perfected. Oral narratives, by contrast, are composed of regular and memorable sequences that are repeated in various forms. They are often redundant, ensuring that audience members who missed hearing a section will still get all the information. The oral narrative that is not repeated disappears quickly into the past.

Walter Ong, an authority on the historical transition from oral to written culture, notes that oral cultures are often combative, engaging in stylized verbal hostility:

> Proverbs and riddles are not used simply to store knowledge but to engage others in verbal and intellectual combat: utterance of one proverb or riddle challenges hearers to top it with a more apposite or a contradictory one. Bragging about one's own prowess and/or verbal tongue-lashings of an opponent figure regularly in encounters between characters in narrative. (Ong 2002, 43)

At times, /b/ has the feel of a crowd, a faceless, anonymous mob. Ephemerality gives it an insistence on speedy action; act now or it will be too late. The transgression of viewing its hostile and shocking images gives the adrenaline rush that comes from taking part in a forbidden activity.

Though Stack Overflow and 4chan/b/ could hardly be more different, they share some key structures. They both use knowledge boundaries (CAPTCHAs) as protection against spam; they both allow anonymous postings (though they are the norm in 4chan and discouraged elsewhere); they both rely on moderation to eliminate poor-quality postings, and draw from user response to highlight good ones. To varying degrees, these communities police themselves. Participants who have been deemed by other participants to be exemplary contributors gain additional abilities to rate content and establish other users' reputations.

In their very different ways, these systems have all implemented the infrastructures that Ostrom observed were characteristic of successfully managed commons. They have boundaries and rules about proper usage, and the community itself has the ability to enforce those rules. Their rules are "adapted to local needs and conditions," resulting in the generation of knowledge on the Stack Exchange sites, the fast exchange of news on Slashdot, and the creation of a bizarre and trenchant culture on 4chan.

It will be interesting to see how these sites will evolve in the ever-changing context of the Internet (had we studied Usenet in 1990, we would have made a very different assessment about its long-term viability). 4chan, for example, is financially unsupportable. Although it is one of the most heavily trafficked sites on the Web, it takes in very little advertising revenue; few companies want to be associated with its offensive content. The Stack Exchange model seems to work very well for technical areas, but as it has expanded into more social topics, the results are uneven. Some topics, such as parenting or personal productivity, lend themselves to a more social format than this model's rigid voting and removal of questions that "will likely solicit opinion, debate, arguments, polling, or extended discussion."

None of these sites requires participants to use their real-world identity. Slashdot uses permanent pseudonyms; /b/ discourages even pseudonymous identities (but then again it embraces much of the behavior that real-world identity is lauded for hindering). Even the most serious of the Stack Exchange sites do not require real names. MathOverflow's introductory page says:

> Using real names reminds everybody that they are corresponding with real people, and it demonstrates a certain level of personal investment in your MathOverflow identity. If you use a pseudonym and you get into some kind of trouble (e.g. fights in comment threads or spammy-looking posts), the moderators are much less likely to give you the benefit of the doubt.[31]

At the same time, they recognize that someone might have good reasons use a pseudonym, ranging from insecurity (is my question so naive that I should be embarrassed asking it?) to confidentiality (my question is about a paper that I am reviewing anonymously).

CONCLUSION

The "human net" of electronically connected people that fascinated the early ARPANET and Usenet participants goes "beyond being there" by dissolving the spatial and temporal boundaries that limit face-to-face interactions to currently present, nearby people. It also dissolves the boundaries of conversational and organizational scale. Online, we can converse and create with multitudes.

But boundaries are not merely constraining limits, forbidding people from accessing what they want. They are also essential for establishing community. Without boundaries, communication becomes chaotic. The key challenge for online communities is to figure out how to structure the new boundaries—how to make them porous enough so that new people and new ideas can enter, yet impervious against those who would disrupt the community.

It is easy for us to see the need for boundaries in physical spaces, to see how a commons of fish stocks or pasturage can be wasted by excessive use. But it was not obvious, at first, that this would always be true in the online world. Full openness seemed like a good idea: the more people who have access to the public good of knowledge, the better. But online communities are complex ecosystems. Not all contributions to a conversation are of equal value, readers' time and interest are limited, and there are destructive forces the community must guard against. For the designer of tomorrow's communities (and thus of their boundaries), the history of Usenet vividly illustrates how boundaries evolve in response to changing circumstances, and what happens when they fail.

The concept of boundaries draws heavily on the metaphor of walls and containers. But online boundaries are made of information—codes one must know, points one must acquire, levels of status one must attain. The challenge for designers is to understand the social impact of these various types of knowledge walls and data gates: how do they influence how people contribute? Who and what do they exclude?

We have looked at several online boundary strategies in this chapter. Identity is often—but not always—the foundation. Identity enables reputation, so a community can welcome or reject someone based on his or her past behavior. This identity may be pseudonymous, but it must be persistent. In general, people act more conservatively the more that is known about them, and the more they risk if their actions are deemed inappropriate. There are also boundary strategies that do not rely on identity, assessing instead the value of the contribution, without necessarily knowing who the contributor is. Here the burden of assessing the material is greater, but the range of contributions is wider (and wilder).

In the physical world, our bodies anchor our identity. We recognize people by their faces; this is the basis of reputation. We hear a person's words coming from their body: it is easy to associate actions with an individual. We create boundaries that limit where bodies can go, some porous and easily surmounted, such as sidewalks or the rooms within houses, others much stronger, like the prison walls that confine those who transgress society's laws.

Online, there are no bodies, only information. Identity becomes amorphous and the participants in a discussion often blur into an inchoate form. A person banned for misbehavior reappears in easily assumed new guises (Dibbell 1993). However, we can construct information bodies through accumulated data and interaction history. The design of these bodies shapes how identity manifests in the online world. What are the cues we want to use to recognize each other? What are the boundaries we want to enforce?

In later chapters, we will examine two related issues. Chapter 9, "Constructing Identity," looks closely at how we know who others are, both as particular individuals and as social types. Both are relevant for understanding social boundaries: individual identity enables reputation, and social identity allows for including or excluding groups based a few easily assessed cues—something that can be essential for bounding communities, but which is also the basis of harmful prejudice. One of the great early beliefs about the social transformation that the Net would bring was that it would eliminate the boundaries of race and gender; "Constructing Identity" looks at whether this has happened, how desirable it is, and what alternative social framework we may wish to create. In this chapter, we have mostly assumed that the material created in these large conversation spaces is public. Yet not all information is. Chapter 11, "Privacy and Public Space," looks at the social and technical boundaries that separate private from public space. Here the focus is on how we perceive this boundary, for technology can make it porous and invisible.

8

DATA PORTRAITS

How we see people—ourselves as well as others—in the virtual world is perhaps the most challenging problem in the design of online spaces. Online, we have no inherent appearance. This is liberating, for we can rethink and recreate personal identity cues, or omit visual representation altogether. Yet a world in which it is difficult to perceive the inhabitants as distinct individuals can be dull and confusing. We are sensory beings, gaining much of our impressions of people and places through sight and sound. Text is excellent at communicating information, but a dry text interface does not provide the feel of a vibrant society. If we are to create more immersive and sensorial interfaces for social communication, one of the fundamental problems we must solve is how to represent the participants.

Data portraits are depictions of people made by visualizing data by and about them. These data can be anything: a portrait of someone's medical history (Plaisant et al. 1996), travels (Rekimoto, Miyaki, and Ishizawa 2007), shopping lists (Sherman 2006), and so on. We will focus here on the data people create in their online interactions: their email exchanges, status updates, and contributions to online discussions.

I call these depictions "portraits" rather than "visualizations" to emphasize the subjectivity of the representation. The goal of a visualization is often accuracy; it is a tool for scientific or sociological analysis. A portrait is an artistic production, shaped by the tension among the often-conflicting goals of the subject, artist, and audience. The subject wants to appear in the best possible light; the audience wants to gain insight about the subject; and the artist has his or her own aesthetic message to convey, as well as mediating between the subject and audience. The data portrait artist has an enormous number of choices to make in creating the portrait, beginning with deciding what data to show. Even given the decision to use, say, one's history in a conversation, decisions remain about which patterns to show and how to depict them. This is not to deny that data portraits are visualizations; they are. The distinction is in the conceptual framing.

The portrait framework helps us see that these decisions can be in cooperation or in conflict with the subject. Is it in the tradition of the commissioned portrait, where the subject has the final say on what is shown and what hidden? Or is it more like a street photograph, where the artist captures a starkly revealing image, fascinating to the audience but perhaps appalling for the subject? Visualizations share these issues, and certainly data portraits are a form of visualization. But there is a distinction.

The term "portrait" emphasizes that the representation is an evocative depiction, meant to convey something about the subject's character or place in society.[1] A portrait provides a salient, recognizable, characteristic, evocative, or symbolic representation of its subject. Facial portraits are the archetypal form—which is unsurprising, given that we are neurologically predisposed to recognizing other humans by facial structure. (If dogs were artists, perhaps they would portray each other via creatively rendered scents.) A person's face can tell us something about his or her place in society, character, and approach to the world.

The goal of portraiture—evoking a person's essential qualities—is a difficult challenge. Looking at traditional portraits, we see that many images of people's faces are not deeply evocative; many paintings barely capture a likeness, let alone an essence. Even many photographs, which are accurate recordings of the person's appearance at one particular place and moment, convey little of their subject's character (and often barely resemble them). The difficulty is not only in the rendering, but also in the source data; the face itself is a fallible indicator of character. We make inferences about personality and intention based on structural characteristics such as a heavy brow or weak chin, which in fact are very poor predictors of these traits. Creating portraits from data has the same challenges: one must base the portrait on salient and emblematic data and then represent it in a legible and intuitive form.

The "essential qualities" of a person vary from one culture to another. Medieval portraits emphasized one's position in a rigidly hierarchical society; nineteenth-century portraits showed an increasing interest in human psychology. Data portraits (besides their general context in the twenty-first-century world of computational analysis, algorithmic rendering, and online social media) reflect the mores of the community for which they are made, whether composed of health-measuring life-loggers, argumentative tabloid readers, or weapon-collecting role-playing gamers.

A data portrait can serve several purposes. It can be a mirror designed for private viewing of the data that exist about oneself and for managing the impression they make. It can function as a public portrait, whether as a work of art or as an avatar, representing the subject in an online interaction space. It can be used to make an activist statement about privacy, surveillance, and power in our culture.

For online communities, data portraiture can create recognizable and meaningful renderings of the participants. One of the big problems in these communities is that it is difficult to keep track of the other members (Hancock and Dunham 2001). For a newcomer to the community, or any participant in a very large group, it is hard to figure out others' roles and contributions. Even if you can see, for instance, all the comments that someone has made in an ongoing discussion, this unwieldy archive does not easily provide you with a clear picture of his or her role in the community. You would need to spend hours poring over transcripts, piecing an impression together through scattered remarks. Visualization reifies this data and condenses it into something we can easily perceive, compactly embodying a tremendous amount of information and making it possible to see years of activity in a single glance. Data portraits like this can help members of a community keep track of who the other participants are, showing the roles they play and creating a concise representation of the things they have said and done. Here, the portraits act as proxies for the subjects, affecting how others in the community act toward them.

Communities flourish when their members have stable identities, and upholding local norms enhances social status. Anonymity and its effective equivalent, cheap pseudonyms are, in general, antithetical to community. Yet a stable identity need not be a singular identity, nor does it need to be based on one's real name or tied to one's offline self. In the physical world, we can maintain separate personas in different contexts; but online, where searches can easily aggregate everything said and done under a particular identifier, using one's real name for all interactions eliminates the contextual privacy we take for granted in everyday life. Strong pseudonymous identities can have extensive histories and reputations within their community. They can thus provide the stability and motivation for social cooperation that we associate with "real" identity, yet also maintain privacy. Data portraits support pseudonymity by providing an effective way to see these histories and reputations; they are a picture of the person's actions in the local space, rather than merely a photo of his or her offline appearance.

Data portraits also function as mirrors. Voluntarily or not, we all leave an increasingly detailed trail of data behind us—a history not only of deliberately published interactions, but also of our searches, movements, and the mentions others make of us. Being able to see the patterns of these data trails—the impression given off by our recorded actions—can help us decide how we want to modify our behavior to shape our virtual persona. Looking at yourself through such a lens could, with the relevant data, make it easy to see if you talk more or less than others, or if you answer your share of questions in addition to seeking advice. On the positive side, this is socialization; we see ourselves as others see us and modify our behaviors to conform to our community's standards and to gain status according to its values. On the negative side, we have the chilling effect of ubiquitous surveillance, where our self-awareness of the inferences that might be drawn from what we do causes us to greatly curtail our comments and actions.

Data portraiture raises many questions, including who controls the depiction, what purpose can it serve, and how can we create a vivid portrayal of a person using data about him instead of creating an image of his physical features? To address them, we will start by seeing how artists of different eras, with their varied conceptions about what is important to know about a person, have represented people. We will then look at recent examples of data portraits, and the varied approaches they use to translate material such as their subject's online interactions into a visual depiction. Finally, we will look at the big conceptual changes that arise when the "artist" is a machine: how does it affect the negotiation between subject and artist about how the former should be portrayed? What brings insight to the mechanical eye?

A BRIEF HISTORY OF PORTRAITURE

A portrait reflects its era's concepts of identity. Throughout history, portraits have been about much more than simply showing what someone looks like. Their purpose is to convey something about who their subjects are, though what is considered significant varies among cultures. Our notions of identity,

FIGURE 8.1
Bartolo di Fredi, *Nativity and the Adoration of the Shepherds* (14th c.).

Medieval art was not concerned with creating an illusion of reality; the role of the image was to remind the viewer of the symbolic significance of the depicted people and objects, rather than their appearance. Spiritual relationship, not the demands of perspective or cohesive narrative, guided the placement of things (Dunning 1991). Bartolo di Fredi's panel (figure 8.1), for example, presents "the Adoration of the Christ Child" and "the Annunciation to the Shepherds"—events that took place at different times and places—in a single image; it depicts Mary as larger than the shepherds, showing her greater spiritual significance, not her physical size.

Although the concerns and beliefs of today's online world are vastly different from the mystical, nonscientific worldview of the Middle Ages, art from that distant time can provide inspiration for using the screen as a symbolic space in which to depict relationships, events, and status.

of the constancy of a person in different circumstances and throughout life, are culturally constructed; as notions of identity change, so do portraits.

The Middle Ages did not hold immediate, fleshy reality in high regard, rejecting material life in favor of the spiritual. Early medieval portraits of rulers often did not depict the actual appearance of the living person. Instead, they used the image of the long ago Roman emperor in whose succession the ruler claimed to be standing. The portrait thus showed the historical, political, and social context in which the subject wished to be viewed, rather than the earthly, physical visage (Schneider 2002).

The Late Middle Ages and the Renaissance saw a renewed fascination with the surrounding world. Lifelikeness became the goal of portraiture, and painters acquired great technical skill in recreating the appearance of their sitters and in rendering the richly symbolic clothes and objects that represented class and status in an increasingly complicated world. The relationship between artist and subject also became more complicated. Although lifelikeness was the artist's goal, most sitters also wanted a flattering rendering, and the sitter's patronage was important to most artists (Woods-Marsden 1987).

Until photography, a painting was the only way to capture and preserve how someone looked at a certain time, or to convey that image to others at a distance. When King Henry VIII of England was seeking a new queen after the death of his third wife, he sent Hans Holbein to paint portraits of various prospective brides, including Anne of Cleves, whom the King eventually chose as his fourth wife. Although Henry had found her portrait attractive and, on the basis of it and other descriptions, contracted to marry her, once he met her in person he was repelled by her, and the marriage was quickly annulled (Warnicke 2000). Paintings could be proxies: a painting of a ruler in his chair was accorded the same gestures that would be given to the monarch himself (viewers uncovered their heads and were careful not to turn their backs to the portrait); portraits of criminals who could not be found could be executed in their stead (Schneider 2002).

By the twentieth century, serious art was increasingly abstract. One reason is that photography brought an easy ability to capture a moment of reality, and thus verisimilitude became its provenance. Yet it was not only in reaction to this new technology that painting moved increasingly toward images that explore the nature of form, light, or movement, or diverge from representation completely.

FIGURE 8.2
Pablo Picasso, *Portrait of Daniel-Henry Kahnweiler* (1910).

The publication of Freud's *Interpretation of Dreams* in 1899 ushered in a century in which psychology and its attendant questions about how the mind works would be very influential. "Are we to paint what's on the face, what's inside the face, or what's behind it?" Picasso is famously said to have asked (see figure 8.2). A related intellectual theme was the increased awareness of the subjectivity of all perception (Baumer 1977). In painting, this was manifest in a shift to seeing the artist's vision, rather than the subject, as the primary point of an artwork. Twentieth-century painted portraits are far from the venerating images of the Renaissance: the subject is often distorted or otherwise made grotesque.

FIGURE 8.3
Queen Elizabeth I (the Darnley Portrait), artist unknown (c. 1575). Queen Elizabeth I kept tight control over how she was portrayed, and her portraits show her to be beautiful, strong, and powerful. The Darnley Portrait was an official portrait and the model for her face in later paintings: the Queen aged, but her image did not.

Five hundred years later, Lucien Freud painted a portrait of Queen Elizabeth II that was described by the chief art critic of the *Times* of London as "painful, brave, honest, stoical and, above all, clear sighted." Others were more blunt. The royal photographer for the *Sun* said, "Freud should be locked in the Tower for this" ("Freud royal portrait divides critics," 2001). The contrast between the images of these two Queen Elizabeths, five hundred years apart, reflects the greatly diminished power of the monarchy and the subsequent greater freedom of its portrayers. Had someone dared paint the first Elizabeth in an equivalent manner, it is likely that he would in fact have been locked in the Tower. (The Royal Collection Trust refused to grant permission to reproduce Freud's painting in this book.)

> The project of "portraying somebody in her/his individual originality or quality of essence" has come to an end. But portraiture as genre has become the form of new conceptions of subjectivity and new notions of representation. (van Alphen 1996, 254)

By mid-century, photography had become an inexpensive and popular hobby. Capturing reality was possible for anyone with a camera, not only a few skilled artists. It became the norm to photograph events such as vacations and birthdays; schools provided portraits of the pupils each year. It became clear, too, that simply capturing how someone looked at a given moment with a snapshot, though accurate, did not necessarily create an evocative portrait.

Today, we are in the age of information. Vast databanks collect details of our everyday life. The human genome is decoded. Although facial portraits, abstract and distorted though they may be, still define the genre, there are noteworthy works that use recordings and data to depict their subject. Sophie Calle's *Address Book* (1983) portrays her subject through other people's opinions. Upon finding a stranger's address book in the street, she called some of the numbers in it and asked about the owner. With the transcripts of these conversations and pictures illustrating what she had learned were his favorite activities, she created a portrait of a man through the words of his acquaintances. It's a fascinating work in its depiction of a person through the multiple lenses of varying acquaintances. And, it is a disturbing work in its invasion of the privacy of the man who had the misfortune to drop this collection of personal data, his list of contacts, at that particular place and time.

Portraits of people through their possessions (the inventory portrait) are physical data portraits. Some draw upon our cultural understanding of objects to express meaning. Peter Menzel's *Material World* (Menzel 1994) is a series of photographs of families around the world, with all their possessions displayed in front of their home. Although each family was chosen because it was deemed to be "statistically average" for its country, the photographs still read as highly individual portraits of specific people, evoked through the objects they live with. Rachel Strickland's *Portable Effects* (Strickland 1998) was an installation in which visitors were requested to empty whatever bag they had with them—a backpack or purse—and the contents and owner were photographed separately. The resulting images were exhibited in a gallery, where viewers were asked to try to match the right face to its possessions, testing the resemblance between face and data.

Others evoke their subject through the intimacy between a person and his or her objects. Christian Boltanski created a series of portraits called *Inventory of Objects Belonging to a Young Woman of Charleston, Inventory of Objects Belonging to a Woman of Bois-Colombes*, and so on, in which he selected a person, photographed his or her possessions, and published the images in a book. The art historian Ernst van Alphen argues that these non-representational portraits can evoke their subjects more successfully than the more traditional form:[2] "This success is due to the fact that one of the traditional components of the portrait has been exchanged for another semiotic principle. Similarity has gone, contiguity is proposed as the new mode of portraiture" (van Alphen 1996, 250).

Many contemporary self-portraits depict the artist through an intimately personal inventory. Tracy Emin's *Everybody I Have Ever Slept With* is a tent in which she appliquéd the names of 102 people she had slept with, from her grandmother with whom she had napped as a small child to her recent lovers (see figure 8.4). Here, the inventory is data: a list of names, not actual objects. As a self-portrait, for most viewers its concept is its most evocative feature:

FIGURE 8.4
Tracey Emin, *Everyone I Have Ever Slept With 1963–1995* (1995). Appliqued tent, mattress, and light. Copyright the artist. Courtesy White Cube. Photo: Stephen White.

we get an impression of someone almost aggressively eager to shock. It presents another level of legibility to viewers within her community who know, or know of, some of the people listed.

Emin's work is a forerunner to the social network portrait, in which we see a person through the set of people with whom she is connected; these portraits gain vividness only when we know something of the connections, as we saw in chapter 4. Such knowledge may come from being part of the artist's community, but it can also be part of the self-portrait, if it is itself made from evocative portraits of others.[3]

Not all data are expressive. Steve Miller's *Genetic Portrait of Isabel Goldsmith* is a beautiful, abstract-seeming painting of chromosomes cultured from its subject's white blood cells (see figure 8.5).[4] The depicted data

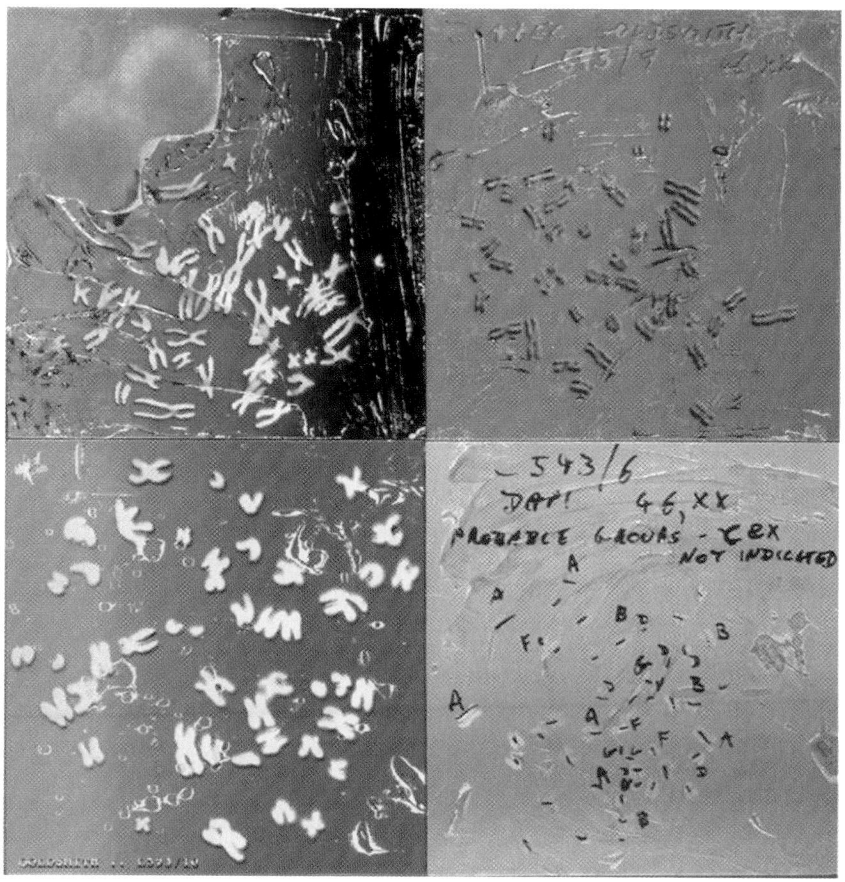

FIGURE 8.5
Steve Miller, *Genetic Portrait of Isabel Goldsmith* (1993).

comprise very much the essence of the person: DNA is what, at the biological level, makes the individual. But pictures of DNA are effectively meaningless; though so much is encoded in them, as a visual representation they are no more informative than random squiggles. What fascinates the viewer—and they are intriguing, enough so that a company now sells custom DNA portraits; you send them a sample and several hundred dollars and they send you a colorful wall-sized print of your DNA (DNA Art by DNA 11 2012)—is the idea that this indecipherable pattern is the key to who someone is. It is a portrait of a concept, not a person.

DESIGNING DATA PORTRAITS

In the late 1990s, my students and I began experimenting with ways to represent participants in online discussions. The Web, with its wealth of information and easy navigation, was attracting huge numbers of people online.[5] Discussion sites were having difficulty keeping up with the accelerating influx of newcomers who were unfamiliar with the customs and social rules, and people were having a hard time figuring out where the interesting discussions were. We wanted to make visualizations that would function as maps, guiding people where to go. More fundamentally, we were interested in making visualizations that would help people make sense of the other online participants and of the evolving social mores.

Making sense of the different personalities and complex social dynamics in a big online discussion is difficult, especially for newcomers. You see a person frequently referred to in other postings. Who is that person? Why does everyone seem to be ignoring one person's questions but eagerly answering another's? You say something and someone criticizes you. Are you dealing with a crank or with an authority in the group whom you need to take seriously? You might be able to answer some of these questions by painstakingly reading all the back correspondence, but there is also the problem of keeping track of people for whom you have no visual referent. In most online discussions, people are represented by email addresses or screen names. Sometimes these are quite memorable, but often they are either cryptically obscure or forgettably common. If there are four or five "Dans" in a group, it is easy to conflate them.

One solution is to add a visual representation of the participants; indeed, many discussion sites make it possible for people to accompany their postings with a photo or graphic. These images are of limited value. Photos are most useful for groups in which the participants know each other face to face, where they serve as a reminder of a familiar person. But a photo of oneself is not useful for anyone who wishes to be pseudonymous, or for those who do not wish their gender or race to be the most notable aspects of their identity. Arbitrary graphical icons are similar to a self-chosen screen name; they are arbitrary. A photo can be faked, and a graphic can falsely imply a skill or affiliation. Furthermore, they are far from unique, and popular ones, from sports team logos to cute cats, share many users.

The key problem was how to make a recognizable graphical image that would meaningfully represent a person. The most salient material, we decided, would be the actions of the person him- or herself. So we decided to visualize people's conversation history, with the goal of creating a compact representation, a portrait that would show the patterns of their actions within that context. Over the next several years, we made many portrait sketches, experimenting with approaches to rendering textual history.

The two big problems in creating a data portrait are choosing what data to show and designing the visual representation for it. In reviewing these portrait sketches, I will focus on the visual representation problem and, in particular, on the question of what makes a data portrait intuitively legible. A traditional portrait has a face, body, and expression—features in which we can easily read the subject's age, gender, and often also something of his or her character, social position, and dominant mood, even across cultures. But the data portrait is abstract. Making it intuitively legible, or intriguing enough that one is willing to learn to read it, is a key goal in designing data portraits.

Abstraction and Metaphor: *Authorlines* and *PeopleGarden*

Authorlines (Viégas and Smith 2004), a companion piece to *Newsgroup Crowds* discussed in chapter 6, uses a bubble graph to show the different roles individuals play within a group (see figure 8.6). Each column is a week, and the bubbles represent conversations the subject has been part of; the larger the bubble, the more posts she has written. Conversations that the subject has initiated appear as orange circles above the middle line; those initiated by others are yellow circles under the line.

Certain patterns of behavior are immediately apparent. Spammers almost always only initiate conversations (at least as of the time this work was

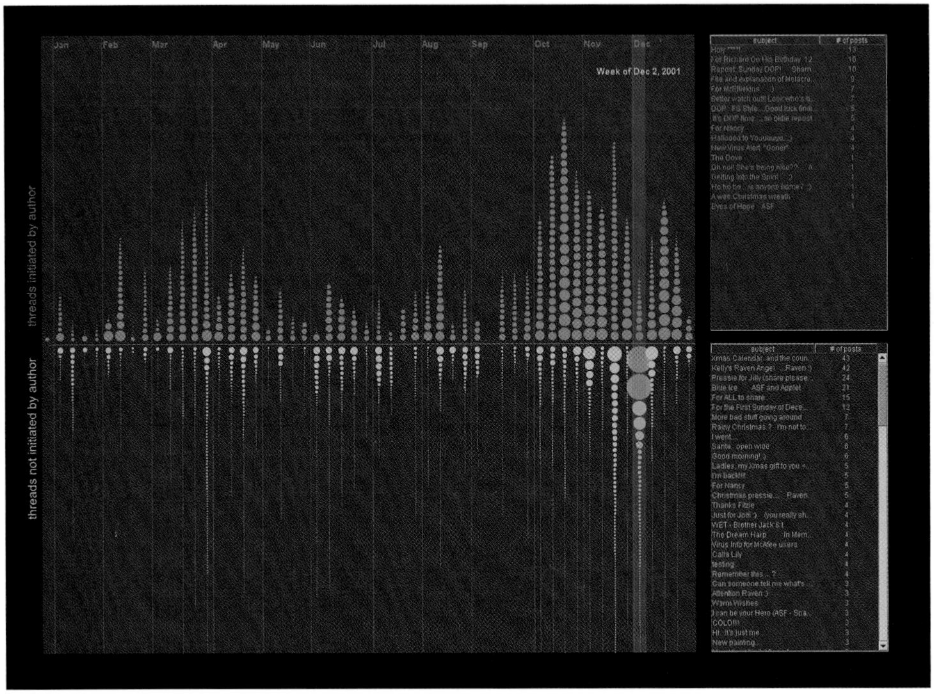

FIGURE 8.6
Fernanda Viégas and Marc Smith, *Authorlines* (2004).

created; they have since become more savvy about insinuating themselves into ongoing discussions) and do not follow up on their posts; their portrait shows lots of small bubbles, all above the midline. Someone who takes the role of an expert has a very different portrait. They initiate fewer postings but are likely to respond to others' questions, sometimes with a couple of postings. The portrait of people who take on the role of answerer has small but not uniform bubbles primarily in the response zone. Highly argumentative people may either initiate or respond; their portrait is recognizable by its large circles showing where they have gotten deeply embroiled in a disagreement.

Authorlines is clear and legible. It would be an invaluable tool for helping a participant or, especially, a newcomer, assess who is who within the community. However, the form of the portrait is itself part of the message-bearing content. Without knowing what the data is, one would never guess that it represented people rather than, say, mortgage failure rates or gross national product. It shows you statistics about a person but you do not think of it as a proxy for the person.

FIGURE 8.7
Rebecca Xiong and Judith Donath, *People Garden (thriving)* (1999).

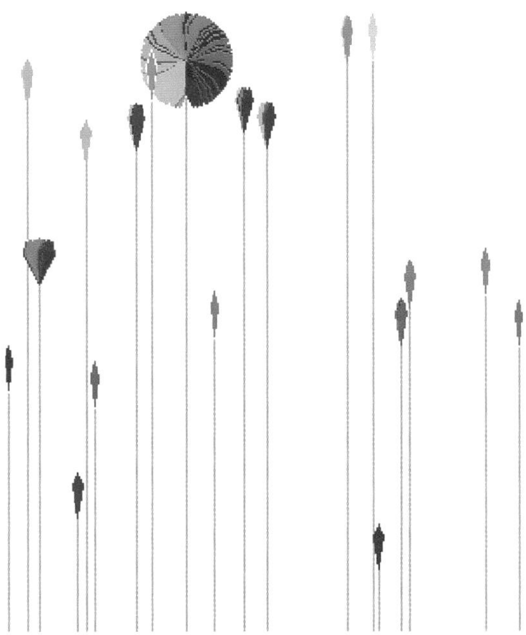

FIGURE 8.8
Rebecca Xiong and Judith Donath, *People Garden (abandoned)* (1999).

An early Sociable Media Group project, *PeopleGarden** (Xiong and Donath 1999), used organic forms to stand for the person (see figures 8.7 and 8.8). Its metaphorical poetics, which portrays the participants in a discussion group as flowers and the group as a garden, makes interpreting its meaning intuitive. As the height of a real flower indicates its age, the height of a *PeopleGarden* flower indicates how long someone has been posting to the group. The number of petals represents posting frequency; a lush blossom indicates an engaged contributor. A petal's color indicates whether it is an initial posting or a response and the color fades over time; it is easy to remember that a faded flower is an inactive participant. The flower metaphor makes the portraits easily legible. It gives them visual appeal and a sense of vitality; rather than a dry statistical graph, here the data appear as an enticing garden. The drawback is that the metaphor overwhelms the content it depicts. *PeopleGarden* portrays everyone as pretty flowers no matter how hostile or gruesome their comments are.

Metaphor is a powerful, but sometimes tricky, way to introduce meaning. The challenge in using metaphor is to abstract sufficiently from the source. A less figural representation could still draw meaning from our familiarity with natural forms without looking like a blossom; it could use growth and height to indicate age, brightness and fading to show recent presence, denseness of detail to indicate activity. This way, the representation achieves legibility without relying on literal depictions.

A key point to notice in the difference between *Authorlines* and *PeopleGarden* is neutrality. *Authorlines*' graphs are legible, but neutral. You can easily understand that larger quantities of circles and more of them represent an increase in some quantity, but you do not know whether this is desirable. Even after learning the key to the mapping, it is up to the viewer to interpret it, to decide what a "desirable" dataset is. *PeopleGarden*'s design implies values: we want the garden to be lush, to have many flowers with lots of petals. We may find it more attractive when the flowers are diverse, with different colors and heights.

Designers need to be aware of the values their visualizations promote. A discussion group with only three or four participants might still be quite useful and successful, but could appear scraggly and sparse in a *PeopleGarden*-like portrayal, unless, for example, the designer added a rule to keep interacting participants tightly bunched, distributing them at a distance from each other only if they communicated very little. The designer of any visualization, but especially one that functions as a proxy for a person, needs to be cognizant of what values the representation promotes.

Data in Human Shape: *Anthropomorphs* and *Lexigraphs I*

Another experimental interface from the Sociable Media Group, *Anthropomorphs** (Perry and Donath 2004), portrayed its subjects as humanlike forms, encoding numerous statistics into the size, shape, and posture of these bodies (see figure 8.9). For example, the more messages they had written, the higher their arms are raised; the higher the proportion of replies to initial posts they sent, the wider open their eyes; the more central they were to the group, measured by how many responses they received, the larger their legs are and the wider apart they are set. Each box on their body stands for one message the subject has sent, so the more prolific the subject, the bigger his or her abdomen. Their facial expression and body color reflect the emotional tone of their postings.

There were earlier attempts to use human forms as a medium for visualization. Herman Chernoff proposed representing data by varying the size, shape, and position of facial features (Chernoff 1973).[6] His idea was that since people are so good at recognizing faces and detecting the minute differences between them, we should be able to exploit this ability for depicting data. The problem with this is that the effect of moving and changing facial features has nonlinear perceptual results; making a single feature larger can change the overall expression and appearance of the face. A seemingly small change in a feature can appear significant, and vice versa.

FIGURE 8.9
Ethan Perry and Judith Donath, *Anthropomorphs* (2004). "PeterH has written a single message and has received no responses. Nova has posted three messages that have an anxious tone on average and has received a couple of responses. Ali is a more central figure in the group with several dozen messages and a variety of replies and responses" (Perry and Donath 2004).

Unlike Chernoff faces, *Anthropomorphs* makes use of the viewer's social and psychological interpretation of the work's humanoid form. It attempts to match the meaning of the data to the expression of the visualization. For example, how open the figure's eyes are indicates the subject's ratio of replies to initial postings: someone who is actively paying attention to others (making a lot of replies) would be depicted with wide-open, alert eyes. The width of the figure's stance indicates the number of responses the subject receives: the wide-set legs of the person who receives many responses is meant to show someone sturdily ensconced in the community.

Here, the problem is that the humanlike forms are too intuitive—we read too much into them. The prolific poster, who in *PeopleGarden* appears as a lush flower, here is big-bellied, his girth appearing to push his arms up from his sides; the novice looks, by contrast, compact and self-possessed. And I say "he" because this rendering, from the blue body to the wide stance, reads as male, though there is no reason to assume the subject is not, in fact, female. Furthermore, these particular human forms are quite cartoonlike. Some users found them cute and attractive, but to others they were cloying.

Although *Anthropomorphs* was not an entirely successful visualization, as an experiment we learned several things about the advantages and pitfalls of using human forms for depicting data. The central issue is that of unintended interpretations. When mapping a numerical quantity to growth in the form, one needs to be careful about making the form larger, not heavier. Different postures can indicate different emotions; unless you want the visualization to express these feelings, take care not to have it look dejected or triumphant, for example. In particular, if the portrait functions as a proxy for a person, it balances on a fine line between something that you can identify with and something that has an identity of its own.

One of the problems with *Anthropomorphs* was that the faces created characters. In a game environment, when one is playing a fictional role, a proxy with its own identity may work well. But for typical discussion groups, the proxy should not compete with the subject for human(like) identity. To address this, we designed a subsequent version with more abstract anthropomorphic visualizations. These had silhouette heads, with no faces, and elongated bodies. These were less cute and personable, which is more suitable for many applications (see figure 8.10).

The humanlike form has the advantage of immediately reading as a person. A group of such portraits is intuitively perceived as a group of people;

FIGURE 8.10
Ethan Perry and Judith Donath, *Anthropomorphs* (2004). Abstract and silhouetted version.

it does not risk being mistaken for a chart of mortgage rates or baseball statistics. The key is to find the right balance between figurative images and abstraction. Part of the appeal of the anthropomorphic depictions is that they read as individuals; the disadvantage is that they can easily convey unintended expressions and personalities. A more abstract rendering reduces the expression, but can also lose the individuality. One purpose for data portraits is to humanize the online experience, make us recognize these collections of words and statistics as representing real people. For this, the humanlike visualization form, problematic as it is, can often be a good solution.

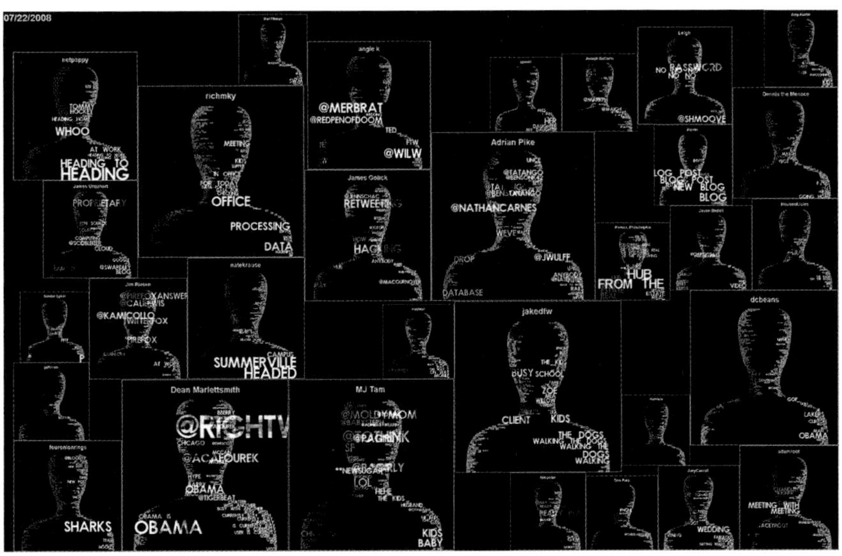

FIGURE 8.11
Alex Dragulescu and Judith Donath, *Lexigraphs I* (2009).

Another approach to using human forms in data portraiture is to use the form as a frame for the visualization, but not as a carrier of information. *Lexigraphs I** is a group portrait of Twitter users (Dragulescu 2009). Each person appears as a silhouette outlined in words derived from their updates, animated by the rhythm of their postings (see figure 8.11). The silhouettes are identically shaped; the individuality of the portrait is in the specific words and rhythms. The silhouette is thus purely decorative; it bears no specific information. Yet setting the words in the shape of heads contributes greatly to the sense that one is looking at portraits of individual people. It is important that these head shapes are themselves quite abstract; there are no features, simply the impression of a human. Edward Tufte, in his influential writings about graphical design, inveighed against "data ducks," decorative elements that distort or overwhelm the information the graphic should convey. Is making a data portrait in the outline of a head a form of data duck? Although the shape of the head does not provide data about the individual, I would argue that it is not a pointless decoration, but a design that immediately clues the viewer into perceiving the visualization as a portrait of a person. A community thus rendered becomes an inhabited cityscape, an online space where people-watching is an entertaining and informative pastime.

Incorporating Text

Words are the raw material of many data portraits, and incorporating the text itself into the portrait provides immediate context and detail. The challenge is to compress what may be a large body of words into a quickly readable image. For this reason, textual analysis is a key element in the design of data portraits. One approach is to highlight the most evocative words. *Lexigraphs I* analyzes word usage to find ones used with unusual frequency. The technique (discussed in greater detail below) is similar to that of creating a caricature: one finds the norm and highlights the ways that the subject deviates from it (Brennan 1985).

As with any portrait, there is a trade-off between expressivity and accuracy: the artist's vision, which can render the subject distinctly and vividly, also distorts the portrayal. An interface that allows the viewers to delve more deeply into the source material for the portrait—to see the original text and context from which the portrait was made—gives them both the concise representation of the portrait and the ability to form their own impression of the subject. This is especially important in situations, such as online communities, where the portrait functions as a proxy for the subject.

Multiples

> At the heart of quantitative reasoning is a single question: Compared to what? Small multiple designs, multivariate and data bountiful, answer directly by visually enforcing comparisons of changes, of the differences among objects, of the scope of alternatives. For a wide range of problems in data presentation, small multiples are the best design solution.
>
> —Edward Tufte (1990)

Data portraits usually exist in a series, created by applying an algorithm to the data of numerous subjects. The ability to compare among multiples makes these abstract depictions legible; it is primarily in the context of other portraits of similar design that we can understand a portrait's nuances and vocabulary. *Lexigraphs I*, for instance, shows a group of Twitter users, portraying each with salient words from their current and past updates. It animates with the rhythm of each user's postings. While we would get some impression from a single portrait, only upon seeing the whole group can we judge whether the person is notably prolific or unusually personal in their postings; these are relative qualities, and one needs to see the community to understand its individuals.

THE PORTRAIT'S TRIANGLE: ARTIST, SUBJECT, AUDIENCE

> A portrait photographer depends upon another person to complete his picture. The subject imagined, which in a sense is me, must be discovered in someone else willing to take part in a fiction he cannot possibly know about. My concerns are not his. We have separate ambitions for the image. His need to plead his case probably goes as deep as my need to plead mine, but the control is with me.
>
> —Richard Avedon, foreword to *In the American West* (1985)

Every portrait has an artist, a subject, and an audience. The tension between them is what creates the portrait: The subject wishes to appear in a positive light. The artist wants to create a good artwork, to represent the subject truthfully while also keeping him or her happy. The audience wants to get a sense of what the subject is like. When the subject's good will is very important to the artist, presenting him or her favorably will be paramount. The portrait must still have some resemblance to its subject, yet here the subject has great influence over the artist, and may request a flattering depiction. This can produce blandly agreeable depictions, such as the photographs of board members and CEOs that line corporate hallways. Yet it can also produce deeply insightful and empathic works (Cohen 2003). The great Renaissance portraits (e.g., Holbein's paintings of Henry VIII, Medici portraits) were commissioned works, and the painters could not offend the powerful merchants and royalty who were their subjects. Still, they managed to create revealing and compelling portrayals. When the subject is not a patron, the portrait may be far more stark and revealing. This is the relationship of the artist and subjects in Renaissance Dutch "genre" painting (Jan Steen, Franz Hals, Judith Leyster) and in contemporary art, from painting to street photography (Robert Frank, Lisette Model). What the viewer learns of the subject varies not only by the dynamics of the artist–subject relationship, but also by the artist's skill and inclination. There are great and revealing portraits of powerful patrons, as well as opaque ones made by artists whose interest is in surface and design, rather than in portraying the subject's psychology.

At the extreme are passport photos and mug shots, utilitarian images made for identifying the subjects, who in these cases have no say at all as to how they wish to appear. Here, the audience—immigration and law officials—is in control; there is no artistic vision set on furthering a career, and no desire on the subject's part to be thus immortalized. Though even here, especially with the mug shot, where the subject is likely to be feeling angry, frightened, or defiant, a strong sense of personality can seep through the regimented form. Mug shots of arrested civil rights workers, for example, show pride and dignity in their deliberate civil disobedience (Etheridge, Wilkins, and McWhorter 2008).

The photographer Richard Avedon pointed out that although photographic portraits are always accurate—light really did bounce off the subject's face in that particular way at some time—that does not mean they are objective; they present the artist's viewpoint. And, being accurate does not mean that they are true; they do not, he claims, get at some fundamental story or observation about the subject. In his foreword to *In the American West*, he argues: "A portrait is not a likeness. The moment an emotion or fact is transformed into a photograph it is no longer a fact but an opinion. There is no such thing as inaccuracy in a photograph. All photographs are accurate. None of them is the truth."

In the world of information visualization, the goal is to depict the data as objectively as possible. This is the opposite of art, where the artist's subjective vision is central. Data portraits sit between these extremes: their techniques come from the world of statistical analysis, but their purpose is artistic. Some may be closer to one extreme or the other; neither is "right," but understanding where a particular portrait falls in this subjectivity continuum is important to understanding its function.

One of the key aspects of art is choosing what not to show. Even in traditional painting, the artist chooses among all the possible poses and settings, omitting all but one. In creating a data portrait, the first decision is what data to show. Who controls the information a data portrait includes? Is it legitimate for the subject to omit data? If the portrait derives from my contributions to a conversation, can I edit my words? If it is made from, say, the times I punch in and out of work, can I change these data? There are no clear-cut answers to these questions. They depend on the purpose of the portrait, the intentions of the subject, and what message the portrait conveys about its relationship to accuracy.

Portraits that show one's history within a community usually cannot be edited. Their function is not simply to depict people as they are, but to promote acting within the norms of the group and pursuing the achievements that bring high status in that context. One changes one's portrait not by editing it after the fact, but by modifying one's actions. Such portraits are common in online role playing games, where the player profiles show such data as the player's role, skills, and achievements in the game (see figure 8.12). They are also used in "serious" sites. Stack Overflow, for example, is a successful knowledge-building site in which participants ask and answer questions about computer technology. It has a strict hierarchy of privileges, making status, in the form of "reputation points," highly sought after and valuable. The user profiles on this site feature subjects' total reputation points, the questions they have asked, and the community's assessment of them, as well as the answers they have supplied and how well they were received; it

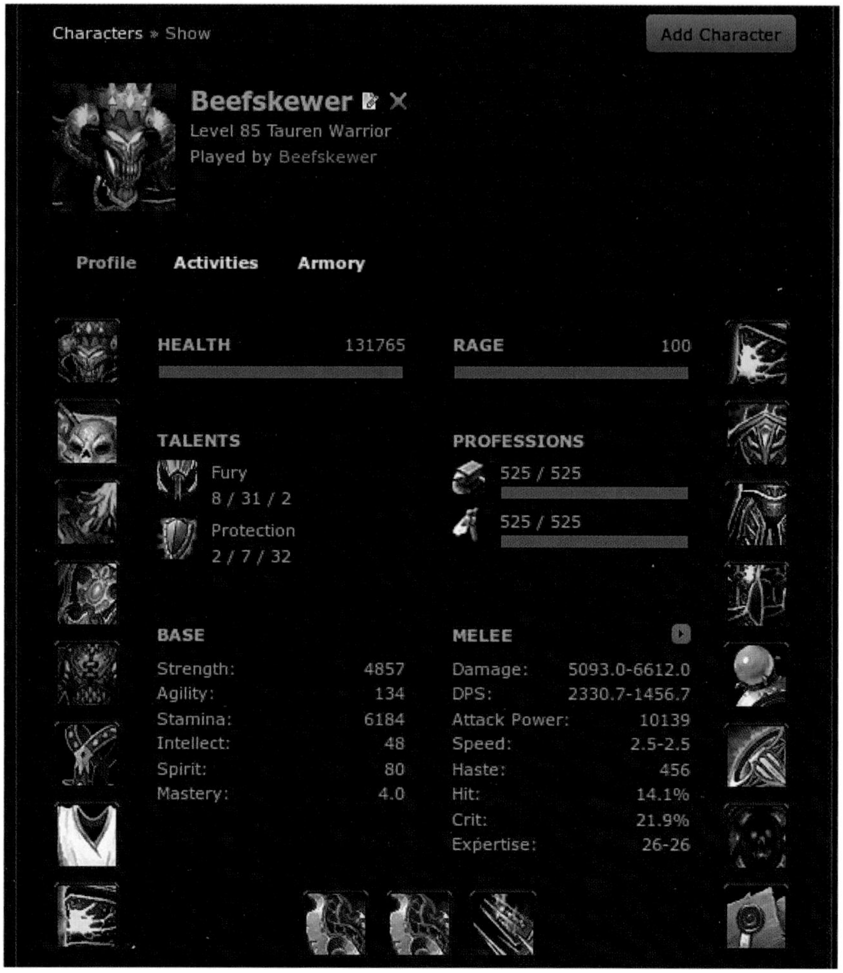

FIGURE 8.12
World of Warcraft profile.

also shows the topics to which they contribute, and other details about their participation on the site (see figure 8.13). Some Stack Overflow users remain pseudonymous, providing little information about their age, nationality, role in the physical world, and so on, yet they are vivid personas within the site, portrayed through its distinctive lens.

Other data portraits give the subject more control of the depiction. Today's self-written online profiles are primarily text, but people increasingly include data, whether as a link to their Twitter stream, statistics from various monitoring services (How far did you run this week? How many hours did

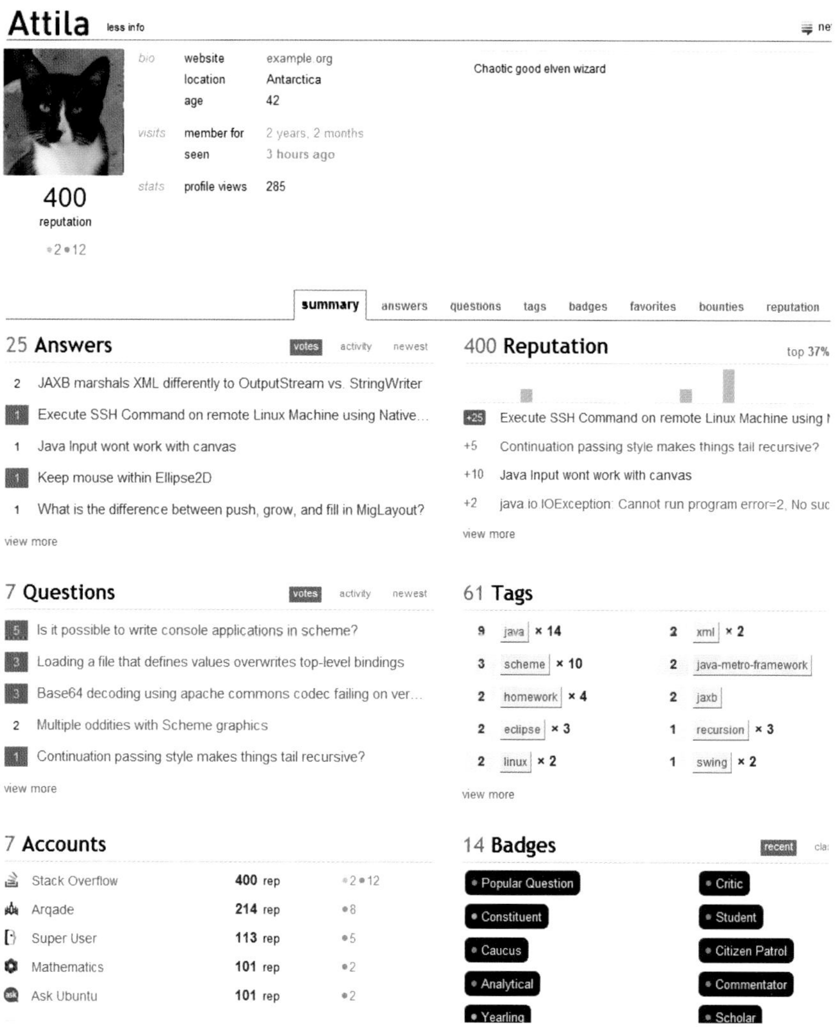

FIGURE 8.13
Stack Overflow profile.

you work?), updates on their travels, the music they are listening to, and so on. One can choose which of these data streams to include in one's self-portrait, but cannot alter the data itself. If I am embarrassed by how sporadically I exercise or how unadventurous my musical taste is, I can choose not to include this data stream in my profile, but I cannot—or at least, should not—falsify it.

Deception is possible, of course. The economics of honesty tell us that if the gains from being deceptive are high, people will lie; and if the cost of being deceived is high, the audience will demand more reliable signals (Donath 1998, forthcoming). For example, sites for self-monitoring athletic achievements allow users to record their daily statistics. In the general community, there is little concern about this; most viewers have little to lose if they falsely believe an acquaintance has been running steadily, when in actuality he's been sitting on the sofa.[7] In events such as races, however, self-reports do not count, only official measurements made by an outside authority. Here, cheating can be very tempting for some racers, but can be very costly to other, more honest ones, as well as to the audience who expects to see a fair race. Control over one's own portrayal of oneself works in situations where trust is high or where the cost of being deceived is low.

Giving people greater freedom to portray themselves, even falsely, can be revealing; discerning audiences can read a great deal into an untruthful self-portrait. The profiles in online dating sites are self-written descriptions. There are no technical controls to enforce honesty, yet people often reveal more than they intend. No one sets out to write a profile that says, "I am whiny and needy, quick to blame those around me for all my shortcomings," or "I am officious and pompous, ready to take over any gathering with my long-winded pronouncements"; yet such subtexts can be read into what the writer intended as a flattering self-depiction.[8] As data portraits become increasingly common forms of online self-representation, subjects, artists, and viewers will need to address the issue of what is acceptable data-retouching, and how to convey the existence or absence of such adjustments.

Having some measure of control over what data about oneself are made public is essential to maintaining privacy. Personal data can be very embarrassing if revealed out of context, to the wrong person, or at an inappropriate time. The obvious examples are things such as treatment for STDs, sappy love notes, or drunken pictures from one's youth. But many things can be embarrassing if taken out of context. Grocery lists—part of your personal database if you shop online or use a supermarket loyalty card—reveal our private eating habits. These facts might be perfectly ordinary, but they are still part of one's private domestic world, unsettling if revealed without your permission. The words of endearment I use with my children can embarrass me in front of my colleagues, while the professional jargon I use at work can seem stilted and pretentious in front of my family.

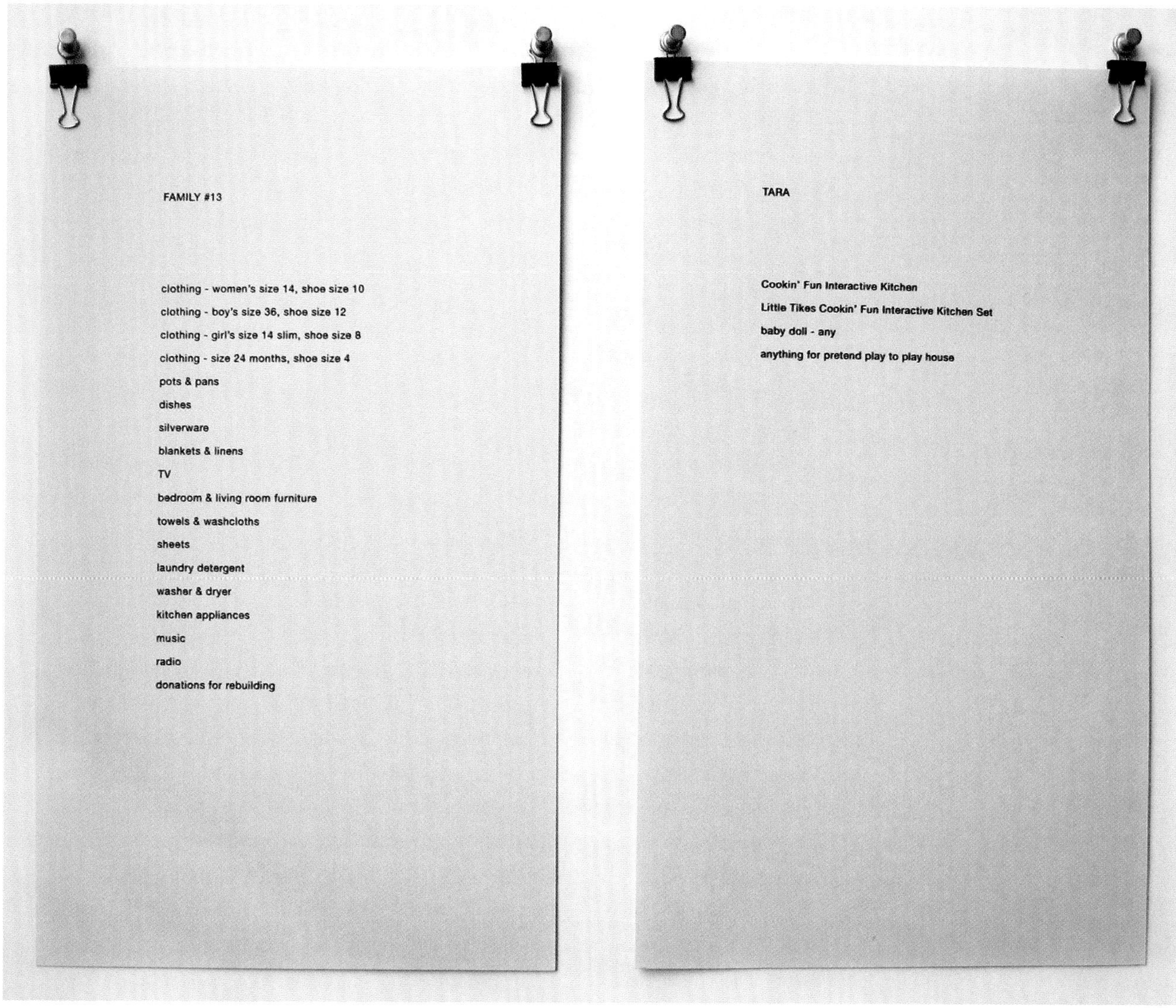

FIGURE 8.14
Kelly Sherman, *Wish List* (2006). Courtesy the artist and Barbara Krakow Gallery.

The artist Kelly Sherman has exhibited a series of portraits titled *Wish Lists* (Sherman 2006). Each was a person's wish list found online, typed onto a sheet of paper (see figure 8.14). One, for instance, called "Tara," listed:

scrapbooking supplies
non-breakable dishes and glasses
silverware
bathroom rugs and shower curtain
gift certificate for Ross
boom box with LL Cool J CD
fingernail polish

These simple lists are quite evocative. Like people-watching from a café seat, one can read these lists and make up stories about the people they represent, and make guesses about their age, home, and relationships. As with the imaginary biographies we compose about the passersby on the street, these are probably inaccurate, but nonetheless vivid. But *Wish Lists* does not feel intrusive. It is not a privacy violation, because there is no way to recognize the identity behind the list. The impression is vivid, but also anonymous. It does, however, highlight how evocative even the most innocuous information can be. This does not mean that we all need to hide our wish lists, grocery receipts, and all such mundane, telling details. We should, however, be aware of the how vividly they portray us. Removing information is one solution; so is adding it. If one's data portrait seems skewed and uncharacteristic, the solution may be to provide more information, to round out the portrayal and place the different details of one's daily life in their broader context.

THE MECHANICAL ARTIST/ALGORITHMIC PORTRAITS

Most data portraits are created algorithmically: the artist designs a program for making portraits, rather than the portraits themselves. Each step in the process—mining for data, analyzing it, and then depicting it—involves creative choices. But it is still an automated process—a final stage, perhaps, in the increasing mechanization of portraiture.

The traditional portrait was painted by hand, the artist consciously shaping each brush stroke. The advent of photography changed the artist's role in the work's creation; the photographer's eye and intention remained actively involved, but creating the image itself became the job of a machine.[9] Data portraits automate the process even further, raising questions about the artist's participation in his or her creation and about the source of meaning and artistic interpretation in these works.

Indeed, two aspects of automation distinguish the hand-painted portrait from the computer-generated one. First, there is the automation of rendering. Painting is a physical act, with each brushstroke laid by hand (Donath 2011). The algorithmic portrait, like a photograph, is produced by a machine; the artist need not ever touch the final object. Second, and more radical, is the automation of observation. Though a photograph is machine made, the artist observes the subject, decides when to shoot, and often chooses the most evocative (or flattering) shot among numerous images. With the algorithmic portrait, the artist, having finished designing the algorithm, need never see the subject or the subject's data. Photography automated the hand; algorithmic portraits automate the eye.

Traditional artists create portraits based on their responses to individual sitters, often spending days, even months, in close quarters with the subject. The artist with a portrait-machine can depict people without establishing any relationship with them; indeed, data-portraitist and subjects usually never meet. The subjects of data portraits, like the subjects in street photographs, are often unaware that they are being portrayed.

Yet in some ways, the line between algorithmic and handmade portraits is not as clear as it first seems. Artists bring their existing set of skills and techniques to each portrait. Some are highly attuned to each sitter, while others churn out rote images, applying their technique identically to each sitter. You need not look further than fifteen-minute pastel portraits commissioned for $20 in many tourist districts, or even at a gallery filled with nearly identical white-ruffed seventeenth-century nobility, to see that handmade portraits can be inexpressive and conventional, efficiently produced by following a set of painterly rules.

On the other hand, following rules and having a degree of separation from your subject do not rule out the creation of expressive and evocative portrayals. It depends on the rules and tools. Computational portraits can incorporate sophisticated algorithms that highlight the most salient features for evoking the individual. The programmer/artist, who never sees the subject nor touches the portrait, can in effect respond individually and meaningfully to different subjects.

One approach is to highlight how the subject differs from a given norm. Caricature works this way, by exaggerating the features that differentiate the subject. A facial caricature exaggerates features such as a prominent nose or small eyes:

> [Caricature] is a transformation which amplifies perceptually significant information while reducing less relevant details. The resulting distortion satisfies the beholder's mental model of what is unique about a particular face. Caricature ... can be considered a sophisticated form of semantic bandwidth compression. (Brennan 1985, 170)

What makes a caricature expressive is which features the artist chooses to amplify. For eyes alone, one could consider their overall size a feature, or how widely spaced they are, or their shape or angle. One could exaggerate the lines around them, the bags under them, or the eyelashes lining them. The artist's task is to determine which of the myriad possible features distinguish the subject in an interesting way.

We can use a caricature-like approach to highlight characteristic words and phrases in a body of text. "Term frequency–inverse document frequency," or TF-IDF (Salton 1988), is a statistical method of determining how significant a word is in a collection of words. Given some definition of normal word-frequency distribution, this method compares how frequently a given word occurs in a collection relative to its expected frequency. A word receives more weight the more frequently it appears, offset by giving little weight to common words.

Caricature exaggerates perceptually significant features that differ from a given norm (see figure 8.15). A traditional artist works from an internalized model of what constitutes an ordinary face. Different norms will result in highlighting different features as unusual and significant. Caricatures of people of a different race than the artist's norm will exaggerate the differences in typical facial structure between the two races.

Verbal portraits that use caricature-like techniques to highlight significant words must also choose their norms carefully. *Lexigraphs I*, which visualizes English-speaking Twitter users, compares their words with the norm of a large collection of Twitter updates, rather than the English language as a whole. Words such as "tweet" or "follower" are relatively rare in general, but very common on Twitter; using this corpus prevents words that are common

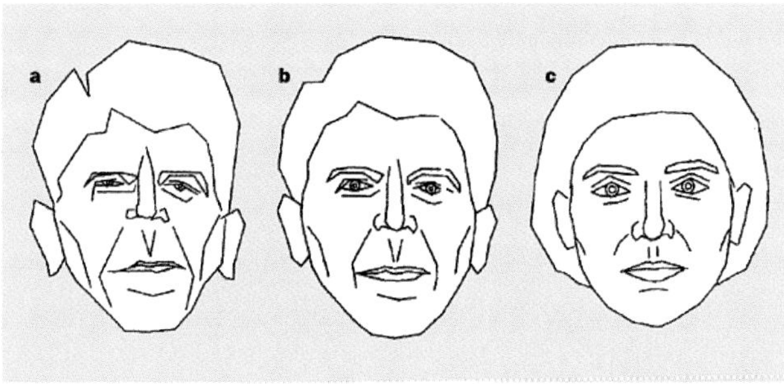

FIGURE 8.15
Susan Brennan, *Caricature Generator* (1985). Susan Brennan's *Caricature Generator* (Brennan 1985) was a program that created facial caricatures algorithmically. Here, the subject is Ronald Reagan. The image on the right is the norm, the middle is undistorted (source) image of Ronald Reagan, and the image on the left is Reagan caricatured by this program using that norm and source.

in this setting from being part of the portrait. If, however, you wanted to exaggerate for an outside audience the clichés of Twitter jargon, you could use ordinary English as the norm: the resulting portrait would be an exaggerated version of what makes someone's Twitter-speech so different from ordinary verbal exchange, and might feature, along with mentions of tweets and followers, many shortened words, abbreviations such as MT (modified tweet), and also different subject matter: a big proportion of my postings to Twitter—much bigger than their role in my everyday conversation—are mentions of political news stories and design innovations.

Themail, described in a previous chapter, varies the norms it uses in order to create a multilayered portrait of a pair of people. The background shows the words that typify all their correspondence in the context of general English usage, while the foreground shows how their discussion topics changed over time, found by setting their words for that period against the corpus of all their interactions.

Refining this technique further can produce even more vivid portraits. We can develop the requisite heuristics by creating portraits by hand, with the goal of articulating, and ultimately automating, the design decisions.

Like the automated word-frequency portraits, the handmade *Rhythm of Salience** emphasizes characteristic words (Abrams and Hall 2006; Donath 2006). It is a group portrait of the participants in a conversation; I made it by highlighting the words and phrases each person used that seemed to exemplify what I took to be their favored topics and typical speech patterns (see figure 8.16). For example, "Janet" was a facilitator of the conversation; her highlighted phrases include "common ground," "invitation," "question," and "expand that for me." Warren is a media theorist, and among his highlighted

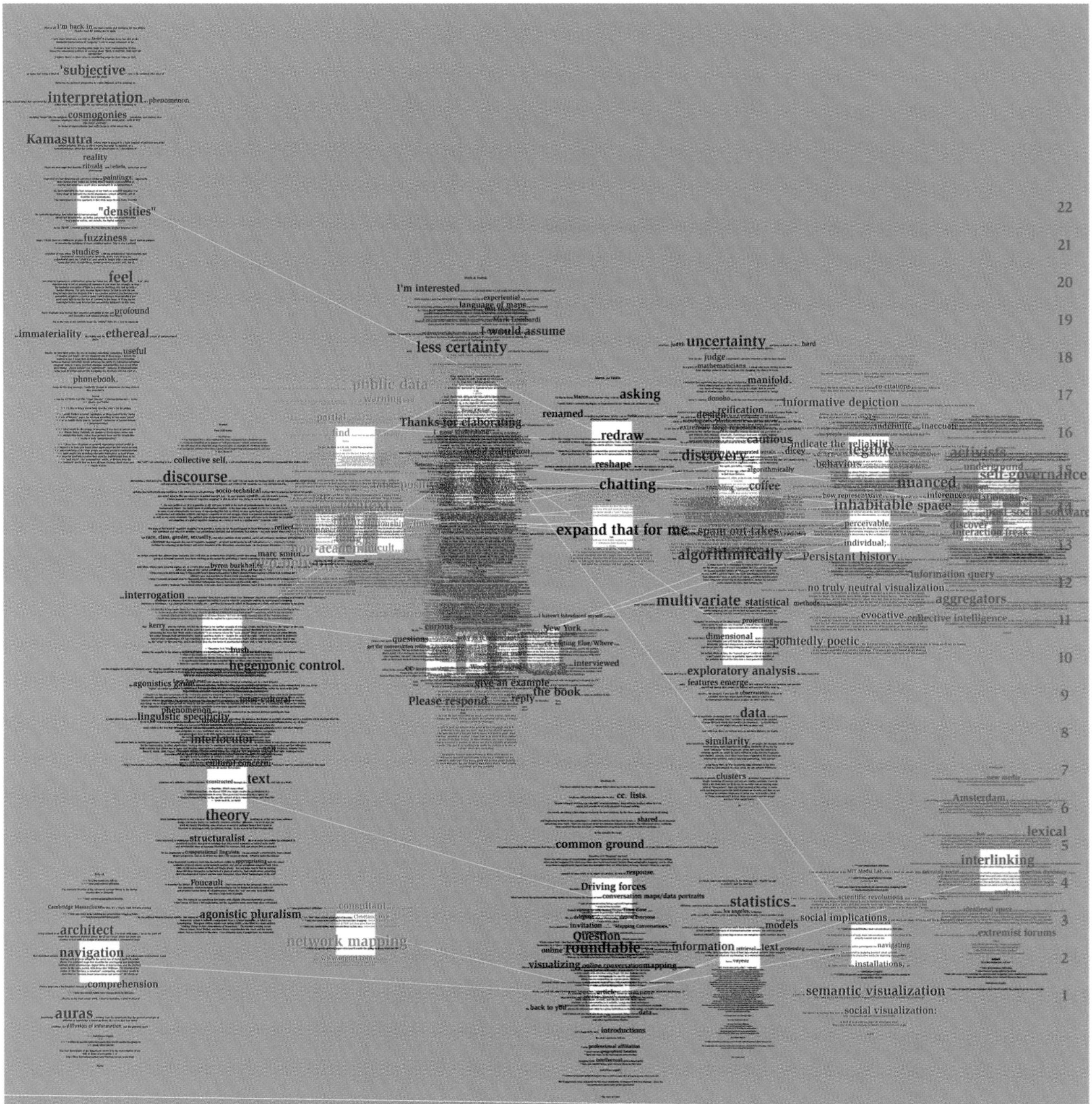

FIGURE 8.16
Judith Donath, *The Rhythm of Salience* (2006).

phrases are "agonistic pluralism," "hegemonic control," "discourse," "interrogation," and "Foucault." Also highlighted were common words such as "text" and "theory," which in his case were equally evocative. The portrait of Mark, a statistician, included "data," "similarity," "clusters," "statistics," and "multivariate"; "rambling" and "coffee" round out his portrayal. Note that with the basic TF-IDF algorithm, words such as "similarity" or "text" would manifest the same degree of significance regardless of who said them, but with this personal topic-based approach, they are given higher weight in the profile of someone who was typified by a relevant topic or role.

Rhythm of Salience is a handmade data portrait. The typifying topics were the artist's general impression of each person, and the highlighted words were ones that seemed to fit with that impression. Could this process be automated? To some extent, yes. Topic modeling is a rapidly developing field and computers are increasingly able to extract topics, emotional tone, and other semantic content from text (McCallum, Wang, and Corrada-Emmanuel 2007; Pang and Lee 2008). More difficult would be the humanizing details that help a portrait come alive, such as including the references to coffee and the self-conscious remark about rambling in the portrait of Mark the statistician.

If we gave ten people the raw data of the *Rhythm of Salience* and told them to highlight the most evocative phrases, we would see ten different portraits. It is easy for us to imagine such an exercise, and to understand that each artist would see the subjects from a different perspective and would find in their words different phrases to capture that impression. But it is important to remember that automated portraits are also subjective, that the mechanical artist has a point of view. The algorithmic artist expresses a vision for society by choosing which patterns to highlight and how to depict them. Even the most "objective" data portrait has some subjectivity in the data it shows and the color it uses. The visual style of a portrait can indicate its degree of subjectivity. The statistical graphs in *Authorlines* imply that it is an objective, factual depiction, whereas the cartoon figures in *Anthropomorphs* suggest a more subjective view, suited to its computational analysis of emotional content.

Furthermore, objectivity and accuracy are different, and a computational portrait can approach objectivity without being accurate. *Personas** is a piece that critiques the role of the machine as "artist" (Zinman 2009).[10] It creates a portrait based on the results of a Web search for the subject's name. It

FIGURE 8.17
Aaron Zinman and Judith Donath, *Personas* (2008).

analyzes the resulting texts and attempts to characterize the person by fitting him or her into a set of categories of roles and interests (see figure 8.17). The result is sometimes surprisingly apt, but can also be very far off, given the computer's inability to distinguish different people with the same name and its errors in language comprehension. *Personas* is a reminder of the fallibility, social naiveté, and opacity of the computer as portrayer in an era when such computer analysis of people is increasingly prevalent.

THE FUTURE—OR END—OF THE PORTRAIT

The art historian Richard Brilliant ends his book *Portraiture* with a warning:

> Indeed, before long, one may expect that instead of an artist's profile portrait the future will preserve only complete actuarial files, stored in some omniscient computer, ready to spew forth a different kind of personal profile, beginning with one's Social Security number. Then, and only then, will portraiture as a distinctive genre of art disappear. (Brilliant 1990, 174)

Is a data portrait—created by a machine, visually abstract, depicting a person through data—inherently dehumanizing? I argue that it is not. Data portraits have the potential to evoke the individuality of their subjects in ways that are not possible with traditional forms.

For example, a person's role in her social world—not her status, which traditional portraits have long depicted with displays of prized possessions and carefully chosen clothing, but her web of social ties, whether numerous and diverse, or fewer but dense and close—is a major part of her identity. Yet, with the exception of group portraits that depict a small family or corporate circle, the subject's social connections are at best implied in existing portraits. As we saw in the "Mapping Social Networks" chapter, depicting a person's social network and the communication that flows through it can be meaningful, evocative, and, owing to its great complexity, best rendered by machine.

We are still only novices in this field, still learning what kinds of data are expressive, still developing the vocabulary to display these data. This process involves all three parties, not just the artists. The viewers' understanding of the visual vocabulary must evolve along with that of the artists, and the subjects—who could be all of us—need think about how we wish to appear in the information world.

9

CONSTRUCTING IDENTITY

With only minimal cues, we are able to form vivid and detailed impressions of other people. In person, we see another's face, clothing, perhaps hear him speak—and after less than a minute, will have formed a strong opinion about his personality and his role and status in society. This impression helps us decide whether to trust him, and shapes our expectations of what he will do and our understanding of how we should act toward him. These impressions may, of course, be wrong—they are subjective and stereotypical, based on our previous experiences and influenced by our culture's mores and prejudices. But without this ability, we would be unable to make sense of society: each new person or situation we encountered would be completely novel, and we would be reduced to the social illiteracy of the tourist in a completely foreign culture, unable to understand how to act toward others or what to expect from them, unable to judge if others were acting appropriately or not.

Online, the process is the same, but the cues are different—and sparser. In many settings we do not see the other's face. There is no voice to hear, no clothing to evaluate. We may have only a screen name and a few lines of commentary to go on. With too little data, the result is a cipher. But with just a bit more information—sometimes even just a few words or an evocative name—we again form vivid, if not necessarily accurate, assessments.

With its different identity cues, the online world offers the intriguing possibility of being a place in which we can make sense of other people in fundamentally different ways. In particular, it raises the promise of eliminating the stereotypical impressions we form based on physical characteristics. In person, physical characteristics dominate our initial impressions. Although we do make some insightful judgments, physical cues also lead us to make erroneous, though pervasive and strongly held, assumptions about others.

Online, we can create spaces where identity is firmly tethered to one's real-world self, and where the impression you make online is as close as possible to the way you appear in person. We can create spaces where identity floats freely and fantastically, and you can claim to be whoever or whatever you please. We can create spaces where your history anchors your identity, but where many of the physical features people would see immediately in person are unknown.

In this chapter, we will take a close look at how we form impressions of others, with these questions in mind: Do we need the context of real-world identity to make sense of each other? Can we design social spaces in which people make better sense of each other than they do face to face—that ameliorate the prejudices stemming from physical trait–based impressions, while also avoiding the confusion and deceptions of easy, ungrounded identity claims?

CYBER UTOPIA

In the late 1980s and early 1990s, online social interaction—and identity experimentation—was becoming a mainstream experience. Colleges had begun routinely providing online access to incoming students, away from home for the first time and primed for self-reinvention. America Online and other consumer services offered easy access to disposable identities and anonymous chat-rooms. In 1993, the *New Yorker* published what would become its most reprinted cartoon ever, a picture of a dog sitting at a computer, telling his canine companion, "On the Internet, nobody knows you're a dog."

Many greeted this new, potentially post-gender, post-racial, and disembodied world with enthusiasm. "Cyber-utopian" writers predicted a future in which people judged each other on the merits of their words rather than their skin color, and where anyone could experience what it was like to be a man, or black, or fantastically beautiful—transformative experiences that might even carry over to reforming face-to-face society.[1]

In *Life on the Screen* (1995), psychologist and MIT professor Sherry Turkle wrote about the therapeutic value of online identity play:

> When people adopt an online persona … some sense the possibilities for self-discovery, even self-transformation. A more fluid sense of self allows a greater capacity for acknowledging diversity. … We do not feel compelled to

> rank or judge the elements of our multiplicity. We do not feel compelled to exclude what does not fit. (Turkle 1995, 260)

Turkle was writing about MUDs,[2] online fantasy worlds that Howard Rheingold, writing at around the same time, described as

> the wild side of cyberspace culture, where magic is real and identity is a fluid. ... MUDs are part of the latest phase in a long sequence of mental changes brought about by the invention and widespread use of symbolic tools. ... Similar to the way previous media dissolved social boundaries related to time and space, the latest computer-mediated communications media seem to dissolve boundaries of identity as well. (Rheingold 1993, 149)

In this view, "real life" is constraining, with limits imposed by social conventions, by accidents of birth, by lack of money. Online, one is free to imagine anything. If you are curious about what it is like to be the opposite sex, you can simply create a character of that gender and experience it. If you have always wanted to be a darkly mysterious foreigner, or a blond cheerleader, or a flying elf, online you could find a community where you could identify yourself as such, and others would go along with the fantasy. And if it was not too farfetched—that is, if you claimed to be a gifted male graduate student (though in fact were a forty-two-year old mother of three) rather than, say, a talking, clairvoyant frog—there was a good chance that the others would not just humor you, but would actually believe you, since any evidence to the contrary was sparse. Turkle quoted one MUD user:

> You can be whoever you want to be. You can completely redefine yourself if you want. You can be the opposite sex. You can be more talkative. You can be less talkative. Whatever. You can just be whoever you want, really, whoever you have the capacity to be. You don't have to worry about the slots other people put you in as much. It's easier to change the way people perceive you, because all they've got is what you show them. They don't look at your body and make assumptions. They don't hear your accent and make assumptions. All they see is your words. (Turkle 1995, 184)

It was not only the fantastical worlds of MUDs and role-playing games that provided opportunities to explore new identities. All over the Net, people were engaging in discussions with others whom they had never seen face to face, people whose race, attractiveness, and habitual expressions were unknown. Even if their names were known, in this disembodied world, identity was still markedly freer than in face-to-face experience. Discussing the WELL, an early online text-based community where people gathered to discuss anything from headache remedies to world politics, Howard Rheingold observed:

> Because we cannot see one another in cyberspace, gender, age, national origin, and physical appearance are not apparent unless a person wants to make such characteristics public. People whose physical handicaps make it difficult to form new friendships find that virtual communities treat them as they always wanted to be treated—as thinkers and transmitters of ideas and feeling beings, not carnal vessels with a certain appearance and way of walking and talking (or not walking and not talking). (Rheingold 1993, 11)

Today, elements of this ideal persist in various forms. News articles spark lively discussions among readers identified only by screen name on topics ranging from foreign policy to health care to vacation tips. Virtual worlds are lauded as places where the disabled can dance and autistic children learn to socialize. Millions of people worldwide play online role-playing games, in which they assume the guise of mythical figures, join guilds with other players, seek treasures, battle enemies, and live out an alternative existence.

But, as is often the case with idealistic visions, reality has proven to be more complex. Many people have found the fluidity of online identity to be deceptive rather than empowering; they do not enjoy finding out that the beautiful girl they had been flirting with is really a man, or that the expert advisor is still in junior high school.

Moreover, the ease of creating and abandoning identities has allowed people to misbehave without repercussions. In the earliest days of online communication, one's account was attached to one's position in a university or corporation, a connection that helped ensure responsible behavior. But by the early 1990s—the time of much of the most enthusiastic cyber-utopian writing—consumer Internet access was available for a monthly subscription, and Web-based sites, which are often anonymous, were rapidly gaining popularity.[3] These online identities are not only mutable, but disposable. And disposable identity has proved to be incompatible with community. Sites allowing anonymous postings are almost instantly flooded with pornography, commercial spam, and vicious hate speech. It appears that many people, freed from the responsibility of being their real-world self, behave rather badly.

Partly in reaction to the slipperiness of much online identity, social networking sites such as Facebook, which ground identity with solid ties to one's real-world self, became prominent in the early 2000s. These sites are the antithesis of the "wild side of cyberspace culture," for they make identity less fluid than it is even in face-to-face experience. In everyday life we typically maintain separate facets of identity: we play different roles in different social contexts, and may consciously try to reinvent ourselves at times of major personal disruption, such as moving away from home to college, and so on. Social network sites collapse these contexts, thus compelling their users to attempt to present a single identity that is appropriate across all situations.[4]

One can argue that reality has deflated the cyber-utopian dream and that the explosive growth of networking sites featuring participants' real-world identity shows where the future lies. Online discussions increasingly require participants to register with a verified and sometimes network-based identity; this not only reveals name and gender, but clearly situates the person in his or her real-world social position (Donath 2007; Ellison, Steinfield, and Lampe 2007; Jernigan and Mistree 2009; Utz 2010; Walther et al. 2008). Using a pseudonym and wanting not to connect your online actions with your real-world self is seen as suspicious: why, if your intentions are good, would you want to appear under a fake name? Anonymity is associated with trolls, scammers, and fringe activist groups.

It is easy, in this atmosphere, to forget the excitement and idealism that identity experimentation and anonymous communities sparked a couple of decades ago. Underlying the cyber-utopian ideal was a critique of the physical world as one in which people are tethered to identities based on immediately visible facial and bodily features—many of which, such as age, gender, and race, trigger deep-seated and often prejudicial stereotypes. Inherent to the ideal was the belief that these embodied social identities are not innate but culturally imposed, and that their markers are features only of the body. Online, where there is no body, the identities could vanish.

It is a controversial ideal. Does the absence of the body and of the visibly prominent and embodied features of race, gender, age, attractiveness, and so on lead to an absence of prejudice based on physical cues? Or are the cues to our real-world identities more than skin deep? Is identity volitional—a performance rather than an inherent state of being—and how does technology change this? What, if anything, is fundamentally different about how we make sense of other people online compared with face to face? To answer these questions, we need to look more closely at how we construct and perceive identity.

HOW WE MAKE SENSE OF PEOPLE

To start, we need to clarify what we mean by identity. The word "identity" refers to two different but intertwined phenomena. One is individual identity: who you are as opposed to any other person. This is the identity of social security numbers, fingerprints, passports, DNA testing, face recognition, and the like. The other is social identity: the type of person you are and your role in society.

Individual identity is fundamental for forming relationships: if you are my friend or lover, you are not replaceable with a similar other, no matter how strong the resemblance. We develop a shared history with individuals; as time passes, each relationship becomes more detailed and distinct. We base our decisions about future interactions with others on our knowledge of their past actions. In addition to immediate experience, this knowledge can come via reputation (the experiences of others) or history (records of the person's past actions), both of which require individual identity, the ability to connect memories and stories to a specific individual. We look more closely at issues around individual identity and identification online in chapter 11, "Privacy and Public Space."

This chapter focuses on the other phenomenon that the word "identity" refers to, social identity, a loosely defined concept that includes personality, interests, and social role. If you ask about a person "What is he like?" you are asking about social identity. Social identity is how people make sense of you—it is how they understand what sort of person you are, what type of relationship they might have with you, what behaviors they can expect from you, and how they should act toward you (Holland and Skinner 1987). We want to shape the impression others have of us so that they will act in desirable ways toward us (Goffman 1959).

These two aspects of identity are intertwined. The identifiers that we use to recognize and refer to an individual also reveal varying bits of social information. Numeric identifiers such as social security numbers reveal relatively little (though some encode social and demographic data), whereas names may indicate gender, ethnicity, social class, and so on.

Perceiving Social Identity

In a 1908 essay entitled "How Is Society Possible?" Georg Simmel, a founder of the field of sociology, presented the question of how we make sense of other people:

> The picture of another man that a man gains through personal contact with him is based on certain distortions. … We see the other person generalized, in some measure. This is so, perhaps, because we cannot fully represent to ourselves an individuality which deviates from our own. … We cannot know completely the individuality of another. …
>
> We conceive of each man—and this is a fact which has a specific effect upon our practical behavior toward him—as being the human type which is suggested by his individuality. We think of him in terms not only of his singularity but also in terms of a general category. This category, of course, does not fully cover him, nor does he fully cover it. …
>
> … Just as we compensate for a blind spot in our field of vision so that we are no longer aware of it, so a fragmentary structure is transformed by another's view into the completeness of an individuality. (Simmel 1959, 10)

Imagine being introduced to someone at a party. You observe that he is a man, white, middle-aged. You see the clothes he wears; you know the setting in which you are meeting; perhaps you see some of his acquaintances or exchange a few words. After even a brief meeting, you are likely to feel able to make a good guess about many unobserved characteristics—is he a sports fan? Would he like this joke? Whom did he vote for in the last election?

We can make these guesses because we have in our minds types of people. These types provide information about many features of their members; once we have classified someone as being of a particular type, we infer a much broader set of beliefs about him of her than our observations alone would bring.

These inferences may be wrong. Indeed, as Simmel pointed out, they are inevitably distorted. We develop types based on our experience. Since each person's experience is different from every other person's, each person's types are different, and thus the inferences they make about another, given the same observations, are different. For example, upon returning from a dinner party, a couple may discuss the people they had met that evening. Although both participated in the same experience, their impressions may be quite different.

"What did you think of the woman that Danny brought with him?" "She seemed very interesting. So artistic and creative." "You think so? She was certainly weirdly dressed, with everything mismatched and asymmetrical. But I didn't hear her say anything particularly interesting." Is Danny's date imaginatively talented or just an eccentric dresser? She may be both—or neither. The two people who are discussing her have formed different impressions based on their individual experiences and personal categories. Such conversations highlight the subjectivity of the participants' interpretations of the same social information.

Such conversations also help people develop shared cultural models, as they exchange and refine their viewpoints (Holland and Skinner 1987). One's own personality and experiences affect individual perceptions, but the basic types that we perceive, as well as our vocabulary for thinking about them and discussing them with others, we share across our culture. Our culture shapes our impressions of other people.

Prototype Theory

In the hundred years since Simmel wrote about our perception of people as different social types, anthropologists and cognitive scientists have learned more about how our social cognition works. To understand how we categorize people, it is useful to first look at how we comprehend everyday objects.

Classification is at the heart of how we make sense of the world—it is how we can see a new piece of furniture and know that it is a chair and can be sat upon, or meet a new person and know that she is a sweet old lady and should be deferred to. How do we do this? One might think we have definitions, for example, chairs are the set of objects with four legs and a platform big enough to sit on and a back on one side. But, while formal systems such as mathematics and biological classification are based on definitions (even numbers are whole numbers that are divisible by 2; mammals are warm-blooded vertebrates that have hair or fur and nurse their young), that is not how we make sense of our everyday world. Instead, we understand the world through prototypes (Lakoff 1987; Rosch 1975; Rosch et al. 1976).

Prototypes are the most central member of a category, its clearest example. Think of a bird. Chances are the bird you imagined resembles something like a robin or a sparrow and not a chicken or a penguin, even though those are birds, too. The bird in your imagination—your prototype of the category bird—might not be any specific species of bird, but it is distinct enough so you can note that some birds (robins, sparrows, finches) resemble it quite closely whereas others, such as owls, are less similar, and others, like ostriches, are more distant still. Robins and finches are termed prototypical members of the category bird: they closely resemble our conception of the typical member of the category.

These categories are learned and subjective. If you grew up in a world where penguins were the dominant avian species, your idea of the prototypical bird would be quite different. Culture also influences categories—even if you grew up surrounded by penguins, but your schoolbooks featured illustrations of typical English garden birds, you might still think of robin-like creatures as prototypical birds, although they were outside of your personal experience. Categories do not exist as independent external entities; we construct them through our interactions with the world and with each other.

Although the categories into which we classify physical things—birds, chairs, cars, trees, shades of red—are socially constructed, they are not arbitrary; they reflect the structure of the objects themselves. We also have many categories into which we classify social things—family, mother, geek, spinster, untouchable, hippie, hipster, and so on. These too are not arbitrary; they reflect the larger framework of how a culture structures the world. To understand why some unmarried men are "bachelors" and others are not (gay men, Catholic priests, men confined to mental institutions or in long-term, cohabiting relationships) requires understanding the culture notions about eligibility for marriage (Lakoff 1987).

Much can go unsaid in conversations with friends who share your cultural models, for you can simply refer to a shared prototype to conjure up a detailed picture. Discussions with people with different beliefs or from different cultures can be more difficult, for disparate types may populate your social worlds. Even where you share the basic types, your assessments of them may differ. A mother offers to introduce her twenty-year-old daughter to her friend's son, a nice boy who has a steady job in a bank and volunteers at church on the weekend; mother and daughter may share enough cultural foundation to agree upon the type of person he is, but may differ significantly on their assessment of whether it makes him desirable.

Some cultural categories exist only within a small community. In *To Kill a Mockingbird*, Miss Caroline, a new first-grade teacher in town, tries to lend a quarter to a boy who did not bring any lunch to school. Jean, another first-grader, attempts to explain to her why he will not accept it (Lee 1962).

> I rose graciously on Walter's behalf: "Ah—Miss Caroline?"
> "What is it, Jean Louise?"
> "Miss Caroline, he's a Cunningham."
> I sat back down.
> "What, Jean Louise?"
> I thought I had made things sufficiently clear. It was clear enough to the rest of us: Walter Cunningham was sitting there lying his head off. He didn't forget his lunch, he didn't have any. He had none today nor would he have any tomorrow or the next day. He had probably never seen three quarters together at the same time in his life.

The students in the class, as inhabitants of the town, shared a common knowledge of the different clans and neighborhoods; they knew what to expect of each and how to act toward them. Ordinarily, they would never state this knowledge out loud. However, the presence of a newcomer, who did not understand any of this and yet was in a position of authority, required that they explicitly describe their cognitive model of the local society.[5]

Online, the cues to identity are different and sparse, but the cognitive process of impression formation is the same,[6] and we can still form vivid impressions of others. In one study of this process, a participant, given simply a screen name, filled in the details as follows:

> JoshSamBob's name sounds like a white southerner. He fits my idea of a stereotypical frat boy. He's just under 6 feet tall, medium build, blonde hair, blue eyes, his lips are a bit thin. He's particular about what he wears and is in general very neat. He tends to fidget a lot and would much rather be out playing sports than sitting in a lecture hall or library. He enjoys horseplay and being where the action is. (Jacobson 1999)

Sparse cues can have the paradoxical effect of producing more intense impressions: absent specific individual details, we rely more heavily on our internal prototypes, including exaggerated stereotypes,[7] to fill in the blanks (Hancock and Dunham 2001).

Not all cues are evocative. A generic name, with no clear cultural meaning, such as gss93, will conjure up very little. But in the absence of information, we do not perceive others to be complete ciphers; instead, we bestow upon them what we imagine to be the typical identity in that setting. If you see a generic name in an online forum that you imagine to be populated by white men in their thirties, you will ascribe the qualities you associate with that type to an otherwise unmarked person.

Online discussions bring together people from around the world, with greatly varying cultural models. In the example above, you can imagine that the name "JoshSamBob" would evoke a different impression (or none at all) in a participant unfamiliar with the college culture of the American South. A name or behavior that makes a vivid impression on one person will imply something quite different to another. One challenge in making cross-cultural discussions work is to help people recognize these underlying differences and work toward creating common ground.

Mistaken Impressions

It is remarkable how much we can sometimes accurately infer from very little data. Studies estimate that people accurately assess personality about 70 percent of the time after observations as brief as thirty seconds (Ambady and Rosenthal 1992). Certain traits are more readily observable: people quickly recognize whether another is outgoing or introverted, dominant or passive, anxious or confident, warm or chilly. Other traits, such as creativity and intelligence, are harder to detect. Too, some people are more legible than others—unsurprisingly, those who are outgoing and confident provide more cues about themselves (Ambady, Hallahan, and Rosenthal 1995; Ambady and Rosenthal 1992; Funder 1995). And, the best judges are the "socially vulnerable": women, shy people, and people with lower self-esteem; they need to be more alert to the moods and intentions of others. Confident, outgoing people—less dependent on the whims and wishes of others—tend to be less accurate judges.

Overall, we are "good enough perceivers" of social traits (Fiske 1993): although we make many errors in our assessments of other people, we generally do well enough to make sense of and function in the world.

However, we do make pervasive errors in assessing others. The leaps of categorization that allow us to quickly make sense of a diverse social world also lead us to the distorted and harmful assumptions of racial prejudice and gender stereotypes. Studies have shown that people judge essays, job applications, musical performances, and the like lower when they think they were produced by a woman rather than a man (Bertrand and Mullainathan 2003; Goldin and Rouse 1997; Steinpreis, Anders, and Ritzke 1999).

Furthermore, we overgeneralize, too broadly assuming that a feature implies that a person has certain character and personality traits (Zebrowitz 1997; Zebrowitz and Montepare 2008). For example, Leslie Zebrowitz and colleagues have found that people ascribe characteristics such as naiveté and trustfulness to strangers who have small chins, upturned noses, big eyes, and other childlike features—although having those facial features does not correlate to actual personality differences. Zebrowitz hypothesized that our evolved response to babies and children—to nurture them, to expect naive behavior from them—was also triggered by individuals who happened to have those sorts of features as adults.

PERFORMING IDENTITY

One of the key visions the cyber-utopian writers set forth for online society was to have people's words and actions assessed on their merits rather than filtered through someone's belief that, say, black people or young mothers or people who speak with an accent are less intelligent and able. Merit-based assessment is possible online because embodied cues such as facial features that reveal gender and race or a receding chin that is equated with weakness can be unseen.

The desirability of masking an identity cue online depends on one's assessment of the validity of the prototypes it triggers. Let's say that the cue "female" tends to make people think of someone nurturing, passive, risk-averse, emotional, not intellectually rigorous. If you think that this is an accurate model for the prototypical woman, then you will see the cue of gender as being a very useful guide for understanding the other. If you think this prototype distorts the way people see women, then you may believe that eliminating the cues to gender can help women be perceived more accurately. These controversial questions arise about all aspects of identity: they are at the center of debates about racial and ethnic profiling, women's role in combat, men's parenting instincts, and so on.

In a society where roles are immutable, no such controversy arises. It is when roles are changing that claims about what traits are cultural or innate become hotly contested. The Internet, with its novel opportunity for identity reinvention, arrived at a historical moment that was already wrestling with these questions.

In medieval Europe, rulers and religious leaders exhorted their subjects to be content with their station in life, for it was divine will that made unequal positions and placed people in them (Herlihy 1973). Since then, rigid ideas about innate identity have been steadily loosening. Five hundred years ago, the appearance of guilds and a growing merchant class shook up the highly codified social structure of medieval feudalism. The eighteenth century saw the rise of democracy over inherited monarchy. In nineteenth and early twentieth-century America, slavery was abolished and voting rights were extended to all women. Today, although we still have many entrenched stereotypes, we accept that many aspects of someone's identity, including social status, religious beliefs, and the like, can change over time.

By the mid-twentieth century, the notion of identity as performance arose in both popular culture and intellectual writing. Popular fashion reflected a growing ambiguity in gender roles with the acceptance of women dressing in pants and other traditionally male garb. The world of ideas included works such as Erving Goffman's influential book *The Presentation of Self in Everyday Life* (1959), which used the metaphor of theater to describe society: daily life is a performance in which people attempt to create a desirable impression, within the constraints of their role in a particular context and their social (acting) abilities.

This dramaturgical model of society resonated strongly with growing social movements that questioned traditional roles. For generations, women had not been allowed to vote, own property, or pursue most careers—constraints based on the argument that women were biologically unfit owing to their smaller brains, excitable hormones, and destiny as child-bearers. As the women's movement gained force and these constraints were lifted, it became clear that women's lesser abilities were mostly culturally imposed. Girls acted silly not because they were silly, but because they were taught to do so.

In her book *Gender Trouble* (1990), radical feminist Judith Butler took this argument further, positing that all of masculinity and femininity is performance, separable from the physical shape of male or female bodies. Radical as her writing might be, she noted that the response to it had been even more extreme than she intended: “One of the interpretations that has been made of *Gender Trouble* is that there is no sex, there is only gender, and gender is performative. People then go on to think that if gender is performative it must be radically free. … What’s interesting is that this voluntarist interpretation, this desire for a kind of radical theatrical remaking of the body, is obviously out there in the public sphere. There’s a desire for a fully phantasmatic transfiguration of the body” (Osborne and Segal 1994, 110–111).

By the late twentieth century, traditional stereotypes based on visible characteristics were under attack, in realms ranging from academic cultural theory to everyday life. A growing body of laws, especially in Europe and the United States, forbade discrimination based on gender, race, or age. These traits, which people a generation earlier had assumed were legitimate, commonsense cues about a person’s character and suitability, have now become legally invisible. Although the goals of such legislation are less extreme than those of race- and gender-bending activists, they are evidence of a worldview in which identity is seen as personally constructed rather than anatomically destined.

It is into this cultural atmosphere that online communication arrived. It is thus not surprising that many idealistic visions for the technology focused on the opportunity to create social spaces in which one’s physical traits were unknown.

In the face-to-face world, even if it can be shown that most of the personality and cognitive traits associated with categories such as race and gender are culturally produced, many of the cues that place a person in these categories are inborn and immediately visible in one’s appearance, making it difficult to escape from them as basic ways of organizing the physical world.

But the online world seemed to present no such difficulty. With no body, you could just claim to be, well, whatever you wanted. Or could you?

Identity cues are given off in many forms, not just appearance. Writing—the medium of online communication—also provides cues to gender. Susan Herring, a linguist who has carried out numerous studies of gender online, notes that, in general,

> males are more likely to post longer messages, begin and close discussions in mixed-sex groups, assert opinions strongly as “facts,” use crude language (including insults and profanity), and in general, manifest an adversarial

> orientation towards their interlocutors. … In contrast, females tend to post relatively short messages, and are more likely to qualify and justify their assertions, apologize, express support of others, and in general, manifest an "aligned" orientation towards their interlocutors. (Herring 2000)

In the absence of visible cues to gender, verbal cues can reveal it.

Misclassifying someone—whether because he or she claimed to be a different identity or had provided no cues and we had made an erroneous assumption—distorts our interpretation of his or her behavior. The norm for women is to be more polite than men. Thus, if I correctly assume that a particular writer is a woman, and she writes in a typical female fashion, I will mark her neither as unusually nice nor aggressive. But let's say her screen name gives no indication of her gender and I initially assume she is male. I will then read "his" words differently—they will sound quite deferential, even meek. My impression of this person—a woman writing in a normal tone for a woman—would then be one of a rather submissive and self-effacing man.

This distortion in social perception happens as well in the face-to-face world when a person's behavior does not match the expected cultural norm. One of the problems facing women who seek leadership positions is that candidates for these roles are expected to be outspoken and assertive. A man with these qualities is perceived to be authoritative; a woman with them is seen as bossy, shrill, and aggressive.

In an online discussion, a woman with strong, clear opinions might find her ideas received more favorably with her gender masked—those who would reject the suggestions of a "strident woman" might welcome them when they thought they came from an authoritative man. Yet this is not an ideal solution; at best, it effects improving perception by guiding others to a better-fitting, but still quite inaccurate, stereotype.

Negative stereotypes, which unfairly denigrate their subject, are clearly harmful. But even positive ones can cause harm, if they make someone seem to be more trustworthy or well-meaning than he or she actually is. One goal for an ideal society is thus not to eliminate social categorization—it's essential for helping us make sense of the world—but to make the prototypes and their triggering cues more closely aligned with actual behavior.

To truly effect change in how people are understood, the cultural models themselves need to change.

Changing Cultural Models

Changing cultural models is a slow process. It is often easier simply to miscategorize the other rather than to adapt to a new worldview. In the famous husband-and-wife architect team, Robert Venturi and Denise Scott Brown were equal collaborators, but Venturi gained far more acclaim: the prototypical architect was male. Scott Brown said that no matter how forcefully she and Venturi explained that that were equal partners, people assumed she did not have a creative role: "Whatever you say to them, they say, 'Well, she must be something else. Maybe a planner, maybe a typist, maybe she takes photographs. It has to be something else!'" (Cook 2013). People found it easier to distort their own observations than to change their assumptions about women in architecture.

Pervasive cultural stereotypes are especially hard to change because one's distorted perception will be reinforced by the similar beliefs of one's peers. If a population of observers thinks that all white people are greedy or all Asians are treacherous or all black people are violent, their shared stereotype allows them to be in agreement without being accurate (Allport 1979; Lee, Albright, and Malloy 2001).

Yet cultural models do change and new types arise.[8] By the end of the 1960s, most Americans could identify a person with long wild hair and tie-dyed clothing as a hippie, a type that had not existed a decade earlier. They could make numerous assumptions about the latter's politics and lifestyle and would have beliefs about how to act toward him or her—whether as the person they would gravitate to at a party or as the one they would forbid their daughters from befriending.

Online, new social types have emerged in many communities. People discuss what they are, how to recognize them, and most importantly, how to act toward them. Disruptive types get much attention, because figuring out how to discourage them is necessary for the community to thrive: "newbie," "bot," and "troll" were among the most widely recognized and discussed in early text-based discussion groups (Golder and Donath 2004). "Trolls" initially pretend to be legitimate participants but become increasingly disruptive, often by making offensive statements designed to derail the discussion (Donath 1998). Communities developed detailed cultural models of this type, as they analyzed whether an offensive user was actually a troll or simply an abrasive individual and then debated how to respond. Understanding the trolls' motivations was essential for figuring out how to discourage them, and once they were seen as pranksters poking fun at the infuriated response they drew, it became clear that ignoring them would be most effective response. "Newbie" is a somewhat derogatory term for newcomers to the online community; they are people who do not yet know the rules of behavior. One description of newbie says that a "well-constructed" troll's post "induces lots of newbies and flamers to make themselves look even more clueless than they already do, while subtly conveying to the more savvy and experienced that it is in fact [deliberate]" (Raymond 2003). Newbies are those who have not yet learned about cultural categories such as trolls.

Interface design can help shape culture by making cues to the qualities that are important to the community prominent. The data portraits we discussed in an earlier chapter are one way to do this. Seeing others via a representation that highlights actions such as responsiveness, the things they talk about, and the rhythm of the interactions, as opposed to one that provides cues to features such as gender, race, and age, could help create a society in which those traits form the basis of new prototypes—and become the primary models for a community's structure.

How big a change can design make? One answer comes from evolutionary psychologists who suggest that the categories associated with race would be relatively easy to transform (Cosmides, Tooby, and Kurzban 2003; Kurzban, Tooby, and Cosmides 2001). They argue that, whereas people immediately and automatically encode new individuals by age, gender and race, age and gender are more fundamental, while race is a "by-product" of adaptations for detecting coalitions and alliances.

> Our subjects had experienced a lifetime in which ethnicity (including race) was an ecologically valid predictor of people's social alliances and coalitional affiliations. Yet less than 4 min of exposure to an alternative social world in which race was irrelevant to the prevailing system of alliance caused a dramatic decrease in the extent to which they categorized others by race. This implies that coalition, and hence race, is a volatile, dynamically updated cognitive variable, easily overwritten by new circumstances. If the same processes govern categorization outside the laboratory, then the prospects for reducing or even eliminating the widespread tendency to categorize persons by race may be very good indeed. (Kurzban, Tooby, and Cosmides 2001, 15391)

Human society organizes around in-group and out-group clustering. We may not be able to change this tendency, but we can change the features that define the clusters.[9]

As for gender and age, although we may never be able to fully tease apart the innate from the cultural, we can design spaces that make these features more or less prominent, depending on their relevance in the context. Your gender should not be relevant in a forum on math, but may be in a discussion on sexism—or rating shoes.

The anonymous comments on *New York Times* stories provide an interesting example of people choosing to selectively reveal different facets of their identity. Depending on the story, people will note relevant aspects of their identity, to provide context for their opinions and establish their authority on the subject. An article about Trayvon Martin (Barry et al. 2013), a black teenager shot and killed while visiting his aunt by a white vigilante who though he was a trespassing criminal, had comments with identifiers such as: "I'm an old white guy and I formed the opinion that when the dispatcher said 'we don't need you to do that' Zimmerman should have stopped and met the police as he was instructed to do," and "Even though my husband and I are white, we could never live in a state where the law enforcement fails its citizens and stands behind such an ill conceived law as 'Stand Your Ground.'" People commenting on an opinion piece by Sherry Turkle (2012) bemoaning the growing use of social technologies at the expense of face-to-face interaction often mentioned their age: "Although I'm in my late 60's and lived most of my life without anything like email, even I now find that emails are an important part of my life"; "I'm twenty-five & rather prone to anxiety. I don't use Twitter or Facebook, I don't have a smartphone or tablet computer, I don't watch TV. I own an iPod but no longer use it." These writers all felt that others needed to be aware of these aspects of their identity in order to understand their opinions.

Identity Play versus Deception

In the examples above, nothing prevents the anonymous writers from falsely claiming an identity (if the accounts were pseudonymous, one could still make false claims, but would need to stick with them. One could not be a twenty-year-old one week, and fifty the next). The comments on a news article may not be the weightiest of texts, but the reader is still arguably harmed by such deceptions. I might feel that, for example, a stand against vigilante patrols in the Trayvon Martin case would be more powerful coming from a middle-aged, white Southern male—the type many people would imagine support such patrols—but it is deceptive and misleading to falsely claim this identity to give my comments a credibility that they have not earned. Even worse would be using a false identity to make trouble; this is the behavior of an Internet troll.

Yet, you might ask, in the last section we talked about masking identities to be more accurately perceived—is that not deceptive also? Not generally, in cases where identity information was simply absent, and the perceiver made the wrong assumption; we cannot be responsible for all the mistaken assumptions people make (though one could argue it is deceptive if the mistake was very likely and the person counted on it being made). A more ambiguous case is the one in which the person deliberately provides misleading identity information—but with the intention of avoiding being inaccurately stereotyped. We can think of examples that fit this model that we would call deception and others that we would find acceptable. Here we want to assess whether the motivation was to avoid misjudgment by an erroneous stereotype and whether the resulting assessment proved beneficial to the perceiver.

In 2011, during the "Arab Spring," a time of great political unrest in the Middle East, a blog appeared with the title "A Gay Girl in Damascus." The author, Amina Abdallah Arraf, wrote about being gay and a woman in an oppressive society. People were fascinated by her story and the insight it provided into Syrian culture; she had many online supporters and journalists covered her story. In June, she was abducted. Activists lobbied for her release, even getting the attention of the US State Department. Soon, however, the hoax was uncovered. Amina turned out to be neither gay, nor a girl, nor in Damascus, but instead was the creation of a white male graduate student in Edinburgh, invented in order to attract attention and garner credibility for his views on the Middle East. In his apology, Tom McMaster, Amina's creator, defended the righteousness of his actions: "I feel that I have created an important voice for issues that I feel strongly about. … I do not believe I have harmed anyone" (quoted in Whitaker 2011). Yet his creation was harmful: besides misleading people into believing they were gaining real insight into the world and thoughts of a gay woman in Syria, the journalists who had written about Amina lost credibility, legitimate Syrian bloggers faced increased scrutiny and doubt about their veracity, and the people in Syria who attempted to rescue her took serious risks trying to save a fictional character (Addley 2011; Hajratwala 2011). Here, real social identity matters a great deal—not individual identification; if Amina were a real person, revealing her name would put her in danger from a repressive government (a fact that helped sustain the deception)—but the writer's actual cultural identity. For many stories, authenticity matters.

Had McMaster written an openly fictional account, these harms would not have occurred.[10] Many acclaimed novels show the world through the eyes of a character far removed from the author's identity. The make-believe of fiction takes place with the reader's consent.

Online, there are numerous sites where fictional identities exist by common consent. Yet even in social spaces that encourage creative identity, such as the graphical worlds (The Palace, There, Second Life) that come in and out of online fashion every few years, most people create an online persona that strongly resembles their real-world self—or quickly devolves back to it. Maintaining a fiction is hard. For the most part, what people want to do is shape the impression they make. The online environment changes what elements we can play up or tone down, but in the theater of social life, we mostly want to be performing as ourselves.

The extremely popular massively multiplayer online role-playing games (MMORPGs) are an interesting example. The roles are predesigned by the game makers: the players inhabit an elaborate costume, typically including a fictional racial type (role-playing games neatly illustrate the hypothesis that people can quickly and fervently adapt to arbitrary ethnic divisions) and clearly defined characteristics. At first glance, they appear to be worlds in which everyone plays a character far removed from their mundane selves. Yet while the participants interact as fictional characters, many build close friendships that carry over outside of the game.[11] Nicholas Yee, a social scientist who studies behavior in online games, argues that these games provide an advantageous environment for developing relationships. The real physical identity cues are all hidden (age, gender, attractiveness, etc.) and the resulting pseudonymity encourages self-disclosure: people are more open than they might be face to face. At the same time, the vivid mask of the role makes each player memorable. Unlike many other forums, where interactions are fleeting, players in these games work as teams and spend considerable amounts of time together online. The gameplay itself provides a proving ground for character: players get to see who takes risks to help others, who acts selfishly, and so on. Participants thus form impressions of each other based on many and various shared experiences, before they learn what the other looks like (Yee 2009).

Popular as they are, MMORPGs are not to everyone's taste. But they demonstrate the feasibility of one cyber-utopian goal—to have a place where people can get to know each other without immediately resorting to preconceived opinions based on real-world physical appearance. They show that to achieve this in a meaningful way, simply making up an identity is insufficient. The identity needs to be persistent and needs to exist within a community with shared goals and activities.

Another cyber-utopian goal—that playing another ethnicity or gender online would give someone special insight into what it is like to have that identity in the real world—has proven less promising. Much online identity play has ended up being rather shallow. People create a character, claim a gender, but soon forget about the role, like a masquerade party when, after the first excitement of seeing the costumes, the Supermen and witches and ghosts sit around eating dip and talking about sports and the PTA. Social scientist Lisa Nakamura used the phrase "identity tourist" to critique the notion that radically free identity choice is a transformative experience: "It gave users a false notion of cultural and racial understanding based on an episodic, highly mediated experience" (Nakamura 2008, 1675). Being able to painlessly assume the appearance of a different identity does not provide an understanding of the social consequences to being seen as, raised as, and living as male or female, or black, white, or Asian, and so on. At most, it gave people the opportunity of experiencing how others act toward the claimed identity.

MULTIPLE IDENTITY SPACES

Identity is not monolithic: there is not a singular, unchanging self that is you. But neither is it a constantly shape-shifting shroud. We have inner qualities—our beliefs, personality, knowledge, and experience—that make up who we are. We have roles in society that shift over time and vary by context, ranging from our individual relationships to our position in a large-scale community. We try to make a desired impression on others. We may wish to appear tough, kind, cool, or loving. Sometimes the impression we wish to give to others is a great match with our inner self and social role, and sometimes it is quite divergent. Whether this divergence is deception, ambition, role-playing, or self-expression depends on the person's intentions. A man who presents himself as a woman online may be doing so for a range of reasons. He may enjoy fooling people (e.g., a troll on a dating site), he may wish to understand better the experience of being a woman, or he may feel that he is in fact more female than male and it is his body that is at odds with reality. The level of reinvention people find acceptable depends on the context. There can be great freedom in games and role-playing spaces, whereas in other situations we want to maintain a level of honesty, ensuring that the impression and information we get from each other is reliable. Almost anyone who has posted anything online—which is now a sizeable percentage of the world's population—has had to think about identity. What name to use? What tone to take?

What we want to know (or ought to know) about the identity of another depends on context. In a technical support forum, it may be better if the social identities of the customers and technicians remain hidden, the better to avoid immediate, perhaps even subconscious assumptions that, say, a non-white non-male is technically illiterate. On a dating site, gender is quite relevant. Age, too, can sometimes be important. Numerous sites on the Web today explicitly forbid minors or children under a certain age from entering, because the content and activity is not appropriate for them; at the same time, other sites are set aside to be places for children to interact with other children (and hopefully not with forty-year-olds pretending to be kids).

The design of an online space can make it easier for people to fabricate claims about themselves, or it can make it more likely that one will see, over time, sufficient detail about another to form a well-grounded sense of them. Online, it is technologically easy to create a space where little or no information is given about the effectively anonymous participants; it is only a bit harder to create one that insists on a real name for identity. The key challenge is in creating online spaces that are in between, where we are known but not entirely transparent. The design goal is to create a space in which the most obvious and salient properties that we see of the other are the qualities around which we want society to structure itself.

10

EMBODIED INTERACTION

In the physical world, our interactions are embodied. Much of our communication is not in the words we speak, but in our gestures, movements, and facial expressions. Even before we say a word, our appearance tells much about who we are: faces often reveal gender, age, and race, while clothing and hairstyle convey economic status and cultural affiliations. Our movements communicate. We stand close to people we feel very comfortable with, and we back away from those we find off-putting or aggressive. Our expressions help convey how we feel about what we are saying or hearing, and they provide important cues for others about how to respond. Am I looking intently at you as you speak, or is my attention wandering as I steal glances at my watch?

In previous chapters, we focused on words, looking at ways of visualizing and extracting patterns from text conversations—a form of communication in which gaze, gesture, and other forms of nonverbal expression are for the most part missing. This chapter looks at the issues involved in bringing these inherently physical forms of interaction to the mediated world.

Text is an excellent medium. It is easy and convenient to both read and write; it is good for reviewing one's words before sending them off; and it affords anonymity if needed. But the information we convey by text is very different from what we communicate by nodding, by looking in a particular direction, and by the subtle changes in our expression as we listen or our voice as we speak. Text is deliberate, and although it can convey nuance beautifully, making it do so requires considerable effort. With our nonverbal physical actions, we express attention, emotion, and so on almost subconsciously; indeed, it requires more effort to conceal our feelings than to reveal them.

Interfaces in which each participant has some visible representation—what I am calling "embodied interactions"—provide a medium for conveying these nonverbal aspects of communication. These representations also convey presence, the feeling that you are "with" the others in a common space. But, along with their richer communication channel and sense of presence, embodied interfaces bring new design challenges and problems. The first challenge is sensing the actions: how does the medium sense the person's emotions or attention? The second is display: how does the medium convey what was sensed from one person to another?

We will first discuss approaches based on sensing and conveying the participants' appearance. Most straightforward is video, recording how one person appears and sending this image to another; it transmits emotions, for example, by showing the person's face and expressions. It holds the promise of recreating the experience of "being there" as faithfully as possible. Yet simple video has a big drawback for interactive communication—it lacks a common virtual space, and thus gaze and its attendant cues of attention and interest are misleading. The ultimate solution is to create a virtual reality (VR) system, which senses the movements of each participant, and re-renders them in a common, virtual space. Along with solving the common space problem, VR opens the possibility of transformation: changing the person's appearance to mask identity or to explore creative representations. However, VR is burdensome, requiring participants to don special equipment and be in a controlled space; it is fascinating for special purposes, but impractical for everyday communication.

We will next look at approaches that sense nonverbal communication in other ways, ranging from keyboard input to biometric sensing. Here, the participants are represented by avatars and questions about their design, such as the benefits of realism versus abstraction, and the representation of nonverbal cues are central. A problem with most avatar interfaces is the mismatch of input to display: they convey more than the user can control. Humanlike forms in particular portray a tremendous amount of social info, but when the avatar has expressive features (e.g., a smiling face, a slouchy posture) that the user did not prompt, it can be worse than no image at all, for it gives a misleading impression. We will look at an alternative approach: very simple, minimalist avatars that existing input streams can fully control. Our challenge here is designing the interface to make these expressive.

Ultimately, communication is about conveying the thoughts, feelings, and intentions of one person to another. We gather clues by reading—and reading into—people's words and by scrutinizing their expressions. But whether we gather them at a distance or face to face, from deliberately typed text or a subconscious frown, these cues are still surrogates, indicators of what we want to know, not the thing in itself. What if we could perceive the feelings of others more directly? Arguably, we can, using biosensing techniques such as measuring skin conductivity, heart rate, or, most directly, brain activity.

A communication system that uses biosensed data as its input is radically different from traditional communication forms. Unlike gestures and expressions, which evolved to communicate, these forms of direct sensing did not. Though it may take effort, we can usually master our expressions—and many other common media, such as written text, are far easier to control. In contrast, our bodies' internal physiological response to—indeed its formation of—our thoughts and feelings is far less manipulable. Does such a medium open a new pathway to empathy, or does it invade the privacy of anyone who uses it? We can design embodied interactions with a wide range of input controls, and the chapter will conclude with a discussion of the social and communicative implications of the range of possible input technologies for controlling online representations.

THE ALLURE AND CHALLENGE OF "BEING THERE"

People like seeing other people. Though we may complain about crowds, most of us are drawn to places buzzing with human activity. We derive comfort from the presence of others and stimulation from seeing and processing the wealth of information that people's faces, clothing, and actions provide. When we speak in the physical world, we know who is listening, whether it is one companion or an audience of hundreds.[1] We can see if our listeners are attentive or distracted, whether they are nodding in agreement or looking doubtful. In face-to-face conversation, listeners as well as speakers continuously convey information.

Online text conversations are very different. The audience is invisible. There is no shared space, no gestures, and no visible identity. Even in synchronous text chats, where all the participants are online at the same time, there is relatively little sense of presence. You are visibly present so long as you are typing, but quickly fade away if you are inactive, even if you are in

Reducing information—and thus changing the available social cues and mores—is another way for video conferencing to go "beyond being there." In 2010 a site called "Chatroulette," a video chat system that connected people with random strangers, enjoyed sudden popularity. You saw yourself in one window and the stranger in the other. You could chat, and either party could disconnect with a "next" button, at which point the system connected you to a new random stranger. Simple as it was, Chatroulette fascinated people: it was the fastest rising search term on Google in 2010. What was its appeal? It resembled the random text chat-rooms that were popular in the early days of online socializing, where people went online using easily replaceable pseudonyms and chatted with strangers, making up identities as they went. Here, there was a voice and face, but the absence of names, the searchable identifiers that tie an online presence to a real-world person, lent it an aura of anonymity.

Chatroulette required little work. You didn't need to be witty, or make the effort to invent a character, or even type. You just needed to appear, and there was enough interest in the appearance of others to make it work. Of course, not everyone is interested in everyone else. One visiting journalist (Anderson 2010) reported how dispiriting it was to get onto Chatroulette and then be repeatedly "nexted" as people swiftly found nothing of interest in his single, male, older-than-thirty self (his wife was much more successful). Chatroulette's combination of video and anonymity meant that the deviant behavior of similar online text spaces could play itself out visually and vividly: there were many exhibitionists, seekers of anonymous virtual sex, and people hoping to shock or disgust anyone who chanced to be connected to them. Although Chatroulette's moment of popularly has ended, it is relevant here because it is an intriguing example of how removing information—in this case, the identity of the other, including any way of building

fact paying close attention. In some forums, an effectively invisible audience of lurkers makes up about 90 percent of the participants (Nonnecke and Preece 2003). Thus, although text conversations have many benefits, from their simplicity and clarity to their freedom from distracting and potentially misleading social cues, there are also reasons to want interfaces with embodied interactions, ones that approach the richness of being in the presence of other people.

Remote presence captures our imagination. One of the most famous scenes in the *Star Wars* movies shows Princess Leia as a holographic image, begging Obi-Wan Kenobi for help. This archetypal science-fiction technology also appeared in the 2008 election coverage, when CNN showed a "hologram" of distant guests who appeared on host Wolf Blitzer's set as if present. Though shown in the supposedly factual world of news coverage, it was fiction: actual holographic presence is well beyond current technology (the guests were actually blue-screened into the video image using numerous camera views; the host simply saw a red dot that helped him direct his gaze as if he were seeing a projection of his guest [Welch 2008]). Although this episode did not display an existing (or even a foreseeably plausible) technology, it did demonstrate our fascination with the dream of realistic telepresence.

In practice, realistic telepresence—faithfully recreating the experience of "being there"—is technologically very difficult. Making a real two- (or more) way holographic communication system would require capturing highly detailed three-dimensional visual information about every participant and transmitting it to all the others, appropriately reconstructed for their perspective. Recording and transmitting the data is challenging but solvable. The problem of creating a common space and perspective, however, presents basic conceptual difficulties.

The fictional "holograms" we have seen in *Star Wars* and on television dazzle the viewer, but they omit a key element: what does the holographic visitor see? In CNN's sketch, what was Jessica Yellin, the reporter, supposedly seeing when her hologram stood in front of Wolf Blitzer? To experience "being there," she would need a representation of everyone at the studio: if that freestanding, three-dimensional "hologram" were real, the distant guest herself would see nothing unless there was equivalent "hologramming" of the host and his surroundings. As depicted, even if Wolf Blitzer actually saw Yellin instead of the red circle on the floor that, in fact, stood in for her, it would be a one-way experience with no shared space, no common ground, no way for gaze to be meaningful.

Indeed, these fictional depictions of telepresence may seem intuitive to the casual viewer, but they are conceptually based on teleportation, a technology that is even more fantastical (and far from achievable) than holographic communication. They function as if what had been transmitted was not simply one's appearance and sound but a stand-in for the actual body (albeit one with scan-lines and blurry edges).

up a history or reputation—creates a very new-seeming medium. The newness here is the opportunity to see and interact with others, minus the ability to affect them or know much of anything about them.

Teleportation, the ability to conquer distance by instantly appearing in another place, has been a dream of people from ancient to modern times. Several hundred years ago, the genies in the Arabic tale *Aladdin and the Magic Lamp* transported people instantly from one place to a distant other. More recently, the TV show *Star Trek* frequently featured teleportation, and in the popular *Harry Potter* books expert wizards can "apparate"—move instantaneously from one place to another. Yet, outside of fiction, the laws of physics make teleporting humans impossible (Davis 2003).

Holographic communication does not suffer from the fundamental physical impossibilities that plague teleportation, but it is still an extremely distant goal. In the meantime, people do the next-best thing given existing technologies, and use video to recreate the experience of "being there."

The Next-Best Thing to "Being There"?

The telephone was invented in 1876; three years later, *Punch's Almanack* published a cartoon envisioning a "telephonoscope" that would transmit pictures as well as sound (see figure 10.1). Seeing distant friends and family, as well as hearing them, was a popular element in futuristic scenarios. A 1910 French postcard from a series called *En l'an 2000* (In the year 2000) shows a man conversing with a far-off woman whose image is projected on a screen (see figure 10.2). Many other predictions of its day still exist only in fantasy, but video telephony arrived early, well before 2000 (Fischer 1994). Prototypes existed in Germany in the late 1930s; the first commercial version, the Picturephone, came out in the 1960s. Although the Picturephone never became successful and was discontinued in the 1970s, there have since been many technological improvements, and today video telephony is commonplace. For business, there are elaborate conferencing rooms with large screens and high bandwidth. For everyday use, webcams make video chat easy and inexpensive, and camera-equipped mobile phones make video calls possible everywhere.

FIGURE 10.1
George du Maurier, *Edison's Telephonoscope* (1879). From *Punch's Almanack for 1879*. The caption reads:

> (Every evening, before going to bed, Pater- and Materfamilias set up an electric camera-obscura over their bedroom mantel-piece, and gladden their eyes with the sight of their Children at the Antipodes, and converse gaily with them through the wire.)
>
> *Paterfamilias (in Wilton Place).* "Beatrice, come closer. I want to whisper."
>
> *Beatrice (from Ceylon).* "Yes, Papa dear."
>
> *Paterfamilias.* "Who is that charming young Lady playing on Charlie's side?"
>
> *Beatrice.* "She's just come over from England, Papa. I'll introduce you to her as soon as the Game's over!"

Video telephony has several noted benefits. Seeing the other is a great advantage when there is a deep emotional bond. Here, where one would ideally have the real person to see and hold, the increase in media richness—in getting a picture as well as sound—is valuable (Ames et al. 2010; O'Hara, Black, and Lipson 2006). It is also useful when the other is a stranger, to get a sense of meeting him or her. It is popular with the deaf community, who communicate via sign language. And it does help people understand and react to pauses and other disruptions in a conversation and be more interactive listeners, able quietly to convey understanding and reaction (Hirsh, Sellen, and Brokopp 2005; Isaacs and Tang 1994; O'Hara, Black, and Lipson 2006; Whittaker 1995). Finally, it is useful for showing things to the other person, rather than simply describing them with words.

Yet, while certainly more popular than in the days of the Picturephone, video telephony remains a minor form of communication (Hirsh, Sellen, and Brokopp 2005). This seems, at first glance, to be surprising. The face is the locus of identity, and its expressions, along with our range of other gestures, are richly communicative. The ability to see each other while speaking should greatly improve our interactions. Why, then, is a technology that provides

FIGURE 10.2
Villemard, *Imagining Video-Telephony as It Would Be in 2000* (1910).

this ability so modestly successful? Is the flaw technical—a problem of cost or bandwidth? Is it that there are too few people to call, the sort of flaw that better and more widespread technology would fix? Or is there a deeper issue in the design and experience of remote video communication?

Conceptually, video telephony is very appealing, but in practice, it is awkward and often not well liked. Video reveals where you are and how you are dressed. When we meet face to face, we are, by definition, in the same place. But on the phone, our situations may be mismatched: you may be in your office, dressed for work, while I am working at home in sweats, with a pile of dirty dishes in the background. In an audio call, I can project a professional aura with a businesslike tone and command of the discussion material, but for a video call, I would need to prepare my appearance and background as well. This demand may be reasonable for some situations, such as when the video call's purpose is to meet a new person virtually, but it is too onerous for other conversations. Video also constrains our motion. In face-to-face meetings, we can look around the room; sharing the environment, our companions can follow our gaze and understand our shifting attention. A video meeting roots us to our desks, staring at the camera. On an audio-only call, people walk and talk; they wash dishes, water plants, walk to work. Although technically one could participate in a video call while walking around with a mobile phone, as one participant in a study noted, no one wants to "be a prat and walk into a lamp post" (O'Hara, Black, and Lipson 2006).

To achieve a coherent communication, common ground is required. In the physical world, our interactions occur in a shared space. If a passing distraction interrupts your thoughts as you speak, I understand what is happening since I can see it too. The shared environment is a stage for our interactions. We move within the space to enter and leave conversations; we face people to pay attention to them and turn our back on those we want to ignore. In audio calls, people create a common space in their imagination: watch someone talking on the phone as he nods and gestures at his of course unseeing partner. Mobile phone users often struggle to manage their dual existence in the real space of their physical surroundings and the conceptual space of the call (Ling 2002).

Video does create common ground when used specifically to invite the other to see something in one's own space: a prototype you are both designing, the cute new kitten, scenes from a concert. Here it functions as a one-way transmission of images rather than a conversation, a function that has proved to be relatively successful (O'Hara, Black, and Lipson 2006). When video is used for two-way conversation, however, it introduces a new and conflicting visual space, common to neither (Hirsh, Sellen, and Brokopp 2005). This conflict is most apparent in problems with gaze in video communication.

One of the most important nonverbal cues is gaze.[2] Gaze conveys personality. Someone who is shy or otherwise uncomfortable may have trouble making eye contact, whereas someone who is more aggressive or intent on appearing sincere may hold eye contact for uncomfortably long stretches. Gaze can convey aggression or modesty: it shows how willing you are to follow social rules. It is rude, for instance, to focus on your conversational partner's cleavage, no matter how alluring. Gaze also helps manage conversations, and its choreography goes far beyond simply looking at the person you are conversing with. We use gaze to manage turn-taking, to show that we are considering what to say next, to wordlessly convey that we are listening. In a two-person conversation, the speaker usually looks at her companion only about one-third of the time, while the listener looks at the speaker almost twice as much, but far from a nonstop stare (Argyle 1993). This is partly because looking at another person is cognitively demanding: there is a lot to observe and think about when we see a face. Thus, as we speak, we often look away in order to focus on preparing our words rather than assessing our listener. Though the listener may look away for a moment, if his gaze does not return once the speaker has finished it will seem as if he had ceased paying attention and was lost in his own thoughts.

Gaze shows our reactions to the world around us. If I hear a noise, I look in that direction; my gaze provides a cue about where my attention lies. In person, I barely notice if you look down as you pick up a pencil or glance at the window as a truck goes by; these changes of gaze are unremarkable given what I can see of our shared environment. If we were talking via video, however, you would seem to me to be looking inexplicably away or to have disappeared from the screen entirely. Seen through the limited window of the screen, your ordinary responses to your environment seem disruptively odd. To seem attentive on video, we need to be more still and focused than we normally are in unmediated encounters. We also need to look into the camera, which means that the camera then becomes our focus, not the face of our interlocutor. Video calls tether us to the screen and camera.

If we accept constrained activity, elaborate technological setups can improve mediated gaze (Carson et al. 2000; Dumont et al. 2009; Lanier 2001; Vertegaal, Weevers, and Sohn 2002). In these systems, multiple cameras capture each participant and eye-trackers follow their gaze. The system also knows the location of the other participants' images on each person's screen. By tracking where a person is looking, it can deduce whom she is looking at and then, using the images from the various cameras, recreate her image showing her looking at the object of her attention.

Creating a common virtual space remains a challenge. Commercial videoconferencing services achieve the illusion of one by building carefully matched, austere rooms and having the participants travel to these sites for their virtual meetings. Still, distractions and other events in one space are not shared with the others. And, in practice, people choose media that are easy to use. One often-cited reason why high-quality videoconferencing is used so infrequently is that it requires too much effort. People don't want to go to a special room to make a call (Hirsh, Sellen, and Brokopp 2005); they like technologies that are lightweight and simple.

The ultimate solution to "being there" is immersive virtual reality. Here, you shut out all views of the physical world and see only a synthetic environment, a shared "third space" that is neither your actual surroundings nor

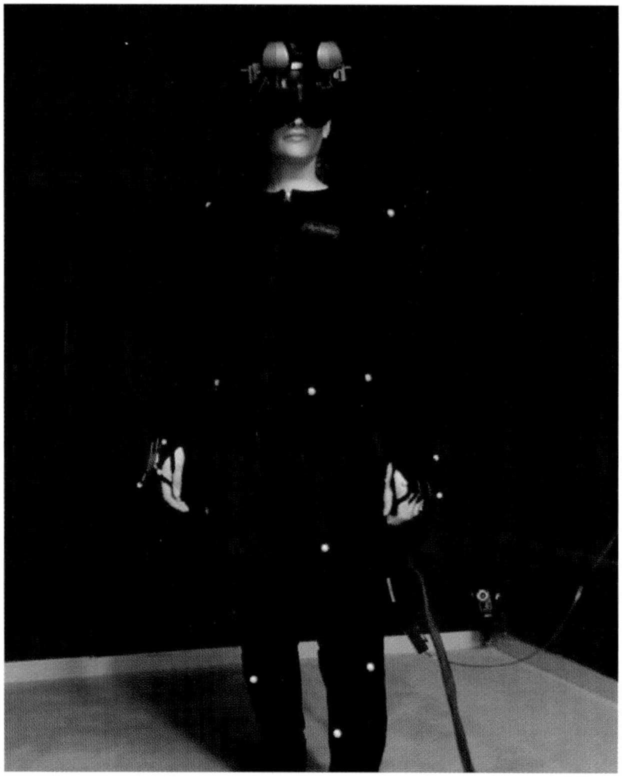

FIGURE 10.3
Virtual reality suit, eventLAB, University of Barcelona (2011).

your partner's, but instead an artificial world you both inhabit (Bailenson and Beall 2006). All of your movements must be tracked by sensors (which might be video cameras); if you appear as yourself in this world, your image must have been previously recorded: it is synthetically re-rendered (see figure 10.3).

Yet if we are going to go through all the effort of participating in a highly instrumented and synthetic experience, why limit it to recreating the mundane experience of being there? A virtual environment has infinite possibilities: the "table" can visualize the conversational patterns, there can be interactive objects in the setting, and the people themselves can be transformed (Bailenson and Beall 2006; Yee and Bailenson 2007). Why not explore what else we can do in a fully computational and synthetic environment? Once we have all the data and instrumentation we need to fully recreate "being there," we also have the potential to go far beyond.

AVATARS AND THE WORLDS BEYOND BEING THERE

Virtual worlds are shared online environments. Participants move through a simulated geography in which they can communicate with each other and affect the environment in various ways. Virtual reality is one form of virtual world—one in which the participants' every move is tracked and recreated in the space, and where each person is immersed (using gear such as helmets and goggles) so that all they perceive is the synthetic world. But virtual worlds can also be quite simple.

Some are text based; words describe the environment and the users navigate via text commands. Others (the ones we will focus on here) are graphical worlds, in which people appear in the guise of avatars (graphical images representing the user). Avatars can range from quite realistic human forms to abstract shapes. They can provide a sense of presence, expressivity, and other features of embodiment, while allowing identity to be fluid. As a medium for embodied online communication, graphical worlds are the opposite of video: the shared space is inherent to the medium, but appearance is arbitrary, and conveying expression is challenging.

In this section, we will look at virtual worlds that enable various aspects of embodied interaction. Our focus will be on avatar design, on the images and behaviors representing the user and the ways of communicating through them. We will start by looking at existing avatar implementations, both in games, where they are quite popular, and in more "serious" and social settings, which have been rather less successful. Are they inherently suited only for fantasy?

To use avatars as a communicative medium, the key problem we must solve is how to match the expressive capability of the representation with the user's means of controlling it. I will argue that the problem with typical humanlike avatars is that their appearance and movements implicitly convey a tremendous amount of social information, but the user's input is very limited. The avatar has eyes: Where should it be looking? What expression should its face have, what mood should its gait convey?

One approach is to program the avatar to be "smarter," able to carry out complex behaviors programmatically, without detailed instructions from the user. This makes for a more lively and expressive avatar, but whose feelings is it conveying? We will look at the distinction between creating an autonomous character and creating a personal representation.

A different approach is to design simpler avatars, in which the amount of detail in the representation matches the input the user provides. Starting with a very basic interface in which the avatars are colored circles, we will explore ways to build increasingly expressive systems from a simple foundation.

The communicative capacity of an interface ultimately depends on the extent and subtlety of the user's input to it. If typing is the only input, graphics may illustrate the words, but the user's message is still bound by what the text conveys. Interfaces that sense other actions—for example, that record and then represent gestures or facial expressions—can convey additional and potentially more candid meaning, especially when they are easier and more intuitive actions than typing words. We will start by exploring ways to use common input devices to convey expressive gesture, and will then examine the issues that arise with measurement of subconscious and private reactions.

Humanlike Avatars

By far the most popular use of virtual worlds and avatars is in online games. Millions of people play MMORPGs, "massively multiplayer online role playing games."[3] In these fictional worlds, players wander about, find companions, seek treasure, fight battles, and so on. Role-playing an imaginary character is not only accepted but required. There is a strong social component to many of these games: the players need to work closely in teams to achieve their goals and sometimes develop friendships that transcend the game.[4] However, although these games feature detailed graphics and complex strategy, the usual communication medium is traditional text or audio chat, and the avatar design has focused on role-based costume, not the subtleties of social interaction (see figure 10.4).

There have been repeated attempts to make social (as opposed to quest-oriented gaming) graphical worlds. In the mid-1980s the first commercial one, Habitat, was developed (Morningstar and Farmer 2008). Several, like Worlds Away and The Palace, were created in the mid-1990s as home computer use became increasingly widespread. Though these sites debuted with much excitement, interest in them soon faded. In 2004, a more technologically complex graphical world called Second Life launched. Its users could wander about a three-dimensional landscape and sculpt the face, hair, and clothing of their detailed avatar. Second Life included a virtual economy:

FIGURE 10.4
Avatar ("Undead") from World of Warcraft, Blizzard Entertainment.

users could build and own objects, and buy and sell them in an internal market. As Second Life grew in popularity, enthusiasts predicted that it would be the successor to the Web. Many companies (perhaps remembering how irrelevant they had thought the Web would be when it appeared in the early 1990s, and how unprescient they had seemed when, soon after dismissing it, they needed to buy back the URL with their company's name for their now clearly obligatory corporate homepage) were quick to jump onto the Second Life bandwagon. They bought up virtual islands, built virtual showrooms, and gave out virtual branded gifts. Years later, Second Life, though still in existence, is fading out of sight. It is likely that at some point it will disappear entirely, or at least drastically transform itself. It is equally likely that in a few years another avatar-based world will appear, again promising to be the ultimate future of online communication.

What makes the concept of an imaginary social world seem so intriguing, yet in practice not particularly compelling, if not outright unappealing, for most people? Is it a matter of getting the technology and design right? Or is there a deeper problem with the concept of inhabiting a virtual avatar?

Avatars let you be anything; an avatar need not, and frequently does not, resemble the user. Whether this free identity is desirable depends on the situation. In the fantasy game worlds that comprise the vast majority of avatar use, the ability to play as an imaginary and fantastical self is a key part of the game. But here, while the avatar is nonrealistic, it is not free form. Role-playing games usually assert strict control over an avatar's appearance, which usually functions like a professional uniform, displaying its player's class and other rigidly maintained aspects of role. Only through achieving a series of goals can the player display various badges and other marks of status.

In the online social realm, the value of free-form identity is ambivalent. For those who see these virtual worlds as primarily fantasy spaces, places to try out different imagined characters or characteristics, they can be quite appealing. Notably, there has been considerable use of Second Life by disabled users, who find the ability to be physically attractive and mobile in a world that values appearance to be very empowering (Cassidy 2008). These cases are very vivid, and they epitomize what many people enjoy about the site: the ability to interact in a setting where physical attractiveness counts highly, while having the freedom to specify their own appearance. Others find it less appealing. Chimerical avatars are the visual equivalent of the text world's "cheap pseudonym" (Friedman and Resnick 2001). Where it is easy to appear as anything you want to be, appearance loses its significance.

Communicating via avatar changes the social dynamics. It introduces an element of fantasy that keeps interactions in the space at a certain remove. When using text alone, you can interact with others while remaining ignorant of their appearance and all that it implies about them. When interacting via avatar, although you are consciously aware that the other may look quite different in real life, having a moving, acting, vivid image in front of you makes it hard not to think of it as a lifelike depiction of the other. This simultaneous belief and nonbelief keeps the space suspended in a limbo between realism and imagination.

FIGURE 10.5
Avatar faces from Second Life. We read meaning from faces (Bruce and Young 1998; Donath 2001; Zebrowitz 1997), including from the faces of avatars. Imagine each of these saying: "I have some land to sell to you" or "Do you want to go to a party?" Even though both faces could belong to anyone, and the difference between them was made in a couple of minutes by changing a few parameters in Second Life's face-editing program, we interpret the words through the context of the personalities we read into these two different, fictional faces. Whereas it is equally easy to make fictional self-descriptions in text, the vividness of visual imagery makes it harder to stand back and remember that it may be a completely imaginary representation.

Though it is technically possible to have any appearance in an avatar site, stylistic norms exist. Second Life avatars tended to be young and hip looking: the female avatars wore tight jeans and midriff-baring outfits, and the males, who were also in tight-fitting clothes, looked as if they spent hours in the gym every day.[5] For the business users eager to embrace Second Life as the next platform for commerce, this presented a dilemma. You go to your corporate job dressed conservatively; it is the rule and the standard. Then you are sent to attend a virtual meeting, for which you need to create an avatar. Because it is for work, you should go as a virtual version of yourself; in this context, it is not a fantasy space. (The colleague who shows up to a virtual business meeting as his favorite after-hours wizard avatar, with blue flowing hair and a wand, will be quite out of place.) However, if you create a too realistic version of yourself, it also could seem oddly, almost freakishly out of place. You certainly do not want to wear the slightly sci-fi, sexy clothes that are the avatar norm, but an avatar in a business suit appears to be in corporate drag. Creating a body is complicated. If in real life you are rather plump, showing up online as a skinny, shapely avatar is problematic. Does it mean you think you look like that, wish you looked like that, or feel that you must portray yourself like that even if you are quite happy with how you actually look? But depicting yourself with your real-life shape can also be awkward. Though it might be quite unremarkable in the physical world, it would stand out as hyper-realistic in this land of air-brushed fantasy. The avatar worlds are fantastical at heart, well suited for situations that thrive on imaginary experience; those that do not can be at odds with their inherent playfulness.

A fundamental problem with contemporary avatars is that they are not very responsive. Avatars have faces, arms, and bodies. We thus expect them to move and interact as people do, but their expressions and reactions are limited. Increasingly realistic avatars, with highly detailed faces and bodies, set up increasing expectations of responsiveness and subtlety that they are not equipped to fulfill. Perhaps most disturbing is their blank stare; set to look in one direction, they do so until the next time the user remembers to move their virtual gaze point.

The source of problem is that the avatars have expressive detail beyond their users' means to control. A typical computer has a keyboard, mouse or other pointing device, and perhaps a camera. The keyboard and mouse are the primary inputs; they are ubiquitous, and interpreting their simple and unambiguous input is easy. But there is little in the way of graceful and intuitive mapping when going from these devices to moving an avatar. Many systems employ a combination of input techniques; you can control the avatar by typing the name or shortcut for a gesture as part of the text (e.g., "\laughs at a story") or you can pick it from a menu. This is far from the spontaneous expression of feeling that gestures and expressions communicate when we perform them with our bodies. Interacting via avatar is not so much like inhabiting another body as it is about manipulating a puppet. It may be fun, but it is work; it may be expressive, but it is not spontaneous.

Without either internally generated intelligence or an external applied control, the avatar stands around looking dumb. A person surrounded by other people is seldom still. Even if he is not talking, he is nodding at this one, making room for that one, watching the action over there, smiling at something here. Contemporary avatars, however, simply stand still. They are vacant, like dolls waiting for a child to pick them up and bring them briefly to life. Their appearance is much more sophisticated than the inputs that control their behaviors. To solve the vacant doll problem we can program autonomous behaviors to make smarter avatars or implement new input pathways to create avatars that are more communicative. Or, we can avoid the problem by designing simpler avatars.

Autonomous Behaviors

The simplest avatars are just pictures; they have no movements or behaviors. One moves them by dragging them across the screen. More advanced avatars have algorithms for complex actions built into them. For example, to get the avatar to walk somewhere, the user simply indicates a destination, and the avatar's walking programs animate its gait. Doing so by hand would be extremely tedious.

An avatar can also be programmed to perform social actions. For example, upon greeting another avatar, it could give a slight bow or shake hands, and its face and eyes could be animated to look lifelike when it is speaking. An avatar can have programs for greeting, leaving, appearing raptly

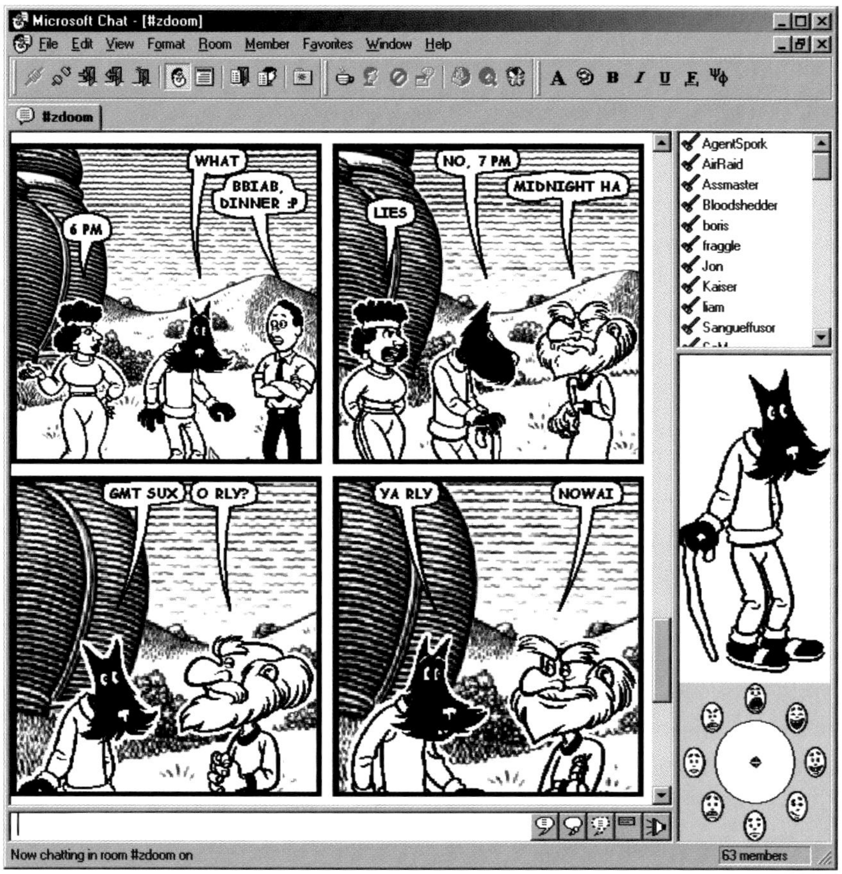

FIGURE 10.6
Comic Chat (1996). Software by David Kurlander, Microsoft. Artist: Jim Woodring.

interested, or rudely bored. In Cassell and Vilhjálmsson's Body Chat program, if two avatars were talking and the user of one texted "goodbye," the program would have the avatar look at the other, nod its head, and wave (Cassell and Vilhjálmsson 1999; Vilhjálmsson and Cassell 1998). Similarly, an avatar can have programs that give it a set of actions to perform when idle (check its virtual phone, take out a magazine and appear to read, do its virtual nails). Microsoft's Comic Chat not only gave the avatars social expressions, it placed them on the screen as if in a comic book (see figure 10.6). Adopting the sequential art form (Eisner 2001) solved the problem of what to do with the avatars between moments of dialogue: instead of continuous motion, Comic Chat desplayed a series of still images, rendered only as needed (Kurlander, Skelly, and Salesin 1996).

Virtual worlds have markets for behaviors, where one can buy algorithms for one's avatar to make it bow more gracefully, obsequiously, or minimally. One can purchase a high level of politeness, turn it on, and forget about it. Similarly, one can purchase an aggressive persona or a suggestively flirtatious one. Cheap behaviors are poorly rendered, and truly sophisticated interactions cost quite a bit. Though these algorithmic behaviors make avatar interaction smoother and more entertaining, what can we really learn about our companions through such an interface? In our unmediated encounters, politeness and other social behaviors tell us a great deal about each other. It takes work to be extremely gracious; one must both know the social rules and make the effort to perform them consistently and well. Acting graciously signals one's knowledge of and commitment to the rules and mores of society.

If the avatars and their algorithmic behaviors are made well, they can evoke personality and character quite convincingly. We form strong impressions of others based on their social actions without necessarily being aware of what has influenced us (Ambady and Rosenthal 1992). However, displaying these traits via a "smart" avatar only shows that the person behind it can afford to buy the social behavior program; it says nothing about whether he has these traits in real life. The "cheap pseudonym" problem becomes one of cheap affect. In a world where politeness and aggression are commercially available styles that one can put on or remove at will, these behaviors have no deeper significance than easy verbal claims like "I'm a nice guy."

Autonomous conversational agents are not new: chatterbots—programs designed to converse with people and often to try to pass as human—have been taking part in online interactions since the early 1990s (Mauldin 1994) and are increasingly common in commercial settings as companies automate consumer relations. Adding graphics and behavioral mimicry to a chatterbot can make it more convincing, for the avatar's image and gestures can distract the viewer, and they are easier to synthesize than sustained and believable verbal interaction (a problem that is still unsolved; Gratch et al. 2002).

For games and fantasy spaces, this ability to create vivid characters that not only look but also act their role is exciting. For social interactions, its benefit is more dubious. We respond to the avatar using the social knowledge we have developed through years of interacting with other people, easily forgetting that a program, rather than an emotion or intention, motivates its behavior. Once the avatar is smart enough, there need not be any human acting behind it.

Sometimes we care only about external behavior, and sometimes we care about the motivation behind it. If we think of the other as just an agent acting for our benefit, whether to buy a ticket or to entertain us, then the smart avatar, or perhaps even the autonomous one with no person actually directing it, is desirable. In this case, we want the experience to be smooth and enjoyable, and it is fine if the smiles and nods are merely simulations of sociability.

Yet if the purpose of our interactions with the other is, at least in part, social (we want to get to know another person, create a social tie, or see how others respond to us), then the avatar with simulated social behaviors is a barrier. How long someone holds your gaze, whether they say "thank you" and with what expression, the minute lift or frown of their brow—these innumerable social gestures, both big and small, provide us with cues about the other's thoughts and opinions that we cannot perceive otherwise. If the gestures are simulated, we may feel that we are getting to know the other, but we are actually responding to a mask.

Simulated and algorithmic behavior can make an interaction seem smoother, but they make it less communicatively reliable. A wholly autonomous, "intelligent" avatar can be quite an entertaining performer, but it conveys little about its user other than the taste she demonstrated by choosing it as her representative. To be communicative, the user must guide the avatar.[6]

Simpler Avatars in Abstract Spaces

Humanlike avatars have faces and bodies that give off social signals, often disconnected from their users' intentions. Their familiar forms set up expectations of humanlike behavior that are often unobtainable.[7]

The less realistic the avatar, the lower our expectations are for it to behave in a humanlike way, and the more likely it is to satisfy these expectations. Simpler avatars have fewer details that require continuous updating. Yet this does not mean that the representation cannot be expressive: even simple lines and shapes can be eloquent. The faces of Charlie Brown and the other characters in the very successful *Peanuts* series are circles, with dots for eyes and lines for mouths.

In the late 1990s, the increased popularity of online socializing and the growing power of home computers prompted a wave of graphical chat sites. Users chose avatars to represent themselves and then went from room to room looking for people to chat with. A big appeal of these worlds was the sense of presence they provided (Biocca 1997; Nowak and Biocca 2003). In nongraphical text-only chats, one sees other people only when they talk, and though the invisible listeners might be listed somewhere, a list of names does not feel like a group of people surrounding you. In the graphical chat sites, as in real life, everyone present was visible.

Yet the design of these virtual environments was awkward. The avatars—which could be human forms, frogs, cars, hearts—floated like haphazardly placed paper cutout dolls against backdrops such as a living room, a palace throne room, or outer space. Neither the shape of the avatar nor the contents of the room had functional meaning. The avatars had limbs but no gestures, faces but no changing expression. They portrayed vivid characters, but there was little meaning to being a wizard, a queen, a fox, or a little girl when each was just an arbitrary picture. You could be a grapefruit or a judge; it made no difference. The environments, too, were all surface representation without any deeper significance. One could have a setting of medieval riches, depicting thrones and knights and hanging tapestries, or one of urban blight, showing a run-down street with burnt-out buildings and rusting cars; functionally, both were the same. The freedom to be anything and anywhere meant that there was little significance to any of it.

Chat Circles

My students and I created *Chat Circles** in response to these avatar worlds (Donath, Karahalios, and Viégas 1999; Donath and Viégas 2002; Viégas and Donath 1999). We liked the idea of having visible presence and a graphical context for interaction, but not the imagery of the avatar worlds. So we set

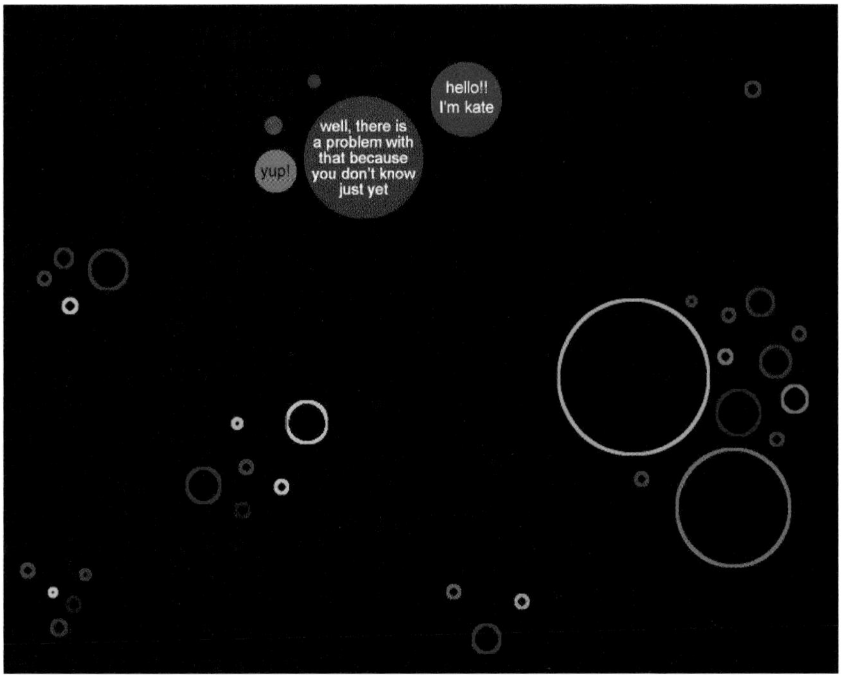

FIGURE 10.7
Fernanda Viégas and Judith Donath, *Chat Circles* (1999).

out to design a very simple graphical social space, based on the idea of form following function (Sullivan 1896), in which the visuals would reflect what the user could convey.

In *Chat Circles*, the "avatar" was simply a colored circle (see figure 10.7). When you typed, your words filled the circle, which expanded to hold them, and then they would slowly fade and the circle would shrink. To see what other people were saying, you needed to be close to them. If someone was outside of your "hearing range" you would see their circle only as hollow outline. You could not see the words when they spoke, but you could see the circle expanding and contracting. Thus, you could see activity at other parts of the space, but could only participate in conversations near you. Hearing range was symmetric: if you saw someone else as a solid circle (and could thus see his words), you knew he could see yours. If he was just a muted outline to you, then you were the same to him. In The Palace and other avatar worlds of the time, there were seating areas for conversation; but avatars do not need to sit, their virtual legs do not get tired. Since the seats and specific areas had no function, people just floated anywhere on the screen. *Chat*

Circles' hearing range gave meaning to proximity. You needed to show that you were interested in a conversation to join it. And if someone irritated you, you could, in effect, walk away.

Chat Circles was designed to be a starting point from which we and others could build worlds of increasing complexity and greater functionality. There were numerous directions to pursue. "Hearing range" functioned as a simple sensory organ for the basic circle avatar. What other senses might we create? The space itself was empty; how could we create functional environments in which to act? The avatars were simple circles; how might we make their appearance richer and more expressive?

*Talking in Circles** was a project we built on the *Chat Circles* foundation (Rodenstein and Donath 2000). Here the users communicated via voice instead of text. The basic look was similar: you appeared as a colored circle that grew and shrank with the amplitude of your voice. While visually simple, it added several useful features to the typical phone conference. You could easily see who was present; even a listener who never said a word was clearly there. You could also easily tell who was speaking (which can be quite difficult in audio-only conferences, unless you know the people well enough to distinguish their voices). In addition, it made it very easy to have quick side conversations: if you and I needed to discuss something together, we could just move our circles to another part of the screen and talk, returning to the main group as soon as we were done, much as people do in real conversations.

A graphical conversation interface turns the screen, which in traditional chats is still a typewriter-like linear stream of text, into a two-dimensional inhabitable space. To make use of this space, we need to design avatars with senses—such as hearing range—and environments with spatially varying functionality. With these features, people have reason to move about the space and to congregate in a location; they have the foundations to create their own social mores.

Talking in Circles had listening areas, places where one could go to listen to music or a newscast. They were meant as gathering places; for example, people could get together to listen to and discuss current events (later versions of *Chat Circles* similarly had pictures in the background; Donath and Viégas 2002). However, they had no interaction function; other than providing information, they did not change the affordances of the space. A later project, *Information Spaces* (Harry and Donath 2008), experimented with functional areas (see figure 6.16). For example, in some areas, conversations were archived, while other spaces were designated for ephemeral discussions. One could make some areas anonymous, where all circles/avatars would be identical and nameless. Some areas could require an invitation to enter.

Another variation of *Chat Circles* experimented with contagious appearance: the avatars were simple shapes and colors, which "wore off" on each other. If you spent a lot of time talking with one person, your colors would both start moving toward an intermediate point. In an alternative version, one retained an "inner core" of original color while changing "social color" in an external ring. Such imitation could have a subtle effect on how people act. When we see people presenting a common appearance, whether in the long term (e.g., similar clothing styles) or short term (similar gestures), we think of them as having something in common. Kurzban, Tooby, and Cosmides (2001) have claimed that we encode coalitions by arbitrary markers; race is a familiar one in everyday life, but they can be anything, even the color of one's avatar. For the participants, reactions would depend on many things, including how divided the user population was. If the interface was being used to stage discussions between hostile groups, participants might refuse to go near opposing members, appalled at the idea of the other's shape and color rubbing off on them. In a more sociable setting, people might find it entertaining that their appearance shifted to resemble the people with whom they had spent time. Alternatively, we could make such imitation volitional: one might need to be both close to someone and indicate that one wanted to adopt some of the other's appearance. Here, it gains communicative value and the potential to evolve social meanings; would it seem rude to not adopt something of your companion's appearance? Would some people seem fawningly imitative? In real life, "mirroring" is hypothesized to be at the heart of our ability to empathize with others (Bailenson and Yee 2005; Chartrand and Bargh 1999; Heyes 2001; Meltzoff and Decety 2003; Sebanz, Bekkering, and Knoblich 2006). We imitate other's facial expressions and gestures, which may help us empathize and feel that we are experiencing what they experience.

In a system that gives people the ability to control appearance and action, cultural meanings evolve with use. In a world where, for example, height is an easily modified attribute, we can imagine a culture developing expressions of politeness related to height. This could manifest in how you show awareness of your current status in a particular context, perhaps by growing when you wish to take the floor in a discussion or shrinking as a form of respect to another.

We can extend the simple circle in many other ways. One could encode history by making a space where everyone starts as a plain-colored circle, but gains visual complexity over time. Algorithms might encode participation patterns in shapes, evolving eventually from generic circle to individual data portrait.

The plain circle was not set forth as the ultimate representation of the online human, but as a foundation on which to build. It was able to go "beyond being there" not by adding complexity, but by taking it away—by thinking of the avatar in terms of communicative and sensing functions, rather than as a humanlike representation.

THE PALETTE OF REPRESENTATIONAL CHOICES

Embodied interactions include a broad palette of representational choices. Appearing as your recognizable physical-world self is inherent to video, but once we move from video to the computationally rendered world of avatar interfaces, the choices multiply. Your avatar could be realistic, looking exactly like you, or it can appear as a distinctive human—but different from your real-world appearance. You can be some other humanlike form, cartoonlike but socially legible, or you can be a fanciful form, or an abstract shape.

Identity is one criterion for choosing between a realistic or fantastic representation. When we see another's face, even briefly, we learn a lot about his or her social identity: race, age, and gender, as well as social affiliations. Does she have a conservative haircut? Multiple piercings? This provides a useful context for interpreting her words and developing a relationship with her; it can also provide the basis for distorting the meaning of her words because of stereotyped social models (see chapter 9). In person, we have little choice; our faces reveal many identity cues. Online, however, we can choose: we can use media, such as video, that display these cues, or ones that do not. We can also design media that provide alternative identity cues, avatars that reveal the user's recent interactions or that the user shapes to appear as she wishes others to see her.

Different representational choices have a variety of other social effects. Here we will discuss two of them: how people react to faces and how transforming basic body features, such as height, can alter social dynamics.

A Face in the Interface

Faces humanize the interface. We react socially to faces—we are nicer, but also less forthright and revealing, when talking to a face. This socialized behavior occurs even when the "face" is the interface to a machine.

In one experiment, people were administered a questionnaire by a computer, which was sometimes simply a text interface, sometimes a neutral face, and sometimes a stern face. People said they did not like the stern face, but they took more time responding to the questions posed by it and answered them more thoroughly, even though they reported finding the experience less comfortable (Sproull et al. 1996). They also presented themselves in a more positive light when the computer had a face.[8] In all cases the subjects typed their answers. The difference in how forthright and engaged they were was due not to their own communication medium, but to the appearance of their conversational partner. One explanation is that when communicating with a face, we bring our sense of sociability to the interaction. Although the subjects knew that they were corresponding with a machine, they still attempted to make a good impression on it when it was more humanlike.[9]

Similar effects occur when the interface connects two people. When a conversational partner appears only through words, there is less sense of being connected with that person. In an experiment that compared how people respond when communicating via video and audio or with audio only, the subjects reported feeling a greater sense of the presence of others when they could see them, but also disclosed less about themselves (Bailenson et al. 2006). People find it easier to be rude to another whose face they do not see. Thus, if you are building an interface where you want people to enter their medical history, a text interface is better: you want people to disclose their full history and not be embarrassed about past conditions. If you want people to behave politely and strive to make a good impression, seeing the other person (even if synthesized) can help.

The Social Impact of Physical Transformation

In the physical world, we choose our clothes to present a certain image: a man in a suit projects far more authority than does one in a T-shirt and swim trunks. Similarly, modifications to how we appear in a virtual world can strongly affect the impression we make. Jeremy Bailenson at Stanford

University has carried out a series of experiments in immersive virtual settings examining how even subtle transformations of appearance affect social interactions (Yee and Bailenson 2007).[10]

In one experiment, Bailenson and colleagues demonstrated that people are more trusting of others who resemble themselves. They took pictures of political candidates and, unknown to the subject, morphed the subject's face with the candidate's, subtly enough that few detected it. The subjects showed a measurable preference for candidates when they were more similar to themselves (Bailenson et al. 2009). Another experiment showed that programming avatars to automatically imitate another's gestures makes them more influential (Bailenson and Yee 2005).[11] The subtlety of the modifications makes them even more powerful, for the receiver is not likely to notice the manipulation. Indeed, it can be invisible: in another experiment, one subject's avatar was made to appear taller than the other avatars, *but only to that subject*; the others saw it as the same height as the rest. The subjects then engaged in a negotiation. The ones who perceived themselves to be taller did better: simply seeing yourself with this advantage changes how you act toward others. These experiments demonstrate the potential of virtual spaces to, in Bailenson's words, "transform social interaction," and they provide a rigorous and provocative foundation for thinking about design.

Let us consider the height example. In the face-to-face world, height influences both personal and professional success. Yet, although tall people are *perceived* to be more competent and effective, height does not predict better actual performance, and for most jobs, "the practice of favoring tall individuals amounts to little more than pure bias" (Judge and Cable 2004). One of the big advantages of the text-based online world is that these influential but irrelevant physical features are invisible: on the Internet, no one knows you are short. If we reintroduce these features in embodied interfaces, can we do so in a way that is socially beneficial?

In the novel *Snowcrash*, Neal Stephenson posits a world in which avatars are legally required to be the same height as the person they represent. But we can design any rules. We can make worlds in which everyone's height is strictly equal, or where height is determined by how long one has been a participant or by how esteemed one is by others. We could make a world where the quietest people are taller, to give them more confidence. We could make ones in which height is randomly distributed, changes every day, or is available for purchase. The avatar is a canvas for data portraiture, and Bailenson's studies show the power of these representational changes.

A key point of Bailenson's experiment is that transformations of physical appearance have significant social affects even if visible to only one participant—that seeing yourself as taller (or more attractive) makes you more confident and authoritative, even if no one else sees it. This raises the question of whether an interface should be objective, showing a common view to all participants, or subjective, adjusting to the preferences of each. Should I be able to depict, for my own private viewing, the others in my group as unattractive in order to boost my confidence? Alternatively, should people be able to specify how they appear to others, and if so, with what if any constraints? Or should the system determine each participant's appearance? In a face-to-face meeting, if I nod with vigorous agreement to one person, everyone sees that I have aligned myself with her; if I subsequently express the same support to someone expressing the opposite opinion, I will seem to be either exceedingly persuadable or excessively sycophantic. Yet one could design a virtual meeting system where I can designate who sees me agreeing with one speaker, and a different group would see me nodding with another. Or, as in Bailenson's study, each person could see a version of me that slightly resembles themselves, and that subtly mimics their gestures.

Attempting to make ourselves appear more attractive, powerful, or persuasive has been an integral part of human culture throughout history. Archaeologists have found both terrifying masks and pigments for cosmetics in prehistoric sites. Venetian women in the Renaissance risked blindness in the pursuit of beauty when they dilated their pupils with drops of belladonna (Feinsod 2000). Today, magazines and lifestyle coaches tell us how to "dress for success"—what styles and colors make us appear more powerful and intelligent; lawyers instruct their clients on how to look innocent and law-abiding. We learn to control the tone of our voice to convey authority or to mask our emotions. Executives gathering for an important meeting seek seats that place them at the greatest advantage. Our daily life comprises numerous ways in which we work to burnish our image in the eyes of others, perhaps subconsciously, perhaps quite deliberately. Are the computer-aided transformations we describe above a continuation of this striving for self-enhancement, or are they something new? Are they within the boundaries of what we consider acceptable, or are they too insidious or deceptive?

There are no easy answers to these questions. Much depends on the intention of the person performing the transformation—is it primarily for his personal gain? Would the receivers agree to it if they were informed? A teacher running an online classroom and using these techniques to motivate students and give confidence to shy ones is quite different from a politician persuading voters to elect him by making himself appear more trustworthy through personalized manipulation.

BIOSENSING: INNER STATE AS INPUT

Communication can be frustrating. We misunderstand and are not always straightforward with each other. The thoughts of others are in many ways unknowable, and often this is by design: we deliberately conceal much of what is on our minds. Even when two people want to know each other better—lovers, for example—it is a fraught and difficult process.

People often imagine that communication would be much easier if we could telepathically read one another's thoughts. No more misunderstandings, no more reticence holding us back from something we ought to say.

Without telepathy,[12] we rely on cues to others' emotional state and intentions. We hear their words and observe their gestures, expressions, and tone of voice. Yet these cues are not in themselves the states of mind; they are signals of them, of greater and lesser reliability (Donath forthcoming). A smile, for example, generally denotes happiness or amusement, though there are also polite smiles, sarcastic smiles, and smile-like grimaces. What we often want to know is the feeling behind it; is it a genuine smile of warmth, or a forced smile masking discomfort?[13]

An intriguing possibility for improving communication is technological telepathy: using sensors to "read" what someone is thinking or feeling.[14] These biosensors measure bodily changes that are associated with different affective states, cues that are not ordinarily perceivable in our everyday interactions. These include heart rate, skin conductivity (how sweaty your hands are), and, ultimately, the electrical and chemical activity in your brain.

One use for this data is to supplement a less expressive medium (Picard and Cosier 1997). *Conductive Chat** (Fiore, Lakshmipathy, and DiMicco 2002), for example, combined text chat with affective sensing. Users wore gloves that measured galvanic skin response (GSR) as they typed their messages. When their skin response became elevated, a sign of increased emotional intensity, the application made the text they were sending larger and brighter.

Supplementing text chat with biosensed emotional information is an appealing idea. People use this medium for social interaction, where emotion is an important part of the message, but its speed and brevity make conveying the subtleties of affect quite difficult. Emoticons, which extend punctuation beyond the exclamation point and the question mark to convey sadness, happiness, irony, and so on, evolved and proliferate in this sparse medium, but they are still a limited emotive supplement. Because people often use text chat on mobile devices and in other circumstances where ease is important, a simple sensor that sends affective information and provides the chat with a layer of extra meaning without imposing any extra effort on the user is appealing.

Yet this is a significantly different type of affective communication from ordinary nonverbal expression and gesture. The main issue is the degree of control you have over what you convey. Our face and voice are under our control, though imperfectly. Learning this restraint is part of socialization; babies express their feelings nakedly; by even a few years old, children learn to mask particular emotions in certain contexts (Zeman and Garber 1996). In contrast, pulse, skin conductance, and other such bodily manifestations of emotional state are generally not under our control: they did not evolve for communication, and we are not socialized to manage them in the same way.

Biosensing raises privacy concerns. Today, such sensors are used mostly in coercive situations, such as lie detection. Here the person has information he wants to keep to himself and interrogators use sensors against the subject's will, attempting to gain access to his private thoughts. Literary portrayals of mind reading often portray it as aggressive and invasive. For example, "legilimency" in the *Harry Potter* books is the ability to read the thoughts of others against their will—and plant false memories in them.

Yet there are also positive accounts that portray it as an enviable skill, generally between people who are already very close, such as twins. A key criterion for evaluating direct affective communication is whether it is coerced or free, whether the participants are willing to experience this more direct and intimate connection.

Privacy is less of a concern, too, when the results are collective rather than individual. A promising scenario for such a device is distance lecturing. When you give a talk in person, you get feedback from the audience; you see people nodding or laughing. You can also notice if you are losing your audience; you see people moving about, rustling papers, perhaps getting ready to leave. Lectures given at a distance, however, receive little ongoing audience feedback. Sensing devices could convey the level of group-wide attentiveness.

Biosensing could also be used to influence people's affective states. For example, online discussions often become vitriolic forums where people get angry and abusive. Imagine an interface that conveyed reliable affective information about each participant—and the system made your words smaller and blurrier the angrier you became. You would need to work on being calm, rather than loud and aggressive, in order to get your point across. An experimental game uses brainwave sensing to teach people to relax: only when the subject is calm do the controls work as desired (Nijholt, Bos, and Reuderink 2009). Conversely, one could design rather nefarious games in which players need to work themselves into an actual fury to win a battle.

Affective sensing is still in its early stages. It includes the measurement both of social signals, communicative expressions that have evolved to convey emotion (like facial expression), and bodily responses that correspond to different affective states that neither evolved nor have been previously been used for communication. We are far from a time when people will put on lightweight, stylish helmets and convey their feelings directly to each other. But, as different types of sensing do become available, it is useful to think through the potential impact of such communication. To understand affective sensing, we need to have a more nuanced understanding of how and why our ability to convey emotion, using our normal communicative expressions as social signals, evolved as it did.

Further, the amount of control we have over our expressions is an open question. A popular view of expression (both facial expressions and gestures) is that their function is to be a readout of our internal state. As we become socialized, our visible expressions are filtered through social convention, so while the "natural" expression would be the pure emotion readout, the socialized, filtered expression represses much of that. To maintain social correctness, we struggle to keep the expression of felt emotions at bay. The psychologist Alan Fridlund has argued against this view that deems "fake" those expressions that result from complying with social rules or otherwise conveying a false image (Fridlund 1997). Fridlund critiques what he calls the "crypto-moralistic view of deception"—that an authentic self is hidden under false surface expressions, but detectable through "leaked" expressions (Ekman

1992). Fridlund argues that we would not have evolved a communicative function that was often at odds with what we wanted and with our best interests. Instead, he posits a model based on behavioral ecology: our expressions and gestures evolved as communicative functions, coevolving with responsiveness to them. As communication, their function is to cause a response from the recipient; for example, babies cry in order to get a response from a caretaker. Although some inner state—discomfort, hunger, fear—may trigger the crying, the baby may not be consciously trying to attract attention. The purpose of the crying, and the reason it survived as an evolved trait, is to gain care and attention. The response to babies' cries coevolved with them. In this model, the "leaked expressions" that Ekman claims are cues to deception are rather the result of being conflicted about what message to send. People who have no ethical conflict about the deception they are making, like sociopathic liars and people who believe that the lie they are telling is morally justified, do not show this "leakage" of truth. This is unsurprising in the behavioral ecology view, as they have no internal conflict about what they are saying.

Framing expressions and gestures as communicative acts, rather than outward displays of inner feelings, puts more starkly the difference between sensing our traditional expressions and biosensing our internal states. The biosensors measure internal states that have to do with our preparedness to respond: fight or flight, for example. They provide a readout of emotion that reflects the physiology of our emotional experience. In this view, the function of our facial expression and gestures is quite different. Our emotional state shapes our facial expression, but so does the social context: whom we are with, the situation, our history with this person, who else is here, what we want to happen, what we want the other person to think, how we want to influence him or her, and so on.

Face and voice are under our control—imperfectly, but trying to control them is part of our socialization process. The physiological correlates of emotion that biosensors measure are not under our control, nor did they evolve for communication. Today's heart rate and GSR sensors—even today's fMRIs and other brain activity monitors—produce crude measurements, but they will improve. As a thought experiment, imagine a biosensor capable of "mind-reading," something that gives us an accurate readout of someone's internal state. Would we want this?

Of course, we also do not know what such a readout would be. Our mind and memory shape our experience of how we think, even how we see our surroundings, into a coherent narrative. When I look at the world around me, it seems stable, familiar. But the unfiltered, unprocessed perception I have of it is one where my eye is in constant saccadic movement, where the colors change radically with changes in light, where perspectives shift as I move. Our minds take care of smoothing all of this into the familiar sensations we have of seeing a panorama of solid surroundings. Similarly, our thoughts and emotions are much more chaotic than we consciously experience them to be. For this thought experiment, let's imagine a sensor that can detect the thoughts we have at a conscious level—something perhaps like the stream of consciousness that modern writers such as James Joyce and William Faulkner have tried to capture. This is the interior space of our unshared thoughts; it is our experience of being bored but looking attentive, of noticing the egg stain on a colleague's shirt. What is most noticeable is the great discrepancy between our thoughts and our normal outward expression. Though one might call it deceptive, that word is appropriate only if we believe that the purpose of our social interactions is to perceive the inner core of the other.

Such naked revelation is far from social. Sociability requires a balance between revealing and restraint. Face to face, we see this in the struggle we have at times to conceal our emotions. We have a great deal of control over what we reveal, but it is far from complete. On the whole, society functions with this balance. We cannot always get away with hiding our thoughts or motivations, but neither are they open for all to read. As we design new social media, we need to think about where we want to set this balance (Farah 2005; Racine and Illes 2007). At one end of the spectrum are interfaces where you can be anything, where concealing much of yourself is easy. At the other end is the futuristic world where direct neural interfaces remove the social barriers we place between our thoughts and what we communicate to others.

Why should we be concerned about these distant future issues? One reason is that it helps us to see the inadvertently revealing aspects of our normal communication as part of a continuum. Even in text, a medium in which we have much editorial control, we reveal a lot, especially if we are writing quickly without careful review. Face to face, our voice, facial expressions, and so on reveal quite a bit, and we inevitably read character into faces (even if we tend to be wrong; Zebrowitz 1997).

Another reason is that at least some versions of biosensing are not all that far off in the future—and are possible without one's consent. Computer analysis of video images of one's face on a webcam can reveal blood pressure, pulse, and breathing rate; these biometrics can be used to infer affect (Picard, Vyzas, and Healey 2001; Poh, McDuff, and Picard 2011). What are the implications if, unknown to you, the person you are chatting with via video is conducting this type of analysis?

In the next chapter, we look at further privacy issues that arise with new technologies.

11

PRIVACY AND PUBLIC SPACE

Technology is radically changing what is private and what is public in our daily lives. Our personal, professional, and financial interactions increasingly take place online, where almost everything is archived and thus potentially permanently searchable and publishable. Cameras are ubiquitous in public plazas; our strolls are recorded by storeowners, government agencies, and, of course, our friends, who post and tag pictures of us. We share our location both deliberately via updates to locative social media and inescapably via our location-aware smartphones.

Historically, human interaction was local and ephemeral; only those nearby could witness it, and the words, once spoken, disappeared in the passing of time. Today, however, our interactions, and other's observations of them, can reach across space and persist in time. Surveillance cameras open seemingly private rooms to distant and unseen observers; archives retain casual conversations and outgrown profiles, forever enabling their out-of-context and possibly inopportune redisplay. These technologies make it difficult to distinguish between what is private and what is public. We are often unaware of the recording of our words and actions, and do not intuitively grasp that casual interactions, once fleeting and ephemeral, are now permanently etched digital artifacts.

Privacy is about maintaining control of information about ourselves. This can include what we are thinking, what we said to another person, what we did last night, our undressed body, our favorite book, and so on. Privacy is also contextual (Nissenbaum 1998, 2004). I may discuss my family problems with one friend, but not another, and I certainly would not want them to be publicly broadcast. I may be comfortable naked with my spouse, but not my

Communication technologies have been disrupting our notion of privacy for over a century. In 1890, Warren and Brandeis wrote "The Right to Privacy," one of the fundamental legal articles on privacy, and many of the concerns it raises are still troubling today.

> Recent inventions and business methods call attention to the next step which must be taken for the protection of the person, and for securing to the individual what Judge Cooley calls the right "to be let alone." Instantaneous photographs and newspaper enterprise have invaded the sacred precincts of private and domestic life; and numerous mechanical devices threaten to make good the prediction that "what is whispered in the closet shall be proclaimed from the house-tops." (Warren and Brandeis 1890, 195)

coworkers. Privacy varies from situation to situation and culture to culture. I can freely share my taste in books if it is innocuous, if it is congruent with the mores of my community, or if I live in an open and tolerant society. But if my taste reveals my deep religious commitments in a vehemently secular context or, vice versa, proclaims my atheism in a religious world, I may prefer to keep my reading habits more private—not necessarily secret, but limited to the people who I feel are accepting of my beliefs.

Privacy is important because access to private information about us by the wrong person or agency can be harmful. The direst concern is with an intrusive and repressive government, like Big Brother of *1984* and the spies and agencies of recent and ongoing totalitarian regimes. Even for those of us lucky enough to live in a more open society, history shows that governments are in constant flux, and there is no guarantee that today's democracy will be free forever. The data now collected for innocuous reasons may be used tomorrow by a less benign authority.

There are also concerns about employers and insurers who can hire, fire, and deny services based on information they have been able to glean about us. More insidiously, there are people and institutions who may not directly harm us, but whose motivations do not align with our own. Marketers, for example, are among the most voracious amassers of information about what people do and say online. Are they working for us, helping us find the goods and services we need? Or are they working against us, manipulating our tastes and values to make us believe we have a ceaseless need for new purchases?

In these examples, we are concerned about protecting our privacy from outside agencies, from governments and corporations that seek to constrain and influence our beliefs and behaviors. But there is another, social aspect of privacy. We need privacy to maintain a variety of relationships with diverse people (Rachels 1975). I may tell an off-color joke or use profanity in front of my friends, among whom it is an accepted way of speaking. But I would not use this language in front of my great aunt, who would be shocked, or my children, to whom I try set an example of model behavior, or my colleagues, whom I want to think of me as composed and dignified. Thus, I would be quite discomfited to find that a recording of my friends and me joking around in this manner was circulating among my relatives, kids, or coworkers. Until recently, it was unlikely that such a recording would exist. Today, camera-equipped phones, designed for easy and instant publishing of their content, are present in most social situations, making every acquaintance a potential paparazzo. Dinner-party attendees post live updates from the table about the conversation and the food. Both online and off, it is becoming harder to discern who is privy to one's words and easier to promulgate conversations and other activities to people outside the intended audience. Technology is eroding our ability to keep separate the many facets of our lives.

Privacy is important, but more privacy is not always better. We can protect our privacy by saying nothing and leaving no traces. Taken to an extreme, a very private world is anonymous, lonely, and anarchic. We need to have public realms, where we encounter new people and new ideas and where self-imposed constraint on actions, rather than the absence of watching eyes, maintains privacy. Vibrant public spaces are of great value to a community. Public spaces are for celebrations and protests, for commerce and socializing; by being out in public, we see how others appear and act. There is an energy that comes from being seen by others and making the effort to act in our public role.

In some ways, technology is making our world more private. It was not so long ago that we could easily see what our fellow subway riders were reading because their books and magazines were clearly visible. Today, tiny screens hide what people are reading or listening to on digital media. This is a small but significant loss in the social vividness of the city, as taste in books and music is one way people define their social identity. Many workplaces have become eerily silent, as employees who once gathered to chat at water coolers now stay in their offices (or even at home), communicating mostly online. The sociability that was once available simply by being in a public space is diminishing.

In other ways, technology is creating new public spaces. The Internet provides numerous platforms for public speech; we can voice our opinions, display our photographs, and publish our songs to a global audience with unprecedented ease. *What* we do in these new, mediated public spaces is much the same as what we do in traditional public spaces: we seek out entertainment, support political causes, and meet new people. But mediated public spaces are significantly different; words and images persist indefinitely, audiences are often invisible, and people's identities range from wholly anonymous to extensively documented. These new forms of public information can help reinvigorate public space, but they can also be a nightmare of violated privacy and repressed behavior. (And the line between physical and mediated spaces grows blurrier. We enter mediated public spaces when we go online from the privacy of our computer screens. We also enter them, perhaps unwittingly, when we walk into a space where cameras and other recorders are transforming ephemeral physical actions into archived data traces.)

The design of new technologies shapes private life and public space.[1] Design can make a camera invisible or prominent, and it is a design choice to publicly display its video to the people it records or to show it secretly only to a distant watcher. It is a design choice for a social network site to allow its users to present different facets of themselves to different people or to insist that they present the same view to all. Yet knowing which design to choose is complicated. Privacy is not an unmitigated good: it involves trade-offs with public life, sociability, safety, and convenience. Furthermore, a design that seems to protect privacy may ultimately compromise it. For example, if I write something today in a conversation that is kept private among a small group, but my words persist into an unprivate future and are eventually publicly revealed, might my privacy have been better protected if I had never had the expectation of privacy and acted accordingly?

Privacy and publicity are complementary and need to be in balance. A world in which everything is private, in which you see little of your fellow inhabitants, is a world without society. It is a world where people act in isolation, one where social mores have no place to develop. Alternatively, a world in which everything is public is one where social control is overwhelming, where every act and expression is open to scrutiny. We need public space, where we can encounter the new and unexpected, where we can see and be seen by others. And we need private space, free from the constraining norms of the greater world, in which to act as an individual and with a smaller group.

Indeed, public and private form a continuum. Many of our actions are public to some group—our family, our coworkers, our fellow cross-dressers or cat fanciers—but private to our other social groups and the rest of the world. The street is obviously public, but even in "the privacy of your own home" your family is also a public, with its own set of rules for how one behaves. How much control you have over the norms of a situation affects whether you perceive it to be public and controlled by others or private and controlled by you. danah boyd notes that teenagers think of the family as public space and their friends as the private world, whereas adults perceive the opposite (boyd 2006).

Tolerance also affects our need for privacy. The drawbacks of a highly public world—intense social control, endless scrutiny—are ameliorated in a society that accepts and protects diversity of opinions and behaviors. When the public sphere is liberal and gives people much freedom, there is less urgency for privacy.

Many of the designs we discuss in this book change the balance between privacy and public space. For example, visualizations of interaction history can make past actions accessible to new, unforeseen audiences for far longer than if they had passed into the back pages of the digital archive. A designer who is aware of the privacy issues involved can modify the visualization to create the desired balance, in this case possibly by limiting the amount of older material that is included or personalizing the view so that people see only material they would have had access to at the time it was created. The goal of this chapter is to help the reader think through what that "desired balance" is in different situations, for we need to balance the public and the private, the collective good and personal liberty, for society to thrive.

DESIGNS THAT DEMARCATE THE PUBLIC AND THE PRIVATE

In a plaza, we assume that other people in the space can see us; we may be aware, too, of those looking out the windows of overlooking buildings. But new technologies make it harder for us to see those who see us. We are often unaware of the cameras that make us observable from miles away and for years to come. Online, we may know that we are posting a remark in a public forum, but we may not intuitively grasp the scale of the audience, nor the ways that this remark may become part of our growing virtual persona. Design plays an important role in enhancing privacy by clarifying the scope and boundaries of our ambiguous public spaces; it can help us understand what is public and what is private.

The illusion of privacy induces people to act, erroneously, as if they were in a private space. Online, many spaces feel as if they are very private—that one's actions are seen by no one and that one's words are perused by only a few. In fact, these actions are happening in a space that is not only public, in that many eyes can see it, but is also hyperpublic in that it can be seen for an extended time, in many contexts.

Designs can mislead us about the public extent of a space or they can make it quite legible: a hidden camera breaks open a space without the knowledge of those observed, a visible camera makes them aware of the possibility of being recorded and watched from afar, and a prominent live video feed makes it more vividly and intuitively clear that what happens in the space can be seen by distant and future viewers. We act differently in private than in public and need to be able to perceive those distinctions in order to act appropriately. Our knowledge is, however, inevitably asymmetric: a public display of the images and data gathered in a space provides proof that it is public, but just because there is no such display does not mean that the space is private.

Individuals' standards of personal privacy vary; some desire attention whereas others seek isolation. A well-designed space, whether virtual or physical, should help them see who can see them and understand how far their words and actions can travel. It is then up to the person to choose how to act and what to reveal.

Making Audiences Visible

In our face-to-face communication, we take for granted the ability to see who is listening. Online, however, the audience is often invisible; we are aware of the people who participate actively, but we forget about the silent readers, who may greatly outnumber the vocal ones (Nonnecke and Preece 2003). This lack of audience awareness helps create the feeling of intimacy that can characterize even very large online discussions: people feel—and thus write—as if they are addressing only a few known companions, not the multitudes who may actually be reading. This can be good; the intimate tone of informal speech and personal revelation makes for more interesting reading than the stiffly self-conscious voice of someone addressing a vast audience. Yet this lack of awareness can create a voyeuristic dynamic in which people reveal far more than they would were they aware of the scale of the discussions.

We can redesign discussion sites to make the audience visible. One approach is to show the size of the audience without revealing the individual readers' identity. We see such audience counters on Web pages; they are anonymous[2] and do not discourage people from reading. However, they are not very intuitive: a page with a note at the bottom saying that there have been 10,000 visitors is not viscerally different from one that claims only 50. A graphical approach, even one simply showing dots for visitors, would provide a more vivid impression (figure 11.1).

Making the size of the audience visible transforms the social dynamics of the interaction. A writer who becomes more aware of how large her audience is or how many strangers are in it might write more formally and disclose less

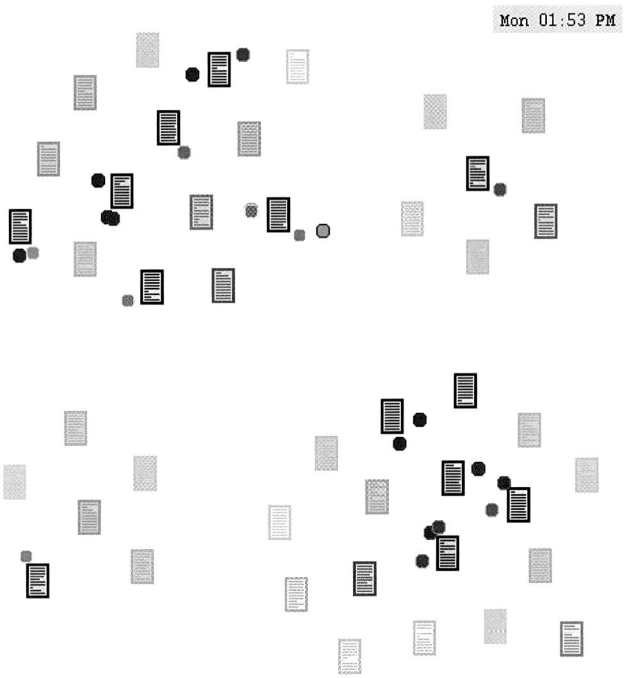

FIGURE 11.1
Nelson Minar, *Visualizing the Crowds at a Website** (1999). This visualization sketch displays visitors to a page as colored dots and one can see them move from page to page. Pages with recent visitors are bright (Minar and Donath 1999).

personal information.[3] Publicly disclosing the identities of the readers would have an even greater impact, making them more circumspect about what they could be seen perusing.

For readers, the obvious privacy concern is with controversial or embarrassing material. But making readers visible would also affect behavior around seemingly innocuous social material. Let us look at how this would affect, for example, status updates. As an invisible reader, I can peruse the updates of many friends and acquaintances, stopping to comment on only a very few, if any. The friends whose proud achievements, vacation photos, or latest jokes receive no comment from me do not know if I have said nothing because I do not care, cannot think of something to say, or simply have not seen them. As a named and visible reader, I would need to be more selective about what I read. And because it would be apparent that I was aware of something, I would often feel obligated to respond. I might choose not to read what promises to be an accounting of an important event, because I do not have the time to respond properly and do not want people to know that I have read and am aware of the event, but have said nothing. Visible readers have greater social responsibilities.

Our existing social norms influence our understanding of privacy. If we frame online writing as conversation, we often expect all participants to be visible. This is why, as we saw in chapter 7, nonparticipating readers may be called, pejoratively, "lurkers" even though as readers they benefit the active participants. In a face-to-face conversation or a telephone call, the norm is to be aware of the audience; an unseen listener is an eavesdropper. Allowing the speaker (or writer) to see who is listening is courteous rather than invasive. On the other hand, if we frame the writing as publication, we expect privacy for the readers. Reading privately is a revered right. Thus, if we think of social media as being like publishing, then making the audience visible is itself an invasion of privacy, reminiscent of asking libraries to reveal their patrons' borrowing records or the concern over electronic books keeping tabs on their readers (Ozer and Lynch 2010). Naming the readers of, say, an online political tract has unpleasant overtones of state surveillance.

To support privacy, designs need to clarify the conceptual model underlying participants' expectations of what they can see and what they can hide. The publishing model, with its invisible audience, is suitable in some situations, and the conversation model, with its mutually visible participants, is suitable in others. A social medium can follow either model; designing it to support privacy means providing cues to ensure that participants' expectations match the medium's affordances.

Seeing Surveillance

In some situations, the best way to protect privacy is to remind people that they are in public and that their audience may include unintended watchers. Mistaken expectations about privacy are frequent at work (Nord, McCubbins, and Nord 2006), especially as communication technologies blur the distinction between office and home. We chat online with friends while in the office, and keep up with professional duties from home. Employees often feel that their email and other communications are private, but they actually are not, especially if they are using company equipment and accounts. If a company says that management may scrutinize all email, it is important that the employees habitually think of their email at work as public communication.

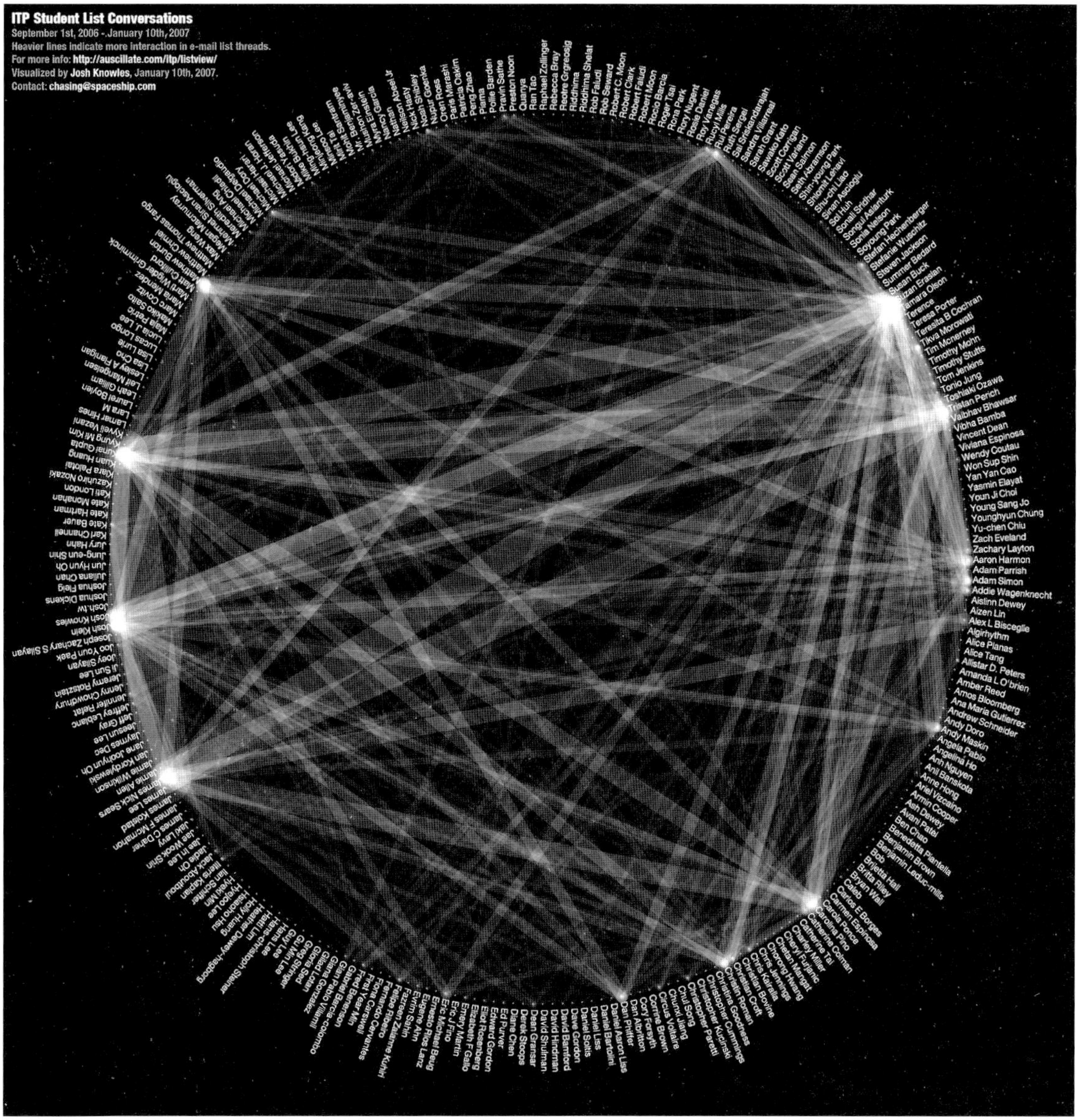

FIGURE 11.2

Josh Knowles, *ITP Student List Conversations* (2007). This visualization shows the quantity and variety of email contact between students in an academic department (Knowles 2007).

Yet although they may receive notices that their correspondence may be read and their online activities monitored, employees frequently do not understand that there is not a zone of privacy for personal correspondence or forget they may be observed.

Imagine a workplace common area with a big dynamic display that shows the flow of email in the company (see, for example, figure 11.2). Such a display is interesting as a social map of the company, but it also functions as a visceral reminder that these emails are not private. If I am secretly dating someone in the next department, it would make me think twice about sending him a note via company email. Do I want a connection between us to show up in a public display? If not, I need to find another way to reach him. If I want to schedule a confidential meeting with Human Resources to complain about my boss, it reminds me that he may read my email. Perhaps I should call, instead.

The display would not reveal the contents of the email; you could still send confidential company email to coworkers without any of the material being revealed to casual visitors, but you would be reminded and come to intuitively feel that your actions, when using the company's communication technologies, are open in various ways within the company. It makes the virtual space semi-public, like the glass-walled offices that are popular in many businesses. We can close the door so no one hears what we are talking about, but anyone can see who is meeting with whom. This type of display would have a chilling effect on users, but that can be a good thing. Given that the employees' correspondence is already monitored, they benefit from greater awareness, and the company benefits by having employees focus on work-related issues. (One might argue against tightly monitoring employees, but then the solution is for the monitoring to stop or be limited, not for it to exist while its subjects are only vaguely aware of it.) Design needs to balance the benefit of providing people with the knowledge that they are or might be watched with the cost to them of the pervasive anxiety this knowledge can cause.

In 1785, the English philosopher Jeremy Bentham proposed the "panopticon," a prison designed so that prisoners could be under surveillance at any time but would be unable to tell at any given moment if they were actually being observed or not (see figure 11.3). Though at any particular time they might be unobserved, they would need to act at all times as if they were under an omniscient and omnipresent eye (Bentham 1791). The concept of the panopticon resonates in a world where surveillance is increasingly ubiquitous.

FIGURE 11.3
Statesville Prison in Illinois is one of many prisons built on a panoptic model. A single guard in the center tower could watch hundreds of prisoners in their surrounding cells.

Social theorist Michel Foucault wrote in *Discipline and Punish*, his history of prisons and punishment, "The panoptic schema, without disappearing as such or losing any of its properties, was destined to spread throughout the social body; its vocation was to become a generalized function" (Foucault 1979, 207).

Though the phrase "ignorance is bliss" sounds unsettlingly like the Party's slogans in *1984*,[4] it actually comes from an eighteenth-century poem that suggests that given the inevitability of suffering and death, it is better to enjoy life without being consumed with thoughts of the misery to come (Gray 1753). How much should we be aware of the possibility of surveillance? When is it better to know, and to anxiously limit what we say and do, and when is that self-censorship itself a problem? The answer depends on who is watching.

Who Is Watching Us?

Our feelings about being observed depend on who is observing us. Why are they watching us? Is it for our own good, or does it harm us? Is it an asymmetric observation, where they watch us while we are unaware of them? Or is it an experience of mutual assessment? This book focuses on private and public social interaction, where controlling and revealing personal information is part of negotiating trust and establishing bonds among individuals. Yet we need to be aware of others who observe our actions—governments, employers, insurers, marketers—whose purpose may be detrimental to us. They add a cost to our interactions that may be steep enough to make us rethink how we act or demand a greater degree of privacy in our social spaces.

Most readers of this book live under nearly constant government surveillance in public spaces. Security cameras, increasingly able to recognize faces, monitor stores, parks, and streets. This surveillance is increasingly pervasive in seemingly private spaces too. Private phone conversations may be surreptitiously recorded and one's shopping, Web browsing, and travel activity analyzed. The aim of this surveillance is to combat terrorism and crime; many citizens support it, especially at times and in places where fear of attack is high. It is benign to the extent that the government's laws and actions are just. Yet even a just government can have corrupt or overzealous departments and individuals. And governments change, whereas databases last forever.

Governments are not the only watchers. Corporations watch, too. They want to know if you are credit worthy, insurable, or employable. Many people in Europe and the United States see this as a more immediate concern than government repression, for though they think of themselves as generally law-abiding, they have done things that could make them ineligible for a desired service or position. Feeling that all your actions, everywhere, must conform to a company's ideal puts tight constraints on behavior. Yet, some of this observation is for our own benefit. Having our data used for medical purposes is generally helpful, letting us and/or our doctors make better decisions for our health. However, insurers' use of that same data is often harmful to us when they seek information that allows them to refuse to reimburse us for medical expenses.

Surveillance can be indirectly beneficial. The government may intrude on our privacy for our own good, claiming that it needs information about everyone to protect against terrorists and criminals (Baker 2003; Cole and Dempsey 2006). We may benefit from the government having access to other people's information, but we do not derive any benefit from—and arguably are harmed by—their access to our own information. Here we need to weigh the benefits against the privacy costs. (What has been disturbing in the years since 9/11 is the claim that fighting terrorism is infinitely important, trumping all costs.) Can the government maintain security with lower privacy costs, for example, by diligently destroying information as soon as it is reasonably deemed irrelevant? And what are the social costs? If the government uses the data it finds this way for suppressing dissent, the cost is extremely high.

Whether marketers' use of our private information is beneficial or not is up for debate. They claim that by being able to better target advertising to our wants and needs, they can provide information that is more relevant to us—which sounds helpful. However, the "benefit" of being persuaded to consume more, of ever more skillfully and subtly being made dissatisfied with what we have, benefits the advertiser and its client, but is arguably quite costly to us—and the environment.

The benefit to us of employers, school admission offices, and the like having access to private information is also complex. Admission and employment are generally zero-sum games; someone will be hired, and one person's loss is another's gain. The key issue is whether the information the employer is using is relevant to the decision. If it is—if it helps her make a better decision and is in line with what the community thinks is pertinent information for assessing that sort of job or opportunity—then it is beneficial. Though it may cost one person the job, another, presumably better-suited person does get it. The problem is when the information used is not materially relevant to the decision. This is a matter for the community to decide (though what constitutes the community and how they made this decision is not always clear). The United States as a country is a community that has outlawed racial and other forms of discrimination in hiring. Interviewers are privy to the applicants' race and gender, but are barred from using it in their assessments. We need to make similar determinations about the use of all kinds of private data: health information, online comments, photographs, and so on.

A very different category of observers is other people in a social setting: "Although Big Brother actions may threaten life and liberty, it is interpersonal privacy matters that figure primarily in decisions about technology use on an everyday basis" (Palen and Dourish 2003, 130). This is the privacy of

In his essay "On Face-Work," Erving Goffman wrote:

> Every person lives in a world of social encounters, involving him either in face-to-face or mediated contact with other participants. In each of these contacts, he tends to act out what is sometimes called a line—that is, a pattern of verbal and nonverbal acts by which he expresses his view of the situation. … The term face may be defined as the positive social value a person effectively claims for himself by the line others assume he has taken during a particular contact. … A person may be said to have, or be in, or maintain face when the line he effectively takes presents an image of him that is internally consistent, that is supported by judgments and evidence conveyed by other participants and that is confirmed by evidence conveyed through impersonal agencies in the situation. … A person is said to be in the wrong face when information is brought forth in some way about his social worth which cannot be integrated … into the line that is being sustained for him. (Goffman 1967, 5)

social mores, of social expectations, of keeping face and experiencing embarrassment. This social privacy is changing as our interactions move online, where they are stored, archived, collated, visualized, and permanently retrievable. We are entering a world where the impression we make comes not just from our present demeanor, but also from a vast shadow of past words, photos, and others' comments. Much has been written about technology and changing expectations of external privacy, but the impact of new media on social privacy and public space is not as well understood. Why do people want to know private information about each other, and why do people want to provide it? Is this beneficial or not? Who benefits? Who loses?

MANAGING IDENTITIES

In the physical world, we maintain privacy through the separation of different facets of our lives. Coworkers with strongly differing political or religious beliefs can get along by not discussing those facets of their lives at lunch together; parents of young children can be silly and warm at home yet in charge and imposing at work. For everyday privacy, the distance between work and home, or between different sets of friends, can be sufficient to keep different aspects of our identity separate. Online, we need stronger walls between the aspects of our lives we wish to keep distinct.

We all work to create an impression on other people—to make them think a certain way about us. This impression, or "face," changes given different audiences and varying contexts (Goffman 1966). Sometimes we may want to seem authoritative and knowledgeable, while at other times, with other people, we may want to seem loving or sinister, empathetic or helpless. But we cannot always present the face we ideally wish to show. I may want to show my boss that I am really brilliant and responsible, but if my job is very menial, I may have little opportunity to do so. Or, information may surface that is contrary to what I want the others to know—that disrupts and distorts the face I wish to present. For example, if I'm out with a group of new and old friends, one who has known me for a long time might tell revealing stories from my past that contradict my current image. Such disruptive information is a form of privacy violation: information that was meant for one context has been revealed in another one (Rosen 2000). These violations need not be malicious or even intentional. Indeed, simply being in the presence of people you know from disparate social contexts makes such privacy violations likely.

It can be awkward to encounter people from various social circles together—simply choosing which voice to use means that to some members of the mixed audience you will seem to be acting out of character.

Mixing social contexts can also be beneficial, providing depth to the impressions we have of each other. It is nice to know that your friend is a well-respected expert in her professional life, or that your highly efficient colleague is sweet and silly with his toddler. Politicians running for office strive to keep a balance between the humanizing effect of allowing us to see them with their families and maintaining the aura of authority and competence that their official image conveys.

Technology Collapses Contexts

In the pre-Internet face-to-face world, it was relatively easy to keep one's social contexts separate. Online, however, these contexts often collapse. On a social network site, readers of your updates and the writers of comments about them may include your colleagues, your anarchy-espousing college roommate, and your prim great aunt (Donath and boyd 2004). Technology, including search engines and social network sites, makes it more difficult to maintain the separation we have in the physical world between different roles and facets of our personality. Sometimes this is deliberate. Mark Zuckerberg, the founder of Facebook, has stated that one of his goals is to break down these social walls between people; and Facebook's design strongly encourages people to present personal updates, including photos of family vacations, announcements of work travel, statements of political opinion and religious belief, in a single undifferentiated context. "You have one identity," Zuckerberg has said; "having two identities for yourself is an example of a lack of integrity" (D. Kirkpatrick 2010, 199).

This demand for a single, un-nuanced self-presentation oversimplifies the complexity of human personality and human social existence. Furthermore, this stance is at best naive about the importance of privacy to people outside of the mainstream, whose beliefs and practices leave them vulnerable to harassment or persecution. It is easy to espouse the extreme transparency of an unprivate life when your religion, tastes, and lifestyle align with the values of those in power.[5] For others, privacy is essential to be able to safely discuss their ideas, practice their religion, show affection for their lover, and so on. However, not only the marginalized seek privacy to avoid conflict. Our ability to have a diverse society—to build communities of people who are different, and who disagree about things—depends on our ability to mask our differences when necessary. Indeed, "politeness" is primarily concerned with preventing overly honest interactions; we learn to be gracious when we are actually irritated, to say thank you when we are disappointed, and to act calm when we are seething inside.[6] Both in the course of trying to present ourselves in as good a light as possible and in striving to be nice to others, we may act in ways that are at odds with how we actually feel.

What is the social effect of being unable to present different facets of ourselves in different circumstances? One possibility is that people will be more circumspect. They will keep more information offline, and say mostly innocuous, even banal things. Many users of Facebook have said they follow this strategy in order to not offend or act out of character to the diverse set of people who are privy to their updates (Lampinen et al. 2011). Another, perhaps utopian, possibility is that people, upon seeing more about each other, will become more tolerant. In 1985, the communication theorist Joshua Meyrowitz argued that media (at that time, primarily mass media) were breaking down the barriers between social groups by exposing facets of their lives and ideas that had previously been hidden from each other (Meyrowitz 1985). Understanding the role of technology in pushing society toward tolerance or divisiveness is complex. Online forums bring together very diverse groups of people, but these gatherings often result in highly polarized antagonisms. Simply throwing people with fundamentally different beliefs together does not by itself promote tolerance; usually the opposite occurs. Time can bring better results, as when you learn that someone with whom you already have some bond is less similar to you than you had thought; here the existing tie motivates learning more about why the other holds these disparate beliefs.

As a group of people gets to know one another better, the experience of being together transforms from the public experience of being amidst strangers to the more trusting and private experience of being among friends. As strangers, we are circumspect about what we tell each other and unable to predict each other's actions. As we learn anything about another, it helps us to categorize him, to feel as if he is a familiar type, and to know what to expect from him. Furthermore, we may exchange confidences with someone, private information that functions as a social currency which we trade to establish trust. This engenders trust through secrecy; confidants have the bond of trusting each other with information they do not share with others. Telling something to me and no one else signals that you trust me; if you tell me along with one hundred other people, there is no longer a special significance. Sharing information widely diminishes the trust achieved through shared confidences.

To connect with others we need to be somewhat vulnerable, somewhat open. We must reveal a bit of ourselves. It is part of the constant trade-off of privacy versus accessibility in the social sphere.

Creating Context with Pseudonyms

Online, the extremes of identity—anonymity and real-name identity—are relatively easy to implement. It is the gray space of everyday life that is difficult to replicate, the incomplete but functional privacy that comes from the spatial and temporal separation of home and work, friends and family. We can attempt to recreate our faceted identities, using multiple identifiers—pseudonyms—for different roles. People do this by using one email address for games or dating, another one for work, a third for shopping or political activity, and so on. Face to face, the separation in place and time between our social, familial, and professional worlds is usually sufficient to give us the privacy we need to maintain the distinct facets we present to each. Online, however, search engines conglomerate all data and activities carried out under a particular identifier, requiring a more radical separation of different identities. These separations are delicate, for once there is a single public connection link between the two personas, the identities are linked.

The notion of "local" is central to privacy. In the physical world, the difference between private and public is often a distinction in space: you are in your room (private) or out in the street (public). Between these extremes is "locally public." Many private spaces are locally public: a classroom, restaurant, office, a party at someone's house. A private matter can be locally public, within a small group; the privacy violation occurs when it spreads beyond the bounds of the intended group. As our actions and interactions move online, privacy centers around identification: you are anonymous (private) or named (public). Pseudonyms are local identities; they are identifiers that maintain history and reputation, but are distinct from their creator's real-world identity; one can have multiple distinct and separate pseudonyms.

I can create a pseudonym that I will use, say, for doing product reviews online. We would like these reviews to not be anonymous; part of their value is that we can see a whole history of someone's taste, so you know if it aligns with yours. A pseudonym keeps these reviews from being part of my public persona. Why should I care? I may be reviewing personal products, whether medicine for itchy feet, or the book I just read, or even just the restaurants I eat at or the hotdogs I buy. Is this private information? Some of it is. What parts of it are private is a personal decision. One person might like to have all the fantasy novels that he read be part of what all people know about him; for others, it is a private taste and not part of the public persona that they wish to fashion. One person might want others to know about the elegant restaurant he visits (indeed, this display might be for him the main point of the visit), while another might feel uncomfortable about publicly displaying such extravagance. I may want to discuss controversial political matters without my opinions being part of my real-life public identity. I may simply want to keep private how I spend my days: I might have no problem with others knowing that I read the *Times* or buy Palmolive, but I do not want the fact that I spend hours embroiled in virtual discussions to be part of my identity.

There is a whiff of the illicit about this, for in our ordinary life we seldom, unless engaging in a forbidden activity, resort to using a false name. Yet pseudonyms provide both accountability and privacy if they are implemented in a manner that encourages people to establish a good history and reputation with them. (The data portraits we discussed in chapter 8 are one approach to creating a memorable representation of an individual without relying on his or her real name and physical appearance.) Online, pseudonymity recreates the level of personal privacy we expect in our everyday lives.

HOLES IN THE BOUNDARIES OF SPACE AND TIME

Twentieth-century America was in many ways the most private of societies. Huge numbers of people migrated to the relative anonymity of cities, surrounded by strangers. It was the century in which going to the bank went from a social exchange with a clerk with whom you exchanged pleasantries and greetings to the much more efficient but impersonal interaction with a bank machine. Big companies transferred their employees every few years, resettling them in new faceless suburban tracts with wide and empty streets. Television moved entertainment from public theaters to private homes. Not only did we not know our neighbors' secrets, we did not even know their names. Privacy slid into isolation. Yet at the same time, it was becoming the most public of societies. At the beginning of the twentieth century, women ventured out only if properly covered up from wrist to ankle; by midcentury, they were on beaches wearing bikinis. Television let ordinary people expose their personal quirks in front of millions, coyly at first with programs such as *The Newlywed Game*, and accelerating to today's relentless broadcasts of plastic surgeries, family court battles, childbirth close-ups, and hoarders' piles of dirty laundry.

Entering the twenty-first century, American society is also, for the most part, a tolerant one. This, plus the abundance, if not excess, of privacy, creates a world in which many people place a low value on privacy. We post updates about our dates, our health, and our political beliefs. At the extreme, we allow cameras to follow us day and night, discuss our family's unhappiness on TV, and describe the minutiae of our daily life in tell-all blogs and memoirs. The openness of our society appears to be self-perpetuating: the more we see and hear of others' thoughts and actions, the less shocked we are by differences and the more tolerant our society becomes—and the less value we place on privacy.

America is the "Wild West" of privacy in two opposite ways. First, the myth of the frontier, of the endless ability to move West and start over as an unknown, history-free stranger, is deeply rooted in its culture; this is privacy through reinvention (Copple 1989). Second, however, privacy is not well protected. In America, it is open hunting season on data, as compared to Europe, where numerous laws govern the collection and use of citizens' information (Bignami 2007). Europe does not have the mythology of endless reinvention: many people still live in the towns and villages of their ancestors, deeply aware of how long one's history can linger. Europeans also have more immediate and vivid memories of the horrors a totalitarian regime can inflict and how it can use records to terrorize people. Thus, as we attempt to understand the rapid, technologically precipitated changes in our current experience of public and private, we need to keep in mind that our sense of "normal," of the proper balance between the two, was formed in a particular place and time, and is neither culturally nor historically universal (Solove 2002).

In the 1990s, it was difficult to find out much about a person who was neither famous nor personally known within one's social group. Today, whenever you come across a new person—a name mentioned in a news article, a person seated across from you at a business lunch, a potential

Richard Sennett, in his book *The Fall of Public Man* (1976), traces changing expectations among the upper class in the eighteenth and nineteenth centuries about how much knowledge one was expected to have in advance about new acquaintances. Eighteenth-century court society was a small world in which everyone knew or knew about everyone else. Upon introduction, the greeting convention was for the person of lower social standing to flatter the other extensively, mentioning his accomplishments and position. The assumption was that while you might meet new people, they would not be total strangers, but known-of entities within your greater community. As the center of social life moved from the court to the city, such meetings, even in the same rarified upper class, became encounters between strangers who as the decades passed knew less and less about each other. Public space became a world of encounters with strangers and people became more private in their public behavior; for example, public clothing became more guarded and less expressive.

babysitter—the first thing you are likely to do is to Google him. For some people, there is still very little information. But many others have extensive dossiers: pages of links to papers they've written; articles about them; photos at parties; blog postings reaching back several years; court records of their divorce and custody battles; their arguments in forums; and their reviews of shoes, hotels, and antifungal creams. Our social expectations are changing. It now seems strange if no information comes up in a search on someone you meet in a professional context. Has she really left no mark online, not even a posting? Has she not inspired anyone to say anything about her? Today we expect to be able to find data about others. This also changes what we expect others to know about us. If I am meeting someone for the first time, say, a researcher from a distant university, how much should I know about him? If I know nothing, it can seem a bit insulting, as if I did not think he was important enough to look up. Yet if I do such a search, and now I know that his dog recently died or he spent several years living in Mumbai, how do I bring up this personal knowledge I have about someone who had been a stranger only minutes before? We need new etiquette to help us appear to be interested and attentive, but not creepy stalkers.

Like celebrities who both crave fame yet complain about the cameras that follow them, we are ambivalent about whether we want more publicity or more privacy. People's reactions to these social changes vary greatly. A newspaper article about sharing in social media described people who enthusiastically and publicly post such things as what they ate, the clothes they bought, and where they are (Stone 2010, A1):

> Mr. Brooks, a 38-year-old consultant for online dating Web sites, seems to be a perfect customer. He publishes his travel schedule on Dopplr. His DNA profile is available on 23andMe. And on Blippy, he makes public everything he spends with his Chase Mastercard, along with his spending at Netflix, iTunes and Amazon.com.
>
> "It's very important to me to push out my character and hopefully my good reputation as far as possible, and that means being open," he said, dismissing any privacy concerns by adding, "I simply have nothing to hide."

It prompted an outpouring of almost unanimously negative comments, such as:

> Lack of common sense. That's all I can attribute it to. Seriously, what real or tangible purpose does posting everything you do or purchase serve. You can call me old fashioned, but privacy is something I (and countless other millions) would like to continue to enjoy.

And:

> I am a very private person and find appalling this need people have to expose everything about themselves on the web. I do not understand it. But I generally find the entire culture, from the worship of vapid celebrities to 50 percent high school drop out rates, appalling. None of it bodes well.

And:

> Years from now, when we look back, this sort of thing will be to the 2010s what polyester pants were to the 1970s.

Is this sharing part of a growing trend toward decreasing privacy, or is it a temporary fad? Perhaps it is more akin, in its risks and long-lasting repercussions, to taking acid in the 1960s than to wearing polyester pants, but nonetheless it still could be a passing fashion. By the time you read this, many of the websites mentioned will be gone.[7] In a couple of years, the way we provide information will have transformed, so that today's "status updates," "tweets," and "check-ins" will indeed sound dismally out of date. However, the concept of sharing extensive and seemingly mundane information online may well continue, for its social value goes beyond satisfying narcissistic tendencies.

Permanent Records

Judge Benjamin Cardozo wrote in 1931: "What gives the sting to writing is its permanence in form. The spoken word dissolves, but the written one abides and perpetuates the scandal."[8] The online world is a hyperpublic space that extends in time. The biggest transformation in privacy and public space the Internet has created is the retention of data into the indefinite future. Our spoken words are ephemeral, disappearing as soon as we utter them. Our traditional written words on paper are relatively controllable, individual objects: photos and diaries can be destroyed. But the words and images that reside online are tenacious. They are easily copied and live on in backups and other archives long after you think you have erased them. Although some things do indeed disappear, it is reasonable to assume that anything published online is there forever.

We think of the past as private, with time creating a curtain that shields our present self from our earlier days. Our mobile society has a mythology of personal reinvention and redemption. We believe in moving on, in creating a new life for ourselves. More prosaically, you may have spoken openly when you were young and single and jobs were plentiful, but now you want a more serious job or insurance. Or, you are now going through a difficult custody battle and wish to be able to present yourself as being as mainstream and vanilla as possible. But an ineradicable data shadow makes the past a part of the present.

A generation ago, students went off to college as blank social slates, able to start fresh, create a new identity independent of their high school role. Of course, not entirely new: personalities, skills, and interests did not change, and the careless, charismatic athlete was quickly distinguished from the awkward and introverted mathematician. But they could escape the roles they had outgrown; in entering a new social ecology, they could find a new niche. Today, students arrive with roommates already friended on Facebook, already calling them by the nicknames they had wished to shed.

For those of us who grew up in a time when every move was a fresh start, this new inescapability seems invasive. Yet those dislocating moves were a painful severance as well as a liberation, a harsh chopping away from the past as well as a fresh start. The new inescapability is also a new continuity, ending an era of disposable pasts. Our ineradicable data shadows certainly present enormous challenges to privacy. Yet making the past go away can be undesirable. The nightmare of *1984* is not only the pervasive surveillance, but also the constant rewriting of history. Winston, the novel's protagonist, works in the Ministry of Truth; his job is to revise past news stories to keep them in line with the Party's current positions.

We are living in an experiment, shifting rapidly from a culture in which reinvention was singularly easy, owing to great mobility and the relative anonymity of city life, to a culture in which the past is inescapable, a culture in which everything goes into your permanent record. Perhaps the cultural response to this will be a great belief in personal transformation. We may be more empathetic if we know more of the struggles someone had in becoming the person he is now. Or perhaps we will discount the past when it is too dissonant with the present. Many teens have been mortified when their mother brought out their baby pictures to entertain their date; but these pictures, no matter how embarrassing, seldom affect the date's impression of the present-day self. The diapered baby is too distant to connect to the current person.

Some legal scholars have proposed "reputation bankruptcy" as a potential (but problematic) solution to temporal privacy issues. The idea is to allow people to make a fresh start by removing some or all of their history from the online record (Rosen 2010; Zittrain 2008). There are legal precedents; convictions can be expunged from one's records, and one of the important tasks for a trial judge is determining what evidence—what tales from the past—can be heard during a trial.

Leaving out the considerable (and given the reproducibility of information, probably insurmountable) technological problems of instituting "reputation bankruptcy,"[9] a fundamental social question remains: what about the past do we as a society feel is legitimate to erase? We have rules about what constitutes normal personal information polishing and what verges on deception. Your resume, for example, is a history of your past jobs and education. You may omit things, and even rearrange the document to obscure these omissions (for example, the years you were out of the job market because of family, cult membership, or incarceration). But you are not allowed to pad it with nonexistent accomplishments; if caught doing so, you could face losing your job and possible legal prosecution. Social situations are murkier. Advice columns frequently feature questions from people unsure about what they must tell a new romantic partner about their past—other lovers, financial bankruptcy, marriage, an arrest?

In the physical world, we take for granted that we spend time and money crafting our appearance. We need to learn to craft our virtual self, too. For most people, the notion of consciously shaping what is online about you is still an abstraction. Those who frequently study other people's online data, who have a visceral sense of the portrait that data can draw, are the ones most likely to monitor and craft their online presence (Madden and Smith 2010). The visualizations of conversations and other social data that we discussed in the first half of the book are useful not only for perceiving others—they are an invaluable mirror for reflecting and grooming one's virtual self.

Observed Everywhere

Walking down a street today, I can see many people (strangers) going about their business. Although we are all out in public together, we retain quite a bit of privacy. I do not know where they are going or why, nor do I know much about them beyond what they have chosen to reveal about themselves. Our privacy comes not from being hidden, but from being obscure. Today, the footage from the increasingly ubiquitous surveillance cameras in public spaces effectively shows anonymous people going about their unknown business. Only when there is reason for suspicion, like a robbery, is the effort made to figure out who they are.

But once computers can recognize people and attach to their physical selves the vast hoards of official, commercial, and social information about them, obscurity evaporates. As face recognition improves (and in our online socializing, many of us unwittingly help by tagging images of our friends and ourselves), anyone will be able to point a camera at a stranger on the street, identify her and see a vivid portrait of the data she has generated, the reputation she has accrued, and the records she has left.

Today, this seems creepy; it is the end of privacy. Think of how self-conscious you feel when someone is looking closely at you. Now imagine that he can see a tremendous amount about you—not just your face, hair, clothes, and body, but also all the information that is publicly available about you. Maybe this is not such a bad thing for you. Maybe all the public records about you are things you are proud of: your job success, the articles you have published, and the winning races you have run. However, maybe there are things about you online that make you cringe: a negative article; an embarrassing photograph—maybe you were drunk, or maybe the picture just makes you look as if you were; the nasty flame war you got into years ago, the one that ended with everyone calling each other Nazis. Did you write a review for bad breath remedies, or for a book you read on what it is like to be married to an alcoholic? What about your search history? How much time do you spend watching celebrity meltdowns, how much do you spend on weight-loss products? You might well find the merging of the virtual and physical selves uncomfortable, knowing that anyone else in the park or the café who might be curious about you could see all this.

But the future inhabitant of that hyperpublic city, upon looking back at our current world, might find it unsettlingly opaque. Enigmatic strangers surround us. Yes, the astute observer can read quite a bit of identity information from passersby; we can recognize businesspeople versus construction workers, wealthy versus poor. Yet some wealthy people seek to be inconspicuous, whereas others who are poor strive to appear successful, and many people are reticently indeterminate, hiding lives of extraordinarily complexity under an unremarkable exterior. Our unaugmented public display, though not entirely uninformative, provides a layer of privacy through vagueness, ambiguity, and the ease of imitation.

Perhaps most unsettling to the time-traveler from the future would be our ignorance of whether the strangers around us are dangerous. Is the man on the playground park bench just reading his book or is he a child molester scouting his prey? Is the passerby who offered to help us with our flat tire a kind Samaritan or a potential thief? Because of this ignorance, we treat everyone with suspicion. If our car breaks down, we are told to stay inside with the doors locked, telephone the authorities for help, and check their (low-tech) ID carefully through the window before accepting aid. Safety concerns such as these may give us our first taste of widespread social augmentation. It is not hard to imagine a government deciding that in the name of security, all convicted felons or sex offenders must virtually broadcast their status, perhaps with an easily read RFID (radio-frequency identification) tag. For the traveler from the augmented, hyperpublic, fully identified future, accustomed to knowing so much about everyone, our current world would seem unnavigable, its inhabitants socially blind.

In a world of ubiquitous surveillance, being in private requires being unidentifiable: surveillance cameras glean little about a hooded and masked populace. If people feel oppressed by the watching eyes, they may respond, like paparazzi-hounded celebrities, by venturing out only if thoroughly disguised. But intense suspicion may fall on anyone who cannot be recognized. The question of how identifiable one must be in public is already a subject of intense debate: "On grounds of security … I believe that both coverings [niqab and burqa] should be banned, as one cannot have faceless persons walking the streets, driving cars, or otherwise entering public spaces" (Pipes 2006).

World Changing

> In 1999, Sun Microsystems chief executive Scott McNealy: "You have zero privacy anyway. Get over it" (quoted in Sprenger 1999).
>
> In December 2009, Google chief executive Eric Schmidt: "If you have something that you don't want anyone to know, maybe you shouldn't be doing it in the first place" (CNBC 2010).
>
> In January 2010, Facebook founder Mark Zuckerberg: "People have really gotten comfortable not only sharing more information and different kinds, but more openly and with more people. That social norm is just something that's evolved over time" (quoted in M. Kirkpatrick 2010).

There is good reason to think that privacy, as we have known it, is disappearing. As we shop, socialize, and gather information online, we build a detailed and persistent trail of data about our interests and intentions. We build some of it ourselves, with our check-ins, status updates, political rants, and product reviews. Even without ever touching a computer, we amass a personal data shadow. Cameras—whether hidden surveillance eyes or the ubiquitous snapshots of the tourist panopticon—transform our physical movements into archived data. Marketers and others who stand to gain immensely from knowing us better, whether to guide our purchasing or influence our opinions, work to ensure that our daily tasks, whether virtual or real, are heavily instrumented to record our every action. The move to less privacy is perhaps inevitable and unstoppable. We may not, at least in the foreseeable future, without some catastrophic upheaval, turn back on the data collection of this new information age. The coming century will be one in which more and more is known about everyone. And as we lose our privacy, we gain a more public world. What does this mean?

In a world where there is a great deal of privacy, where we know little of each other, people are free to act as they will, and there is little social pressure on them to conform. Privacy supports diversity; where people have protected private space, they have the freedom to be different from the public mainstream ideal. The more we know about each other, the more we can enforce social norms. The more information that individuals must reveal about themselves in a society, the more influence the society has over what they do.[10]

Thus, the permissiveness and openness of a society determines the value of privacy. In an intolerant society, privacy is very valuable, especially if you in any way deviate from the accepted norm. Many forms of behavior are unacceptable and those who engage in them must do so secretly. On the other hand, a society that is publicly intolerant but also provides a great deal of privacy might seem to us to be hypocritical, but it provides its members opportunities for private liberty while also having the benefits of a conforming public culture.

Repressive regimes are intolerant of dissent both in public and in private. When imposed by the government, this is totalitarianism. But people also sometimes choose to live in highly conformist societies with little privacy; for example, they may join a strict religious group. For those whose individual norms fit well with those of the group, this can be a satisfying communal, cooperative life (Sosis 2003). How pleasant life is in any community in which everyone knows everything about everybody depends on how narrow the community's norms are, and for the individual, how well they fit them. In a liberal and tolerant society, privacy is less valued because the society does not seek to tightly control the individual; revealing personal data about yourself does not result in negative societal consequences. In a very open (and so far, utopian and theoretical) society that tolerates and even celebrates differences among people, extreme transparency is possible because there is no cost to being different; privacy here would be pointless.

In practice, privacy protects diversity. It can be very difficult to tolerate those who are significantly different from us, which brings up the issue of the tolerance of intolerance. When we believe in something strongly, we see those who do not share our beliefs as wrong. By permitting people to have private space, a society can give people room to have their own beliefs, to act according to their practices—to, in the privacy of their home or their church, be less tolerant than is required in the greater public space.

In a society where diversity thrives through privacy, people of different beliefs are segregated from each other. Alternatively, in a society that has little privacy but is flexible and tolerant, people of different beliefs have the benefit of exposure to each other. As we contemplate a future of diminished privacy, we must seek this societal ideal. But the more diverse the society is, the more difficult it is to ensure tolerance. Nor is it guaranteed over time. A society that is open minded today—about your religion, sexuality, political beliefs, behavior—may not be so open minded tomorrow.

Ultimately, to retain freedom and safety—the benefits of privacy—our designs must address the larger issue of safeguarding tolerance and supporting individuality in a growing public sphere.

12

SOCIAL CATALYSTS

In the 1970s and '80s, urban designer William H. Whyte walked the streets of New York City, watching, recording, and analyzing how people move, sit, and strike up conversations in urban streets and plazas. His goal was to discover what actually attracted people to city spaces, what were the features that created vibrant areas. He found that many of the things people claimed they wanted, such as wide-open spaces and vendor-free districts, were not what they actually liked and sought out; big plazas, the celebrated feature of many new big building sites, were actually sterile and empty. Based on his observations of where people chose to walk, sit, and linger, he developed a set of guidelines for creating lively and sociable urban spaces.

One of the factors he cited as essential for creating a vibrant environment was what he called triangulation: "The process by which some external stimulus provides a linkage between people and prompts strangers to talk to each other as if they were not" (Whyte 1988, 154). This stimulus, or social catalyst, could be a performer, a minor altercation, a striking view, a popular food truck, and so on. Social catalysts change the relationship of the people in the space with each other, providing them with a shared experience and a reason to acknowledge each other. Public spaces have the potential to be social spaces; the purpose of the social catalyst is to unlock that potential.

In this final chapter, we will look at how communication technologies can function as catalysts that change the social dynamics of a physical space (Karahalios 2004). These works open the space to outside voices, give people new means with which to interact with each other, or change what the people in the spaces know about each other. Online, engaging in a discussion with strangers is a common experience. Face to face, however, such interactions

One might say, as a general rule, that acquainted persons in a social situation require a reason not to enter into a face engagement with each other, while unacquainted persons require a reasons to do so.
—Erving Goffman, *Behavior in Public Places* (1966)

are rare, especially in cities, where one can encounter thousands of people but greet no one. The goal of putting social catalysts in public spaces is to bring some of the online world's open sociability to the physical world.

What is the value of interacting with strangers face to face, and why are there high barriers to doing so? In the city, one reason is that the vast multitude of strangers makes it impossible to acknowledge each person. Louis Wirth, the early urban sociologist, wrote: "The reserve, the indifference and the blasé outlook which urbanites manifest in their relationships may thus be regarded as devices for immunizing themselves against the personal claims and expectations of others." Were city dwellers expected to greet each passerby, life would come to a halt, gridlocked by graciousness.[1] In a small community, however, people walk down the street amid a web of relationships, greeting many passersby, each nod reflecting a history of interactions and knowledge. Such communities need not be rural; even the largest of cities have village-like enclaves, neighborhoods where families have lived for generations (Young and Willmott 1992).

There are costs to making a connection: the small but still real effort required to be properly sociable (Goffman 1966); the responsibility you take on for helping the other if needed; and the possibility that you have just made yourself vulnerable to someone who could turn out to be oppressively strange. When people feel insecure, pressured, or intimidated, they may retreat from interaction. Several years ago, I was in a New York subway when a large and rather threatening man got on and began gesturing and shouting. Before this, people had been making the minute acknowledgments of everyday life, saying "Excuse me" if they bumped into each other, or looking quietly around at each other. But with the arrival of the ominously volatile man, everyone in the train looked down at their feet, and all conversation and eye contact stopped. By retreating to their private space and ceasing to acknowledge the presence of others, they were removing themselves from responsibility. Would they have helped each other if needed? Possibly, though less likely than if their immediate response had been joining together rather than retreating to isolation (Milgram 1964).

Mobility can create a lonely crowd. A suburban town inhabited mostly by newcomers and commuters living in perpetual transit can still feel isolated, even though it may be dressed up with quaint, village-like facades. When we are hurrying to get somewhere, late for work or late getting home, the cost of time in engaging with others—particularly in an urban space with its seemingly inexhaustible supply of strangers—is high. Rushing commuters avoid eye contact; they don't want to be stopped to give directions. They want the street to be an efficient means for moving from one place to another.

Yet efficiency is not always the goal. In thriving, vibrant parts of our cities there are people sight-seeing, shopping, sitting in cafés, walking dogs, caring for children, or heading from one place to another—but not in a frenzied rush.[2] People enjoy even brief interactions: the storeowner who chats with customers, the short conversation with a stranger catalyzed by a street performance. Interaction is an investment in a relationship, no matter how fleeting. These minor engagements still create a sense of connection with others and begin to dissolve the wall that says that they are not my responsibility.

Wirth observed that, in the life lived among strangers, "whereas the [urban] individual gains, on the one hand, a certain degree of emancipation or freedom from the personal and emotional controls of intimate groups, he loses, on the other hand, the spontaneous self-expression, the morale and the sense of participation that comes with living in an integrated society" (Wirth 1938, 12). The bonds between strangers and the sense of responsibility we each have to each other are tentative and delicate. Fostering them helps make a place not just more pleasant but safer (Milgram 1964, 1970).

Technology has exacerbated the problem of isolation in the city. People are involved in their own world of music and mobile updates, their eyes and ears focused on private entertainment, oblivious to the sights and sounds around them. Though the reader of a traditional print book might have been immersed in the story, the book's cover itself could be a catalyst: "Is that as good as his last book?" people might have asked in a café or park. The move to electronic books removes the last vestige of public display from the act of reading.[3] Yet technology need not be only an alienating force. Redesigning personal media devices to publicly display images related to the user's reading, viewing, or listening would reintroduce the communicative and catalytic aspect (see figure 12.1).

On a larger scale, technology can transform the nature of a public space, making deeper awareness of and communication with those around you into an inherent part of being there. That is not to say that all people want, all of the time, to engage with others. But many do, at least some of the time. Our goal here is to find the means of making this happen and to understand the contexts in which it works.

FIGURE 12.1
Christine Liu and Judith Donath, *UrbanHermes** (2006). In public spaces, media consumption has become more private, while at the same time it has become more public online. People post playlists and reading lists, their running times, pictures of the lunch they are about to eat, and scene-by-scene updates of the movie they are watching. These online displays invite others to respond, by commenting or passing on and spreading a striking phrase or image. In redesigning media devices for public display of musical, literary, and cinematic taste, we can also adopt elements of the social ecology of online updates. We designed *UrbanHermes* as an experiment in bringing social media to the physical world. The user displayed an image or saying, which anyone nearby (who had the compatible *UrbanHermes* gear) could choose to copy and transmit, should they find it appealing. Here, virtual memes spread through physical proximity (Liu and Donath 2006).

Mediated discussions and interactive games, performed in public spaces, can function as especially intriguing social catalysts.[4] They can, like the street performer, function as entertainment. But they can also change the nature of what is public about a space, and by doing so, redraw its boundaries. They can add to a space by annexing other spaces through communicative portals. They can change the ephemerality of the space, bringing in additional history or recording for posterity. And they can introduce new roles and new players into the urban mix, ones that raise questions about volition and responsibility.

This chapter is about designs whose purpose is to provoke thought and conversation in public space. The variety of possible designs is immense. We will focus on three areas: video connections that establish a visual link between two spaces, telepresence systems that enable people to move and act in distant venues, and augmentation that adds virtual information to people and objects. These technologies each have the ability to catalyze social connections, but with different implications for the participants' sense of safety, privacy, and engagement. I will primarily discuss works that have been built and installed in public, because seeing how people reacted to them is useful and often surprising. Most are artworks, rather than commercial projects; the goal of the former is to change how people relate and to make them think and talk, whereas the latter, which may well function as catalysts, usually have marketing as their ultimate goal.

PORTALS TO DISTANT SPACE

Our senses define what is "near," but each one does this a bit differently. Touch is quite limited; we can only feel things within the diameter of our arm span, just a few feet. We can see much farther: several miles, given an open horizon and a clear, sunny day. In the city, though, unless you are high up in a skyscraper, your view is quickly blocked by buildings. We cannot hear as far as we can see, but sound does travel through walls and around corners. The boundaries of what is proximate are set by our senses. For this reason, interfaces that connect us to other spaces, that expand proximity, seem magical. Today, we are somewhat accustomed to communicating with people at a distance, but there is still something extraordinary about a window through which we can see a distant scene as if it were a continuation of our own. Scale, setting, and interaction matter here. Live video streaming onto a computer screen at home seems just like TV. But a full-scale window into another space is like a doorway into another world, one that you could almost step inside of and be transported.

The first public creation of such a portal was Kit Galloway and Sherrie Rabinowitz's aptly named *Hole-in-Space* (see figure 12.2), which connected a big display window of The Broadway department store window in Los Angeles with a window at Lincoln Center in New York City (Galloway and Rabinowitz 1980; SFMOMA 2008). Passersby could see and speak with their life-size counterparts in the other space. The connection ran for three nights,

FIGURE 12.2
Kit Galloway and Sherrie Rabinowitz, *Hole-in-Space* (1980).

initially with no explanatory materials. The first night, people discovered and explored the installation, and on subsequent nights they were joined by others who had arranged to meet up with distant family and friends via the installation or to sing and dance with the bicoastal audience. Though there were some design problems, including off-center gaze and confusion about the symmetry of the communication, the installation was very successful (Karahalios 2004).

> *Hole-In-Space* suddenly severed the distance between both cities and created an outrageous pedestrian intersection. There was the evening of discovery, followed by the evening of intentional word-of-mouth rendezvous, followed by a mass migration of families and trans-continental loved ones, some of which had not seen each other for over twenty years. (Galloway and Rabinowitz 1980)

Since then, other similar projects have been developed (see Karahalios 2004). Sometimes these electronic portals invite interaction, but simply connecting two spaces with video and audio does not automatically catalyze interaction between them. Often, passersby would see the people and activity from the other side, but would not attempt to communicate. For designers, the question is why do some installations, such as *Hole-in-Space*, work so well while others fail?

Galloway and Rabinowitz had taken care to make *Hole-in-Space* feel like an extraordinary spatial connection rather than a mundane videoconference. The display was bright, accessible, and easy to interact with. People appeared life-sized, and the picture filled the window to its edge, leaving no television-like frame: the distant people appeared to be right behind the glass. It was installed in busy public places, which drew crowds of entertainment-seeking shoppers and theater-goers. It was also made at a time before fast Internet connections and cheap cameras made live, two-way video common.

Framing, both physical and metaphorical, is important. Often, installations that attempt to capture the magical feeling that *Hole-in-Space* created miss it because their physical setting is off. For instance, when the distant scene is shown on a screen, even a life-size one, the frame of the screen breaks the illusion of common space, and the on-screen people seem no more present in the room than does the anchor on the evening news. An unexpected setting can help. A more recent project, *Hole in the Earth*, used video to

FIGURE 12.3
Maki Ueda, *Hole in the Earth* (2001). Looking in.

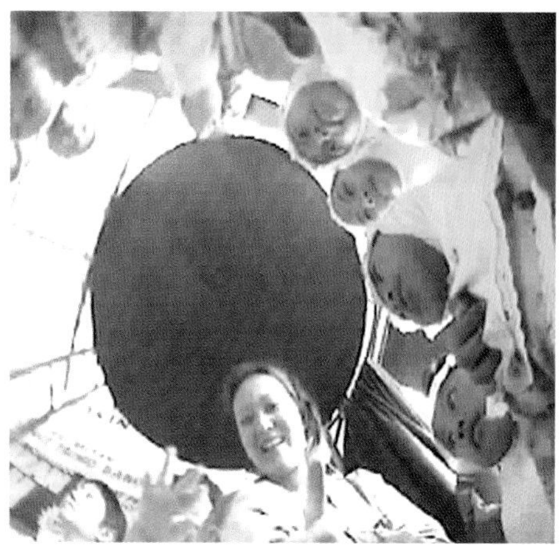

FIGURE 12.4
Maki Ueda, *Hole in the Earth* (2001). The view through the "hole."

connect a public square in Rotterdam, the Netherlands, with a popular mosque in Bandung, Indonesia, theatrically framing the work as a hole cut through to the other side of the earth (see figures 12.3 and 12.4). Although less gracefully intuitive than *Hole-in-Space*, it did succeed at making the now commonplace experience of video connectivity again seem extraordinary, reminding people of the distance, the sheer physical separation, between the two ends of an Internet connection (Ueda 2006).

Hole-in-Space ran for a limited time (it used very expensive satellite communication), which made it into an event; this created a much denser crowd and festive atmosphere than if it had been an ongoing installation. It is hard to know how people would have responded if it had been left up as a permanent feature in the New York and Los Angeles urban scenes. Would people continue to see it as a space where spontaneous street performance was allowed, where one could talk to and make faces at complete strangers? Or would it have faded into daily life, the people seen walking on the other side of its glass no more open to random interactions than any actually local person walking behind an ordinary storefront window?

Artificial Realities

Video portals such as *Hole-in-Space* and *Hole in the Earth* are about being there. They seek to reconstruct the experience of being in the presence of the other; their magic is in their erasure of distance. A video connection can also engage people by going beyond being there. Artificial reality pieces create an imaginary third space in which the distant participants interact. This computational third space can have its own "magical" effects and physics; exploring them is the catalyst for interaction.

One of the earliest artificial reality installations, Myron Krueger's *Videoplace*, featured this symmetrical common ground (Krueger, Gionfriddo, and Hinrichsen 1985; Krueger 1991). Krueger's work showed participants as silhouettes, and he used those forms to explore the nature of interaction, creating scenarios with different rules of engagement.

In Krueger's work, people interact with gestures, their silhouettes bumping up against each other with surprising but believable effects. In one scenario, your silhouette is a tiny form, and you move it about the screen with gestures: lifting an arm up makes it jump up and pointing in a direction causes it to go that way (see figure 12.5). The silhouette is simultaneously a depiction of self and a control device.

FIGURE 12.5
Myron Krueger, *Videoplace* (1991).

Krueger designed *Videoplace* to connect people in separate spaces (though many of its applications work well on their own also). Discussing the aesthetics of artificial reality, he noted:

> The relationship of one viewer to another can … be the explicit subject of the work. Thus, for the first time, the artist can compose relationships between friend and stranger where the very nature of the interaction can be changed as casually as we change the subject in a conversation. … Rather than isolating people further from one another, the challenge for artificial realities is inventing new ways to bring people together. (Krueger 1991, 93)

Erving Goffman (1966, 126) noted that although in many circumstances it was not acceptable for unacquainted people to spontaneously speak to each other in public, there were a number of exceptions. One was when people were engaged in an "unserious sport." The movements and gestures that people make to interact with a system such as *Videoplace* are light and unserious; by getting people to move in this way, the interface changes the rules of engagement.

Works that connect two spaces need to ensure that there are people at both sides, or else function gracefully in their absence. *Hole-in-Space* connected two very populous public spaces for a limited time; it did not matter that it was not interesting when the other side was vacant, for there was no lack of audience at either end. Many installations, however, are in places with

FIGURE 12.6
Karrie Karahalios and Judith Donath, *Telemurals* (2004).

fewer passersby—a pair of lobbies, common rooms, or cafés—where it is important that the screen present something interesting when only one space is occupied. Several of Krueger's projects work well as standalone installations, able to entertain a solo visitor as well as connected ones.

Karrie Karahalios's *Telemurals** addressed this problem by functioning as a mirror as well as a portal (Karahalios and Donath 2003, 2004). Like Krueger's pieces, *Telemurals* featured silhouettes of the participants interacting in a common, artificial space (see figure 12.6). As the participant moved, the silhouette became increasingly detailed, while lack of movement made it fade and fray. The goal with this visual transformation was to encourage people to gesture and move. This fading and filling in works even if no one is at the other location. Passersby became intrigued by it, and stopped to explore the installation, increasing the likelihood that they would be there when someone came by the other side. People could talk to each other, too. The audio was straightforward, but the screen also displayed their words as text, and the imperfections in speech recognition made this transcript (deliberately) more comical than redundant. By making speech into an entertaining game, this simultaneous mistranslation encourages people to talk at greater length than the stilted "hellos" that often make up much of the conversation among strangers in other mediated spaces.

Social Catalysts in Semipublic Spaces

In a public space such as Times Square, anyone can walk by. Connecting such a space to another, distant one does not fundamentally change how public it is. Semipublic spaces, however, are more limited. In an office, a common area may be public to the employees of the company, but not to the world at large. A company with widely dispersed satellite offices may want to have a way to connect these far-flung groups and provide a sense of connection, but that connection needs to function within the expectations of privacy and control of the semipublic space (Dourish and Bly 1992; Mantei et al. 1991).

Attempting to encourage sociability by placing a video connection in a space where people expect some privacy, as in an office, can backfire, causing people instead to limit their conversations to neutral and impersonal topics or to avoid the space altogether. Control and awareness are the important factors: giving people control over when the system is operational and providing intuitive indications of what is visible and audible to others help ensure that the connection works as a social catalyst rather than a deterrent (Bellotti and Sellen 1993; Dourish et al. 1996; Langheinrich 2001).

In a space where I have control over who enters physically, I should similarly have control over who enters virtually, including the ability to turn the system off. I don't expect to be able to disable a system running in a public space, but I do expect to be able to do so if it is in my office, my home, or a conference room where I am running a meeting. Control also tests the installation's value: when people have the ability to turn a system off, it must provide a sufficiently strong benefit for them to turn it back on again.

Awareness determines how easily people can intuit what others see of them. If I am unaware that there is a camera in my space and people elsewhere can see me, then I am under covert surveillance. Users or administrators of public video installations sometimes attempt to create awareness by putting up signs announcing that cameras are operating in an area. Though their wording may be more cheerful, these signs have the same chilling effect as the warnings near surveillance cameras: you are being watched and should constrain your behavior accordingly. This effect is desirable for a security system, but not for a social catalyst. Plus, people tend to overlook such signs; they are just one more notice in an environment overloaded with information.

A more graceful way to foster awareness is with an interface that makes the connection to another space intuitively apparent. An interface that resembles a window, such as *Hole-in-Space*, provides awareness since we assume windows have two-way visibility: when the other space is empty, we know no one is there to see us, and when it is occupied, we assume those present can see us, just as we see them. The window illusion is essential, for an interface that simply appears as a video screen does not engender this assumption of symmetry; we see video screens all the time without thinking that the people in the programs can see us (indeed, believing that the people on TV are watching you is a sign of mental instability). A common virtual space can also create awareness of distant others and their perception of you, but how vividly or intuitively it does so depends on its design. Both *Telemurals* and *Videoplace* present a common virtual space to both sides, but in those unfamiliar environments, users may initially be unsure of what the distant viewers see or even that there is another set of viewers.

EMBODIED TELE-INTERACTION

The screen-based works discussed above emphasize the appearance and movements of the participants. Being flat, they are always in the role of window or wall. They are works that emphasize symmetry, making a connection between two spaces where each site has a screen and camera, and each user can see and be seen. A different type of social catalyst allows remote visitors to interact with people in the space via a physical object, essentially a sculptural or robotic avatar. This embodied tele-interaction opens up the public space to interactions with people from outside, whose own location and identity may be unknown. Here, aspects of the online world, such as frictionless entry and exit from conversations and anonymous participation, enter (or intrude upon) the face-to-face, local environment.

One design goal of embodied tele-interaction is to give heft to the remote visitor. If you have ever sat in a meeting where some people participated via speakerphone you know that locally present people attract one's attention more than an invisible virtual presence does; when the distant participants are not speaking, people quickly forget about them. The shape and scale of the physical avatar can give them significant presence in the space. We designed the *AgoraPhone* and the *Chit Chat Club* projects to explore the forms and interactions that would provide remote participants with substance, while not overwhelming their personality and message.

FIGURE 12.7
Kelly Dobson and Judith Donath, *AgoraPhone* (2002).

At the same time, the remote participant has less at stake in maintaining the civility of the space. We know that when people can make anonymous comments online, the quality of discourse plunges. People do not behave this way when out in public because they are identifiable and because other people, who might become angry and offended, are physically present. Giving voice and presence in a space to people who have the safety of distance and the cloak of anonymity has the potential to invite hostility, rather than make the space more sociable. Thus, another important design goal is to foster constructive remote participation.

The *AgoraPhone** was an installation that gave voice in a public space to distant, anonymous people; it relied on the visual cues of its design to maintain civility (Dobson 2002a). Its physical manifestation was a human-sized and vaguely humanoid sculpture that was installed on a well-traveled walkway plaza (see figure 12.7). It was painted a warm orange, with a big trumpet-like opening for speaking and listening. Postcards and online notices advertised its service:

> *AgoraPhone* is a free, uncensored, and easily accessed communication place. ... Combining increasingly popular mediated communication allowances with old school public interaction, the first installation of *AgoraPhone* consists of a phone number that can be dialed from anywhere, and a communication sculpture installed as an element of urban architecture. From any touch-tone phone anywhere, people can call *AgoraPhone*'s number and be connected to the public place. (Dobson 2002a)

People called from far away, and from cell phones elsewhere in the plaza; they called to play music or seek anonymous advice. It created a public platform in the plaza for the emblematic contemporary speaker, mediated and anonymous. And, it created a spectacle in the plaza that gave the passersby a reason to stop, listen, and respond.

The name "*AgoraPhone*" comes from the ancient Greek word *agora* meaning a public space where people gather for debate, discussion, and other civic and social purposes. Today, many cities have spaces that are set aside for public speech, perhaps the most famous being the Speaker's Corner in Hyde Park in London. Expectations about behavior are different in such places than in ordinary plazas; it is acceptable to stand on a platform to lecture or attempt to rally the gathering crowd, behavior that would seem odd, if not illegal, in many other public spaces. In such a space, anyone can get up and declaim, but the audience is also free to speak its mind and often heckles the speaker. The *AgoraPhone* creates its own speaker's corner, with a local audience and remote speaker. The distance gives the caller safety, a feature that the service's advertisements highlighted: "Is there something you have been aching to express or discuss, but for one reason or another have not yet found a way to feel comfortable doing so? Dial *AgoraPhone*!"

Although anonymous, remote callers to the *AgoraPhone* were surprisingly well behaved. This was partly because of the advertisements, which depicted it as a supportive experience. The interface also played a role. Kelly Dobson, the designer, considered having a website where the remote user could view the plaza, but ultimately decided it would be too surveillance-like, and being able to surreptitiously view the passersby and then speak to them might invite pranksters hoping to surprise and shock people Thus, most remote speakers did not even know if anyone was there when they called; the only way for them to achieve any connection was to attract and engage people who would respond.

The *Chit Chat Club** used a similar technology but was designed to be installed in cafés, a quite different setting. Cafés are semipublic places where people come to sit, observe the passing crowd, and converse with friends; some patrons want to read in solitude, while others hope to meet up with a neighborhood acquaintance or an agreeable stranger. Today remote socializing is common, and many people sit at a table chatting online or talking on a mobile phone. Yet, while the buzz of discussion among physically present people adds to the liveliness of the space, these one-sided conversations are

FIGURE 12.8
Karrie Karahalios, Kelly Dobson, and Judith Donath, "Slim," a *Chit Chat Club* chair (2005).

dissonant, their rhythm and timbre at odds with the surroundings (Ling 2002). *Chit Chat Club* was designed to bring conversations with remote partners fully into the physical present.

Chit Chat Club was a set of human-scale avatar chairs, meant to be placed among regular tables and chairs. Each chair had a camera, a microphone, speakers, and a display (Karahalios and Dobson 2005). Via the Web, a remote person could occupy the chair, see and hear the people at the table, and converse with them. The chairs gave the visitor the scale and voice to be a full presence at the table. Conversation via the avatar chair was novel, yet at the same time natural; since the avatars occupied their place much as a human in a chair would, including them in the conversation and turning to face them when addressing or listening to them seemed quite intuitive.

Chit Chat Club opened the café table to a wider public. The Web interface allowed anyone to occupy a chair; a conversational group could thus become a circle of public discourse rather than a private discussion. For the participants in the café, conversing with the avatar did not bring them to a private world, as the phone does; they could engage with it and with the people and activity around them. And, the avatar chairs gave the distant participant both a better sense of what was occurring in the public space and an audible voice in the conversation. (Interestingly, some people were convinced the chair itself was a very intelligent robot, rather than a physical avatar that a person controlled and was speaking through.)

Chit Chat Club included several different avatar chairs (see figures 12.8 and 3.16). Three had cartoon faces, one featured abstract graphics, and one communicated by text. People found the chairs with faces to be the most natural to talk to, and they were usually the most popular. The text chair was designed in part to accommodate people who did not have a computer microphone or preferred not to speak out loud; it used large animated fonts to display the distant person's written responses. By making text big and striking, it allowed a distant person who was limited to text input to be a full-scale participant in a spoken conversation. The abstract chair was visually striking, but harder to engage with for small conversations. Abstraction, we found, works better for public declamation in which the tele-interactive sculpture is a platform for performance. For the intimacy of conversation, text and figurative interfaces appear more approachable and sympathetic.

Projects such as the *AgoraPhone* and *Chit Chat Club* open up a public space to outside communication. They enable a new hybrid interaction, one that combines the ease of engagement of online forums with a sense of physical presence. They were sculptures, able to transmit words, sounds, and images, but physically inert.[5]

Eric Paulos and John Canny's *PRoPs (Personal Roving Presences)* were remotely inhabitable robots, physical avatars that can move around (Paulos and Canny 1998, 2001). In their various incarnations—a navigable blimp, a wheeled robot—the remote visitor was truly visiting, able to move around, explore the space, and be part of mobile society. The wheeled robot *PRoP* had an abstractly humanlike shape, including a head with a screen that showed the remote user's face, a camera for eyes, and a microphone and speakers (see figure 12.9). Displaying the remote user was an important reminder that the rig was actually a telepresent visitor; otherwise, the robot would seem like an autonomous surveillance tool. Having the camera in the head meant the user would turn the robot to look at people and things; thus intuitively conveying the object of the telepresent person's attention. The wheeled *PRoP* also had a fingerlike pointing device, which made it possible for the remote visitor to indicate specific objects.

FIGURE 12.9
Eric Paulos and John Canny, a wheeled *PRoP* (2000).

Using a *PRoP* was a very different way to experience visiting a remote place than simply appearing on a static screen; you could physically interact with your environment. Paulos and Canny point out that having a large, remotely operated object in a public place requires considerable responsibility and trust. Even a well-meaning but careless operator could cause considerable harm to both the robot and bystanders by, for example, sending it tumbling down a flight of stairs.[6] A difficult and important challenge is ensuring that the operator acts responsibly. The *PRoP* creates a situation of asymmetric presence. The operators' experience of the world is virtual, seen on a screen, but their ability to have an impact on it is real. People online are often less inhibited, and less kind, than they are in person. This disinhibition, combined with the ability to effect remote physical action, means that ordinary people may, from their distance and behind the screen, cause harm they would not inflict in person.[7]

Paulos and Canny were able to limit access to the *PRoP* to trusted colleagues, carefully vetting who was allowed to affect a public space from afar. As more devices are connected to the Net—and already there are robots designed for children with instructions on how to set them up so that "anyone on the Internet … can activate your robot" (Hello Robot Software 2012)—the issue of how to regulate remotely controlled displays, recorders, robots, and other objects becomes increasingly complex (Goldberg 2001).

The moral questions surrounding telerobotics and the ability to effect action at a distance are most stark in the military, where officers seated safely in offices a continent away from the battlefield can send drones, telerobotic weapons, to maim and kill. On the one hand, using unmanned weapons lets a commander fight without risking the lives of his soldiers. Yet "the spectacle of Americans fighting wars with robots runs the risk of reviving the perception of the United States as a cowardly nation unwilling to back up its principles with genuine sacrifice" (Brzezinski 2003). Does saving the lives of one's own soldiers make these weapons not only morally acceptable, but even morally imperative? Or is the ability to kill without cost morally reprehensible? Is it only by paying the cost (in this case, the lives of one's own soldiers) that one can decide fairly whether to fight?[8]

The public plaza is, fortunately, a very different place than the battlefield. In the battlefield, the goal is winning at the ultimate competition, whereas in the plaza the goal is cooperation or at least coexistence. But we can draw useful analogies. To be physically present in the battlefield puts the soldier at risk; removing the soldier to a remote location sets up a situation some would argue is ethically wrong. Are there risks that a person in the plaza faces through his or her proximity to others, and does the loss of these risks affect the ethical balance?

People who share a public space engage in a complex, though often subconscious, performance demonstrating their willingness to conform to the community's rules. This includes being dressed appropriately, maintaining the culturally prescribed distance between people, and using the subtle eye contact and gestures that allow us to, say, navigate who goes first in a narrow pathway (Goffman 1966).[9] They wish to avoid costs ranging from loss of self-esteem ("I don't want people to think I'm a slob") to physical harm ("I don't want those guys to hit me").[10]

It is important to emphasize that in face-to-face social situations, the psychological costs of disobeying norms is, for most people, very high. Stanley Milgram carried out a series of experiments in which he required his graduate students to flout these norms; for example, they had to get on a subway car and request another passenger give up their seat, or intrude in a waiting line of people (Milgram et al. 1986; Milgram 1978). One important observation from the experiments was how difficult these acts were for the students to perform.

> Most students reported extreme difficulty in carrying out the assignment. Students reported that when standing in front of a subject, they felt anxious, tense, and embarrassed. Frequently, they were unable to vocalize the request for a seat and had to withdraw. They sometimes feared that they were the center of attention of the car and were often unable to look directly at the subject. (Milgram 1978, 42)

The students were not afraid of physical reprisal; what challenged them was the fear of disapproval, of being seen as selfish or boorish. It did not matter that the people who would be making that judgment were strangers. It shows the depth to which we do care what strangers think of us; this concern about the regard of others maintains much of our social order.

How can we maintain at least some of that desire to stay in the good graces of others in a tele-interactive system? To start, the remote operator needs to feel that there are potential costs to them for being disruptive. One approach is for the system to impose costs externally, like requiring identified

FIGURE 12.10
Webcam view of Piazza Navona, Rome.

log-ins or requiring a deposit to use the system. You then behave appropriately because you might be fined or banned from using the system again in the future. However, these externally imposed costs require additional effort to monitor and impose penalties. Moreover, they do not inherently motivate people to behave cooperatively. Are there interface designs that would give people an inherent motivation to be cooperative?

Let's start by looking at the opposite, at a (hypothetical) interface that makes it easy to misbehave. Webcams that provide live views of public spaces around the world are quite common. From their high-up, wide-angled perspective, you can see people walking down streets, sitting at tables, or driving their cars (e.g., figure 12.10). Although there is activity, it is not very interesting to watch, for the people are just distant beings milling around in their space. Now imagine that this view is the interface for a tele-interaction system; you can intervene in their space, perhaps just to speak to them, but maybe also to move an object around. You can see the reaction to your actions, the disruption to the others' flow. Doing something that makes them pause for a second is a first step, like when a child, bored of watching ants go about their daily lives, places a twig on the anthill. But that too becomes dull. The child with a stick at first tentatively and then more ferociously pokes at the hole, stirring the ants to frenzied and entertaining reaction. What of the webcam viewer with a telerobot? The people, viewed from above, are faceless, unidentified, resembling ants more than fellow humans. The scale of their reaction is hard to judge. They might be shocked or frightened, but that is invisible in this view. The only reactions that are perceivable are big ones—people running, hiding. Face to face, we see individuals, we recognize and empathize with the emotions in their reactions; but from a distant view, their expression is invisible, and they cease to seem like individuals. Too easily, we can find excitement in action, in the big disruption that causes people to flee, that disrupts their orderly flow and sends them racing wildly in every direction.

Compare the bird's-eye view interface with an installation in which the camera has a human-scale view and the people in the space can walk away from it, ignore it, or shut it off. In the latter case, the remote participant needs to work to keep an audience; engaging them, rather than disrupting them, creates a more interesting experience for all.

What would encourage the remote users of a telerobot to act properly? First, the remote operators need to be able to perceive the social nuances of potential and ongoing interactions. Even the most well-intentioned operator will act boorishly if he cannot discern who is willing to converse. Think about

FIGURE 12.11
Marie Sester, ACCESS (2003). ACCESS is an art installation that allows remote viewers to anonymously target individuals in a public space by directing a robotic spotlight to shine on them. A computer vision system keeps the beam of light on the targeted person, pursuing him as he moves through the space. People react to the piece in various ways: the implied surveillance makes some very uneasy, while others revel in the attention.

how you go about initiating conversation with a stranger—for instance, if you want to ask directions in a strange city. If many people are around, you do not approach the first person you see, but instead seek someone who appears open to this engagement. Some you rule out because they clearly seem in a hurry or avoid making eye contact. Ideally, you will find someone who responds to your initial signals that you are trying to ask something. People communicate their availability for interaction with words, eye contact, gestures, and movement. To engage graciously with people, the tele-operator must be able to perceive these signals (see Paulos and Canny 1997, 2001, for an in-depth discussion).

The people in the physical environment also need the ability to penalize poor behavior on the part of the robot's operator, not only egregious disruption but also any inappropriate and annoying action. For example, we do not ordinarily walk up to random strangers and say "Hi there, honey!" in a goofy voice, but that might be tempting for some users of this system, giddily experimenting with the freedom they feel as distant unreachable actors.

The designers of the *Chit Chat Club*, *AgoraPhone*, and *PRoP*s all note that physical scale is important (Dobson 2002a,b; Karahalios and Dobson 2005; Paulos and Canny 1997). An object that is the height of an average person allows for natural interaction; if taller, it is intimidating, and if shorter, it forces the person to stoop uncomfortably.[11] A balance of vulnerability is necessary between the people in the space and the remote operator. Giving the people in the physical space the ability to deactivate the robot temporarily—perhaps a button that silences it, shuts off its camera, or makes it stand still for a moment—creates this balance. It is not an exact equivalence: the people cannot see the remote operator or intrude upon his space, and the remote operator cannot push a button on a person to make her stand still. But, as we are with other people face to face, each is vulnerable to the other; each has a stake in creating a harmonious interaction.

CYBORG INTERVENTIONS

The robotic *PRoP* could explore spaces and convey the operator's words, but both its range and communicative ability were limited. Getting robots to perform reliably is not a simple task, and the world is full of things that are trivial for people to operate, but almost insurmountably difficult for a machine. For example, the robot *PRoP* could not open doors or operate elevators (indeed, its limited mobility is part of what rendered it safe, for it could be easily confined). Ken Goldberg, a colleague of Paulos and Canny's and a pioneer in telerobotic art (Goldberg 2001), came up with the idea of the Tele-Actor, a setup similar in many ways to the *PRoP*, but with a person in the place of the robot. A tele-operated human is agile and intelligent. One can give it high-level tasks, far beyond the ability of current robots to understand and carry out. "Go to the store and get some water"; "Get a gin and tonic and drink it"; "Flirt with the blond guy in the gray T-shirt." The Tele-Actor concept was used to explore different interaction scenarios (Goldberg et al. 2002).

In *Tele-Direction** (designed by Goldberg, my students, and myself), a group of operators, rather than an individual, would together decide on what directives to send to the Tele-Actor. The actor had a head-mounted camera and microphone, which sent pictures and audio of her surroundings to the directors, and a screen on which she read the directions sent by them.

FIGURE 12.12
Kelly Dobson, Dana Spiegel, Matt Lee, Judith Donath, and Ken Goldberg, *Tele-Direction*, the Tele-Actor (2001).

The simplest sort of representation is strict agency. … So long as I do not, either in person or through my agent, join in the enactment of that by which I am governed, I cannot justly claim to be autonomous.
—Robert Paul Wolff, *In Defense of Anarchism* (1970)

A key observation from this experiment was that the people around the Tele-Actor also needed to read the directions she was carrying out. Although the head-mounted camera and microphone gave some indication that there was something unusual about this person, if you did not understand that remote instructions were directing her actions, her behavior would seem at best disjointed and often bizarre or rude. Once we added a prominent display to the actor's outfit showing the directions, people could better comprehend the situation and her motivations (see figure 12.12).

The project raised interesting questions about autonomy and responsibility. If the directors said to, say, steal someone's phone, or tell someone his hair looked funny, who was responsible? Was it the actor, because after all she was not a robot but a real person with ethics and judgment? Was it the directors? All of them, or only those who voted for the irresponsible act?

With the first iteration of the Tele-Actor, the semi-anonymity of group directing combined with their remoteness created a system in which few directors felt much responsibility for their actions, and the directions reflected it. At a business lunch, the Tele-Actor was told at one point to grab and eat a piece of food off of someone's plate; at another, she was requested to jump on a table and bark like a dog. The slapstick tone of the directions reflects the theatrical feel of the project: the Tele-Actor is a form of street performer, a jester who can both entertain and disturb. The human in the loop here is an intelligent being, but that intelligence was used simply to facilitate blindly carrying out orders. How could the design be changed to inject judgment and responsibility into the system?

A second iteration, the *Tele-Reporter**, explored this question (Tang 2002). The basic setup was the same, with two key distinctions. The role of the actor was changed to reporter, and the controlling software had a new system of rewards and discouragements to encourage constructive behavior.

Tele-Reporter was designed for the public space as agora, a place where people come together for debate and discussion. Many people who want to participate in public discussion—community or work meetings, for example—are unable to attend; they are at work, caring for children, or out of town. With a Tele-Reporter as representative, they could join in the discussion. The directors voted among themselves on the most important points to make and the Tele-Reporter would, after vetting them, convey them as eloquently and assertively as the situation required.

Whereas the Tele-Actor was meant to be subordinate to the directors, the Tele-Reporter was in charge. The Tele-Reporter could veto an inappropriate directive; moreover, anyone who had voted for something that was subsequently vetoed was briefly suspended from participating. Here, the system depends on the reporter's integrity. Is she—can she be—responsible to both the people with whom she is physically present and to the remote people she represents?

These experiments with tele-operated humans were provocations intended to explore some of the complex conceptual and ethical questions in creating remotely controlled interactions. By removing today's primitive robot from the equation and replacing it with an intelligent human (a stand-in for future, smarter robots), they were able to highlight our need for clarity about motivations and explore design solutions for fostering responsibility.

Steve Mann is a computer science professor who has lived since the 1980s as a cyborg, existing in conjunction with a variety of applications, including augmented information about the world and a camera that publishes what its wearer sees. Although video streams of one's life are now rather common online, Mann was among the first to have the ability to automatically post pictures of his surroundings as he navigated them (see figure 12.13); in the process, he set off some of the earliest arguments about which spaces were truly public, and thus fair game for webcams, and which were not. For Mann, his webcam is a response to the increasingly pervasive surveillance under which we live. Stores have cameras to deter theft and to study customer behavior; streets have cameras that were initially placed to prevent major crimes such as terrorism, but which are increasingly used to pursue minor crimes and antigovernment actions (Rosen 2005). Mann objects in particular to the one-sided nature of the recording; stores can, with very little oversight about what they do with this video, record you throughout their premises, while they forbid you from taking photographs in them.

Mann terms his "surveilling the surveillers" *sousveillance*. It is simultaneously a suggestion of collective surveillance, a performance to increase people's awareness of the extensive surveillance they are under, and a dramatic retort to the powerful and secretive surveillers (Mann, Nolan, and Wellman 2003).

Mann's cyborg connectivity seemed bizarrely eccentric in the mid-1990s, when he first began posting images to the Web from his ever-present gear. But webcams quickly moved into dorms, offices, and bedrooms, and other

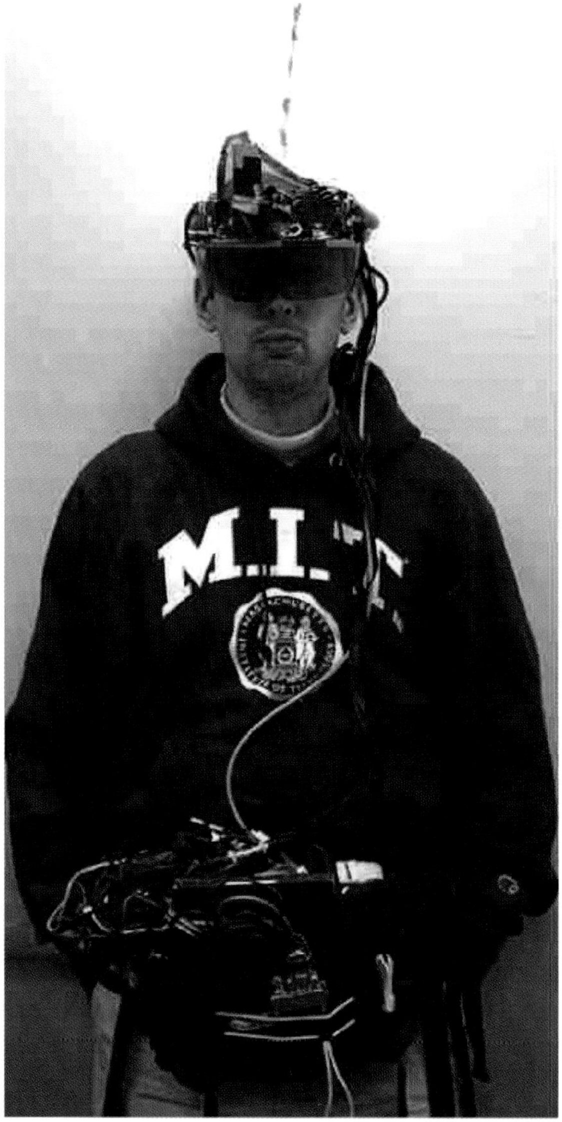

FIGURE 12.13
Steve Mann, *Wear Comp* (early 1990s).

mobile recorders soon followed. Today we are accustomed to acting under the eye not only of innumerable surveillance cameras, but also under the gaze of many other random people's recording devices, taking photos and videos destined to live indefinitely online, probably but not necessarily in obscurity.

A cyborg being combines both the human and the technological. In science fiction, cyborgs may be strange creatures of flesh, metal, and silicon. In our everyday life, as we increasingly augment ourselves with cell phones, computers, and cameras, we are all (or at least those of us who can afford these devices) becoming cyborgs (Haraway 1994; Turkle 2006). Our cyborg selves have already transformed public space. People carve chunks of private space out of the public sphere when their attention is focused elsewhere, on phone calls and messages. Our attached devices change our motivations and volition because we are responding to distant rather than nearby needs. And we become transmitters, too, sending images and sounds from the public space to unknown locations, opening our surroundings to unknown eyes and judges, far away in time or space.

Augmented People

Information is a social catalyst. The more we know about another person, the more likely it is that we will be able to discover common interests or experiences. A good hostess, upon introducing two of her guests to each other, will mention something about each of them that will help start their conversation. Although strangers on a city street today seldom spontaneously introduce themselves, on the rare occasions that they do, it is often because they have figured out that they have something in common (Milgram 1977). Something as simple as a T-shirt with one's college or favorite band on it can thus function as an informational social catalyst.

We can cover ourselves (or our cars) with only so much data about our interests and beliefs. Plus, T-shirts and bumper stickers are not adaptive: they show all the information they have to everyone. Computational mobile devices (smartphones) can selectively make information about their bearer public. Location-based social networks and social connection programs let people control what data about themselves they wish to make available and to whom; if I am in the same location as you and you have allowed me access to your information, these services will tell me of your presence—and about your identity and interests (Eagle and Pentland 2005; Humphreys 2008).

RFID (radio-frequency identification) tags raise privacy concerns. Although it would be difficult to surreptitiously implant a tag in someone, as more consumer goods—clothing, shoes, and so on—come to have embedded tags (for inventory control), we are likely to be walking around emitting various identifiers that can be linked to us. A network of tag readers, for example at store and restaurant entrances, could then build up a detailed picture of our day as we wander about town (Lockton and Rosenberg 2005).

A key technological piece in any augmentation system is the computer-readable identifier of a physical object or person. If an object is large and stationary, such as a restaurant, its location can serve as its identifier. Mobile objects can have identifying tags, such as the RFID (radio-frequency identification) tags used to identify pets, runners, library books, and so on.

An augmented reality device that recognizes objects can provide you with supplementary data about them, such as their botanical name or what they are called in a foreign language. A device that recognizes specific people can tell you everything that is publicly known about them (Starner et al. 1997). Researchers have experimented with providing people in conferences and similarly semipublic situations with "active badges" that both identify people and provide some details about them, such as their work expertise, hobbies, and the like (Borovoy et al. 1998; McCarthy et al. 2004). The goal of these projects is to make it easier for people to introduce themselves to each other. They are especially useful in what we might call proto-communities: groups of people who do not actually know each other, but have some common bond that establishes trust and a feeling of camaraderie and potential interest.[12] Some provide a public display identifying people in the nearby area (Churchill et al. 2004; McCarthy et al. 2004). Others send private messages to people when they pass near each other (Borovoy et al. 1998; Esbjörnsson, Juhlin, and Östergren 2004). These systems work as computational social facilitators, automatically providing introductions that a gracious host would normally offer.

These experiments used opt-in technologies: participants actively chose to wear a tag that identifies them to the system and could remove it at will. They were also able to choose what information the system would reveal about them. The resulting displays were more likely to fail because they were bland (it may not be that exciting to discover that you and Mary share an interest in optical fiber technology) than because they were distressing.

Yet it is increasingly possible to identify people without their consent. Today we can gain a certain degree of privacy in public simply by being somewhat of an enigma to our fellow strangers. Although there may be a lot of information about me available online, someone who sees me on the street but does not know my name cannot connect that material to me. Yet with machines' growing ability to recognize people, this gap is disappearing. Once the computer can attach a name to a face, it can attach the myriad data that accompanies that name.[13]

Augmented reality techniques could let us see a data portrait of each person superimposed on his or her body, either privately, as viewed through computer-aided glasses, or publicly, projected onto the person themselves. In chapter 8 we looked in detail at some of the approaches to and concerns with portraying people in terms of the data about them. What changes when these portraits are attached to an actual, physical person?

How people see the information may be as important as what they see. At one end of the design continuum is the public display, such as a large projection showing a live video of the space with data superimposed on people's images. Here the visualization is public, part of the common experience of everyone in the space. At the other end of the spectrum is surreptitious viewing. Augmented reality glasses are becoming both more powerful and more subtle. Steve Mann's gear from the early 1990s obscured almost his entire head; today, such devices look like slightly awkward glasses. By the time computational face recognition is commonplace, it will not be obvious to anyone that the wearer of the streamlined gear is viewing an augmented world.[14] And though by then one may assume that almost everyone is seeing an augmented scene, it will not be apparent what information they are viewing; the subject will not know she is being so observed.[15] Yet will that allow people to be oblivious to it or cause them to be hyperaware, living in a panopticon-like situation of knowing that they may at any time be secretly observed by someone through both physical and virtual eyes?

We all live now with the possibility that somewhere, someone may be looking at our virtual data. Few of us think about this very often, if at all. And if we do, it is mostly out of concern that we are being ignored rather than a worry that we are being observed: Why has no one responded to my comment? Is anyone reading my posting? Yet something about the idea of people looking at us in person and seeing virtual information seems deeply unsettling. Is the problem the lack of control over what people will see or the combination of the data with our physical self? Perhaps as technologies that map face and data together become increasingly common, people will start thinking about maintaining their virtual profile as an integral part of their public image, their personal grooming.

But let us think for a moment also about the various guises in which public augmentation may occur. One scenario is a nightclub or public art piece, designed to provoke. It could be a wall of pictures of people in the space along with striking data portraits of them. Or, more vividly, a data spotlight that follows people around. Marie Sester's ACCESS (Donath 2008) was a vision-enhanced robotically controlled spotlight that people (or a program) could use to highlight different people in a space (see figure 12.11). Now imagine that same spotlight, but instead of light, it projects your baby pictures, your status updates from years gone by, things people have said about you. Is this an invasion of privacy, or is privacy irrelevant here as the virtual becomes a key part of the search for attention, for status in a hierarchy of short-lived fame?

Today we have districts based on economics, industry, and the like. Places are zoned to be residential, to have no buildings over four stories, to have mixed-income housing, or light industry. In the future, we may have spaces zoned by information use, by the privacy laws that govern them. And similarly, establishments that today attract different clients by having soft, soothing background music or loud hardcore, by having easy-to-clean plastic tables or thick linen, may use personal information to create ambience.

The history that follows us now online will follow us everywhere. Today these scenarios seem intrusive, overly revealing. We can imagine that people would go to great lengths not to be identified, and that the dark glasses and hats of celebrity will become the norm for stepping out of the house. Yet we may well become accustomed to knowing a great deal about the strangers around us, so much so that the days when we knew only the surface appearance of others may seem like a disturbingly dark age of social and civil ignorance. People will think that having no data or being unidentified is a mark of disenfranchisement. They'll want to make sure they are recognizable and that there is good and interesting information about them.

The stranger, as we think of him now, may cease to exist.

CODA: LIVING IN BALANCE

The issue of the stranger exemplifies the contradictions and complexities of life online. On the one hand, we live among strangers, now more than ever. For the first time in history, the majority of the world's several billion people live in cities, and this percentage will keep growing (World Health Organization 2010). Most of us now live surrounded by strangers—people of whom we see only a very narrow slice, a fleeting impression made from a glimpse of clothing or an overheard comment. We are accustomed to not knowing, greeting, or acknowledging the great majority of the people we see. Online, too, we are among a growing population of unfamiliar people, reading comments and relying on recommendations from people devoid of any context of knowing who they are, what they think, or any cue that tells us whether we are similar to them or quite different.

Yet, as mentioned at the end of the previous chapter, at the same time the stranger, as we think of him,[1] may be disappearing. In a world where face recognition is commonplace and your past actions, social connections, favorite books, and starred cat videos are tied not only to your name but to your actual physical self, the stranger as a person about whom nothing is known will exist only as a historical concept, a relic of the risky and benighted (or, one might say, the free and private) past.

The term "surrounded by strangers" evokes lonely alienation, yet it is not a purely negative condition. In an essay entitled "The Experience of Living in Cities," Stanley Milgram wrote:

> Conditions of full acquaintance, for example, offer security and familiarity, but they may also be stifling, because the individual is caught in a web of

> established relationships. Conditions of compete anonymity, by contrast, provide freedom from routinized social ties, but they may also create feelings of alienation and detachment. (Milgram 1970, 1464)

To be a stranger is to be alone, but free. To be amid friends and family is sustaining, but also constraining.

The stranger has multiple guises. Most feared is the dangerous stranger, the one to whom parents warn their children not to speak, the unknown, unmoored person who may randomly attack. Fear stems from lack of control: we have an overly heightened anxiety about things we cannot control, and a corresponding false sense of security about those we think we can. Statistically, you are more likely to be harmed by an acquaintance than a stranger; similarly, few people hesitate to drive while many are afraid to fly, even though airplanes are far safer than cars. Still, the fear of the stranger who is unconstrained by community is not entirely groundless. As we have seen repeatedly online, real anonymity—being truly nameless and faceless, outside the control of social norms and sanctions—unleashes the worst in many people.

More positively, strangers can inspire us. In a short story about a writer struggling with a creative block, novelist Rebecca Miller wrote:

> [He] walked out onto the street again. So many bodies—why weren't they at work? Who were these people? Tourists, students, suits on lunch breaks, mothers killing time till the next school run. Stories in each of them, infuriatingly locked away from him. He peered into their faces for clues. This was what he needed, he thought: he needed to get out more, to be among strangers. (Miller 2011, 226)

The strangers who intrigue us on the street are not blank and impenetrable ciphers, but semi-legible beings, giving off tantalizing clues about what they think, where they've been, and what they've done. In person, we always see something of each other, enough at times even to establish some sense of familiarity. This includes inherent features, such as skin color, body size, and the like, as well as elements of deliberate identity construction, such as the clothing that marks social position and affiliations, for example, hipster, fundamentalist, or country club golfer. Mediated interaction, without physical presence, allows us to go "beyond being there," beyond our accustomed and embodied cues, and to have new and different cues and information form the basis of the impression we make on others. Changing the external manifestations of identity does not itself change who we are, but it can have a profound effect on how we organize society.

Being among strangers may be inspiring, but simply watching a parade of unfamiliar faces pass by is the experience of the tourist, in the city but not of it. The sociologist Richard Sennett claimed that although being among strangers is the source of cities' vibrancy, it comes not just from seeing new people, but meeting them—the transformation of strangers into acquaintances (Sennett 1976). He notes that it is a risky excitement. In the "city" (and Sennett's definition of city—"a human settlement in which strangers are likely to meet"—is an excellent description of many online environments) you meet new people in new contexts, and thus have little, other than their own claims, by which to know their history or to determine whether they are reliable, smart, or well intentioned. Finding acquaintances outside the purview of your existing circle expands your world, bringing in fresh ideas and experiences; but it also makes you vulnerable to someone who may want to take advantage of your trust.

Being a stranger provides the zone of privacy we need in order to enjoy a fresh start with new people and to have the freedom to speak candidly. We need it to see how people respond to us when they do not know who we are. We need it also to try new things—to have the freedom to fail. As a stranger, one can reinvent oneself—a wonderful opportunity to expand and improve; but reinvention can also hide a less than reputable past.

Reinvention is possible only when the past fades away. Social technologies, however, keep the past ever present. We look up new people online, finding work histories, grade school photos, news clippings telling of rewards or arrests; we see the arguments they have engaged in and the jokes they have told. This information provides an instant—and perhaps ersatz—sense of intimacy with people one has just met.[2] Tomorrow, face recognition and other social technologies will make such augmented acquainting quicker and easier; more seamlessly part of just looking at someone. Although knowing things about other people does not alone transform them into friends—we come to know each other through interaction—it does unmask the unknown stranger.

Whether this will be a better world remains to be seen. Balance is the key: balance between being secure and being free; between being part of a

Here we are talking about social surveillance, what people can see of each other. This is different from institutional surveillance—being watched by the government, your employer, insurance companies, marketing groups, and the like. Institutional surveillance is usually one-way, is often markedly antagonistic to the people surveilled, and can make use of more powerful tools to access and extract information—for example, the government can use a search warrant (or more covert means) to demand access to otherwise private data. See chapter 11, "Privacy and Public Space," for more on social and institutional privacy.

community and having a place to be different, alone, a stranger. For many people, the ideal is to have multiple, separate strands to their lives. This need not be as radical as having many full-fledged identities; it can be as commonplace as being able to take part in a protest or religious gathering without telling your colleagues, to dance without being observed by your friends, to go to a bookstore and read in private. The city has historically provided this; such freedom is nearly impossible in a small town, where the bookstore owner is friends with your friends, where comings and goings are noted and newsworthy.

For a while, the online world helped provide this balance. For people enmeshed in tight communities, it provided a place to be separate, to take on a different persona. For those who could not find a community where they fit in, it erased the barriers of distance to bring together scattered people with common tastes and concerns, whether gay teenagers, fans of an obscure music genre, or sufferers of a rare disease. Yet in recent years the balance has been tilting toward identification, tying all activities to one's increasingly searchable real name. The virtual city is becoming the global village, where everyone "knows" everyone else, and myriad eyes watch all activity.

Still, the online world may be the final refuge for privacy and the stranger. If face recognition becomes robust and commonplace, and cameras continue to proliferate in buildings and on foreheads, then data by and about you will augment your physical presence, creating an omnipresent data shadow. There is no facial pseudonymity: your face is coupled to you far more tightly than your real name. In this future, only online will pseudonymity—the ability to maintain separate social contexts and have the level of everyday control over self-presentation we take for granted today—be possible. But people must demand it; if universal real-name identification prevails online, it too becomes a space of collapsed context and casual surveillance.[3]

Too often, it can seem as if technological developments are inevitable—they are not. Yet to change things, to shape new technologies, we need to be aware of what is possible—and of the consequences of different choices. That is why I wrote this book for users as well as designers, for the inhabitants of the spaces, the participants in the discussions, the subjects of the portraits.

This book is a manifesto about what the connected world can be like—a vivid, nuanced space in which the inhabitants have the awareness and tools to shape their world and the impression they make in it. We are not yet there. This is not for lack of data or analytic technologies: today, vivid data portraits and network maps are being made; but they are produced for institutional eyes, to accurately target marketing messages or find criminals (Clifford and Hardy 2013; Gallagher 2013; *Wall Street Journal* 2010–2013). This is, perhaps, due to lack of understanding and vision of what our mediated experiences and interactions can and should be like.

Understanding privacy issues and assessing information is important. But so is recognizing the joy of sociability. Face to face, we surround many of our social interactions with pleasure. We go out to lunch together, or talk while taking a walk; we meet over coffee. We use the setting to enhance the relationship, to imbue our experience and memory of being with someone with pleasant times, enjoyable experiences. The emphasis here on the visual and the aesthetic has been to create this sort of experience. Setting and sociability—interface and impression—are inextricably linked.

In the words of William Whyte, what attracts people the most is other people. The designs in this book are fundamentally about seeing and being with people: about vividly portraying individuals, bringing conversational participants into focus, populating online spaces, and visualizing social patterns. As with being in the city, going beyond being there holds risk for us; but it also holds the promise of inspiration and new connections.

NOTES

Preface

1. This is a tradition we can trace back to Blaise Pascal's seventeenth-century "Addition Machine."

2. The "architecture machine" referred to the computer both as architect's assistant and as the foundation for interactive architecture (Negroponte 1970, 1975, 1996).

1 Introduction: Design Shapes Society

1. Throughout the book, examples marked with an asterisk (*) are of works created by the Sociable Media Group at the MIT Media Lab.

2. Chanting not only spreads the speaker's words to more distant listeners; it also makes the crowd into an active participant in the speech, unified in its chants, yet able to restate and even question the speaker's words. The technology of powered amplification arguably made the audience more passive. See Roueché 1984 on the practice of acclamation in ancient Rome; and see Kim 2011 and King 2012 on the "human microphone" used by the Occupy protestors in 2011, who were forbidden to use any powered amplification.

3. All media transform the messages they carry. The first "media" were human intermediaries, carrying a story from one person to another, perhaps embellishing it on the way.

4. "*Where the Action Is*" is the title of a book by Paul Dourish (2004), one of the leading researchers in social computing and interface design. In it, he argues that understanding the user as a social and embodied being, rather than an abstractly rational calculator, needs to be the foundation of design.

2 Visualizing Social Landscapes

1. For further reading on finding key patterns in social data, see Adamic, Buyukkokten, and Adar 2003; Eagle and Pentland 2006; Hargittai 2009.

2. On sentiment analysis, see Liu 2010; Pang and Lee 2008; on topic modeling, see Blei and Lafferty 2006; McCallum, Wang, and Corrada-Emmanuel 2007.

3. For further reading on the visual and interactive design of visualization, see Keim 2002; Segel and Heer 2010; Shneiderman 1996; Tufte 1986, 1990; Ware 2012.

4. Pad and Pad++ (Bederson and Hollan 1994; Perlin and Fox 1993) were early experiments in designing a zoomable interface. Furnas and Bederson (1995) discuss general problems in multiscale interface design, including what they call "semantic zooming," in which an object's representation changes at different levels.

A beautiful example of the power of zooming is the film and book by Charles and Ray Eames entitled *Powers of 10*, in which the camera zooms out an order of magnitude every ten seconds, going from a close-up of people in a park, all the way out to the size of the observable universe, and then back in (Eames and Eames 1977).

5. See Thrower 2007 on maps and society; Milgram and Jodelet 1976 and Monmonier 1996 on the subjectivity of maps of physical places; Dodge and Kitchin 2000 on maps of virtual world; Abrams and Hall 2006 on new technologies and mapping; and Harmon 2004 on maps and imagination.

6. Twitter trends provide an interesting case story about the subjectivity of algorithms. As of the summer of 2012, there were about 400,000,000 tweets, as the short updates to this micro-blogging site are called, posted each day on Twitter. To help people make sense of this massive flow of information, Twitter publishes a continuously updated list of the top ten trending words and phrases in tweets (worldwide and in various geographic regions). When a topic makes it to Twitter's trends list, it gets a tremendous amount of exposure. People—many who may not otherwise have seen it—click on it to read a stream of all the updates that mention that topic. The trends list also advertises the significance of the topic; it is Twitter's ever-changing crowd-sourced equivalent of the newspaper front page (Lotan et al. 2011). If you have something you want people to pay attention to—whether a product you are marketing or a political story you deem important—having it be listed as a trend is a big boost. So when the protest using the Twitter tag #occupywallstreet did not show up as a trending topic—despite a large and lively presence on the site—people became suspicious that Twitter was censoring the list. It was not, though certainly a different algorithm would have shown it as a major discussion topic (Gillespie 2012, 2013).

But "trending" is not clearly defined. It is not the simply the most popular—it takes into account how rapidly something is increasing in popularity, among how broad a group, how long has it been popular, and more. Twitter does not release the details of the algorithm, in part to prevent marketers and spammers from gaming the system. And they change the algorithm frequently, both in response to attempts to game it and to shape the results. For example, the preteen pop star "Justin Bieber" was a perennially trending topic, until Twitter modified its algorithm to highlight new topics (Lotan 2011).

By changing an algorithm's formulation, a site can highlight or hide the presence of different social groups and types of discussions. Algorithmic analyses and visualizations are objective in that they treat all data equally, but subjective in that they inevitably highlight certain patterns rather than others.

7. "Duckface Mountains" refers to a trend on Facebook of young women posting photographs of themselves with a peculiar pursed-lip pout that became known as a "duckface"; "Bieber Bay" refers to the teen singing star Justin Bieber who was for months the most popular trending topic on Twitter.

8. See Cunningham 2003 and Mindich 2000 for discussions of the complexity of defining journalistic objectivity and the factors that keep it a desirable but unreachable goal.

9. Search engines use algorithms that basically measure the importance of a page by looking at how many pages link to it, how authoritative those linking pages themselves are, and how many links they have; that is, being linked to by a page that is itself quite popular and that links to only a few select pages confers the highest value (Page et al. 1999).

3 Interfaces Make Meaning

1. Some recommended books include: *Visual Thinking* and *Art and Visual Perception*, by Rudolph Arnheim (Arnheim 1974, 2004); *The Ecological Approach to Visual Perception*, by J. J. Gibson (Gibson 1986); *The Design of Everyday Things*, by Donald Norman (Norman 1990); *Envisioning Information*, by Edward Tufte (Tufte 1990); *Eye and Brain*, by R. L. Gregory (Gregory 1990) and *Metaphors We Live By*, by George Lakoff and Mark Johnson (Lakoff and Johnson 1980).

2. It is useful to think of alternatives to the desktop metaphor's businesslike interactions. For instance, imagine information stacked in layers, such as hundreds of old messages piled on each other. What if touching them starts digging down through them or blows the top layer away like a leaf-blower? Though not a good approach if we seek efficiency and organization, it could be useful when the goal is to encourage people to explore a vast dataset, for it encourages serendipitous discovery and makes exploration intriguing. See Abowd and Mynatt 2000; Dourish et al. 1999; and Fertig, Freeman, and Gelernter 1996, for more alternatives.

Many attempts to redesign interfaces suffer from overly determined metaphors. For example, a well-meaning attempt to rethink the "desktop" interface for Chinese users came up with the idea to use a garden metaphor. Although the concept could be promising, the execution was not. They modeled their interface after the formal garden, with overly specific places to put different types of work, including an atrium for arts, a nursery for ongoing projects, and a house for management tools, and they rather awkwardly transformed the file/folder metaphor into pots, plants, seeds, and leaves (Shen, Woolley, and Prior 2006).

3. There have been several studies on how we handle email. Mackay 1988a was among the earliest. Whittaker and Sidner 1996 looked closely at the cognitive difficulties of filing, from creating file names to finding things once they've been filed away. Other major studies include Dabbish et al. 2005; Ducheneaut and Bellotti 2001; Fisher et al. 2006; and Venolia et al. 2001.

4. Gmail, the email service run by Google, is one of the first to use labels rather than folders. However, perhaps in order to seem familiar to people accustomed to folders, the design of the application (as of 2013) is quite similar to traditional folder-based ones. There is a list of labels to one side, and you can click on one to bring up all the messages that bear that label, but you cannot select multiple labels (you can do this through a search window, but it is clunky, requiring typing such entries as "label:travel label:receipt Susie"). And, perhaps in an attempt to innovate while not disturbing traditionalists, it uses both labels and folders, resulting in confusing inconsistencies. An interface that eschewed folders and made labels more versatile, such as being able to click on multiple labels to create complex searches, would be much more useful—and would have made a bigger change in how people think about organizing their data.

5. Designing an intuitive interface for Boolean search presents a challenging problem. For email labels, one is unlikely to need very complex terms, and an interface where you could drag search terms into nestable and negatable "and boxes" and "or boxes," with intuitive labels such as "all of these" and "at least one of these," would be simple yet powerful. See also dynamic queries (Shneiderman 1994).

6. *Metaphors We Live By* (Lakoff and Johnson 1980), the foundational text on conceptual metaphors, states that spatial metaphors are the foundation for other conceptual structures. Cognitive scientist Steven Harnad put forth a similar notion in the context of thinking about machine rather than human intelligence. Harnad (1990) argues that a machine's intelligence needs to be created "from the bottom up"—from sensory physical experience, and from that to more symbolic processes. In contrast, most AI research is "top-down," creating programs that solve problems, rather than recreating the process by which humans generate thought.

7. In the online world of virtual objects, these transformations require similar effort to achieve, but in a real physical space, they are markedly different. Imagine, for example, you are photographing a tree and want its image to be bigger. Zooming is very easy: just press a camera button. But if you want a true close-up, you need to walk closer, i.e., you need translation. Items that had been in the foreground disappear (they are now behind you) and your relationship to other things in the scene also changes. If there is an impassible chasm between you and the tree, this option is not available. Finally, scaling, i.e., making the tree itself bigger, requires waiting a few decades.

8. In most language, the future lies ahead and the past recedes behind, a concept based on walking a path, where the unknown future is unseen around the next bend. But there are rare instances of languages where the past is thought of as in front of you, seen and known, while the unknown future is out of sight behind you. In such languages, greater emphasis is placed on the personal witnessing of events, and imagining future events is denigrated (Lakoff and Johnson 1999; Núñez and Sweetser 2006).

9. Our conceptions of facial expressions are such canonical views: we think of happy people smiling, sad people frowning. But photographs show that the actual expression on faces is seldom so clear, and it is often difficult for viewers to correctly interpret the expression shown in a single shot. Our imagination creates a prototypical image from a series in time (Russell and Fernández-Dols 1997).

10. The most urgent impetus to standardize time came with the advent of the railroad, which brought a real need for a unified, common approach to time (Zerubavel 1982). Before time was standardized, trains ran on schedules based on their parent city's time. As they arrived in other stations, it could become quickly clear that one train's one o'clock was another train's three o'clock. This caused accidents, not to mention an enormous number of missed connections. The railways brought spatial connectedness, which required time to be centralized.

11. Our eyes contain two types of receptors. The rods, which dominate our peripheral vision, are far more numerous and highly sensitive to light, but do not see color. They allow us to see motion and in low light. The cones provide our color vision, and are primarily in the center of the retina (fovea). They provide sharp, clear, color vision, but only with sufficient light. There are three types of cones, each sensitive to different wavelengths. The most numerous ones (nearly two-thirds) are sensitive to the green–yellow–red part of

the spectrum (~580nm); another one-third are responsive to the green part of the spectrum (~520 nm), and the remainder respond to the violet-blue spectrum (~420nm) (Mollon 1990).

You might think that you see lots of color in your peripheral vision, but much of what we perceive to be "out there" in the world is actually built from our knowledge about objects and our recent visual memory. We are also unaware of the constant "saccades" or tiny movements that our eyes make; our foveal vision is in constant motion.

Although the details of the human color vision system are outside the scope of this book, it is a fascinating topic for anyone interested in the question of what is "real" about our perception of the world. Color, as we think of it, does not exist as a property of the external world, but comes about only in our perception of it. What we experience as color is the ratio of the response by the different types of cones in our eyes when a particular wavelength (or wavelengths) of light enters our eyes. Thus, there is a single, pure wavelength we see as "yellow"—and there is also a mixture of other wavelengths (which singly we would see as red and green) that appears to us to be the exact same yellow (Gregory 1990). The equivalence exists only in our vision: the cones in our eyes respond in the same ratio to both the pure spectral yellow and the mix of other wavelengths, so we see them as identical colors, when in fact they come from quite different light sources.

12. A proposed color scheme for document icons had them start new at pale yellow and "age" to duller, deeper browns (Salomon 1990).

13. The colors in the visible spectrum proceed linearly, starting with violet around 380 nanometers and progressing up through red at about 730 nm.

The color in a computer pixel is a mix of red, green, and blue light; to set the color, a program chooses values for each of those lights. This RGB color space is not very intuitive (e.g., you get yellow by mixing red and green) and for many color tasks, it is useful to instead convert to hue, saturation, and lightness (HSL) space. While these are more intuitive to use, they are still representations of the computer's color range, rather than of human color perception.

14. Sound can also bring the feeling of physical realness to the interface. William Gaver's *Sonic Finder* used everyday sounds to provide cues about file system functions. Copying a file, for example, sounded like water filling a glass. Though we are usually unaware of it, the sound does change as the glass fills; this naturalistic accompaniment brought the abstract actions to life (Gaver 1989).

15. The word "ambient" refers to two related concepts in interface design. First, as used here, it refers to designs that are meant to recede into the background and provide data about the ongoing state of some environment, whether natural, financial, social, etc. It can also refer specifically to interfaces that provide such data architecturally, rather than on the screen, in the ambient space of the user's room (Hallnäs and Redström 2002).

16. We need not confine motion to the screen. *Dangling String*, by Natalie Jeremijenko, was an installation at Xerox PARC that showed network traffic via the motion of a dangling string (Weiser and Brown 1996). Hanging in a hallway, it unobtrusively provided useful information to people in nearby offices.

17. Controversy surrounds both the definition of aesthetics and the identification of aesthetic objects. For an overview of the role of aesthetics in interaction design—and an example of how contested a topic this is—see Tractinsky 2012 and accompanying

responses. Other key readings in aesthetics and design include Dunne 1999; Norman 2002; Tufte 1990. For the social foundations of judgments of taste, see Bourdieu 1984; Halle 1993; Thornton 2009.

18. See also Byron and Wattenberg 2008 on the aesthetics of this sort of exploratory visualization.

19. There are times when we want a less social approach. If pure efficiency is the goal, a less sociable atmosphere enables people to be more direct and spend less effort on social niceties (Walther 1996). People are more honest when they perceive the other as machine rather than human (Sproull et al. 1996). And some sites, such as 4chan's /b/ and Chatroulette, thrive on the unbridled harshness of depersonalized interaction (Anderson 2010; Dibbell 2008).

20. The cognitive psychologist Donald Norman has done much to popularize the concept of affordances, especially among designers. He distinguishes between affordances and what he calls perceived affordances (Norman 1999) and stresses the importance of the latter for making legible environments. In the realm of interface design, he claims that "affordances play a relatively minor role … [and] the designer primarily can control only perceived affordances." In his view, it is incorrect to say that an on-screen button affords clicking any more than the rest of the screen does: the fact that things happen when you click that button are "conventions, and feedback, and the like" (Norman 1999, 39).

I would argue that while the button may not have a special "click" affordance, if you click on it, something happens, and that virtual action is an affordance. If the button saves the document you are writing, the button affords saving documents. The button's visual design—for example, a rectangle with the word "save" on it in bold when the document can be saved and gray when it cannot—uses a metaphoric convention to help the viewer perceive the affordance.

21. See Brand 1997 for a discussion of how buildings change over time as people find new uses for them. See Zittrain 2006 for a discussion of the importance of maintaining openness and adaptability, within bounds, online.

4 Mapping Social Networks

1. For an excellent overview of social networks and their evolving role in our changing world, see *Networks in the Global Village* (Wellman 1999) and *Networked: The New Social Operating System* (Rainie and Wellman 2012).

2. Yet even millennia ago, few groups were wholly isolated. In Europe and Asia, travelers passed through and herdsmen wandered from village to village. Hunter-gatherer tribes, often believed to have lived in isolation, probably maintained some contact with neighboring communities (Headland et al. 1989).

3. See Abrams and Hall 2006; Becker, Eick, and Wilks 1995; Brandes, Raab, and Wagner 2001; Freeman 2000; Heer and Boyd 2005.

4. Modeling society as a network has been an increasingly important branch of sociology since the mid-twentieth century, and there have been many studies of small groups and their connections. Some of the main figures in this field include Linton Freeman (Freeman 1979, 2000), Mark Granovetter (Granovetter 1973, 1983), Barry Wellman (Wellman 1999;

Wellman, Garton, and Haythornthwaite 1997), Stanley Wasserman (Wasserman and Faust 1994), and Harrison White (White 1992).

5. This is partly because researchers have had access to only limited information, such as the headers of email, but not the content. Analyses that include the content of conversations can create a very detailed picture of relationships. See, e.g., McCallum, Wang, and Corrada-Emmanuel 2007, which uses corporate email made public as part of the investigation of Enron Corporation's extensive accounting fraud.

6. This layout is only one of many possible layouts we could make with the given data. This particular map does not show the subject, who would be a node in the center with connecting lines to every other node, a design decision that greatly simplifies the graph. A different algorithm gives you a radial layout with the subject in the middle and their acquaintances surrounding them in concentric circles. Different rules for arranging the people in the network map bring different patterns and relationships to the fore. See Freeman 2000 for an overview of different approaches to mapping social networks.

7. A simple design change can help. Indicating the total number of connections a person has (e.g., by making the node larger or darker for those with the most connections) would show if she has few connections on this map because she is a generally isolated person or because she is an otherwise sociable person whose ties with the subject's community are tenuous.

8. Heer is the developer of many graceful and creative visualization techniques (Heer, Bostock, and Ogievetsky 2010); the Vizster program featured several innovative techniques for exploring and making sense of data (Heer and Boyd 2005).

9. For Twitter users more interested in fashion than politics, news of bin Laden's death came via @dkny, the Twitter feed for clothing designer Donna Karan. Verification is always useful; one (facetious) tweet read, "Oh thank god, now @shopbop's [an online retailer] confirmed it. I don't want to rely just on @dkny [a clothing designer] for my Osama bin Laden news" (Grinspan 2011).

10. In fact, Urbahn's tweet was also a rumor-based guess, and he quickly downplayed it with these more cautious postings: "Don't know if it's true, but let's pray it is," and "Ladies, gents, let's wait to see what the President says. Could be misinformation or pure rumor." And, though his role as aide to the former Defense Secretary gave people the impression that his "reliable source" was a government official, it was actually a TV producer who had called saying only that there was a possibility that the announcement would be about bin Laden, and seeking to interview Rumsfeld about it.

11. See Adar et al. 2004; Centola 2010; Gruhl et al. 2004; Romero, Meeder, and Kleinberg 2011; and Weng et al. 2010 for more on information flow in computer-mediated networks.

12. To communicate with someone via this medium, that person too must have chosen to have an account. As Ethan Zuckerman points out, if you are the first person in your country to use Facebook, all your connections will necessarily be international, since none of your fellow citizens are available (Zuckerman 2013).

13. See Zuckerman 2013 for more on the social significance of global connections. Zuckerman (2008) also discusses the impact of airline routes and other forms of transportation on social flow. Paul Butler, who designed the Facebook map, has created other works that

depict time and human motion, including an animation of the Toronto public transit system that maps places by how long it takes to get to them from a given start point (Butler 2013).

5 Our Evolving Super-Networks

1. Social scientists had also been pondering the chain of connections among people. See de Sola Pool and Kochen 1979.

2. It took 125 years, from about 1800 to 1925, for world population to grow from 1 to 2 billion. It then took only 35 years to add the next billion (3 billion by 1960) and just 12 years to reach 4 billion around 1972.

3. Social network sites are websites where users create a self-descriptive profile, link to others on the site with whom they are acquainted (often, but not always, such links require mutual recognition), and explore the connections of the people with whom they are connected (possibly to several degrees out). For more on the history and structure of the first generation of these sites, see boyd and Ellison 2007.

4. Around the time of Friendster's founding, Malcolm Gladwell's best-seller *The Tipping Point* had brought a resurgence of popular interest in Milgram's "small-world problem" experiments.

5. The Friendster profile consisted of a name, photo, perhaps a list of favorite books and movies, and in an especially complete one, a paragraph of self-description and perhaps a "testimonial" from a friend or two.

6. Socioeconomic distances were harder to bridge than were geographic ones. Milgram carried out a subsequent study looking at whether having initial seekers and a target of different races would make a difference—and it did. Only a third as many cross-race attempts were completed, compared with ones where both seeker and target were white (Korte and Milgram 1970). A related study showed that social class mattered: chains composed of higher-status participants were more likely to succeed (Lin, Dayton, and Greenwald 1978). They were more likely to have a more diverse set of acquaintances, a result of a more mobile life (going away to college, meeting colleagues at conferences), and to have similarly diverse friends whom they could afford to burden with this task.

7. Surveys conducted in a later recreation of the small-world experiment confirm this (Dodds, Muhamad, and Watts 2003).

8. It is now newsworthy—and rare—when hitherto isolated people are discovered. There are a few small groups in the Amazon and in New Guinea that are known of, but who are for the most part uncontacted. Occasionally, a lost soldier, hiding from a long-since over war, emerges from the jungle. But otherwise, the world's population is an immense and connected network.

9. Insular dense networks do exist in contemporary urban settings as well as in the rural past. Think of someone who works for his uncle alongside several cousins and whose wife exchanges babysitting and other family care duties with her sisters-in-law; they are part of a big extended family that frequently has dinner together and whose leisure time is often spent celebrating holidays and anniversaries with relatives. See Young and Willmott's 1992 ethnographic study of ties in a close-knit urban community.

10. When resources are scarce, people turn to their immediate community (Oliver 1988). People who are well off seldom need to ask material favors; but if you are poor, you are more likely to need to barter for babysitting, a ride, or a place to stay. Having limited material resources makes having tight-knit, strong ties especially important—and those with neither money nor strong ties are in a precarious position.

The value of strong ties becomes vividly apparent in a disaster, when having close friends and family can be essential for survival (Klinenberg 2003, 2013).

11. Ellison, Steinfield, and Lampe (2007) examine how the use Facebook expands college students' personal networks, helping to "crystallize relationships that might otherwise have remained ephemeral"; Hampton and Wellman (2003) discuss how use of social media increases contact with weak ties and can strengthen local relationships; Tufekci (2008) shows that users and nonusers of social media have similar numbers of close ties, but that social media users have more contact with weak ties; Hampton, Lee, and Her (2011) provide evidence that "an internet user who frequently goes online at work and uses a social networking service has a network that is nearly one-half a standard deviation more diverse than those who do none of these things." See also Boase et al. 2006; Ellison, Steinfield, and Lampe 2007; Hampton, Sessions, and Her 2011.

It is important to note that *how* one uses the medium also has a big effect. Simply reading others' updates on Facebook is very different from actively communicating (Burke, Kraut, and Marlow 2011).

12. Granovetter (1973, 1983) used four dimensions to assess tie strength: time devoted to the relationship, emotional intensity, mutual confidences, and reciprocal services.

13. Weak ties are not necessarily heterogeneous. Some of the follow-up studies to "The Strength of Weak Ties" did not find that weak ties were useful in expanding one's prospects, but closer examination showed that they were too much like the subject's existing strong ties, e.g., relatives of other members of a close-knit family (Granovetter 1983).

14. Strong ties take a lot of time and energy to maintain: they involve providing support and spending time together, talking and sharing experiences. Networks of strong ties are usually homogeneous, for one can maintain a multitude of these costly ties only in the context of a group that does many activities together. The homogeneity of a group of strong ties is both a cause of their closeness (the people have enough similar interests to be doing many of the same things) and an effect (in spending so much time together, they influence each other and become increasingly similar).

15. Declining network capital is not always a sign of a society in distress (but see Kraut et al. 1998; McPherson, Smith-Lovin, and Brashears 2006; Putnam 1995 on the decline of social capital and shrinking social networks). If food and other goods are abundant, and educational and employment opportunities filled by merit rather than connections, people will have less need to maintain strong ties to get by in life (Wellman and Gulia 1999).

16. In the design of online social software, an interesting tension emerges between history and reputation in establishing trust. If I know a lot about your history I can use this to decide whether I trust you and to have a good sense of what you are like, or at least, how you will act—I don't need to establish relationships with mutual acquaintances to acquire this information via their experiences, i.e., reputation. Thus, the data portraits (see chapter 8) are, in effect, a mechanism for establishing trust and predictability and for encouraging

good behavior—all the things for which traditionally we needed close community ties—without relying on community.

17. Robinson and Godbey (1999) analyzed how Americans use their time. After accounting for work, television, household chores, etc., not many hours remain for socializing. That said, it should be noted that not all our social interactions take place as distinct activities: we chat with others at work, we maintain close supportive relationships with family members in the context of household activity, etc.

18. Robin Dunbar has done extensive studies of the cognitive and temporal constraints on human (and primate) sociability. See Dunbar 1993, 1998; Roberts et al. 2009; Stiller and Dunbar 2007.

19. Nicolas Ducheneaut, Nick Yee, and their colleagues have written a series of excellent analyses of social interaction in online games. See, e.g., Ducheneaut, Moore, and Nickell 2007; Ducheneaut et al. 2006.

20. Nicholas Christakis and colleagues have made a series of studies of the spread of behaviors in networks, ranging from smoking and obesity (Christakis and Fowler 2007; Christakis and Fowler 2008) to privacy settings in Facebook (Lewis, Kaufman, and Christakis 2008).

21. Facebook has 1.15 billion monthly active users, as of June 2013: http://newsroom.fb.com/Key-Facts.

22. See Sarah Blaffer Hrdy's *Mother Nature* (Hrdy 1999) for an excellent and extensive survey and history of child-rearing and childcare, among both humans and primates.

23. See Young and Willmott 1992 for an account of how an urban renewal project created similar rifts.

24. The prevalence of nonparent—and nonkin—childcare has varied throughout history; it is certainly not a modern innovation. Wet nurses were common in wealthier households in Asia and Europe, starting in medieval times; they were also, at times, common among the poor, but with far higher infant mortality rates (Hrdy 1999).

25. TaskRabbit (http://www.taskrabbit.com) describes itself as "an online and mobile marketplace that connects neighbors to get things done." The service runs background checks on people who sign up to be "TaskRabbits," who can then bid for the posted errand-like jobs. The company's marketing materials emphasize efficiency: "Wouldn't it be amazing to have a few more hours in your day? Or to be in two places at once? That's exactly what TaskRabbit makes possible," while cloaking the transaction in cozy, feel-good neighborliness: "Neighbors helping neighbors—it's an old school concept upgraded for today."

6 Visible Conversations: Seeing Meaning beyond Words

1. Some useful background readings from the literature on conversation and communication include Goffman 1981, especially the essay "Footing"; Bonvillain 1993; Clark 1996; Clark and Brennan 1991; Saville-Troike 2003; Tannen 2007. See Baron 2005 for comparing one type of online communication (instant messaging) with speech.

2. The anthropologist Robin Dunbar notes that nonhuman primates maintain social relationships through grooming, a process that becomes quite time-consuming as group size

grows. He has hypothesized that speech—particularly social speech and gossip—evolved as a more efficient way to manage relationships in larger and more complex groups: grooming forty or fifty comrades would leave no time for sleeping, eating, or any other activities.

3. The visualizations we discuss in this chapter make social patterns more visible and accessible; the more obvious they are, the easier it is for newcomers to understand and adapt them. But that is not always the goal: when markings of communicative competence are subtle and require one to be a long-term participant in order to be fluent, they function as a way to distinguish established users from outsiders.

4. Fernanda Viégas created all three while she was a doctoral candidate in the Sociable Media Group. *Newsgroup Crowds* was done with Marc Smith at Microsoft, *History Flow* with Martin Wattenberg at IBM, and *Themail* with members of the Sociable Media Group at MIT.

5. That said, the process of designing visualizations can itself inspire new interface ideas. Finding that you cannot depict a key pattern because the necessary data are unavailable suggests that an interface that provides those data would be useful. For example, most text archives tell us nothing about the readers—how many are there? What entries did they read most? To show these data requires an interface that logs it. We will look in greater depth at new designs for conversation interfaces in chapter 10, "Embodied Interactions."

6. There is room here, too, for some additional and salient data. The hue of the circles, for instance, could show the ratio of a person's initial posts to replies, which could distinguish answerers from requesters.

7. Binaries are nontext postings such as music and programs. Most of the binaries posted on Usenet are of dubious legality: pirated songs and software, and pornographic images.

8. On the function of email beyond its basic role as a conversation medium, see Ducheneaut and Bellotti 2001; Fisher et al. 2006; Mackay 1988b; Whittaker and Sidner 1996; on the rhythm of email response, see Dabbish et al. 2005; Tyler and Tang 2003; on email content, see Baron 1998; Panteli 2002; and for additional visualization approaches, see Kerr 2003; Venolia and Neustaedter 2003; Viégas and Donath 2002.

9. *Themail* used an algorithm called TF-IDF (term frequency-inverse document frequency; Salton 1988) to measure the relative importance of words. TF-IDF produces a value for the frequency of a word in a document in the context of a larger collection, which is used to determine the rarity of the word. If two words appear in the document an equal number of times, the one that appears more frequently in the contextual collection, i.e., the more common word, will have a lower value. Changing the context against which you measure rarity thus changes the value assigned each word. "Nymphalidae" is an uncommon word in general English usage, but common in the context of texts about butterflies. *Themail* measured the value of words in a set of messages (all the emails a person and correspondent exchanged in a month or a year) using the entire corpus of the person's email as the context for determining rarity. This creates a personal, subjective depiction of each set of correspondences, showing how each relationship is distinct from one's other interactions. (See also the discussion of caricature in chapter 8, "Data Portraits.")

10. This and the following quotes are from a user study conducted by Fernanda Viégas. See Viégas 2007.

11. See Forte, Larco, and Bruckman 2009; Nov 2007; Viégas, Wattenberg, and Kushal 2004, for more on the social dynamics of Wikipedia.

12. The revision data are only a proxy for really knowing what people read. It is possible, but much more difficult, to reconstruct some notion of what has really been read through download logs (Priedhorsky et al. 2007).

13. Interruption is not necessarily rude. There are supportive interjections, overlap that is part of turn-taking, requests for clarification, etc. (Schegloff 2000; Tannen 1994).

14. Some of the physical qualities that make a leader can be reproduced online, especially in the realm of graphical interfaces. Height, for example, conveys authority, and people to whom tall avatars are given in virtual environments are treated more deferentially and act more aggressively (Yee, Bailenson, and Ducheneaut 2009). And, of course, avatars may be black or white, male or female, ugly or attractive, reproducing online the all of the status-creating distinctions of face-to-face encounters (see chapter 10, "Embodied Interactions").

15. See, e.g., Pang and Lee 2008 on detecting sentiment and the topic of discussion; Blei and Lafferty 2006 on recognizing the topic of discussion; and Pennebaker, Mehl, and Niederhoffer 2003 on assessing personality.

16. "Celebrities" in this context are not (usually) real-world celebrities but rather celebrities in the online forum—highly active on the site, well known by all participants, etc. See Golder and Donath 2004 for an in-depth treatment of celebrities, newbies, lurkers, trolls, and other social roles in online communities. "Celebrities" and "ranters" come from this study; others might choose different names for these particular types, but the overall behavior pattern is recognizable. "Newbies" are newcomers to the site, possibly to the Internet in general. They are often unfamiliar with the accepted ways of behaving and may ask naive questions or repeat queries that have long ago been tabled by the group. "Lurkers" are people who read but seldom if ever write. Unlike the listeners in a face-to-face conversation, lurkers are often completely invisible, for many discussion technologies have no way of detecting or showing who is reading. "Trolls" are deliberate troublemakers. The prototypical troll behavior is to pretend to be a legitimate participant, but one who makes increasingly provocative comments (such as asking if using a stun gun is a good approach to feline training in a cat lovers' group) intended to derail the conversation into rebutting these comments and arguing about whether they were ignorant but innocent, or deliberately malicious.

17. See Welser et al. 2007 for more on computational analysis and visualizing social roles in online conversation.

18. To depict this additional data, we could color the *Newsgroup Crowds* circles shown (figures 6.2 to 6.5) using a ramp of tones from red (maximum responses) to blue (no responses); moving through hues, rather than brightness (dark to light) keeps the depiction neutral. Adding a new statistic to a visualization should make salient patterns stand out better. If it instead becomes more confusing, one needs to rethink both the data choices and the design.

19. Deception is a big part of communication (Donath forthcoming). There are big lies, of course, such as saying you were at work when you were really out partying, but also small, everyday lies, like apologizing for being late because you had such trouble parking, when

really you had just gotten a late start. Polite society requires many deceptions, such as saying you liked a gift when in truth you did not; community could not exist if everyone were always relentlessly honest. Deception decreases common ground for it puts the deceived person's understanding at odds with the deceiver's knowledge.

20. See Zinman and Donath 2009 for an example of incorporating conversation history into a messaging interface to help resolve ambiguity and increase expressiveness.

7 Contested Boundaries

1. See Gillespie 2012, 2013 on algorithms as the walls and borders of virtual spaces.

2. Licklider's essay concluded with a perhaps tongue-in-cheek prediction that "unemployment would disappear from the face of the earth forever, for consider the magnitude of the task of adapting the network's software to all the new generations of computer, coming closer and closer upon the heels of their predecessors until the entire population of the world is caught up in an infinite crescendo of on-line interactive debugging" (1968, 40).

3. Christopher C. Stacy to TCP/IP digest (ARPANET), Jan. 14, 1982, vol. 1, no 12, "For Research Use Only—Not for Public Distribution": http://www.templetons.com/brad/tcp-ip-digest.v1n12.1.txt.

4. For example:

> Several higher authorities believe that the existence of FILM-BUFFS would be pushing the use of the ARPANET too far beyond its research-oriented mandate. Not wanting to jeopardize the lists we have now, I yield to those people's better judgment.
>
> Oh, for the day when such strictures disappear! When WORLDNET lets each interested party EFT his $10/yr for "postage," and Large Lists rule the world! (Hamilton.ES at PARC-MAXC to SF-LOVERS PM digest [ARPANET], May 26, 1981, vol. 3, issue 134, "FILM-BUFFS disappears": http://quux.org:70/Archives/usenet-a-news/FA.sf-lovers/81.05.30_ucbvax.1451_fa.sf-lovers.txt)

5. Ronda Hauben to usenet.hist@weber.ucsd.edu, January 25, 1993, "Re: History of Poor Man's Arpanet": http://shikan.org/bjones/Usenet.Hist/Nethist/0222.html.

6. Steve Den Beste to net.misc (Usenet), March 15, 1982, "Trivia on the Net": http://quux.org:70/Archives/usenet-a-news/NET.misc/82.03.15_dadlaA.98_net.misc.txt. Also in Hauben and Hauben 1997, chapter 10.

7. Mark Horton to NET.news, December 23, 1981: "Proposed Usenet policies." Quoted in Hauben and Hauben 1997.

8. Over time, newsgroup creation became increasingly formalized and restricted, and by the mid-1980s it required the approval of a board of administrators. In response, the alt hierarchy, in which anyone could create any newsgroup, was established in 1987 (Bumgarner 1998).

9. "The World" (world.std.com) was the first (1990) commercial provider of dial-up Internet access (Zakon 1997).

10. See Baym 1999 for an in-depth analysis of one Usenet community (rec.arts.tv.soaps) during this era.

11. See Donath 1998 for more about the dynamics of cheap versus valuable identities in Usenet; and Dibbell 1993 for a narrative about the inability of a community to police itself when identities are easily created and discarded.

12. In 1995, the Church of Scientology got the Finnish police to serve a search warrant to Helsingius demanding he provide the real name of a Penet user who, they alleged, had posted an internal Church of Scientology document (Newman 1996).

13. Usenet's design was open and decentralized. Once a message was posted to Usenet, it would be propagated across the network by different servers: how, then, to block spam? In its early days, only the writer of a message could cancel (withdraw) it; later, it became possible for site administrators to cancel others' messages. When the volume of spam became very high, the canceling of individual messages proved ineffective. In the 1990s the "Usenet Death Penalty" (UDP) was issued against several service providers (including CompuServe; Holt 1997) that had been sources of massive amounts of spam; this entailed automatically canceling all messages from the banned provider—and required the coordination of all the major Usenet administrators.

Because Usenet's code was designed for openness rather than security and its authority was so decentralized, message canceling was both controversial and subject to abuse. The Usenet FAQ on "Cancel Messages" provides an in-depth view on the procedure, problems, and philosophy (Skirvin 1999).

14. 4chan is an image board site where participants, often anonymous, post and comment on pictures. /b/, its most popular board, has a "no rules" policy. It is described on the social news site Reddit as "the utter cesspool of humanity. The very lowest common denominator of humor. The Bottom of the Internet." 4chan is discussed in greater depth later in this chapter.

15. A financial firm that named itself Boston Common Asset Management explains: "Beginning in 1634, the Boston Common served as a common pasture for cattle grazing. As a public good, the Common was a space owned by no one but essential to all. We chose the name Boston Common because, like the Common of old, our work stands at the intersection of the economic and social lives of the community" (http://www.bostoncommonasset.com/about-us.php). They were perhaps unaware that not long after the Common was established for public pasturage, it became overgrazed and, in 1646, just twelve years after the original purchase, grazing was limited to seventy cows at a time.

16. Hardin was not the first to observe this pattern. In the fifth century BCE, Thucydides reported Pericles saying of the Peloponnesians:

> Only after long intervals do they meet together at all, and then they devote only a fraction of their time to their general interests, spending most of it on arranging their own special affairs. It never occurs to any of them that the apathy of one will damage the interests of all. … [Each] thinks that the responsibility for its future belongs to someone else, and so, while everyone has the same idea privately, no one notices that from a general point of view things are going downhill. (Thucydides 1954)

Today, examples of the tragedy of the commons abound. Overfishing has depleted once-abundant stocks. Public parks are so tightly packed with tourists they no longer provide a respite from crowded urban life.

17. Kollock and Smith were referring to the definition in the *Hacker's Jargon File*: "the volume of information per unit time that a computer, person, or transmission medium can handle" (Raymond 2003).

18. It is worth noting that the statement that knowledge is nonrivalrous is debatable. Having knowledge that other people do not have can be quite valuable; this is the concept behind stock tips, trade secrets, fashion, and closely guarded fishing grounds. The model of knowledge as a public good has the (simplified) assumption that the person who makes knowledge available benefits—or at least is not harmed—when it spreads. When knowledge is nonexcludable yet rivalrous (e.g., stock tips) it is more like a commons resource, and Ostrom's commons-sustaining model may again be relevant.

19. Email addresses work well enough as a key in many situations. But email addresses can be hijacked or spoofed. So, if your discussion is going to involve highly sensitive information that unauthorized outsiders will try to access, you will need a more robustly secure identity-authentication system.

20. See DeLaney 1995; Donath 1998 for more on trolls.

21. Luis von Ahn, one of the original CAPTCHA creators, notes that efforts to break CAPTCHAs help advance artificial intelligence. So although we lose a security system, we gain computational ability (von Ahn et al. 2003).

Anh's research has focused on "human computation"—finding ways to motivate people, often online and in large numbers, to solve difficult computation problems. One such project is ReCAPTCHA; here, one of the words in a CAPTCHA is scanned from a digitized book. The many people typing in their best guess of what it says provide disambiguation for words that, due to fading, dirt, etc., are too illegible for automated character recognition. The other, known word authenticates the users (Von Ahn et al. 2008).

22. These sites are at http://slashdot.org/; http://www.wikipedia.org/; http://stackexchange.com/; http://boards.4chan.org/b/; and http://stackoverflow.com/.

23. A 2,500-word directive explains what constitutes a proper question for the site, available at http://mathoverflow.net/howtoask.

24. These are 2013 numbers from http://www.4chan.org/advertise.

25. On 4chan and Rick Astley, see http://knowyourmeme.com/memes/rickroll; on the Church of Scientology, see http://www.wired.com/culture/culturereviews/magazine/17-10/mf_chanology; on antipiracy sites, see http://www.techspot.com/news/41081-fbi-investigating-4chans-ddos-attacks-against-antipiracy-sites.html; and on critical news sites, see http://gawker.com/5590840/4chans-sad-war-to-silence-gawker.

26. To create a tripcode, you write the name you want to use, followed by a hashtag, followed by the seed word for the code <name>#<seed>. The board's software generates a tripcode from the seed text, so the name appears as <name>#<tripcode>. Anytime that seed is used, it will generate the same tripcode (4chan FAQ 2012). See http://ohinternet.com/Tripcode on the negative associations with tripcodes.

27. See http://www.openmediaboston.org/node/1072 for an account of the conflict between 4chan and Sharecash, a spam site.

28. A /b/ invasion is when a group of that board's anonymous participants decide to show up en masse on another site and disrupt it. There have been repeated /b/ invasions of

Habbo, a graphical avatar site for young teens, as well as of Second Life, Tumblr, and others; they have coordinated "Porn Days" on YouTube, uploading thousands of seemingly innocent videos into which they had edited pornographic sequences. Although calls to invasion are banned on 4chan (see http://www.4chan.org/rules), including on /b/, such raids persist, often coordinated from other message boards.

29. Only 160 threads are kept on the board at a time. One study found that the median time a thread was visible before it slipped below that position and was pruned was 3.9 minutes. The researchers noted postings made at an active time and receiving no comments disappeared in as fast as 28 seconds; during their study, the longest that a thread remained alive was 6.2 hours (Bernstein et al. 2011).

30. For a full discussion of "the psychodynamics of orality" and how "writing restructures consciousness," see Ong 2002. For an insightful though fictional take on the study of orality, the cultural transformation caused by recording devices, and the ancient art of surveillance, see Kadare 2002.

31. See http://mathoverflow.net/faq.

8 Data Portraits

1. For further reading on portraiture, the nature of representation, and the complex relationships among artist, subject, and viewer, see Brilliant 1990; Schneider 2002; van Alphen 1996; West 2004; Woods-Marsden 1987.

2. This is in contrast to some more traditional-seeming portraits Christian Boltanski has made, in which he photographed old photos of children who would, by the time he took the images, be adults. Boltanski's point with these photographs was the absence of essence in them: "Today they must all be about my age, but I can't learn what has become of them. The picture that remains of them does not correspond anymore with reality and all these children's faces have disappeared" (Boltanski quoted in van Alphen 1996, 248).

3. See, e.g., the work of photographer Nan Goldin, who photographed her friends over a period of years, often in painful or intimate moments (Goldin 1986).

4. See also Kevin Clarke's *Portrait of James D. Watson*, which also depicts its subject via their DNA sequences. But in this case, it is less of a critique of DNA as an expressive image than an homage to the subject's famed discovery (http://www.wellcome.ac.uk/en/fourplus/art_k_clarke.html).

5. In December of 1995 there were 16 million people online; five years later, 304 million: http://www.internetworldstats.com/.

6. See http://eagereyes.org/VisCrit/ChernoffFaces.html for a detailed critique of "Chernoff faces," a visualization technique of using faces to represent data.

7. Though even for the casual observer, such exaggerations may in fact be costly. We compare ourselves to others, and the positive spin that many people put on their public self-presentation can make others feel unproductive and unsuccessful by comparison (Jordan et al. 2011).

8. See Toma, Hancock, and Ellison 2008 for examples and analysis of deception in online dating.

9. Pop artist Andy Warhol's painted yet mechanistically produced portraits of celebrities are pointed inquiries about the role of the artist and the portrayed meaning of the subject in such a process.

10. *Personas* was initially built as part of a larger Sociable Media Group installation called *Metropath(ologies)*, an immersive art piece about the pleasures and troubles of living in a hyperconnected, information-saturated world.

9 Constructing Identity

1. Highlights of cyber-utopian literature and contemporaneous accounts of gender/race swapping include Danet 1998, Barlow 1996, Turkle 1995, Rheingold 1993, Bruckman 1993; for "dark side" warnings, see Herring 2001; for questions about the depth of identity transformation, see O'Brien 1999.

2. MUD stands for Multi-User Dungeon.

3. See chapter 7, "Contested Boundaries."

4. See chapter 11, "Privacy and Public Space."

5. Or attempt to. The passage continues with Jean's struggle to articulate what "being a Cunningham" means. Though our cultural models may be vivid, they are formed from anecdotes, resemblances to other models, emotional responses, etc., and can be very difficult to describe in words.

6. We read personality into avatars (Nowak and Rauh 2005), websites (Vazire and Gosling 2004), social networking profiles (Barash et al. 2010; Gosling, Gaddis, and Vazire 2007; Stecher and Counts 2008), screen names (Jacobson 1999), online dating profiles (Ellison, Heino, and Gibbs 2006; Gibbs, Ellison, and Heino 2006), and who your Facebook connections are (Utz 2010; Walther et al. 2008). Even in role-playing games, where participants assume the guise of fictional characters, people can form vivid and accurate impressions of other players, based on their behavior in the game's adventures (Yee 2009).

7. I use the term "stereotype" to refer to named, culturally shared prototypes. Whereas prototypes are in general shared in a culture, stereotypes are the culture's recognized types—spinsters, Asians, cops, hipsters. They are often, though not always, negative.

8. In 1991, Robert Venturi was awarded the Pritzker Prize, architecture's top honor; he requested that his wife and equal partner in their practice, Denise Scott Brown, be included in the award but was denied. Over twenty years later, a petition was circulated, with thousands of signatures, including those of several Pritzker Prize winners, requesting that the prize to Venturi be retroactively made into one joint with Scott Brown. In June 2013, the award's jury announced that Scott Brown would not receive the prize retroactively; but it is clear from the quantity of signatures and the many influential theorists and practitioners who signed it that the cultural model of women architects has changed significantly.

9. This does not promise a just or equal society, just one divided along different, and hopefully more relevant, distinctions: "Indeed, in-group favoritism paired with out-group indifference or hostility appears to exist in all human cultures" (Kurzban, Tooby, and Cosmides 2001, 15387).

10. A more critical literary eye might have found little to recommend in his writing. Minal Hajratwala, to whom McMaster sent a memoir he wrote as Amina to seek help in getting it published, described it as narcissistic and stomach turning. See Hajratwala 2011.

11. See Reynolds 2002 on whether players' characters are objects they own or aspects of themselves.

10 Embodied Interaction

1. Except in the case of unseen surveillance, which I discuss in chapter 11, "Privacy and Public Space."

2. See Argyle and Cook 1976 and Vertegaal et al. 2001 for more about the social role of gaze.

3. In fall 2010, there were over 12 million subscribers to World of Warcraft alone.

4. For excellent studies of the social life in online games, see the work of Nick Yee and Nicholas Ducheneaut: Ducheneaut, Moore, and Nickell 2007; Ducheneaut et al. 2006; Yee et al. 2007; Yee et al. 2011; Yee, Ellis, and Ducheneaut 2009.

5. The tight clothes are practical as well as stylish: it is harder to render flowing fabrics computationally.

6. Seemingly mundane greetings convey significant social information. How formally one speaks and how one addresses the other ("Mr. Smith," "Bill," "cuz") confirms the participants' understanding of their social roles and affiliation. Even spare and simple email messages have this social content. "Dear Mr. Smith" represents a different relationship than does "hi bill!"

Performing these greetings can be more difficult in writing than in person. In person, the synchrony of the communication means that if you are unsure of how to address someone, you can wait to see how he or she speaks to you, or try a more formal greeting and see if you are corrected ("Hello Mr. Smith." "No, no, please, call me Bill"). Synchronous interaction has a dancelike quality, as the conversational partners find a style of speaking with which they are competent and comfortable. Furthermore, the ephemerality of the interaction means that a mistake soon evaporates, unless it was so egregious as to cast a shadow on the rest of the conversation (e.g., calling a woman by name of the previous wife of her husband). Written correspondence requires more thought. Do I address my child's teacher as "Mr. Jones" or "Sam"? What if he is much younger or much older than me? Formal paper letters have established rules for these greetings. But although email is thought of as easy and informal, its very informality can make this process more difficult because there are fewer established rules to follow. Mimicking the form of written letters comes off as stiffly formal and anachronistic, while breeziness may still be inappropriate for the situation. And the rules evolve quickly. In email, omitting the greeting and closing entirely once seemed rude, but it has become accepted practice in informal correspondence. Picking up quickly changing conversational styles signals one's ability to observe and adapt to new ways of doing things. Ritual greetings, which on the surface convey no information, are actually dense with social meaning, conveying clues about the participants' roles, how they perceive each other, and their degree of adaptation to the medium.

Autonomous avatars may perform such greetings, but the key issue is whether the intelligence that guides them comes from the user or the designer.

7. One effect of such failed expectations is what the roboticist Masahiro Mori termed the "uncanny valley" (Mori 1970). He hypothesized that humanlike creatures that are close to but do not quite replicate human appearance or movement would inspire revulsion.

8. Personal experience plays a role. Dog owners cooperate with a doglike agent, but people without a history of close relationships with dogs do not (Parise et al. 1996).

9. See also the work of Clifford Nass on anthropomorphizing of computers (Nass, Steuer, and Tauber 1994; Reeves and Nass 1996).

10. Bailenson and colleagues conducted most of their work in full-scale virtual reality environments, with the subjects immersed in the computational space. It is not entirely clear to what extent these effects hold in a less immersive space, such as the screens that are typical of our everyday computer experience, or how they carry over to more abstract and fantastical realms. Research in this area is still sparse, but there are indications that social effects do carry over to less immersive and realistic spaces (Eastwick and Gardner 2009; Nowak and Biocca 2003; Yee et al. 2007).

11. See Chartrand and Bargh 1999 for the original experiments looking at how mimicry among people facilitates social interaction.

12. The existence of naturally occurring telepathy is controversial. Most studies that claim to prove its existence have been shown to be poorly designed; however, some more rigorous ones claim to have evidence that one mind's activity affects another (Dalkvist and Westerlund 1998; Targ and Puthoff 1974). Yet even if telepathy does exist in some form, it is not a practical mode of everyday communication.

13. An excellent introduction to the study of facial expression is Russell and Fernández-Dols 1997. For both machines and humans, understanding affect takes time; it requires "getting to know" someone (Hoque, el Kaliouby, and Picard 2009).

14. Kevin Warwick, professor of Cybernetics at the University of Reading, UK, is a leading proponent of technologically enabled direct brain communication between humans. He experiments with sensing and communicating implants using himself (and in the human–human investigations, his wife) as subject (Warwick and Cerqui 2008; Warwick et al. 2004).

11 Privacy and Public Space

1. This book focuses on design. Yet it is important also to keep in mind technical and legal approaches to maintaining privacy, which are especially important in controlling the observational range of the government, corporations, marketers, insurers, and other external observers.

Technologies such as the use of cryptography can ensure privacy. These are analogous to locks in the physical world, making it impossible for someone without the proper key to access the protected data.

Laws define and protect privacy by establishing who can gather information and how they use it. Antidiscrimination laws, for example, make it illegal for employees to use certain information about a person in hiring and firing. In the United States, the Fourth Amendment of the Constitution forms the basis of much privacy law: "The right of the people to be secure in their persons, houses, papers, and effects, against unreasonable searches and seizures, shall not be violated, and no Warrants shall issue, but upon probable cause, supported by Oath or affirmation, and particularly describing the place to be searched, and the persons or things to be seized." What is "unreasonable"? The Supreme Court defined a test to determine if a person has a reasonable expectation of privacy in a situation: (a) did the person actually expect privacy? and (b) does society think it reasonable to expect privacy in this situation? These expectations can be ambiguous, especially as new technologies of communication and observation emerge.

2. More precisely, the statistics they typically display (how many people have loaded the page) are anonymous. The counters themselves are frequently used to quietly track individuals across a site—or throughout the Web.

3. There are several ways to measure audience size: the potential audience—how many people have access to this material? The actual audience—how many people have read it? The current audience (as in figure 11.1)—how many are reading it now? The potential audience size is useful to the writer as a gauge of how formally or intimately to write; the actual size indicates the work's popularity; and the current size is most relevant when there is a possibility of further engagement with the other readers.

4. "War is Peace, Freedom is Slavery, and Ignorance is Strength" (Orwell 1949).

5. Richard Sennett describes how revelation—both mental and physical—served to empower and bind together ancient Athenians: "Athenian democracy placed great emphasis on its citizens exposing their thoughts to others, just as men exposed their bodies. These mutual acts of disclosure were meant to draw the knot between citizens ever tighter" (Sennett 1996, 33).

6. Politeness is socially mandated dishonesty, necessary because relentless honesty would lead to continual strife. Yet society also cannot function with rampant dishonesty. We need to find the right balance between honesty and kindness, and to achieve politeness without hypocrisy.

A nineteenth-century guide to etiquette recommends avoiding controversial topics: "Discussions on religion, politics, or any subjects upon which there might be strong prejudices should be avoided in society. It is objectionable to controvert what others have to say. Speaking one's mind on all occasions is an evidence of disrespect for the feelings of others."

It also notes that "in every well-ordered community the observance of the usages and forms of social intercourse is an important part of the everyday life of the people. The interests, tastes, education, culture, refinement, employments and aspirations of persons so widely differ, that were it not for certain conventional rules accepted by the members of what we call society, it would be impossible to maintain that concord so essential to human association. The bringing of these diverse elements into relation with each other is the part of etiquette. It may therefore be said that etiquette is the machinery by means of which society is made harmonious and the relations between persons of congenial tastes and pursuits are established and maintained" (Keim 1886, 180).

7. When such sites fold, one of their most valuable assets is their user data, which may, if the user agreement allows, as it often does, be sold to another company. Thus, personal information that had been private on one site may be made more public or mined for other purposes by another (Sherman 2011).

8. *Ostrowe v. Lee*, 175 N.E. 505, 506 (N.Y. Ct. App. 1931).

9. Reputation bankruptcy could technically work for a limited set of sites, given a centralized reputation management structure. But if it was known that eBay, for example, allowed such bankruptcy, there would quickly be a market for archiving eBay reputations, which would not honor the bankruptcy.

An informal version of such bankruptcy exists in any site with history and pseudonymous identity. People trust others who have an established identity, unless that identity has a history of poor behavior. Newcomers need to establish themselves slowly before they are trusted community members. Someone who has acted badly can abandon his tainted identity and return with a new name, a seeming newcomer to the site. This is useful if his goal is to make a fresh start as a constructive contributor, but often it is to continue acting destructively, without the warning of his poor record (see, e.g., Dibbell 1993 for an early account of this phenomenon).

10. Privacy supports the individual; publicity supports the group. Our last century of unprecedented privacy has also been one of unprecedented consumption, a habit that is clearly and urgently unsustainable. We can imagine a less private world, with greater pressure to conform to the public good, in which, for example, people's consumption/carbon footprint followed them visibly about, creating public pressure to consume less. But humans are complex. Conspicuous consumption is still a mark of high status. And, realistically, we are in much less danger of losing privacy for the enforcing of a collective good than we are of losing it to the marketers who use increasingly precise pictures of us to persuade us to consume ever more voraciously.

12 Social Catalysts

1. For further reading on alienation and community in the city, see Wirth 1938; Simmel 1950; Milgram 1970; Sennett 1976. On design solutions, see Whyte 1988; Jacobs 1992.

2. See Whyte 1988 and Jacobs 1992 for analyses of why some urban areas are lively and sociable—and why others, even in wealthy sections, are barren of human interaction.

3. Our public garb also communicates: we display our social roles and affiliations via hairstyle and clothing. Some people choose to be circumspect, but many others put considerable effort into personal displays that mark their political beliefs and subcultural memberships. Taste in media—music, books, etc.—signals cultural affiliation (Lamont and Fournier 1993; Thornton 1996) and is especially reliable when one observes someone actually consuming that media (Voida et al. 2005): I may wear a Motörhead T-shirt just because I think it looks cool, but if I am listening to their music, either I actually like it, or I intensely want people to think I do.

4. See, e.g., Esbjörnsson, Juhlin, and Östergren 2004; Kenton, Glancy, and Robertshaw 2008; McQuire 2006; Paulos and Goodman 2004.

5. One *Chit Chat Club* chair was able to swivel to change its viewpoint.

6. An earlier version of the *PRoP* was a remote-controlled blimp. Although less humanlike in its appearance, one of its features that was touted was how harmless it was as a lightweight floating balloon (Paulos and Canny 1997). It also had the ability to see things that people normally can't see; for example, one could float it up to the top of the *Tyrannosaurus rex* skeleton at a museum. The blimp emphasized exploring space, whereas the robot explored remote human interaction.

7. Ken Goldberg has created numerous experiments exploring the problem he terms "tel-epistemology": what makes people believe in the reality of the scene that they are able to affect telerobotically, but that they only see as a picture on a screen (Goldberg 2001)?

8. In warfare, there is a long-standing moral debate about the rules of engagement, with chivalry at one end and no-holds-barred terrorism at the other. At the chivalric end, it is an engagement among peers, fought on an even playing field. Although today a more nuanced version of history may be taught, when I was growing up in the 1970s, we learned that the clever American revolutionaries fought valiantly against the foolish British red-coats, the latter lined up in proper formation in their brilliant target-red uniforms, by using more sniper-like tactics. Yet from the British perspective, they were facing an unprincipled and amoral army, which broke the rules of civilized engagement. Today, the lines are drawn around issues such as killing civilians and using unmanned tele-weapons. Are those who refuse to use these tactics morally superior, or simply anachronistically idealistic? Having chosen to engage in warfare, what then holds you to a set of rules?

9. Erving Goffman's (1959, 1966) work has been so influential because he astutely describes these behaviors, which are so common and ingrained as to be almost invisible to us; he shows also how difficult these seemingly (but in fact not) innate rituals are for outsiders, especially mental patients, to perform.

10. See Cohen and Vandello 1998 for an interesting discussion of the connection between violent cultures and highly ritualized codes of honor.

11. This is easy to believe in the context of physical-space interactions, but it is also important to keep in mind that even when we are acting in an abstract, virtual world, we react differently to people (and proxies) of different sizes. We are always embodied (Yee and Bailenson 2007).

12. Although most of these experiments have focused on conferences, one (Hocman) connected motorcycle riders passing each other on the highway, playing a sound at the time of the encounter to alert them that another Hocman-enabled rider was near and passing personal URLs between them (Esbjörnsson, Juhlin, and Östergren 2004).

13. Most names are not unique identifiers. This problem is discussed more fully in chapter 8, "Data Portraits." However, it is conceivable that having misattributed information attached to them in public might be what propels people to opt into a universal unique ID tag. A system could recognize your face and know that you are "John Smith," but much of the data it would then attach to you would be related to other "John Smiths." You would want to avoid this by having some means of authenticating as yours and only yours the data you created and the reputation you accrued.

14. Beyond glasses, there is also work on contact lenses that would provide augmentation capability (Parviz 2009).

15. However, whereas one's appearance may not reveal what one is viewing, one's behavior might. Attention is not infinite. We know this already from how distracted people are from their surroundings when engaged in a phone conversation. Reading stories will certainly also distract from the surrounding—and perhaps increasingly mundane-seeming—reality. A full, or even cursory, assessment of the social, psychological, and cultural impact of augmented reality is outside the scope of this book. Most of the work on augmented reality and attention has focused on ensuring that users pay attention to the augmented

material; the question I raise here is how augmentation affects the attention we pay to the real world (Pederson et al. 2007).

Coda: Living in Balance

1. Why "him" and not "her"? "Him" is, in our culture, the unmarked pronoun: it is the default gender you supply when knowing nothing about the person. To refer to someone as "her" shows you have some specific knowledge about the individual—something that makes that person less of a stranger.

2. This is not unique to social media: meeting someone whose memoirs you have read or a public figure whose personal life has been heavily reported provides that same sense of instant, interaction-free intimacy. However, social media and searchable data bring two changes. First, it is now commonplace to be able to peruse such information about anyone, not just famous figures and writers. Second, the information is a broadly mixed collection of data, including deliberate self-portrayal, out-of-context discussion, legal and official material, and so on.

3. Even without real names, there are many ways to connect information about a single person, even if it is created under different identifiers (Jones et al. 2007; Narayanan and Shmatikov 2009; Nissenbaum 1999). Pseudonymity provides casual everyday privacy, not secure secrecy.

REFERENCES

Abowd, Gregory D., and Elizabeth D. Mynatt. 2000. Charting past, present, and future research in ubiquitous computing. *ACM Transactions on Computer-Human Interaction* 7 (1):29–58.

Abrams, Janet, and Peter Hall, eds. 2006. *Else/Where: Mapping—New Cartographies of Networks and Territories*. Minneapolis: University of Minnesota Design Institute.

Adamic, Lada, and Eytan Adar. 2005. How to search a social network. *Social Networks* 27 (3):187–203.

Adamic, Lada, Orkut Buyukkokten, and Eytan Adar. 2003. A social network caught in the Web. *First Monday* 8 (6). http://www.firstmonday.org/ojs/index.php/fm/article/view/1057.

Adamic, Lada, and Natalie Glance. 2005. The political blogosphere and the 2004 U.S. election: Divided they blog. In *Proceedings of the Third International Workshop on Link Discovery*. New York: ACM Press.

Adar, Eytan, Li Zhang, Lada A. Adamic, and Rajan M. Lukose. 2004. Implicit structure and the dynamics of blogspace. In *Proceedings of the Thirteenth International World Wide Web Conference: Workshop on the Weblogging Ecosystem*. New York: ACM Press.

Addley, Esther. 2011. Gay Girl in Damascus hoaxer acted out of "vanity." *Guardian*, June 13.

Ahlberg, C., and B. Shneiderman. 1994. Visual information seeking: Tight coupling of dynamic query filters with starfield displays. In *Proceedings of the SIGCHI Conference on Human Factors in Computing Systems: Celebrating Interdependence*, 313–317. New York: ACM Press.

Ahlberg, C., Christopher Williamson, and Ben Shneiderman. 1992. Dynamic queries for information exploration: An implementation and evaluation. In *Proceedings of the SIGCHI Conference on Human Factors in Computing Systems*. New York: ACM Press.

Aladdin and the Magic Lamp. Project Gutenberg. http://www.gutenberg.org/catalog/world/readfile?fk_files=1441314.

Albers, Joseph. 1975. *Interaction of Color*. New Haven, CT: Yale University Press. Original edition, 1963.

Allport, G. W. 1979. *The Nature of Prejudice*. New York: Perseus Books. Original edition, 1954.

Ambady, Nalini, Mark Hallahan, and Robert Rosenthal. 1995. On judging and being judged accurately in zero acquaintance situations. *Journal of Personality and Social Psychology* 69:518–529.

Ambady, Nalini, and Robert Rosenthal. 1992. Thin slices of expressive behavior as predictors of interpersonal consequences: A meta-analysis. *Psychological Bulletin* 111:256–274.

Ames, Morgan G., Janet Go, Joseph "Jofish" Kaye, and Mirjana Spasojevic. 2010. Making love in the network closet: The benefits and work of family videochat. In *Proceedings of ACM Conference on Computer Supported Cooperative Work*. New York: ACM Press.

Anderson, Sam. 2010. The Human Shuffle: Is ChatRoulette the future of the Internet or its distant past? *New York Times Magazine*, Feb. 5. http://nymag.com/news/media/63663/.

Argyle, Michael. 1993. *The Psychology of Interpersonal Behaviour*. London: Penguin Books.

Argyle, Michael, and Mark Cook. 1976. *Gaze and Mutual Gaze*. Cambridge: Cambridge University Press.

Arnheim, R. 1974. *Art and Visual Perception: A Psychology of the Creative Eye*. Berkeley: University of California Press.

Arnheim, R. 2004. *Visual Thinking*. Berkeley: University of California Press.

Avedon, Richard. 1985. *In the American West, 1979–1984*. New York: Harry N. Abrams.

Bachour, K., F. Kaplan, and P. Dillenbourg. 2010. An interactive table for supporting participation balance in face-to-face collaborative learning. *IEEE Transactions on Learning Technologies* 3 (3):203–213.

Bailenson, J. N., and A. C. Beall. 2006. Transformed social interaction: Exploring the digital plasticity of avatars. In *Avatars at Work and Play: Collaboration and Interaction in Shared Virtual Environments*, ed. R. Schroeder and A. Axelsson, 1–16. New York: Springer-Verlag.

Bailenson, J. N., Shanto Iyengar, Nick Yee, and Nathan A. Collins. 2009. Facial similarity between voters and candidates causes influence. *Public Opinion Quarterly* 72 (5):935–961.

Bailenson, J. N., and Nick Yee. 2005. Digital chameleons. *Psychological Science* 16 (10):814.

Bailenson, J. N., Nick Yee, Dan Merget, and Ralph Schroeder. 2006. The effect of behavioral realism and form realism of real-time avatar faces on verbal disclosure, nonverbal disclosure, emotion recognition, and copresence in dyadic interaction. *Presence* 15 (4):359–372.

Baker, Nancy V. 2003. National security versus civil liberties. *Presidential Studies Quarterly* 33 (3):547–567.

Balzer, Michael, Oliver Deussen, and Claus Lewerentz. 2005. Voronoi treemaps for the visualization of software metrics. In *2005 ACM Symposium on Software Visualization*, 165–172. New York: ACM Press.

Barabasi, Albert-Laszlo, Hawoong Jeong, Zoltan Neda, Erzsebet Ravasz, Andras Schubert, and Tamas Vicsek. 2002. Evolution of the social network of scientific collaborations. American Physical Society Meeting Abstracts: 27012.

Barash, V., N. Ducheneaut, E. Isaacs, and V. Bellotti. 2010. Faceplant: Impression (Mis) management in Facebook status updates. In *Fourth International AAAI Conference on Weblogs and Social Media*. Palo Alto: AAAI Press.

Barlow, John Perry. 1996. A declaration of the independence of cyberspace. https://projects.eff.org/~barlow/Declaration-Final.html.

Baron, N. 1998. Letters by phone or speech by other means: The linguistics of email. *Language and Communication* 18:133–170.

Baron, N. 2005. Discourse structures in instant messaging: The case of utterance breaks. *Language@Internet* 7, article 4.

Barry, Dan, Serge F. Kovaleski, Campbell Robertson, and Lizette Alvarez. 2012. Race, tragedy, and outrage collide after a shot in Florida. *New York Times*, April 1 (online, US section). http://www.nytimes.com/2012/04/02/us/trayvon-martin-shooting-prompts-a-review-of-ideals.html?pagewanted=all#commentsContainer.

Bateman, Scott, Regan Mandryk, Carl Gutwin, Aaron Genest, David McDine, and Christopher Brooks. 2010. Useful junk? The effects of visual embellishment on comprehension and memorability of charts. In *ACM Conference on Human Factors in Computing Systems (CHI 2010)*. New York: ACM Press.

Baumer, Franklin L. 1977. *Modern European Thought*. New York: Macmillan.

Baym, Nancy K. 1999. *Tune In, Log On: Soaps, Fandom, and Online Community*. Thousand Oaks, CA: SAGE.

Becker, R. A., S. G. Eick, and A. R. Wilks. 1995. Visualizing network data. *IEEE Transactions on Visualization and Computer Graphics* 1 (1):16–28.

Bederson, B. B., and J. D. Hollan. 1994. Pad++: a zooming graphical interface for exploring alternate interface physics. In *Proceedings of the Seventh Annual ACM Symposium on User Interface Software and Technology*, 17–26. New York: ACM Press.

Bederson, B. B., Ben Shneiderman, and Martin Wattenberg. 2002. Ordered and quantum treemaps: Making effective use of 2D space to display hierarchies. *ACM Transactions on Graphics* 21 (4):833–854.

Bellotti, Victoria, and Abigail J. Sellen. 1993. Design for privacy in ubiquitous computing environments. In *Proceedings of the Third European Conference on Computer-Supported Cooperative Work*. New York: Kluwer Academic.

Bentham, Jeremy. 1791. *Panopticon, or The Inspection House*. Dublin.

Bergstrom, T., and K. Karahalios. 2007. Conversation clock: Visualizing audio patterns in co-located groups. In Proceedings of IEEE. Los Alamitos, CA: IEEE Computer Society.

Bernard, H. R., E. C. Johnsen, P. D. Killworth, C. McCarty, G. A. Shelley, and S. Robinson. 1990. Comparing four different methods for measuring personal social networks. *Social Networks* 12 (3):179–215.

Bernstein, M. S., A. Monroy-Hernández, D. Harry, P. André, K. Panovich, and G. Vargas. 2011. 4chan and /b/: An analysis of anonymity and ephemerality in a large online community. In *Proceedings of the Fifth International AAAI Conference on Weblogs and Social Media*. Palo Alto: AAAI Press.

Bertrand, Marianne, and Sendhil Mullainathan. 2003. *Are Emily and Greg more employable than Lakisha and Jamal? A field experiment on labor market discrimination*. National Bureau of Economic Research.

Bian, Yanjie. 1997. Bringing strong ties back in: Indirect ties, network bridges, and job searches in China. *American Sociological Review* 62 (3):366–385.

Bian, Yanjie. 1999. Getting a job through a web of guanxi in China. In *Networks in the Global Village: Life in Contemporary Communities*, ed. Barry Wellman, 255–278. Boulder, CO: Westview Press.

Bignami, Francesca. 2007. European versus American liberty: A comparative privacy analysis of anti-terrorism data-mining. *Boston College Law Review* 48:609.

Biocca, F. 1997. The cyborg's dilemma: Progressive embodiment in virtual environments. *Journal of Computer-Mediated Communication* 3 (2).

Blei, David M., and John D. Lafferty. 2006. Dynamic topic models. In *Proceedings of the Twenty-Third International Conference on Machine Learning*. New York: ACM Press.

Boase, Jeffrey, John Horrigan, Barry Wellman, and Lee Rainie. 2006. *The Strength of Internet Ties*. Washingon, DC: Pew Internet & American Life Project.

Bonvillain, Nancy. 1993. *Language, Culture, and Communication: The Meaning of Messages*. Englewood Cliffs, NJ: Prentice Hall.

Borgatti, S. P., A. Mehra, D. J. Brass, and G. Labianca. 2009. Network analysis in the social sciences. *Science* 323 (5916):892–895.

Borges, Jorge Luis. 1998. *Collected Fictions*. Trans. Andrew Hurley. New York: Viking.

Boroditsky, Lera, Michael Ramscar, and Michael Frank. 2001. The roles of body and mind in abstract thought. *In Proceedings of the Twenty-Third Annual Conference of the Cognitive Science Society*. Mahwah, NJ: Erlbaum.

Borovoy, R., F. Martin, S. Vemuri, M. Resnick, B. Silverman, and C. Hancock. 1998. Meme tags and community mirrors: moving from conferences to collaboration. In *Proceedings of the 1998 ACM Conference on Computer Supported Cooperative Work*. New York: ACM Press.

Borovoy, R., Brian Silverman, Tim Gorton, Matt Notowidigdo, Brian Knep, Mitchel Resnick, and Jeff Klann. 2001. Folk computing: Revisiting oral tradition as a scaffold for co-present communities. In *Proceedings of the SIGCHI Conference on Human Factors in Computing Systems*. New York: ACM Press.

Bourdieu, Pierre. 1984. *Distinction: A Social Critique of the Judgment of Taste*. Translated by Richard Nice. Cambridge, MA: Harvard University Press. Original edition, Les Ediitons de Minuit, 1979.

boyd, danah. 2004. Friendster and publicly articulated social networking. In *Proceedings of the Conference on Human Factors in Computing Systems* (CHI '04). New York: ACM Press.

boyd, danah. 2006. Friends, Friendsters, and Top 8: Writing community into being on social network sites. *First Monday* 11 (12). http://firstmonday.org/issues/issue11_12/boyd/index.html.

boyd, danah, and Nicole B. Ellison. 2007. Social network sites: Definition, history, and scholarship. *Journal of Computer-Mediated Communication* 13 (1):210–230.

boyd, danah, Hyun-yeul Lee, Dan Ramage, and Judith Donath. 2002. Developing legible visualizations for online social spaces. In *Proceedings of the 35th Annual Hawaii International Conference on System Sciences* (HICSS'02). Los Alamitos, CA: IEEE Computer Society.

Brand, S. 1997. *How Buildings Learn: What Happens after They're Built*. New York: Viking Penguin.

Brandes, U., J. Raab, and D. Wagner. 2001. Exploratory network visualization: Simultaneous display of actor status and connections. *Journal of Social Structure* 2 (4):1–28.

Brandon, Merel, Simon Epskamp, Thomas de Groot, Tim Franssen, Bart van Gennep, and Thomas Visser. 2011. The effects visual feedback on social behavior during decision making meetings. In *Human Interface and the Management of Information: Interacting with Information*, ed. Gavriel Salvendy and Michael Smith, 6772:219–228. Berlin: Springer.

Brennan, S. E. 1985. Caricature generator: The dynamic exaggeration of faces by computer. *Leonardo* 18 (3):170–178.

Brilliant, R. 1990. *Portraiture*. Cambridge, MA: Harvard University Press.

Brown, Janelle. 1999. What does it take to make a buck off of Usenet? *Salon*, May 24.

Bruce, Vicki, and Andy Young. 1998. *In the Eye of the Beholder: The Science of Face Perception*. Oxford: Oxford University Press.

Bruckman, Amy S. 1993. Gender swapping on the Internet. In *Proceedings of INET '93*. Reston, VA: The Internet Society.

Brzezinski, M. 2003. The unmanned army. *New York Times*.

Bumgarner, Lee S. 1998. Usenet: The great renaming 1985–1988. http://web.archive.org/web/20021012011241/http://www.vrx.net/usenet/history/rename.html.

Burke, Moira, Robert Kraut, and Cameron Marlow. 2011. Social capital on Facebook: Differentiating uses and users. In *Proceedings of the SIGCHI Conference on Human Factors in Computing Systems*. New York: ACM Press.

Burt, Ronald S. 2002. Bridge decay. *Social Networks* 24 (4):333–363.

Butler, Judith. 1990. *Gender Trouble: Feminism and the Subversion of Identity*. London: Routledge.

Butler, Paul. 2013. Bit aesthetics. http://bitaesthetics.com/.

Byrne, David. 2003. Envisioning emotional epistemological information. http://www.davidbyrne.com/art/eeei/index.php.

Byron, Lee, and Martin Wattenberg. 2008. Stacked graphs—geometry and aesthetics. *IEEE Transactions on Visualization and Computer Graphics* 14 (6):1245–1252.

Calacanis, Jason. 2012. This week in startups: Jonathan Abrams, episode 303. http://thisweekinstartups.com/blog/jonathan-abrams-twist-303.html.

Campbell, Heidi A., and Oren Golan. 2011. Creating digital enclaves: Negotiation of the internet among bounded religious communities. *Media, Culture, and Society* 33 (5):709–724.

Card, S. K., T. P. Moran, and A. Newell. 1983. *The Psychology of Human-Computer Interaction*. Hillsdale, NJ: Erlbaum.

Carroll, Lewis. 1893. *Sylvie and Bruno Concluded*. New York: Macmillan.

Carson, Paula Phillips, Patricia A. Lanier, Kerry David Carson, and Brandi N. Guidry. 2000. Clearing a path through the management fashion jungle: Some preliminary trailblazing. *Academy of Management Journal* 43 (6):1143–1158.

Cassell, J., and H. Vilhjálmsson. 1999. Fully embodied conversational avatars: Making communicative behaviors autonomous. *Autonomous Agents and Multi-Agent Systems* 2 (1):45–64.

Cassidy, M. 2008. Flying with disability in Second Life. *Eureka Street* 18 (1):22.

Castells, Manuel. 2000. *The Rise of the Network Society*. Hoboken, NJ: Wiley-Blackwell.

Centola, Damon. 2010. The spread of behavior in an online social network experiment. *Science* 329 (5996):1194–1197.

Chafkin, Matt. 2007. How to kill a great idea! *Inc.*, June 1.

Chartrand, T. L., and J. A. Bargh. 1999. The chameleon effect: The perception-behavior link and social interaction. *Journal of Personality and Social Psychology* 76:893–910.

Chernoff, H. 1973. The use of faces to represent points in k-dimensional space graphically. *Journal of the American Statistical Association* 68:331–368.

Christakis, N. A., and J. H. Fowler. 2007. The spread of obesity in a large social network over 32 years. *New England Journal of Medicine* 357 (4):370.

Christakis, N. A., and J. H. Fowler. 2008. The collective dynamics of smoking in a large social network. *New England Journal of Medicine* 358 (21):2249–2258.

Churchill, Elizabeth, Andreas Girgensohn, Les Nelson, and Alison Lee. 2004. Blending digital and physical spaces for ubiquitous community participation. *Communications of the ACM* 47 (2):38–44.

Clark, Herbert H. 1996. *Using Language*. Cambridge: Cambridge University Press.

Clark, Herbert H., and Susan E. Brennan. 1991. Grounding in communication. In *Perspectives on Socially Shared Cognition*, ed. Lauren B. Resnick, John M. Levine, and Stephanie D. Teasley, 127–149. Washington, DC: American Psychological Association.

Cleland, Kathy. 2004. Talk to me: Getting personal with interactive art. In *Interaction: Systems, Practice, and Theory*. http://research.it.uts.edu.au/creative/interaction/papers/interaction04_43.pdf.

Clifford, Stephanie, and Quentin Hardy. 2013. Attention, shoppers: Store is tracking your cell. *New York Times*.

CNBC. 2010. Inside the mind of Google. http://www.cnbc.com/id/33831099.

Coates, James, Marjorie David, Eric Gwinn, and Clarence Petersen. 1994. Compuserve pries open the floodgates of the 'Net. *Chicago Tribune*, Oct. 7, 69.

Cohen, Dov, and Joe Vandello. 1998. Meanings of violence. *Journal of Legal Studies* 27 (2):567–584.

Cohen, Paula Marantz. 2003. On the death of portraiture. *Yale Review* 91 (3):62–72.

Cole, David, and James X. Dempsey. 2006. *Terrorism and the Constitution: Sacrificing Civil Liberties in the Name of National Security*. New York: New Press.

Cook, Gareth. 2013. What about Denise? *New Yorker*. http://www.newyorker.com/online/blogs/culture/2013/04/what-about-denise.html.

Copple, Robert. F. 1989. Privacy and the frontier thesis: An American intersection of self and society. *American Journal of Jurisprudence* 34: 87.

Corbusier, Le. 1986. *Towards a New Architecture*. Trans. Frederick Etchells. Mineola, NY: Dover. Original edition, London: John Rodker, 1931.

Cosmides, Leda, John Tooby, and Robert Kurzban. 2003. Perceptions of race. *Trends in Cognitive Sciences* 7 (4):173–179.

Cunningham, B. 2003. Re-thinking objectivity. *Columbia Journalism Review* 42 (2):24–32.

Dabbish, Laura A., Robert E. Kraut, Susan Fussell, and Sara Kiesler. 2005. Understanding email use: predicting action on a message. In *Proceedings of the SIGCHI Conference on Human Factors in Computing Systems*. New York: ACM Press.

Dalkvist, J., and J. Westerlund. 1998. Experimental studies on telepathic group communication of emotions. *Journal of Scientific Exploration* 12 (4):583–603.

Danet, B. 1998. Text as mask: Gender, play, and performance on the Internet. In *Cybersociety 2.0: Revisiting Computer-Mediated Communication and Community*, ed. Steven G. Jones, 129–158. Thousand Oaks, CA: Sage.

D'Angelo, A. 2003. BuddyZoo. http://www.buddyzoo.com.

Davies, Lizzy. 2012. Higgs boson announcement: Cern scientists discover subatomic particle. *Guardian*, July 4, 2012.

Davis, Eric W. 2003. *Teleportation Physics Study*. Edwards Air Force Base, CA: Air Force Research Lab.

DeLaney, David. 1995. Net legends FAQ. http://www.faqs.org/faqs/net-legends-faq/.

de Sola Pool, Ithiel, and Manfred Kochen. 1979. Contacts and influence. *Social Networks* 1 (1):5–51.

DeVoto, Jeanne A. E. 1994. The Zumabot's tale. http://www.jaedworks.com/shoebox/zumabot.html.

Dibbell, J. 1993. A rape in cyberspace, or how an evil clown, a Haitian trickster spirit, two wizards, and a cast of dozens turned a database into a society. *Village Voice*, December 23.

Dibbell, Julian. 2008. Mutilated furries, flying phalluses: Put the blame on griefers, the sociopaths of the virtual world. *Wired*, Jan. 18, 2008.

DiMicco, Joan Morris, Katherine J. Hollenbach, Anna Pandolfo, and Walter Bender. 2007. The impact of increased awareness while face-to-face. *Human-Computer Interaction* 22 (1):47–96.

DiMicco, Joan Morris, Anna Pandolfo, and Walter Bender. 2004. Influencing group participation with a shared display. In *Proceedings of the 2004 ACM Conference on Computer Supported Cooperative Work*. New York: ACM Press.

DNA Art by DNA 11. 2012. http://www.dna11.com/.

Dobson, K. 2002a. *AgoraPhone*. Master's thesis, Massachusetts Institute of Technology.

Dobson, K. 2002b. *AgoraPhone*. http://web.media.mit.edu/~monster/AgoraPhone/top.html.

Dodds, P. S., R. Muhamad, and D. J. Watts. 2003. An experimental study of search in global social networks. *Science* 301 (5634):827.

Dodge, Martin, and Rob Kitchin. 2000. *Atlas of Cyberspace*. London: Addison-Wesley.

Donath, Judith. 1995. Visual who. In *Proceedings of the Third ACM International Conference on Multimedia '95*. New York: ACM Press.

Donath, Judith. 1998. Identity and deception in the virtual community. In *Communities in Cyberspace*, ed. Marc Smith and Peter Kollock. New York: Routledge.

Donath, Judith. 2001. Mediated faces. In *Proceedings of Cognitive Technology: Instruments of Mind: Proceedings of the Fourth International Conference*. Berlin: Springer-Verlag.

Donath, Judith. 2002. A semantic approach to visualizing online conversations. *Communications of the ACM* 45 (4):45–49.

Donath, Judith. 2004a. Artificial pets: Simple behaviors elicit complex attachments. In *The Encyclopedia of Animal Behavior*, ed. Marc Bekoff, 3:955–957. Westport, CT: Greenwood Press.

Donath, Judith. 2004b. Social Visualization: MIT MAS.965. MIT Open Courseware. http://ocw.mit.edu/courses/media-arts-and-sciences/mas-965-social-visualization-fall-2004/index.htm.

Donath, Judith. 2006. The rhythms of salience: A conversation map. http://smg.media.mit.edu/papers/Donath/conversationMap/conversationMap.html.

Donath, Judith. 2007. Signals in social supernets. *Journal of Computer-Mediated Communication* 13 (1):231–251.

Donath, Judith. 2008. Technological interventions in everyday interaction. In *Act/React Exhibition Catalog*. Milwaukee, WI: Milwaukee Art Museum.

Donath, Judith. 2011. Pamphlets, paintings, and programs: Faithful reproduction and untidy generativity in the physical and digital domains. In *Switching Codes: Thinking through Digital Technology in the Humanities and the Arts*, ed. Thomas Bartscherer and Roderick Coover, 301. Chicago: University of Chicago Press.

Donath, Judith. Forthcoming. *The Economics of Honesty*.

Donath, Judith, and danah boyd. 2004. Public displays of connection. *BT Technology Journal* 22 (4): 71–82.

Donath, Judith, Karrie Karahalios, and Fernanda Viégas. 1999. Visualizing conversations. *Journal of Computer-Mediated Communication* 4 (4). http://onlinelibrary.wiley.com/doi/10.1111/j.1083-6101.1999.tb00107.x/full.

Donath, Judith, Karrie Karahalios, and Fernanda Viégas. 2000. Visiphone. In *Proceedings of International Conference for Auditory Display*. Atlanta, GA: International Community for Auditory Display.

Donath, Judith, and Fernanda Viégas. 2002. The chat circles series: Explorations in designing abstract graphical communication interfaces. In *Proceedings of ACM Conference on Designing Interactive Systems*. New York: ACM Press.

Dourish, P., W. K. Edwards, A. LaMarca, and M. Salisbury. 1999. Presto: An experimental architecture for fluid interactive document spaces. *ACM Transactions on Computer-Human Interaction* 6 (2):133–161.

Dourish, Paul. 2004. *Where the Action Is: The Foundations of Embodied Interaction*. Cambridge, MA: MIT Press.

Dourish, Paul, Annette Adler, Victoria Bellotti, and Austin Henderson. 1996. Your place or mine? Learning from long-term use of audio-video communication. *Computer Supported Cooperative Work* 5 (1):33–62.

Dourish, Paul, and Sara Bly. 1992. Portholes: Supporting awareness in a distributed work group. In *Proceedings of CHI '92 Conference on Human Factors in Computing Systems*. New York: ACM Press.

Dragulescu, Alex. 2009. Lexigraphs. http://www.sq.ro/lexigraphs1.php.

Dubrovsky, Vitaly J., Sara Kiesler, and Beheruz N. Sethna. 1991. The equalization phenomenon: Status effects in computer-mediated and face-to-face decision-making groups. *Human-Computer Interaction* 6 (2):119–146.

Ducheneaut, N., and V. Bellotti. 2001. Email as habitat: An exploration of embedded personal information management. *Interaction* 8 (5):30–38.

Ducheneaut, N., R. J. Moore, and E. Nickell. 2007. Virtual "third places": A case study of sociability in massively multiplayer games. *Computer Supported Cooperative Work* 16 (1):129–166.

Ducheneaut, N., N. Yee, E. Nickell, and R. J. Moore. 2006. Alone together? Exploring the social dynamics of massively multiplayer online games. In *Proceedings of the ACM*. New York: ACM Press.

Dumont, Maarten, Sammy Rogmans, Steven Maesen, and Philippe Bekaert. 2009. Optimized two-party video chat with restored eye contact using graphics hardware. In *e-Business and Telecommunications* 48:358–372. Berlin: Berlin Heidelberg.

Dunbar, R. I. M. 1993. Coevolution of neocortical size, group size, and language in humans. *Behavioral and Brain Sciences* 16 (4):681–693.

Dunbar, R. I. M. 1996. *Grooming, Gossip, and the Evolution of Language*. Cambridge, MA: Harvard University Press.

Dunbar, R. I. M. 1998. The social brain hypothesis. *Evolutionary Anthropology: Issues, News, and Reviews* 6 (5):178–190.

Dunne, Anthony. 1999. *Hertzian Tales*. London: Royal College of Art.

Dunning, William V. 1991. *Changing Images of Pictorial Space: A History of Spatial Illusion in Painting*. Syracuse, NY: Syracuse University Press.

Eagle, N., and A. Pentland. 2005. Social serendipity: Mobilizing social software. *IEEE Pervasive Computing* 4 (2):28–34.

Eagle, N., and A. Pentland. 2006. Reality mining: Sensing complex social systems. *Personal and Ubiquitous Computing* 10 (4):255–268.

Eagle, N., A. Pentland, and D. Lazer. 2009. Inferring friendship network structure by using mobile phone data. *Proceedings of the National Academy of Sciences of the United States of America* 106 (36):15274–15278.

Eames, Charles, and Ray Eames. 1977. *Powers of Ten: A Film Dealing with the Relative Size of Things in the Universe and the Effect of Adding Another Zero.*

Eastwick, Paul W., and Wendi L. Gardner. 2009. Is it a game? Evidence for social influence in the virtual world. *Social Influence* 4 (1):18–32.

Eisner, W. 2001. *Comics and Sequential Art.* Tamrac, FL: Poorhouse Press.

Ekman, Paul. 1992. *Telling Lies: Clues to Deceit in the Marketplace, Politics, and Marriage.* New York: W. W. Norton.

Ellison, N. B., C. Steinfield, and C. Lampe. 2007. The benefits of Facebook "friends": Social capital and college students' use of online social network sites. *Journal of Computer-Mediated Communication* 12 (4):1143–1168.

Ellison, N., R. Heino, and J. Gibbs. 2006. Managing impressions online: Self-presentation processes in the online dating environment. *Journal of Computer-Mediated Communication* 11(2):415–441.

Esbjörnsson, M., O. Juhlin, and M. Östergren. 2004. Traffic encounters and Hocman: Associating motorcycle ethnography with design. *Personal and Ubiquitous Computing* 8 (2):92–99.

Etheridge, Eric, Roger, Wilkins, and Diane McWhorter. 2008. *Breach of Peace: Portraits of the 1961 Mississippi Freedom Riders.* New York: Atlas.

Farah, Martha J. 2005. Neuroethics: The practical and the philosophical. *Trends in Cognitive Sciences* 9 (1):34–40.

Feinsod, M. 2000. The blind beautiful eye. *Journal of Neuro-Ophthalmology: The Official Journal of the North American Neuro-Ophthalmology Society* 20 (1): 22.

Feld, S.L. 1981. The focused organization of social ties. *American Journal of Sociology* 86 (5): 1015–1035.

Fertig, Scott, Eric Freeman, and David Gelernter. 1996. Lifestreams: An alternative to the desktop metaphor. Conference companion to *Human Factors in Computing Systems: Common Ground*: 410–411.

Fiore, Andrew T., Vidya Lakshmipathy, and Joan M. DiMicco. 2002. Conductive chat: Instant messaging with a skin conductivity channel. Poster presented at the 2002 ACM Conference on Computer Supported Cooperative Work. http://people.ischool.berkeley.edu/~atf/papers/cscw2002_conductive_chat_poster.pdf.

Fischer, Claude. S. 1994. *America Calling: A Social History of the Telephone to 1940.* Berkeley, CA: University of California Press.

Fisher, D., A. J. Brush, E. Gleave, and M. A. Smith. 2006. Revisiting Whittaker & Sidner's email overload ten years later. In *Proceedings of the 2006 20th Anniversary Conference on Computer Supported Cooperative Work*. New York: ACM Press.

Fiske, Susan T. 1993. Social cognition and social perception. *Annual Review of Psychology* 44:155–194.

Forman-Brunell, Miriam. 2009. *Babysitter: An American History*. New York: NYU Press.

Forte, A., V. Larco, and A. Bruckman. 2009. Decentralization in Wikipedia governance. *Journal of Management Information Systems* 26 (1):49–72.

Foucault, M. 1979. *Discipline and Punish*. New York: Vintage Books.

4chan FAQ. 2012. Available from http://www.4chan.org/faq.

Freeman, L. C. 1979. Centrality in social networks conceptual clarification. *Social Networks* 1 (3):215–239.

Freeman, L. C. 2000. Visualizing social networks. *Journal of Social Structure* 1:1.

Freeman, L. C. 2004. *The Development of Social Network Analysis*. Vancouver, BC: Empirical Press.

Freiberger, P., and M. Swaine. 2000. *Fire in the Valley*. New York: McGraw-Hill.

Freud, Sigmund. 2010. *The Interpretation of Dreams*, 3rd ed. New York: World Public Library. (Originally published 1911.)

Freud royal portrait divides critics. 2001. BBC News, December 21, 2001.

Fridlund, A. J. 1997. The new ethology of human facial expression. In *The Psychology of Facial Expression*, ed. J. A. Russell and J. M. Fernández-Dols. Cambridge: University of Cambridge Press.

Friedman, E. J., and P. Resnick. 2001. The social cost of cheap pseudonyms. *Journal of Economics and Management Strategy* 10 (2):173–199.

Fu, Yang-chih. 2005. Measuring personal networks with daily contacts: A single-item survey question and the contact diary. *Social Networks* 27 (3): 169–186.

Funder, D. C. 1995. On the accuracy of personality judgment: A realistic approach. *Psychological Review* 102 (4):652–669.

Furnas, George W., and Benjamin B. Bederson. 1995. Space-scale diagrams: Understanding multiscale interfaces. In *Proceedings of the SIGCHI Conference on Human Factors in Computing Systems*. New York: ACM Press.

Gallagher, Ryan. 2013. Software that tracks people on social media created by defence firm. *Guardian*, February 10.

Galloway, Kit, and Sherrie Rabinowitz. 1980. *Hole-in-Space*. http://www.ecafe.com/getty/HIS/.

Garton, L., C. Haythornthwaite, and B. Wellman. 1997. Studying online social networks. *Journal of Computer-Mediated Communication* 3 (1):1–27.

Gaver, W. W. 1989. The SonicFinder: An interface that uses auditory icons. *Human-Computer Interaction* 4 (1):67–94.

Gavin, Alison M. 2009. In the King's service: Hugh Finlay and the postal system in Colonial America. *Prologue Magazine* 41 (2).

Gavin, Patrick. 2011. Keith Urbahn's tweet heard around the world. http://www.politico.com/click/stories/1105/tweet_heard_round_the_world.html.

Gianotti, Fabiola. 2012. Status of Standard Model Higgs searches in ATLAS. https://indico.cern.ch/getFile.py/access?confId=197461&contribId=1&materialId=slides&resId=1.

Gibbs, Jennifer L., Nicole B. Ellison, and Rebecca D. Heino. 2006. Self-presentation in online personals: The role of anticipated future interaction, self-disclosure, and perceived success in Internet dating. *Communication Research* 33 (2):152–177.

Gibson, J. J. 1986. *The Ecological Approach to Visual Perception*. Mahwah, NJ: Erlbaum.

Giles, Jim. 2005. Internet encyclopaedias go head to head. *Nature* 438 (7070):900–901.

Gillespie, Tarleton. 2012. Can an algorithm be wrong? *Limn* 2. http://limn.it/can-an-algorithm-be-wrong/.

Gillespie, Tarleton. 2013. The relevance of algorithms. In *Media Technologies*, ed. Tarleton Gillespie, Pablo J. Boczkowski, and Kirsten A. Foot. Cambridge, MA: MIT Press.

Girvan, M., and M. E. J. Newman. 2002. Community structure in social and biological networks. *Proceedings of the National Academy of Sciences of the United States of America* 99 (12):7821–7826.

Goffman, Erving. 1959. *The Presentation of Self in Everyday Life*. Garden City, NY: Doubleday Anchor Books.

Goffman, Erving. 1966. *Behavior in Public Places*. New York: Free Press.

Goffman, Erving. 1967. On face-work: An analysis of ritual elements in social interaction. In *Interaction Ritual*, 5–46. New York: Pantheon Books. Original published in *Psychiatry: Journal of Interpersonal Relations* 18 (3), 1955, 213–231.

Goffman, Erving. 1981. *Forms of Talk*. Philadelphia, PA: University of Pennsylvania Press.

Goldberg, K. 2001. *The Robot in the Garden: Telerobotics and Telepistemology in the Age of the Internet*. Cambridge, MA: MIT Press.

Goldberg, K., D. Song, Y. Khor, D. Pescovitz, A. Levandowski, J. Himmelstein, J. Shih, A. Ho, E. Paulos, and J. Donath. 2002. Collaborative online teleoperation with spatial dynamic voting and a human "tele-actor." In *Proceedings of IEEE International Conference on Robotics and Automation*. Los Alamitos, CA: IEEE Computer Society.

Golder, Scott, and Judith Donath. 2004. Social role in electronic communites. In *Proceedings of Association of Internet Researchers*. Bristol, England.

Golder, Scott A., and Michael W. Macy. 2011. Diurnal and seasonal mood vary with work, sleep, and daylength across diverse cultures. *Science* 333 (6051): 1878–1881.

Goldin, Claudia, and Cecilia Rouse. 1997. *Orchestrating impartiality: The impact of "blind" auditions on female musicians*. National Bureau of Economic Research.

Goldin, Nan. 1986. *The Ballad of Sexual Dependency*. New York: Aperture.

Gombrich, E. H. 1981. The sense of order: A study in the psychology of decorative art. *Leonardo* 14 (1):88.

Gosling, S. D., S. Gaddis, and S. Vazire. 2007. Personality impressions based on Facebook profiles. In *Proceedings of 3rd International AAAI Conference on Weblogs and Social Media*. Palo Alto: AAAI Press.

Granovetter, Mark S. 1973. The strength of weak ties. *American Journal of Sociology* 78:1360–1380.

Granovetter, Mark S. 1983. The strength of weak ties revisited. *Sociological Theory* 1:201–233.

Gratch, J., J. Rickel, E. André, J. Cassell, E. Petajan, and N. Badler. 2002. Creating interactive virtual humans: Some assembly required. *IEEE Intelligent Systems* 17:54–63.

Gray, Thomas. 1753. *Designs by Mr. R. Bentley, for Six Poems by Mr. T. Gray*. London.

Gregory, R. L. 1990. *Eye and Brain: The Psychology of Seeing*. Princeton, NJ: Princeton University Press. Original edition, 1966.

Grinspan, Izzy. 2011. Fashion folks learn of Osama bin Laden's death via @dkny. http://ny.racked.com/archives/2011/05/02/death_of_osama_bin_laden_tweeted_by_dkny.php.

Grinter, Rebecca, and Leysia Palen. 2002. Instant messaging in teen life. In *Proceedings of the ACM Conference on Computer-Supported Cooperative Work (CSCW'02)*. New York: ACM Press.

Gruhl, Daniel R. Guha, David Liben-Nowell, and Andrew Tomkins. 2004. Information diffusion through blogspace. In *Proceedings of the Thirteenth International Conference on the World Wide Web*. New York: ACM Press.

Guare, John. 1994. *Six Degrees of Separation*. New York: Vintage. Original edition, 1990.

Guldi, J. 2012. *Roads to Power: Britain Invents the Infrastructure State*. Cambridge, MA: Harvard University Press.

Hafner, K. and M. Lyon. 2000. *Where Wizards Stay Up Late: The Origins of the Internet*. New York: Touchstone Books.

Hajratwala, Minal. 2011. A thousand sighs: Memoir of a hoax. http://www.minalhajratwala.com/2011/06/a-thousand-sighs-memoir-of-a-hoax/.

Hall, R. H., and P. Hanna. 2004. The impact of web page text-background colour combinations on readability, retention, aesthetics and behavioural intention. *Behaviour and Information Technology* 23 (3):183–195.

Halle, D. 1993. *Inside Culture: Art and Class in the American Home*. Chicago: University of Chicago Press.

Hallnäs, L., and J. Redström. 2002. From use to presence: On the expressions and aesthetics of everyday computational things. *ACM Transactions on Computer-Human Interaction* 9 (2):106–124.

Hampton, K., and B. Wellman. 2003. Neighboring in Netville: How the Internet supports community and social capital in a wired suburb. *City and Community* 2 (4):277–311.

Hampton, K., Chul-joo Lee, and Eun Ja Her. 2011. How new media affords network diversity: Direct and mediated access to social capital through participation in local social settings. *New Media and Society*. DOI: 10.1177/1461444810390342.

Hampton, K., Lauren F. Sessions, and Eun Ja Her. 2011. Core networks, social isolation and new media: How Internet and mobile phone use is related to network size and diversity. *Information Communication and Society* 14 (1):1–26.

Hancock, J. T., and P. J. Dunham. 2001. Impression formation in computer-mediated communication revisited. *Communication Research* 28 (3):325–347.

Haraway, Donna 1994. A manifesto for cyborgs: Science, technology, and socialist feminism in the 1980s. In *The Postmodern Turn: New Perspectives on Social Theory*, ed. Steven Seidman, 82–115. Cambridge: Cambridge University Press. Originally published in *Socialist Review* (80), 1985.

Hardin, Garrett. 1968. The tragedy of the commons. *Science* 162:1243–1248.

Hargittai, Eszter. 2009. *Research Confidential: Solutions to Problems Most Social Scientists Pretend They Never Have*. Ann Arbor: University of Michigan Press.

Harley, J. B. 2008. Maps, knowledge, and power. In *Geographic Thought: A Praxis Perspective*, ed. George L. Henderson and Marvin Waterstone, 129–148. Oxford: Routledge.

Harmon, Katherine. 2004. *You Are Here: Personal Geographies and Other Maps of the Imagination*. New York: Princeton Architectural Press.

Harnad, Steven. 1990. The symbol grounding problem. *Physica D: Nonlinear Phenomena* 42:335–346.

Harper, Jim. 2006. *Identity Crisis: How Identification Is Overused and Misunderstood*. Washington, DC: Cato Institute.

Harry, Drew, and Judith Donath. 2008. Information spaces—building meeting rooms in virtual environments. In *Proceedings of CHI '08: Extended Abstracts on Human Factors in Computing Systems*. New York: ACM Press.

Hauben, M., and R. Hauben. 1997. *Netizens: On the History and Impact of Usenet and the Internet*. Los Alamitos, CA: IEEE Computer Society.

Hauben, Ronda. 2002. Commodifying Usenet and the Usenet archive, or Continuing the online cooperative Usenet culture. *Science Studies* 15 (1):61–68.

Headland, Thomas N., Lawrence A. Reid, M. G. Bicchieri, Charles A. Bishop, Robert Blust, Nicholas E. Flanders, Peter M. Gardner, Karl L. Hutterer, Arkadiusz Marciniak, Robert F. Schroeder, and Stefan Seitz. 1989. Hunter-gatherers and their neighbors from prehistory to the present [and comments and replies]. *Current Anthropology* 30 (1):43–66.

Heer, J., M. Bostock, and V. Ogievetsky. 2010. A tour through the visualization zoo. *Communications of the ACM* 53 (6):59–67.

Heer, J., and d. boyd. 2005. Vizster: Visualizing online social networks. In *InfoVis: 2005 IEEE Symposium on Information Visualization*. Los Alamitos, CA: IEEE Computer Society.

Hello Robot Software. 2012.WEBBRICK: Telerobotics made easy. http://www.popbubble.com/Lego/WebBrick/index.html.

Herlihy, D. 1973. Three patterns of social mobility in medieval history. *Journal of Interdisciplinary History* 3 (4):623–647.

Herring, Susan. 2000. Gender differences in computer-mediated communication: Findings and implications. *Computer Professionals for Social Responsibility Journal* 18 (1). http://cpsr.org/prevsite/publications/newsletters/issues/2000/Winter2000/herring.html/.

Herring, Susan. 2001. Gender and power in online communication. Center for Social Informatics Working Papers.

Heyes, Cecilia. 2001. Causes and consequences of imitation. *Trends in Cognitive Sciences* 5 (6):253–261.

Hill, R. A., and R. I. M. Dunbar. 2003. Social network size in humans. *Human Nature* 14 (1):53–72.

Hirsh, S., A. Sellen, and N. Brokopp. 2005. Why HP people do and don't use videoconferencing systems. *Retrieved* 22:2007.

Hochschild, Arlie Russell. 2012. *The Outsourced Self: Intimate Life in Market Times.* New York: Metropolitan Books.

Hogan, B., J. A. Carrasco, and B. Wellman. 2007. Visualizing personal networks: Working with participant-aided sociograms. *Field Methods* 19 (2):116.

Hollan, J., and S. Stornetta. 1992. Beyond being there. In *Proceedings of SIGCHI Conference on Human Factors in Computing Systems.* New York: ACM Press.

Holland, Dorothy, and Debra Skinner. 1987. Prestige and intimacy: The cultural models behind Americans' talk about gender types. In *Cultural Models in Language and Thought*, ed. D. Holland and N. Quinn, 78–111. New York: Cambridge University Press.

Holt, Stannie. 1997. Usenet Bans CompuServe. *PCWorld*, Nov. 18.

Hoque, Mohammed, Rana el Kaliouby, and Rosalind Picard. 2009. When human coders (and machines) disagree on the meaning of facial affect in spontaneous videos. In *Intelligent Virtual Agents*, ed. Zsófia Ruttkay, Michael Kipp, Anton Nijholt, and Hannes Högni Vilhjálmsson, 5773:337–343. Berlin: Springer-Verlag.

Hovers, E., S. Ilani, O. Bar-Yosef, B. Vandermeersch, L. Barham, A. Belfer-Cohen, R. G. Klein, C. Knight, C. Power, and I. Watts. 2003. An early case of color symbolism. *Current Anthropology* 44 (4):491–522.

Hrdy, Sarah Blaffer. 1999. *Mother Nature.* New York: Pantheon Books.

Humphreys, L. 2008. Mobile social networks and social practice: A case study of Dodgeball. *Journal of Computer-Mediated Communication* 13 (1):341–360.

Isaacs, E., and J. Tang. 1994. What video can and can't do for collaboration. In *Proceedings of Multimedia Systems.* http://www.izix.com/docs/Isaacs-VideoCollaboration-mm93.pdf.

Jacobs, Jane. 1992. *The Death and Life of Great American Cities.* New York: Vintage.

Jacobson, David. 1999. Impression formation in cyberspace: Online expectations and offline experiences in text-based virtual communities. *Journal of Computer-Mediated Communication* 5 (1).

Jacobson, N., and W. Bender. 1996. Color as a determined communication. *IBM Systems Journal* 35 (3):526–538.

Jernigan, C., and B. F. T. Mistree. 2009. Gaydar: Facebook friendships expose sexual orientation. *First Monday* 14 (10).

Jia, Yuntao, Jared Hoberock, Garland Michae, and John Hart. 2008. On the visualization of social and other scale-free networks. *IEEE Transactions on Visualization and Computer Graphics* 14 (6):1285–1292.

Johnson, Jeff, Teresa L. Roberts, William Verplank, David Canfield Smith, Charles H. Irby, Marian Beard, and Kevin Mackey. 1989. The Xerox star: A retrospective. *Computer* 22 (9):11–26.

Jones, Rosie, Ravi Kumar, Bo Pang, and Andrew Tomkins. 2007. I know what you did last summer: Query logs and user privacy. In *Proceedings of the Sixteenth ACM Conference on Information and Knowledge Management*. New York: ACM Press.

Jordan, Alexander H., Benoît Monin, Carol S. Dweck, Benjamin J. Lovett, Oliver P. John, and James J. Gross. 2011. Misery has more company than people think: Underestimating the prevalence of others' negative emotions. *Personality and Social Psychology Bulletin* 37 (1):120–135.

Judge, Timothy A., and Daniel M. Cable. 2004. The effect of physical height on workplace success and income: Preliminary test of a theoretical model. *Journal of Applied Psychology* 89 (3):428–440.

Kadare, Ismail. 2002. *The File on H.: A Novel*. New York: Arcade.

Kandinsky, W. 2009. *Concerning the Spiritual in Art*. New York: MFA Publications. Original edition, 1911.

Kaplan, Frédéric. 2000. Free creatures: The role of uselessness in the design of artificial pets. In *Proceedings of First Edutainement Workshop*. http://citeseerx.ist.psu.edu/viewdoc/download?doi=10.1.1.21.4650&rep=rep1&type=pdf.

Karahalios, K. G. 2004. Social catalysts: Embracing communication in mediated spaces. PhD thesis, Massachusetts Institute of Technology.

Karahalios, K. G., and Kelly Dobson. 2005. *Chit Chat Club*: Bridging virtual and physical space for social interaction. In *Proceedings of Conference on Human Factors in Computing Systems*. New York: ACM Press.

Karinthy, Frigyes. 1929. Chain links. In *Everything Is Different*. Translated from Hungarian and annotated by Adam Makkai and edited by Enikö Jankó. http://djjr-courses.wdfiles.com/local--files/soc180:karinthy-chain-links/Karinthy-Chain-Links_1929.pdf.

Keim, D. A. 2002. Information visualization and visual data mining. *IEEE Transactions on Visualization and Computer Graphics* 8 (1):1–8.

Keim, D. A. 2001. Visual exploration of large data sets. *Communications of the ACM* 44 (8):38–44.

Keim, De Benneville Randolph. 1886. *Hand-Book of Official and Social Etiquette and Public Ceremonials at Washington*. Washington, DC

Kelly, J. and B. Etling. 2008. Mapping Iran's online public: Politics and culture in the Persian blogosphere. Berkman Center Research Publication No. 2008-01. http://cyber.law.harvard.edu/sites/cyber.law.harvard.edu/files/Kelly&Etling_Mapping_Irans_Online_Public_2008.pdf.

Kenton, O'Hara, Maxine Glancy, and Simon Robertshaw. 2008. Understanding collective play in an urban screen game. In *Proceedings of the 2008 ACM Conference on Computer Supported Cooperative Work*. New York: ACM Press.

Kerr, B. 2003. Thread arcs: An email thread visualization. In *IEEE Symposium on Information Visualization 2003 (INFOVIS 2003)*. Los Alamitos, CA: IEEE Computer Society.

Kim, Richard. 2011. We are all human microphones now. http://www.thenation.com/blog/163767/we-are-all-human-microphones-now#axzz2a5VfaV3W.

King, Homay. 2012. Antiphon: Notes on the people's microphone. *Journal of Popular Music Studies* 24 (2):238–246.

Kirkpatrick, David. 2010. *The Facebook Effect: The Inside Story of the Company That Is Connecting the World*. New York: Simon & Schuster.

Kirkpatrick, Marshall. 2010. Facebook's Zuckerberg says the age of privacy is over. http://readwrite.com/2010/01/09/facebooks_zuckerberg_says_the_age_of_privacy_is_ov#awesm=~ocDo1KrCEeFwHF.

Kleinfeld, Judith. 2002. The small world problem. *Society* 39 (2):61–66.

Klinenberg, Eric. 2003. *Heat Wave: A Social Autopsy of Disaster in Chicago*. Chicago: University of Chicago Press.

Klinenberg, Eric. 2013. Adaptation. *New Yorker*, Jan. 7, 32–37.

Kling, Rob, Ya-Ching Lee, Al Teich, and Mark S. Frankel. 1999. Assessing anonymous communication on the Internet: Policy deliberations. *Information Society* 15 (2):79–90.

Knowles, Josh. 2007. ITP Student List Conversation Visualization. http://www.auscillate.com/itp/listview/.

Kollock, P. and M. Smith. 1996. Managing the virtual commons: Cooperation and conflict in computer communities. *Pragmatics and Beyond (New Series)*: 109–128.

Komar, Vitaly, and Alex Melamid. 2011. Komar & Melamid: The most wanted paintings. Dia Center for the Arts. http://awp.diaart.org/km/index.html.

Komar, Vitaly, JoAnn Wypijewski, and Aleksandr Melamid. 1997. *Painting by Numbers: Komar and Melamid's Scientific Guide to Art*. Berkeley: University of California Press.

Korte, C., and S. Milgram. 1970. Acquaintance networks between racial groups: Application of the small world method. *Journal of Personality and Social Psychology* 15 (2):101–108.

Krackhardt, D. 1990. Assessing the political landscape: Structure, cognition, and power in organizations. *Administrative Science Quarterly* 35:342–369.

Krackhardt, D., and D. J. Brass. 1994. Intraorganizational networks. In *Advances in Social Network Analysis*, ed. S. Wasseman and J. Galaskiewicz, 207–229. Thousand Oaks, CA: Sage.

Kraut, Robert, Michael Patterson, Vicki Lundmark, Sara Kiesler, T. Mukophadhyay, and William Scherlis. 1998. Internet paradox. *American Psychologist* 53 (9):1017–1031.

Krebs, Valdis. 2004. A brief introduction to social network analysis. http://www.orgnet.com/sna.html.

Krueger, Myron. 1991. *Artificial Reality II*. Reading, MA: Addison-Wesley.

Krueger, Myron, Thomas Gionfriddo, and Katrin Hinrichsen. 1985. VIDEOPLACE—an artificial reality. *SIGCHI Bulletin* 16 (4):35–40.

Kumar, Gautam, and Michael Garland. 2006. Visual exploration of complex time-varying graphs. *IEEE Transactions on Visualization and Computer Graphics* 12 (5):805–812.

Kurlander, D., T. Skelly, and D. Salesin. 1996. Comic chat. In *Proceedings of SIGGRAPH '96*. http://citeseerx.ist.psu.edu/viewdoc/summary?doi=10.1.1.149.2728.

Kurzban, Robert, John Tooby, and Leda Cosmides. 2001. Can race be erased? Coalitional computation and social categorization. *Proceedings of the National Academy of Sciences of the United States of America* 98 (26):15387–15392.

Lakoff, George. 1987. *Women, Fire, and Dangerous Things: What Categories Reveal about the Mind*. Chicago: University of Chicago Press.

Lakoff, George, and Mark Johnson. 1980. *Metaphors We Live By*. Chicago: University of Chicago Press.

Lakoff, George, and Mark Johnson. 1999. *Philosophy in the Flesh: The Embodied Mind and Its Challenge to Western Thought*. New York: Basic Books.

Lam, Francis, and Judith Donath. 2005. Seascape and volcano: Visualizing online discussions using timeless motion. In *Proceedings of CHI '05: Extended Abstracts on Human Factors in Computing Systems*. New York: ACM Press.

Lamont, Michele, and Marcel Fournier. 1993. Introduction. In *Cultivating Differences*, ed. Michele Lamont and Marcel Fournier. Chicago: University of Chicago Press.

Lampe, Cliff, and Paul Resnick. 2004. Slash(dot) and burn: Distributed moderation in a large online conversation space. In *Proceedings of ACM Computer Human Interaction Conference*. New York: ACM Press.

Lampinen, Airi, Vilma Lehtinen, Asko Lehmuskallio, and Sakari Tamminen. 2011. We're in it together: Interpersonal management of disclosure in social network services. In *Proceedings of the 2011 Annual Conference on Human Factors in Computing Systems*. New York: ACM Press.

Land, E. H. 1977. The retinex theory of color vision. *Scientific American* 237:108–120.

Langheinrich, M. 2001. Privacy by design-principles of privacy-aware ubiquitous systems. In *Proceedings of Ubicomp*. Berlin: Springer.

Lanier, J. 2001. Virtually there. *Scientific American* 284 (4):52–61.

Laraqui, Jawad. 2007. Activity based interfaces in online social networks. Master's thesis, Massachusetts Institute of Technology.

Lee, Harper. 1962. *To Kill a Mockingbird*. New York: Popular Library. Original edition, 1960.

Lee, Y. T., L. Albright, and T. E. Malloy. 2001. Social perception and stereotyping: An interpersonal and intercultural approach. *International Journal of Group Tensions* 30 (2):183–209.

Leiner, Barry M., Vinton G. Cerf, David D. Clark, Robert E. Kahn, Leonard Kleinrock, Daniel C. Lynch, Jon Postel, Larry G. Roberts, and Stephen Wolff. 2009. A brief history of the internet. *SIGCOMM Computer Communication Review* 39 (5):22–31.

Lewis, Kevin, Jason Kaufman, and Nicholas Christakis. 2008. The taste for privacy: An analysis of college student privacy settings in an online social network. *Journal of Computer-Mediated Communication* 14 (1):79–100.

Licklider, J. C. R. and R. W. Taylor. 1968. The computer as a communication device. *Science and Technology* 76:21–31.

Lin, Nan. 2002. *Social Capital: A Theory of Social Structure and Action*. Structural Analysis in the Social Sciences. Cambridge: Cambridge University Press.

Lin, Nan, Paul Dayton, and Peter Greenwald. 1978. Analyzing the instrumental uses of relations in the context of social structure. *Sociological Methods and Research* 7 (2):149–166.

Ling, Rich. 2002. The social juxtaposition of mobile telephone conversations and public spaces. *In Proceedings of Conference on the Social Consequence of Mobile Telephones*. Chunchon, Korea.

Liu, B. 2010. Sentiment analysis and subjectivity. In *Handbook of Natural Language Processing*, 2nd ed., ed. Nitin Indurkhya and Fred J. Damerau, 627–666. Boca Raton: CRC Press.

Liu, Christine, and Judith Donath. 2006. Urbanhermes: Social signaling with electronic fashion. In *Proceedings of SIGCHI Conference on Human Factors in Computing Systems*. New York: ACM Press.

Lockton, Vance, and Richard Rosenberg. 2005. RFID: The next serious threat to privacy. *Ethics and Information Technology* 7 (4):221–231.

Lotan, Gilad. 2011. Breaking bin Laden: Visualizing the power of a single tweet. http://blog.socialflow.com/post/5246404319/breaking-bin-laden-visualizing-the-power-of-a-single.

Lotan, Gilad. 2011. Data reveals that "Occupying" Twitter trending topics is harder than it looks! http://blog.socialflow.com/post/7120244374/data-reveals-that-occupying-twitter-trending-topics-is-harder-than-it-looks.

Lotan, Gilad, Erhardt Graeff, Mike Ananny, Devin Gaffney, Ian Pearce, and danah boyd. 2011. The revolutions were tweeted: Information flows during the 2011 Tunisian and Egyptian revolutions. *International Journal of Communication* 5.

MacDonald, L. W. 1999. Using color effectively in computer graphics. *IEEE Computer Graphics and Applications* 19 (4):20–35.

Mackay, W. 1988a. Diversity in the use of electronic mail: A preliminary inquiry. *ACM Transactions on Office Information Systems* 6 (4): 380–397.

Mackay, W. 1988b. More than just a communication system: Diversity in the use of electronic mail. In *Proceedings of ACM CSCW '88: Conference on Computer-Supported Cooperative Work*. New York: ACM Press.

Madden, Mary, and Aaron Smith. 2010. Reputation management and social media. Pew Internet & American Life Project. http://www.pewinternet.org/Reports/2010/Reputation-Management.aspx.

Mann, Steve, Jason Nolan, and Barry Wellman. 2003. Sousveillance: Inventing and using wearable computing devices for data collection in surveillance environments. *Surveillance and Society* 1 (3):331–355.

Mantei, Marilyn M., Ronald M. Baecker, Abigail J. Sellen, William A. S. Buxton, Thomas Milligan, and Barry Wellman. 1991. Experiences in the use of a media space. In *Proceedings of the SIGCHI Conference on Human Factors in Computing Systems: Reaching through Technology*, New Orleans, LA. New York: ACM Press.

Marche, Stephen. 2012. Is Facebook making us lonely? *Atlantic*. http://www.theatlantic.com/magazine/archive/2012/05/is-facebook-making-us-lonely/308930/.

Marketdata Enterprises, Inc. 2012. The U.S. Dating Services Market. http://www.marketresearch.com/Marketdata-Enterprises-Inc-v416/Dating-Services-6773764/.

Marsden, Peter 1990. Network data and measurement. *Annual Review of Sociology* 16:435–463.

Marsden, Peter. 2005. Recent developments in network measurement. In *Models and Methods in Social Network Analysis*, ed. Peter J. Carrington, John Scott, and Stanley Wasserman, 8–30. Cambridge: Cambridge University Press.

Marx, G. T. 1999. What's in a name? Some reflections on the sociology of anonymity. *Information Society* 15 (2):99–112.

Maspero, Gaston. 2005. *History of Egypt, Chaldaea, Syria, Babylonia, and Assyria*, vol. 8 (of 12). Ed. A. H. Sayce. http://www.gutenberg.org/ebooks/17328.

Matei, S., S. J. Ball-Rokeach, and J. L. Qiu. 2001. Fear and misperception of Los Angeles urban space: A spatial-statistical study of communication-shaped mental maps. *Communication Research* 28 (4):429–463.

Mauldin, M. L. 1994. Chatterbots, tinymuds, and the Turing test: Entering the Loebner Prize competition. In *Proceedings of the Eleventh National Conference on Artificial Intelligence*. London: John Wiley & Sons.

McCallum, A., X. Wang, and A. Corrada-Emmanuel. 2007. Topic and role discovery in social networks with experiments on Enron and academic email. *Journal of Artificial Intelligence Research* 30 (1):249–272.

McCarthy, Joseph F., David W. McDonald, Suzanne Soroczak, David H. Nguyen, and Al M. Rashid. 2004. Augmenting the social space of an academic conference. In *Proceedings of the 2004 ACM Conference on Computer Supported Cooperative Work*. New York: ACM Press.

McKenna, K. Y. A., A. S. Green, and M. E. J. Gleason. 2002. Relationship formation on the Internet: What's the big attraction? *Journal of Social Issues* 58 (1):9–31.

McPherson, Miller, Lynn Smith-Lovin, and Matthew E. Brashears. 2006. Social isolation in America: Changes in core discussion networks over two decades. *American Sociological Review* 71 (3):353–375.

McQuire, Scott. 2006. Urban screens: Discovering the potential of outdoor screens for urban society. *First Monday* 11 (4).

Meltzoff, Andrew N., and Jean Decety. 2003. What imitation tells us about social cognition: A rapprochement between developmental psychology and cognitive neuroscience. *Philosophical Transactions of the Royal Society of London, Series B: Biological Sciences* 358 (1431):491–500.

Menzel, Peter 1994. *Material World: A Global Family Portrait*. San Francisco, CA: Sierra Club Books.

Meyrowitz, J. 1985. *No Sense of Place: The Impact of Electronic Media on Social Behavior*. New York: Oxford University Press.

Milgram, S. 1964. The urban bystander. *Nation* 198 (25):602–604. Reprinted in S. Milgram, *The Individual in a Social World*, 2nd. ed., ed. John Sabini and Maury Silver. New York: McGraw-Hill.

Milgram, S. 1967. The small-world problem. *Psychology Today* 1:62–67. Reprinted in S. Milgram, *The Individual in a Social World*, 2nd. ed., ed. John Sabini and Maury Silver. New York: McGraw-Hill.

Milgram, S. 1970. The experience of living in cities. *Science* 167 (3924):1461–1468. Reprinted in S. Milgram, *The Individual in a Social World*, 2nd. ed., ed. John Sabini and Maury Silver. New York: McGraw-Hill.

Milgram, S. 1972. The familiar stranger: An aspect of urban anonymity. In *Division 8 Newsletter, Division of Personality and Social Psychology*. Washington: American Psychological Association July. Reprinted in S. Milgram, *The Individual in a Social World*, 2nd. ed., ed. John Sabini and Maury Silver. New York: McGraw-Hill. July, 1977.

Milgram, S. 1978. On maintaining social norms: A field experiment in the subway. In *Advances in Environmental Psychology: The Urban Environment*, ed. A. Baum, J. E. Singer, and S. Valins. Hillsdale, NJ: Erlbaum. Reprinted in S. Milgram, *The Individual in a Social World*, 2nd. ed., ed. John Sabini and Maury Silver. New York: McGraw-Hill.

Milgram, S., and D. Jodelet. 1976. Psychological maps of Paris. *Environmental Psychology* 2:104–112. Reprinted in S. Milgram, *The Individual in a Social World*, 2nd. ed., ed. John Sabini and Maury Silver. New York: McGraw-Hill.

Milgram, S., H. J. Liberty, R. Toledo, and J. Wackenhut. 1986. Response to intrusion into waiting lines. *Journal of Personality and Social Psychology* 51 (4):683–689. Reprinted in S. Milgram, *The Individual in a Social World*, 2nd. ed., ed. John Sabini and Maury Silver. New York: McGraw-Hill.

Miller, Rebecca. 2011. She came to me. In *New Irish Short Stories*, ed. Joseph O'Connor. London: Faber & Faber.

Minar, Nelson, and Judith Donath. 1999. Visualizing the crowds at a website. In *Proceedings of Human Factors in Computing Systems (CHI)*. New York: ACM Press.

Mindich, David T. Z. 2000. *Just the Facts: How "Objectivity" Came to Define American Journalism*. New York: NYU Press.

Mislove, Alan, Sune Lehmann, Yong-Yeol Ahn, Jukka-Pekka Onnela, and J. Niels Rosenquis. 2010. *Pulse of the Nation: U.S. Mood Throughout the Day Inferred from Twitter.* http://www.ccs.neu.edu/home/amislove/twittermood/.

Mollon, John. 1990. The tricks of colour. In *Images and Understanding*, ed. H. B. Barlow, M. Weston-Smith, and C. Blakemore, 61–80. Cambridge: Cambridge University Press.

Monmonier, M. 1996. *How to Lie with Maps*. Chicago: University of Chicago Press.

Mori, Masahiro. 1970. The uncanny valley. Trans. Karl F. MacDorman and Takashi Minato. *Energy* 7 (4):33–35.

Morningstar, Chip, and F. Randall Farmer. 2008. The lessons of Lucasfilm's Habitat1. In *Cyberspace: First Steps*, ed. Michael Benedikt, 273–302. Cambridge, MA: MIT Press.

Nakamura, L. 2008. Cyberrace. *PMLA* 123 (5):1673–1682.

Narayanan, Arvind, and Vitaly Shmatikov. 2009. De-anonymizing social networks. In *2009 30th IEEE Symposium on Security and Privacy*. Los Alamitos, CA: IEEE Computer Society.

Nass, C., J. Steuer, and E. Tauber. 1994. Computers are social actors. In *Proceedings of the SIGCHI Conference on Human Factors in Computing Systems*, 72–78. New York: ACM Press.

Needham, Joseph, and Ling Wang. 1972. *Science and Civilisation in China: Physics and Physical Technology*, vol. 1: *Physics*. Cambridge: Cambridge University Press.

Negroponte, Nicholas. 1970. *The Architecture Machine: Toward a More Human Environment*. Cambridge, MA: MIT Press.

Negroponte, Nicholas. 1975. *Soft Architecture Machines*. Cambridge, MA: MIT Press.

Negroponte, Nicholas. 1996. *Being Digital*. New York: Random House Digital.

Nelson, L. D., and J. P. Simmons. 2009. On southbound ease and northbound fees: Literal consequences of the metaphoric link between vertical position and cardinal direction. *Journal of Marketing Research* 46 (6):715–724.

Newman, Ron. 1996. The Church of Scientology vs. anon.penet.fi. http://www.thecia.net/~rnewman/scientology/anon/penet.html.

Nijholt, A., D. P. O. Bos, and B. Reuderink. 2009. Turning shortcomings into challenges: Brain-computer interfaces for games. *Entertainment Computing* 1 (2):85–94.

Nissenbaum, Helen. 1998. Protecting privacy in an information age: The problem of privacy in public. *Law and Philosophy* 17 (5):559–596.

Nissenbaum, Helen. 1999. The meaning of anonymity in an information age. *Information Society* 15 (2):141–144.

Nissenbaum, Helen. 2004. Privacy as contextual integrity. *Washington Law Review* 79 (1):119–158.

Nonnecke, B., and J. Preece. 2003. Silent participants: Getting to know lurkers better. In *From Usenet to CoWebs*, ed. C. Leug and D. Fisher. London: Springer.

Nord, G. D., T. F. McCubbins, and J. H. Nord. 2006. E-monitoring in the workplace: Privacy, legislation, and surveillance software. *Communications of the ACM* 49 (8):72–77.

Norman, Donald A. 1990. *The Design of Everyday Things*. New York: Doubleday.

Norman, Donald A. 1999. Affordance, conventions, and design. *Interaction* 6 (3):38–41.

Norman, Donald A. 2002. Emotion and design: Attractive things work better. *Interaction* 9 (4):36–42.

Nov, Oded. 2007. What motivates Wikipedians? *Communications of the ACM* 50 (11):60–64.

Nowak, K. L., and Frank Biocca. 2003. The effect of the agency and anthropomorphism on users' sense of telepresence, copresence, and social presence in virtual environments. *Presence* 12 (5):481–494.

Nowak, K. L., and C. Rauh. 2005. The influence of the avatar on online perceptions of anthropomorphism, androgyny, credibility, homophily, and attraction. *Journal of Computer-Mediated Communication* 11 (1):153–178.

Núñez, Rafael E., and Eve Sweetser. 2006. With the future behind them: Convergent evidence from Aymara language and gesture in the crosslinguistic comparison of spatial construals of time. *Cognitive Science* 30 (3):401–450.

O'Brien, Jodi. 1999. Writing in the body: Gender (re)production in online interaction. In *Communities in Cyberspace*, ed. Marc A. Smith and Peter Kollock, 76–104. London: Routledge.

Offenhuber, Dietmar, and Judith Donath. 2008. Comment flow: Visualizing communication along network path. In *Interface Cultures: Artistic Aspects of Interaction*, ed. Christa Sommerer, Laurent Mignonneau, and Dorothée King. Bielefeld: Transcript Verlag.

O'Hara, Kenton, Alison Black, and Matthew Lipson. 2006. Everyday practices with mobile video telephony. In *Proceedings of the SIGCHI Conference on Human Factors in Computing Systems*. New York: ACM Press.

Oliver, Melvin L. 1988. The urban black community as network: Toward a social network perspective. *Sociological Quarterly* 29 (4):623–645.

Ong, W. J. 2002. *Orality and Literacy: The Technologizing of the Word*. London: Routledge.

Orwell, George. 1949. *1984*. New York: Harcourt, Brace, Jovanovich.

Osborne, Peter, and Lynne Segal. 1994. In *A Critical Sense: Interviews with Intellectuals*, ed. Peter Osborn, 109–125. London: Routledge.

Ostrom, E. 1999. *Governing the Commons: The Evolution of Institutions for Collective Action*. Cambridge: Cambridge University Press.

Ostrowe v. Lee, 175 N.E. 505, 506 (NY Ct. App. 1931).

Ozer, N. A. and J. A. Lynch. 2010. Protecting reader privacy in digital books. Association for the Advancement of Artificial Intelligence Privacy 2010 Symposium. http://ssrn.com/abstract=1588187.

Page, L., S. Brin, R. Motwani, and T. Winograd. 1999. The PageRank citation ranking: Bringing order to the web. http://ilpubs.stanford.edu:8090/422/1/1999-66.pdf.

Palen, L., and P. Dourish. 2003. Unpacking "privacy" for a networked world. In *Proceedings of the SIGCHI Conference on Human Factors in Computing Systems*. New York: ACM Press.

Pang, Alex T., Craig M. Wittenbrink, and Suresh K. Lodha. 1997. Approaches to uncertainty visualization. *Visual Computer* 13 (8):370–390.

Pang, B., and L. Lee. 2008. Opinion mining and sentiment analysis. *Foundations and Trends in Information Retrieval* 2 (1–2):1–135.

Panteli, Niki. 2002. Richness, power cues and email text. *Information and Management* 40:75–86.

Parise, Salvatore, Sara Kiesler, Lee Sproull, and Keith Waters. 1996. My partner is a real dog: Cooperation with social agents. In *Proceedings of the 1996 ACM Conference on Computer Supported Cooperative Work*. New York: ACM Press.

Parviz, Babak A. 2009. Augmented reality in a contact lens. *IEEE Spectrum* 46 (9):36–41.

Paulos, E., and John Canny. 1997. Ubiquitous tele-embodiment: Applications and implications. *International Journal of Human-Computer Studies* 46 (6):861–877.

Paulos, E., and John Canny. 1999. Designing personal tele-embodiment. IEEE International Conference on Robotics and Automation. Los Alamitos, CA: IEEE Computer Society.

Paulos, E., and John Canny. 2001. Social tele-embodiment: Understanding presence. *Autonomous Robots* 11 (1):87–95.

Paulos, E., and E. Goodman. 2004. The familiar stranger: Anxiety, comfort, and play in public places. In *Proceedings of the SIGCHI Conference on Human Factors in Computing Systems*, 223–230. New York: ACM Press.

Pederson, Thomas, Dipak Surie, Haruhisa Ichikawa, We-Duke Cho, Ichiro Satoh, and Hee Youn. 2007. Towards an activity-aware wearable computing platform based on an egocentric interaction model. In *Ubiquitous Computing Systems*, vol. 4836, ed. Haruhisa Ichikawa, We-Duke Cho, Ichiro Satoh, and HeeYong Youn, 211–227. Berlin: Springer.

Pennebaker, J. W., M. R. Mehl, and K. G. Niederhoffer. 2003. Psychological aspects of natural language use: Our words, our selves. *Annual Review of Psychology* 54 (1):547–577.

Perkins, Roderick, Dan Smith Keller, and Frank Ludolph. 1997. Inventing the Lisa user interface. *Interaction* 4 (1):40–53.

Perlin, Ken, and David Fox. 1993. Pad: An alternative approach to the computer interface. In *Proceedings of the 20th annual Conference on Computer Graphics and Interactive Techniques*. New York: ACM Press.

Perry, Ethan, and Judith Donath. 2004. Anthropomorphic visualization: A new approach for depicting participants in online spaces. In *Proceedings of Conference on Human Factors in Computing Systems*. New York: ACM Press.

Picard, R. W., and G. Cosier. 1997. Affective intelligence—the missing link? *BT Technology Journal* 15 (4):151–162.

Picard, R. W., E. Vyzas, and J. Healey. 2001. Toward machine emotional intelligence: Analysis of affective physiological state. *IEEE Transactions on Pattern Analysis and Machine Intelligence* 23 (10):1175–1191.

Pipes, Daniel. 2006. An unveiling: Separate, but acceptable? http://www.danielpipes.org/blog/2006/10/an-unveiling-separate-but-acceptable.

Plaisant, C., B. Milash, A. Rose, S. Widoff, and B. Shneiderman. 1996. LifeLines: Visualizing personal histories. In *Proceedings of the SIGCHI Conference on Human Factors in Computing Systems (CHI '96)*, ed. Michael J. Tauber, 221–227. New York: ACM Press.

Poh, M. Z., D. J. McDuff, and R. W. Picard. 2011. Advancements in noncontact, multiparameter physiological measurements using a webcam. *IEEE Transactions on Biomedical Engineering* 58 (1):7–11.

Preece, J., Y. Rogers, and H. Sharp. 2002. *Interaction Design: Beyond Human-Computer Interaction*. New York: John Wiley.

Priedhorsky, R., J. Chen, S. T. K. Lam, K. Panciera, L. Terveen, and J. Riedl. 2007. Creating, destroying, and restoring value in Wikipedia. In *Proceedings of the 2007 International ACM Conference on Supporting Group Work (GROUP '07)*. New York: ACM Press.

Putnam, R. D. 1995. Bowling alone: America's declining social capital. *Journal of Democracy* 6:65–78.

Rachels, James. 1975. Why privacy is important. *Philosophy and Public Affairs* 4 (4):323–333.

Racine, Eric, and Judy Illes. 2007. Emerging ethical challenges in advanced neuroimaging research: Review, recommendations, and research agenda. *Journal of Empirical Research on Human Research Ethics* 2 (2):1–10.

Rainie, Lee, and Barry Wellman. 2012. *Networked: The New Social Operating System*. Cambridge, MA: MIT Press.

Randall, L. 2012. *Higgs Discovery: The Power of Empty Space*. New York: HarperCollins.

Raymond, Eric S. 2003. The Jargon File, version 4.4.8. http://catb.org/~esr/jargon/.

Reeves, Byron, and Clifford Nass. 1996. *The Media Equation: How People Treat Computers, Television, and New Media Like Real People and Places*. New York: Cambridge University Press/CSLI.

Rekimoto, Jun, Takashi Miyaki, and Takaaki Ishizawa. 2007. LifeTag: WiFi-based continuous location logging for life pattern analysis. In *Proceedings of Location- and Context-Awareness: Third International Symposium (LoCA 2007)*, Oberpfaffenhofen, Germany. New York: Springer.

Reynolds, Ren. 2002. Intellectual property rights in community based video games. http://www.ren-reynolds.com/downloads/RReynolds-MMORPG-IPR.htm.

Rheingold, Howard. 1993. *The Virtual Community*. Reading, MA: Addison-Wesley.

Roberts, Sam G. B., Robin I. M. Dunbar, Thomas V. Pollet, and Toon Kuppens. 2009. Exploring variation in active network size: Constraints and ego characteristics. *Social Networks* 31 (2):138–146.

Robinson, J. P., and G. Godbey. 1999. *Time for Life: The Surprising Ways Americans Use Their Time*. University Park: Pennsylvania State University Press.

Rodenstein, Roy, and Judith Donath. 2000. Talking in circles: Designing a spatially-grounded audioconferencing environment. In *Proceedings of CHI '00*. New York: ACM Press.

Romero, Daniel M., Brendan Meeder, and Jon Kleinberg. 2011. Differences in the mechanics of information diffusion across topics: idioms, political hashtags, and complex contagion on twitter. In *Proceedings of the Twentieth International Conference on the World Wide Web*. New York: ACM Press.

Rosch, Eleanor. 1975. Cognitive representations of semantic categories. *Journal of Experimental Psychology* 104:192–233.

Rosch, Eleanor, Carolyn B. Mervis, Wayne D. Gray, David M. Johnson, and Penny Boyes-Braem. 1976. Basic objects in natural categories. *Cognitive Psychology* 8 (3):382–439.

Rosen, J. 2000. *The Unwanted Gaze*. New York: Random House.

Rosen, J. 2005. *The Naked Crowd: Reclaiming Security and Freedom in an Anxious Age*. New York: Random House.

Rosen, J. 2010. The web means the end of forgetting. *New York Times*, July 25.

Roueché, C. 1984. Acclamations in the Later Roman Empire: New evidence from Aphrodisias. *Journal of Roman Studies* 74:181–199.

Ruffle, B. J., and R. Sosis. 2007. Does it pay to pray? Costly ritual and cooperation. *B.E. Journal of Economic Analysis and Policy* 7 (1):18.

Russell, James A., and José Miguel Fernández-Dols, eds. 1997. *The Psychology of Facial Expression*. Cambridge: Cambridge University Press.

Salaff, Janet W., Eric Fong, and Wong Siu-lun. 1999. Using social networks to exit Hong Kong. In *Networks in the Global Village*, ed. Barry Wellman, 299–329. Boulder: Westview Press.

Salomon, Gitta. 1990. New uses for color. In *The Art of Human-Computer Interface Design*, ed. Brenda Laurel, 269–279. Boston: Addison-Wesley.

Salton, Gerard. 1988. *Automatic Text Processing: The Transformation Analysis and Retrieval of Information by Computer*. Reading, MA: Addison-Wesley.

Saville-Troike, M. 2003. *The Ethnography of Communication: An Introduction*. Oxford: Blackwell.

Schegloff, Emanuel A. 2000. Overlapping talk and the organization of turn-taking for conversation. *Language in Society* 29 (01):1–63.

Schneider, Norbert. 2002. *The Art of the Portrait: Masterpieces of European Portrait-Painting, 1420–1670*. Cologne: Taschen.

Schneier, Bruce. 2011. *Secrets and Lies: Digital Security in a Networked World*. New York: Wiley.

Schubert, T. W. 2005. Your highness: Vertical positions as perceptual symbols of power. *Journal of Personality and Social Psychology* 89 (1):1.

Sebanz, Natalie, Harold Bekkering, and Günther Knoblich. 2006. Joint action: Bodies and minds moving together. *Trends in Cognitive Sciences* 10 (2):70–76.

Segel, Edward, and Jeffrey Heer. 2010. Narrative visualization: Telling stories with data. *IEEE Transactions on Visualization and Computer Graphics* 16 (6):1139–1148.

Sennett, Richard. 1976. *The Fall of Public Man*. New York: W. W. Norton.

Sennett, Richard. 1996. *Flesh and Stone: The Body and the City in Western Civilization*. New York: W. W. Norton.

SFMOMA. 2008. On *Hole in Space*, by Kit Galloway and Sherrie Rabinowitz. http://www.sfmoma.org/explore/multimedia/podcast/aop_tour_413.

Shen, S. T., M. Woolley, and S. Prior. 2006. Towards culture-centred design. *Interacting with Computers* 18 (4):820–852.

Sherman, Erik. 2011. When MySpace goes, what happens to the data and privacy? http://www.bnet.com/blog/technology-business/when-myspace-goes-what-happens-to-the-data-and-privacy/7827.

Sherman, Kelly. 2006. *Wish Lists*. Boston: Institute of Contemporary Art.

Shneiderman, B. 1994. Dynamic queries for visual information seeking. *IEEE Software* 11 (6):70–77.

Shneiderman, B. 1996. The eyes have it: A task by data type taxonomy for information visualizations. In *IEEE Symposium on Visual Languages*, 336–343. Los Alamitos, CA: IEEE Computer Society.

Shneiderman, B. 1998–2009. Treemaps for space-constrained visualization of hierarchies. http://www.cs.umd.edu/hcil/treemap-history/.

Shneiderman, B., and A. Aris. 2006. Network visualization by semantic substrates. *IEEE Transactions on Visualization and Computer Graphics* 12:733–740.

Siebold, J. 1998. Ebsdorf Mappamundi, slide 224. Index of Cartographic Images Illustrating Maps of the Early Medieval Period 400–1300 a.d. http://www.henry-davis.com/MAPS/EMwebpages/224.html.

Simmel, Georg. 1950. The metropolis and mental life. In *The Sociology of Georg Simmel*, ed. Kurt H. Wolff, 409–424. New York: Free Press. Original edition, 1903.

Simmel, Georg. 1959. How is society possible? In *Georg Simmel, 1858–1918: A Collection of Essays*. Ed. Kurt H. Wolff. Columbus, OH: Ohio State University Press. Original edition, 1908.

Skirvin, Tim. 1999. Cancel messages: Frequently asked questions (v1.75). http://www.faqs.org/faqs/usenet/cancel-faq/part1/.

Sloane, P. 1989. *The Visual Nature of Color*. New York: Design Press.

Smith, Aaron. 2011. Why Americans use social media. Pew Internet and American Life Project. http://pewinternet.org/Reports/2011/Why-Americans-Use-Social-Media.aspx.

Solove, Daniel J. 2002. Conceptualizing privacy. *California Law Review* 90:1087–1155.

Sosis, R. 2003. Why aren't we all Hutterites? *Human Nature* 14 (2):91–127.

Sosis, R. 2005. Does religion promote trust? The role of signaling, reputation, and punishment. *Interdisciplinary Journal of Research on Religion* 1:1–30.

Sprenger, Polly. 1999. Sun on privacy: "Get over it." *Wired*, January 26.

Sproull, L., and S. Kiesler. 1991a. Two-level perspective on electronic mail in organizations. *Journal of Organizational Computing* 1 (2):125–134.

Sproull, L., and S. Kiesler. 1991b. *Connections: New Ways of Working in the Networked Organization*. Cambridge, MA: MIT Press.

Sproull, L., R. Subramani, J. Walker, S. Kiesler, and K. Waters. 1996. When the interface is a face. *Human-Computer Interaction* 11:97–124.

Starner, T., S. Mann, B. Rhodes, J. Levine, J. Healey, D. Kirsch, R. W. Picard, and A. Pentland. 1997. Augmented reality through wearable computing. *Presence* 6 (4):386–398.

Stecher, K., and S. Counts. 2008. Thin slices of online profile attributes. In *Proceedings of the Second International Conference on Weblogs and Social Media*. Palo Alto, CA: AAAI Press.

Steen, Elisabeth Waelgaard, Mariann Komissar, and Alfhild Birkeland. 2002. Made in Africa. http://www.khm.uio.no/tema/utstillingsarkiv/madeinafrica/.

Steinpreis, Rhea E., Katie A. Anders, and Dawn Ritzke. 1999. The impact of gender on the review of the curricula vitae of job applicants and tenure candidates: A national empirical study. *Sex Roles* 41 (7–8):509–528.

Stiller, James, and R. I. M. Dunbar. 2007. Perspective-taking and memory capacity predict social network size. *Social Networks* 29 (1):93–104.

Stone, Brad. 2010. For Web's new wave, sharing details is the point. *New York Times*, April 23, A1.

Strickland, Rachel. 1998. Portable EFFECTS. http://www.portablefx.com/.

Suh, Bongwon, Gregorio Convertino, Ed H. Chi, and Peter Pirolli. 2009. The singularity is not near: Slowing growth of Wikipedia. In *Proceedings of the 5th International Symposium on Wikis and Open Collaboration*. New York: ACM Press.

Sullivan, L. H. 1896. The tall office building artistically considered. *Lippincott's Magazine*, March.

Surridge, Alison K., Daniel Osorio, and Nicholas I. Mundy. 2003. Evolution and selection of trichromatic vision in primates. *Trends in Ecology and Evolution* 18 (4):198–205.

Sutton, J., L. Palen, and I. Shklovski. 2008. Backchannels on the front lines: Emergent uses of social media in the 2007 Southern California wildfires. In *Proceedings of the 2008 Information Systems for Crisis Response and Management Conference (ISCRAM 2008)*. Washington, DC.

Tang, D. J. 2002. The Tele-Reporter: A collaborative interface for goal-oriented teledirection. Master's thesis, Massachusetts Institute of Technology.

Tannen, D. 1994. *Gender and Discourse*. New York: Oxford University Press.

Tannen, D. 2007. *Talking Voices: Repetition, Dialogue, and Imagery in Conversational Discourse*. Cambridge: Cambridge University Press.

Targ, R., and H. Puthoff. 1974. Information transmission under conditions of sensory shielding. *Nature* 251: 602–607.

Thornton, S. 1996. *Club Cultures: Music, Media, and Subcultural Capital*. Middletown, CT: Wesleyan University Press.

Thornton, S. 2009. *Seven Days in the Art World*. New York: W. W. Norton.

Thrower, N. J. W. 2007. *Maps and Civilization: Cartography in Culture and Society*. Chicago: University of Chicago Press.

Thucydides. 1954. *The History of the Peloponnesian War.* Translated by Rex Warner. London: Penguin. Original edition, 431 B.C.E.

Toma, Catalina L., Jeffrey T. Hancock, and Nicole B. Ellison. 2008. Separating fact from fiction: An examination of deceptive self-presentation in online dating profiles. *Personality and Social Psychology Bulletin* 34 (8):1023–1036.

Tractinsky, Noam. 2012. Visual aesthetics in human-computer interaction and interaction design. In *Encyclopedia of Human-Computer Interaction*, ed. Mads Soegaard and Rikke Friis Dam. Aarhus, Denmark: The Interaction-Design.org Foundation.

Travers, Jeffrey, and Stanley Milgram. 1969. An experimental study of the small world problem. *Sociometry* 32 (4):425–443.

Tufekci, Zeynep. 2008. Grooming, gossip, Facebook, and Myspace. *Information Communication and Society* 11 (4):544–564.

Tufte, E. R. 1986. *The Visual Display of Quantitative Information*. Cheshire, CT: Graphics Press.

Tufte, E. R. 1990. *Envisioning Information*. Cheshire, CT: Graphics Press.

Tufte, E. R. 2006. *Beautiful Evidence*. Chesire, CT: Graphics Press.

Turkle, S. 1995. *Life on the Screen*. New York: Touchstone.

Turkle, S. 2006. Always-on/always-on-you: The tethered self. In *Handbook of Mobile Communications and Social Change*, ed. James E. Katz. Cambridge, MA: MIT Press.

Turkle, S. 2012. The flight from conversation. *New York Times*, April 21 (online, Opinion section). http://www.nytimes.com/2012/04/22/opinion/sunday/the-flight-from-conversation.html?src=recg#commentsContainer.

Turner, Gerard L'Estrange. 1983. *Nineteenth-Century Scientific Instruments*. Berkeley, CA: University of California Press.

Turner, T., M. A. Smith, D. Fisher, and H. T. Welser. 2005. Picturing Usenet: Mapping computer-mediated collective action. *Journal of Computer-Mediated Communication* 10 (4). DOI: 10.1111/j.1083-6101.2005.tb00270.x.

Tyler, J. R., and J. C. Tang. 2003. When can i expect an email response? A study of rhythms in email usage. In *Proceedings of the Eighth European Conference on Computer Supported Cooperative Work*. Amsterdam: Kluwer Academic.

Ueda, Maki. 2006. *Hole in the Earth* homepage. http://www.ueda.nl/earth/index.html.

Uncontacted Tribes. Survival International Charitable Trust. http://www.uncontactedtribes.org/.

US Political Madness Forum: A call to rename "US Political Madness" forum to "The United States False Left Right Paradigm." 2011. http://www.abovetopsecret.com/forum/thread697159/pg1.

Utz, Sonja. 2010. Show me your friends and I will tell you what type of person you are: How one's profile, number of friends, and type of friends influence impression formation on social network sites. *Journal of Computer-Mediated Communication* 15 (2):314–335.

van Alphen, Ernst. 1996. The portrait's dispersal: Concepts of representation and subjectivity in contemporary portraiture. In *Portraiture: Facing the Subject*, ed. Joanna Woodall, 239–256. Manchester: Manchester University Press.

Van Vleck, Tom. 2001. The history of electronic mail. http://www.multicians.org/thvv/mail-history.html.

Vazire, S., and S. D. Gosling. 2004. E-perceptions: Personality impressions based on personal Web sites. *Journal of Personality and Social Psychology* 87 (1):123–132.

Venolia, G., L. Dabbish, J. J. Cadiz, and A. Gupta. 2001. Supporting email workflow. Technical Report MSR-TR-2001-88. Redmond, WA: Microsoft Research.

Venolia, G., and C. Neustaedter. 2003. Understanding sequence and reply relationships within email conversations: A mixed-model visualization. In *Proceedings of the SIGCHI Conference on Human Factors in Computing Systems (CHI '03)*. New York: ACM Press.

Vertegaal, Roel, Robert Slagter, Gerrit van der Veer, and Anton Nijholt. 2001. Eye gaze patterns in conversations: There is more to conversational agents than meets the eyes. In *Proceedings of the SIGCHI Conference on Human Factors in Computing Systems*, 301–308. New York: ACM Press

Vertegaal, Roel, Ivo Weevers, and Changuk Sohn. 2002. GAZE-2: An attentive video conferencing system. In *Proceedings of CHI '02: Extended Abstracts on Human Factors in Computing Systems*. New York: ACM Press.

Viégas, Fernanda. 2007. Revealing individual and collective pasts: Visualizations of online social archives. PhD thesis, Massachusetts Institute of Technology.

Viégas, Fernanda, and Judith Donath. 1999. Chat circles. In *Proceeding of the CHI '99 Conference on Human Factors in Computing Systems*, 9–16. New York: ACM Press.

Viégas, Fernanda, and Judith Donath. 2002. PostHistory: Visualizing email networks over time. Paper presented at the International Sunbelt Social Network Conference XXII, New Orleans, LA, March 1–2.

Viégas, Fernanda, Scott Golder, and Judith Donath. 2006. Visualizing email content: Portraying relationships from conversational histories. In *Proceedings of SIGCHI Conference on Human Factors in Computing Systems*. New York: ACM Press.

Viégas, Fernanda, E. Perry, E. Howe, and J. Donath. 2004. Artifacts of the presence era: Using information visualization to create an evocative souvenir. In *Proceedings of IEEE Symposium on Information Visualization*. Los Alamitos, CA: IEEE Computer Society.

Viégas, Fernanda, and Marc Smith. 2004. Newsgroup crowds and AuthorLines: Visualizing the activity of individuals in conversational cyberspaces. In *Proceedings of 37th Annual Hawaii International Conference on System Sciences (HICSS'04)*. Los Alamitos, CA: IEEE Computer Society.

Viégas, Fernanda, Martin Wattenberg, and Dave Kushal. 2004. Studying cooperation and conflict between authors with *history flow* visualizations. In *Proceedings of the SIGCHI Conference on Human Factors in Computing Systems*. New York: ACM Press.

Vilhjálmsson, H. H., and J. Cassell. 1998. Body Chat: Autonomous communicative behaviors in avatars. In *Proceedings of ACM Second International Conference on Autonomous Agents*, 269–276. New York: ACM Press.

Vinge, Vernor. 2006. *Rainbows End*. New York: Tor Books.

Voida, Amy, Rebecca E. Grinter, Nicholas Ducheneaut, W. Keith Edwards, and Mark W. Newman. 2005. Listening in: Practices surrounding iTunes music sharing. In *Proceedings of the SIGCHI Conference on Human Factors in Computing Systems*. New York: ACM Press.

Von Ahn, L., Manuel Blum, Nicholas J. Hopper, and John Langford. 2003. CAPTCHA: Using hard AI problems for security. In *Advances in Cryptology—EUROCRYPT 2003*, ed. Eli Biham. Berlin: Springer.

Von Ahn, L., B. Maurer, C. McMillen, D. Abraham, and M. Blum. 2008. Recaptcha: Human-based character recognition via Web security measures. *Science* 321 (5895):1465–1468.

Walther, Joseph B. 1996. Computer-mediated communication: Impersonal, interpersonal, and hyperpersonal interaction. *Communication Research* 23 (1):3–43.

Walther, Joseph B., Brandon Van Der Heide, Kim Sang-Yeon, David Westerman, and Stephanie Tom Tong. 2008. The role of friends' appearance and behavior on evaluations of individuals on Facebook: Are we known by the company we keep? *Human Communication Research* 34 (1):28–49.

Ware, C. 2012. *Information Visualization: Perception for Design*. San Francisco: Morgan Kaufmann.

Warnicke, Reitha M. 2000. *The Marrying of Anne of Cleves: Royal Protocol in Early Modern England*. Cambridge: Cambridge University Press.

Warren, Samuel D., and Louis D. Brandeis. 1890. The right to privacy. *Harvard Law Review* 4 (5):193–220.

Warwick, K., and D. Cerqui. 2008. Prospects for thought communication: Brain to machine and brain to brain. In *Ethical, Legal, and Social Issues in Medical Informatics*, ed. P. Duquenoy, C. George, and K. Kimppa. Hershey, PA: IGI Global.

Warwick, K., M. Gasson, B. Hutt, I. Goodhew, P. Kyberd, H. Schulzrinne, and X. Wu. 2004. Thought communication and control: A first step using radiotelegraphy. In *IEE Proceedings—Communications* 151 (3):185–189.

Wasserman, S., and K. Faust. 1994. *Social Network Analysis: Methods and Applications*. Cambridge: Cambridge University Press.

Wattenberg, M. 2005. Baby names, visualization, and social data analysis. In *Proceedings of IEEE Symposium on Information Visualization (INFOVIS)*. Los Alamitos, CA: IEEE Computer Society.

Wattenberg, M., and J. Kriss. 2006. Designing for social data analysis. *IEEE Transactions on Visualization and Computer Graphics* 12 (4):549–557.

Watts, D. J., Peter S. Dodds, and M. E. J. Newman. 2002. Identity and search in social networks. *Science* 296:1302–1305.

Weiser, M., and J. Brown. 1996. Designing calm technology. *PowerGrid Journal* 1.01. http://www.ubiq.com/weiser/calmtech/calmtech.htm.

Welch, Chris. 2008. Beam me up, Wolf! CNN debuts election-night "hologram." http://edition.cnn.com/2008/TECH/11/06/hologram.yellin/.

Wellman, Barry, ed. 1999. *Networks in the Global Village: Life in Contemporary Communities*. Boulder, CO: Westview Press.

Wellman, Barry, Laura Garton, and Caroline Haythornthwaite. 1997. Studying online social networks. *Journal of Computer-Mediated Communication* 3 (1). http://onlinelibrary.wiley.com/doi/10.1111/j.1083-6101.1997.tb00062.x/full.

Wellman, Barry, and Milena Gulia. 1999. Net surfers don't ride alone: Virtual communities as communities. In *Networks in the Global Village*, ed. Barry Wellman, 331–367. Boulder, CO: Westview Press.

Wellman, Barry, and Scot Wortley. 1990. Different strokes from different folks: Community ties and social support. *American Journal of Sociology* 96 (3):558–588.

Welser, H. T., E. Gleave, D. Fisher, and M. Smith. 2007. Visualizing the signatures of social roles in online discussion groups. *Journal of Social Structure* 8 (2). http://www.cmu.edu/joss/content/articles/volume8/Welser/.

Weng, Jianshu, Ee-Peng Lim, Jing Jiang, and Qi He. 2010. TwitterRank: Finding topic-sensitive influential twitterers. In *Proceedings of the Third ACM International Conference on Web Search and Data Mining*. New York: ACM Press.

West, Shearer. 2004. *Portraiture: Oxford History of Art*. Oxford: Oxford University Press.

Wall Street Journal. 2010–2013. What they know.

Whitaker, Brian. 2011. Gay girl in Damascus was an arrogant fantasy. *Guardian*, June 13.

White, Harrison C. 1992. *Identity and Control: A Structural Theory of Social Action*. Princeton, NJ: Princeton University Press.

Whittaker, S. 1995. Rethinking video as a technology for interpersonal communications: Theory and design implications. *International Journal of Man-Machine Studies* 42 (5):501–529.

Whittaker, S., and C. Sidner. 1996. Email overload: exploring personal information management of email. In *Proceedings of CHI'96 Conference on Computer Human Interaction*. New York: ACM Press.

Whittaker, S., Loren Terveen, Will Hill, and Lynn Cherny. 1998. The dynamics of mass interaction. In *Proceedings of 1998 ACM Conference on Computer Supported Cooperative Work*. New York: ACM Press.

Whyte, William H. 1988. *City: Rediscovering the Center*. New York: Doubleday.

Wilkinson, D. M., and B. A. Huberman. 2007. Cooperation and quality in Wikipedia. In *Proceedings of the 2007 International Symposium on Wikis*. New York: ACM Press.

Wirth, L. 1938. Urbanism as a way of life. *American Journal of Sociology* 44 (1):1–24.

Wolff, Robert Paul. 1970. *In Defense of Anarchism*. New York: Harper & Row.

Woods-Marsden, Joanna. 1987. "Ritratto al Naturale": Questions of realism and idealism in early Renaissance portraits. *Art Journal* 46 (3):209–216.

World Health Organization. 2010. *Hidden Cities*. http://www.hiddencities.org/report.html.

Xiong, Rebecca, and Judith Donath. 1999. PeopleGarden: Creating data portraits for users. In *Proceedings of the ACM Symposium on User Interface Software and Technology (UIST)*. New York: ACM Press.

Yee, K. P., D. Fisher, R. Dhamija, and M. Hearst. 2001. Animated exploration of dynamic graphs with radial layout. In *Proceedings of the IEEE Symposium on Information Visualization*. Los Alamitos, CA: IEEE Computer Society.

Yee, N. 2009. Befriending ogres and wood-elves: Relationship formation and the social architecture of Norrath. *Game Studies* 9(1). http://gamestudies.org/0802/articles/yee.

Yee, N., and J. N. Bailenson. 2007. The Proteus effect: Self transformations in virtual reality. *Human Communication Research* 33 (3):271–290.

Yee, N., J. N. Bailenson, and N. Ducheneaut. 2009. The Proteus effect: Implications of transformed digital self-representation on online and offline behavior. *Communication Research* 36 (2):285–312.

Yee, N., Jeremy N. Bailenson, Mark Urbanek, Francis Chang, and Dan Merget. 2007. The unbearable likeness of being digital: The persistence of nonverbal social norms in online virtual environments. *Cyberpsychology & Behavior* 10 (1):115–121.

Yee, N., Helen Harris, Maria Jabon, and Jeremy N. Bailenson. 2011. The expression of personality in virtual worlds. *Social Psychological and Personality Science* 2 (1): 5–12.

Yee, N., Jason Ellis, and Nicolas Ducheneaut. 2009. The tyranny of embodiment. *Artifact* 2:1–6.

Yi, Ji Soo, Youn ah Kang, J. T. Stasko, and J. A. Jacko. 2007. Toward a deeper understanding of the role of interaction in information visualization. *IEEE Transactions on Visualization and Computer Graphics* 13(6): 1224–1231.

Young, Michael D., and Peter Willmott. 1992. *Family and Kinship in East London*. Berkeley, CA: University of California Press. Original edition, 1957.

Zakon, Robert. 1997. Hobbes' Internet Timeline, 2000: The Internet Engineering Task Force. http://www.ietf.org/rfc/rfc2235.txt.

Zebrowitz, L. 1997. *Reading Faces*. Boulder, CO: Westview Press.

Zebrowitz, L., and J. M. Montepare. 2008. Social psychological face perception: Why appearance matters. *Social and Personality Psychology Compass* 2 (3):1497–1517.

Zeman, Janice, and Judy Garber. 1996. Display rules for anger, sadness, and pain: It depends on who is watching. *Child Development* 67 (3):957–973.

Zerubavel, Eviatar. 1982. The standardization of time: A sociohistorical Perspective. *American Journal of Sociology* 88 (1):1–23.

Zinman, A. 2009. Personas. http://personas.media.mit.edu.

Zinman, A., and J. Donath. 2007. Is Britney Spears spam? Paper presented at the Fourth Conference on Email and Anti-Spam, Mountain View, CA.

Zinman, A., and J. Donath. 2009. Signs: Increasing expression and clarity in instant messaging. In *Proceedings of 42nd Hawaii International Conference on System Sciences (HICSS '09)*. Los Alamos, CA: IEEE Computing Society.

Zittrain, Jonathan. 2006. The generative Internet. *Harvard Law Review* 119:1974–2040.

Zittrain, Jonathan. 2008. *The Future of the Internet—And How to Stop It*. New Haven, CT: Yale University Press.

Zuckerman, Ethan. 2008. Mapping: infrastructure and flow. http://www.ethanzuckerman.com/blog/2008/12/26/mapping-infrastructure-and-flow/.

Zuckerman, Ethan. 2013. *Rewire: Digital Cosmopolitans in the Age of Connection*. New York: W. W. Norton.

Zuk, Torre, and Sheelagh Carpendale. 2006. Theoretical analysis of uncertainty visualizations. In *Proceedings of Visualization and Data Analysis (SPIE 6060)*. DOI: 10.1117/12.643631.

INDEX

Note: Page numbers followed by "f," "n," or "s" indicate figures, notes, and sidebars, respectively.